# BEAUTIFUL COUNTRY
# BURN AGAIN

**Ben Fountain** is the author of *Billy Lynn's Long Halftime Walk*, which won the National Book Critics Circle Award, the Flaherty-Dunna First Novel Prize, and the Los Angeles Times Book Prize for Fiction, and was a finalist for the National Book Award, in addition to being made into a feature film directed by Ang Lee. Fountain's short story collection, *Brief Encounters with Che Guevara,* was a national bestseller and winner of the PEN/Hemingway Award for Debut Fiction, the Barnes & Noble Discover Award for Fiction, and a Whiting Award for Fiction. Fountain graduated from the University of North Carolina at Chapel Hill and Duke University School of Law. A former practicing attorney, Fountain has taught at the University of Texas at Austin, and recently completed a two-year appointment as university chair in creative writing at Texas State University.

**ALSO BY BEN FOUNTAIN**

*BILLY LYNN'S LONG HALFTIME WALK*

*BRIEF ENCOUNTERS WITH CHE GUEVARA*

# BEAUTIFUL COUNTRY
# BURN AGAIN

Trump's Rise to Power,
and the State of the Country
that Voted for Him

# Ben Fountain

CANONGATE

First published in Great Britain in 2018 by Canongate Books Ltd,
14 High Street, Edinburgh EH1 1TE

First published in the US in 2018 by HarperCollins Publishers,
195 Broadway, New York, NY 10007

*British Library Cataloguing-in-Publication Data*
A catalogue record for this book is available on
request from the British Library

ISBN 978 1 78689 200 3

Designed by Renata De Oliveria

Printed and bound in Great Britain by Clays Ltd, Elcograf S.p.A.

MIX
Paper from
responsible sources
FSC
www.fsc.org    FSC® C018072

*For John Issac Fountain*
*and Lee Caitlin Fountain*
*and, as ever,*
*for Sharie*

*. . . Beautiful country burn again, Point Pinos down to the Sur Rivers*
*Burn as before with bitter wonders, land and ocean and the Carmel water.*

ROBINSON JEFFERS, "APOLOGY FOR BAD DREAMS"

# CONTENTS

# BEAUTIFUL COUNTRY
# BURN AGAIN

# PROLOGUE
## THE THIRD REINVENTION

2016 was the year all the crazy parts of America ran amok over the rest. Screens, memes, fake news, Twitter storms, Russian hackers, pussy grabbers, Hillary's emails, war, the wall, the wolf call of the alt-right, "hand" size, lies upon lies upon lies and moneymoneymoney—the more money, the more lies, is this politics' iron rule?—they all combined for a billion-dollar stink of an election. This wasn't Democrats versus Republicans so much as the sad, psychotic, and vengeful in the national life producing a strange mutation, a creature comprised of degenerate political logic. The logic of this politics—the logic of the Frankenstein—requires ultimately that the monster turn on its maker. The logic doesn't tell us who wins. That has to play out in the slog of daily gains and losses, but it would be hard to devise a more spectacular conflict than this high-functioning creature of American schizophrenia versus the very system that brought him to power.

To call Donald Trump a hypocrite insults the scale of the thing. Move far enough along the hypocritic spectrum and eventually you cross into schizophrenia, and nothing less than psychopathy serves to illustrate the magnitude of Trump's achievement. In him we had a candidate who proffered family values at every turn, a man twice divorced, a tabloid-fodder serial adulterer and sexual trash-talker. "The least racist person you'll ever meet," he described himself, while animating his campaign with racist appeals so large and livid that neo-Nazis, the KKK, and the alt-right endorsed him in language evocative of second comings. After making his career as one of the most celebrated libertines of our time, he became a Bible quoter and toter on the campaign trail, this self-proclaimed business genius with a complicated history of bankruptcies, bailouts, welched debts, and dealings with mobsters. A draft dodger enamored of the military; macho tough-talker and finicky germophobe; champion of U.S. manufacturing, purveyor of signature-label clothing made overseas; and loud, proud patriot with a mysterious affinity for Vladimir Putin, one of America's most dedicated foes. Trump the billionaire ran as a fire-breathing populist while offering nothing concrete or even coherent in terms of wages, unions, health care, or taxes that might benefit working people, though his tax plan promised huge benefits for the upper class.

None of this was hidden. The Trump disjunct flamed in plain sight for everyone to see, and he owned it with the coarse, loose-cannon style of the consummate New York asshole. All the stranger, then, that this star and symbol of big-city life should become the hero of the heartland, all those millions of wholesome acres of Bible Belts that truss the nation's middle and nether regions. The guy from Sodom and Gomorrah was all right! His insults and earthiness were received as authenticity: here at last was a man who would stick it to the elites after all these years of eating their shit, the sniffy pieties about tolerance and diversity forced down your throat by the pinheads who'd figured it out for the rest of us. It was galling. It got you down on yourself. It made you touchy and weak where you used to be strong, then this badass comes along and puts it right out there every time he flaps his mouth, says all the things you wanted to say all these years as you lived in constant apology just for being who you are, diminished, depressed, bottled up, pissed off, a hundred fuck-yous a day muttered at Obama and his crowd, heavy weather from Washington all the days of the year. A miracle, the white man who says what he wants! Free, free at last!

This may be the most powerful medicine in politics, the leader who delivers a man to his natural self. To be acknowledged as you are, affirmed and blessed from above: one can imagine it as a spiritual experience. A profound burden is lifted. No more doubt, no dark loathings, only the certainty that you are good and on God's side. Ecstasy isn't out of the question. What greater thrill besides sex to be delivered to yourself, liberated from the bad opinion of your enemies? Something of that ecstasy could be heard at Trump's rallies, "Build that wall!" and "Lock her up!" bellowed like Romans watching lions sink their teeth into Christian flesh.

"He tells it like it is." How often we heard him praised in those terms. "He says what a lot of people are thinking." Apparently so; many more than were willing to admit to the pollsters, though one wonders how strong white identity was to begin with, when the basic courtesy that's the face of political correctness is viewed as a monstrous threat. If economic distress is offered as the socially acceptable reason for Trump's election, the fact remains that many millions of his supporters voted against what seems to be their own economic interests. White women voted for him in spite of Hillary's support of equal pay, along with a broad complementary agenda that promised help with the exhausting challenge—most of which falls on women—of juggling home life and job. Working- and middle-class whites voted for him despite his conventional enrich-the-rich policies (rants against trade deals aside) that have, among the poor and working class especially, stunted wages, shortened life expectancy, driven up drug addiction and suicide rates, and made upward mobility the exception rather than the rule. Trump's election seemed to be the triumph of identity politics—white identity politics—over economic interest.

Then again, maybe identity politics *is* economic. Maybe nothing less than hard-core economic realism explains Trump's victory, a well-honed popular instinct for how money and race have always worked in America. It must be said that many millions of Americans implicitly, and not unreasonably, regard freedom as a finite thing: to the extent that any group, tribe, cohort has greater freedom, others must necessarily have less. Then there's the corollary, which gets us closer to the crux: the less freedom you have, the more readily you're subject to economic plunder. Put the two propositions together and you have what could be called the American anthropology, the two horns of a bloody dilemma on which the democratic experiment has balanced for 240 years. Profit proportionate to freedom; plunder correlative to subjugation. In practical terms, the organizing principle has most often turned on race and gender, the bondage of black men and women being the starkest example. It's as plain as the numbers in the account books of a Cooper River rice plantation, race-based chattel slavery as the engine for tremendous wealth creation. Emancipation erased some $4 billion of capital from Southern slaveholders' books. It also literally diminished these slaveholders' freedom with respect to their former slaves; or, to shade it more finely, restricted their prerogative, their license, the field over which their free will could play. Forced labor, assault, theft, rape, torture, mutilation, murder, kidnapping, these were all within the accepted prerogative of slave owners, all mechanisms of control in a social structure organized for plunder on the industrial scale. The power—the prerogative—of literal life and death; a monopoly on freedom, if you will. American slaveholders enjoyed a scope of freedom that we associate these days with drug lords and Third World lunatic dictators.

The plunder continued in slightly less brutal form after Emancipation, but there was an even bigger game afoot, a more universal plunder with race still playing a pivotal role. Jay Gould, the nineteenth-century robber baron, offered a clue when he said, "I can hire one half of the working class to kill the other half." A startlingly frank approach to the politics of division,[1] but Gould overstated the case. He didn't have to hire anybody; thanks to America's racist legacy, it's easy to get the job done for free. Generations of political hacks have done quite well for themselves and their clients by salting the racial divide, the basic message going something like: *Watch out, white people! Blacks are coming for your homes, your women, your jobs, your life!* The move is so standard a part of the hack repertoire that it's come down to us as a political term of art, "the Southern Strategy,"[2] and for the past fifty years it's worked to perfection[3] in distracting the white working and middle classes from the huge plunder of wealth by society's higher reaches.

But with the Great Recession of 2008, that snake oil started to lose some snap. The biggest wipeout of household wealth in eighty years got people's attention: we'd been had, was the general feeling, a sentiment that the government was all too willing to confirm. The financial institutions that caused the crisis received billions in government loans and guarantees, dwarfing funds devoted to things that would help working people—unemployment benefits, mortgage relief, fiscal stimulus. The bankers continued to get huge bonuses; the big financial institutions got bigger; and for all the fraud and speculative flimflam that led to the crash, and despite numerous referrals to the Justice Department for criminal prosecution, only one midlevel investment banker went to jail. What the Tea Party and Occupy movements had in common was the rage of the little guy getting screwed right and left, though how we were getting it, and by whom, these essential questions were ripe for manipulation amid an angry, badly educated, highly propagandized public. Trump rode the rage

---

[1]  Further to this, the comment of Gould's contemporary Henry Adams: "Politics is the systematic organization of hatreds."

[2]  See "American Crossroads: Reagan, Trump, and the Devil Down South" and "A Familiar Spirit," *infra*.

[3]  One looks long across the span of American history for the rare instance when it didn't work.

by coupling easy-to-digest populist rhetoric—the system is rigged!—with bare-knuckle racism, the most reliable play in the American power-grab book. But after all the sound and fury of the most bizarre election in the country's history, the equation hasn't changed. Profit proportionate to freedom; plunder correlative to subjugation. Until the values in the equation change, it's still a chump's game.

**TWICE IN ITS HISTORY THE UNITED STATES HAS HAD TO REIN-**vent itself in order to survive as a plausibly genuine constitutional democracy. In each case, the reinvention was compelled by the profoundest sort of crisis, and each case may be framed as a turning point in the long elaboration of certain words the country has looked to time and again to define itself. The words were there at the start, presented as "self-evident" truths in the Declaration of Independence. "[A]ll men are created equal." All men "are endowed by their creator with certain inalienable rights." Among these rights—bestowed by no less an authority than the creator, thus sacred—are the rights to "life, liberty & the pursuit of happiness."[4]

The Enlightenment philosopher, political genius, and slave owner Thomas Jefferson wrote these words; fair to say that he, too, had the American schizophrenia. But the moral potential was in the words, and a reasonable person could place the center of American history right there, in the contest for fulfillment of that potential. At no point has it ever been a sure thing, or even the common goal. Emancipation, the first reinvention, was brought about by the crisis of slavery. Were people of color to be included among the "men . . . created equal." Were they to have dominion over their lives, their bodies, the profits of their labor. For four years the land literally burned with the question; either the country would be reinvented as a profoundly different social order—with a redistribution of freedom, in effect, a resetting of the values in the freedom-profits-

---

[4] "Happiness" in the eighteenth-century sense of prosperity, economic well-being.

plunder equation—or it would be broken in two. Some seventy years later the existential crisis of the Great Depression forced a second reinvention, and if "existential" reads as an overstatement, that's because we've lost proper appreciation for the turmoil of the early 1930s.[5] Had the country elected as president in 1932 some tragic mediocrity along the lines of a Franklin Pierce or a James Buchanan, it's easy to imagine an antebellum or even Weimar-like drift toward civil war, a totalitarian regime. Another literal burning. Instead we got Franklin Roosevelt and the New Deal, his answer to the threat that unbridled industrial capitalism posed for democracy. Roosevelt articulated as no president had ever done before the link between freedom and profit, subjugation and plunder. Modern life, he asserted, threatened to trap working people in a new kind of bondage, a shell democracy that maintained the forms of political equality while abetting an economic system that denied the great mass of people meaningful agency over their lives. The early 1930s offered plenty of proof for Roosevelt's proposition: the soup kitchens, migrant camps, hobo squats, and railroad yards, not to mention the National Mall in Washington, DC, during the months it was occupied by the Bonus Marchers, were teeming with slat-ribbed citizens who, it may be safely said, had lost meaningful agency over their lives. At the 1936 Democratic National Convention, Roosevelt made his case for a second term and the continuation of the New Deal:

> *The age of machinery, of railroads; of steam and electricity; the telegraph and the radio; mass production, mass distribution— all of these combined to bring forward a new civilization and with it a new problem for those who sought to remain free.*

---

[5] See "The Long Good Deal," *infra*, for reference to the riots, strikes, and armed insurrections of the era. Communism and fascism competed with liberal democracy for space in America's political mainstream. See Ira Katznelson, *Fear Itself: The New Deal and the Origins of Our Time* (Liveright Publishing, 2013), pp. 43–57.

> *For out of this modern civilization economic royalists carved new dynasties. New kingdoms were built upon concentration of control over material things. Through new uses of corporations, banks, and securities, new machinery of industry and agriculture, of labor and capital—all undreamed of by the Fathers—the whole structure of modern life was impressed into this royal service . . .*
>
> *The royalists of the economic order have conceded that political freedom was the business of the government, but they have maintained that economic slavery was nobody's business. They granted that the government could protect the citizen in his right to vote, but they denied that the government could do anything to protect the citizen in his right to work and his right to live.*
>
> *Today we stand committed to the proposition that freedom is no half-and-half affair. If the average citizen is guaranteed equal opportunity in the polling place, he must have equal opportunity in the market place.*

The New Deal reinvented America for a second time—call it the second redistribution of freedom, a radical reset of the values in the freedom-profits-plunder equation. A reset as applied to whites, it must be noted. Powerful Southern legislators saw to it that blacks were largely excluded from the benefits of New Deal initiatives. *All men created equal.* Still not even close. *The pursuit of happiness.* So many forced to run that race on their knees. It would take the civil rights movement to jump-start that unfinished work, but the New Deal reinvention established a structure, a rough framework for equality that wouldn't be seriously challenged until the Reagan era.

There's a touch of the uncanny in all this. Roughly eighty years separate the Revolutionary period from Emancipation. A more or less equal span of time separates Emancipation from the New Deal—about the span of a reasonably long human life, and nearly the same run of years from the New Deal to the present. The long clock, coincidentally or not—historian mystics, dig it!—concurs with the palpable ripeness of our time, an era of insane economics where the top One Percent possesses wealth on the level of sultans and pre-Revolution French kings, while the middle and bottom struggle to manage such basic necessities as health care and educating their kids. This kind of imbalance screams that the freedom-profits-plunder equation is seriously skewed, and is just as seriously incompatible with a system of government that claims to be democratic. Overweening freedom for a few—or call it what you will, autonomy, license, prerogative, privilege—translates, as it always has, into plunder of the many, a state of affairs starkly opposed to Jefferson's foundational principle of equality, and the guarantee of meaningful autonomy—those rights to life, liberty, the pursuit of happiness—that by the same moral logic proceeds from equality.

"Economic tyranny," Franklin Roosevelt called it, the modern capitalist threat to equality of rights that he sought to counter with the New Deal, just as the abolitionist movement—and Abraham Lincoln, in due course—sought to end that earlier form of legalized, race-based economic tyranny. There was reaction, of course. The bloodiest war in the country's history was fought over racial tyranny, a bloodletting that continues to this day. The reaction to Roosevelt's reinvention was confined to the political fringes for almost fifty years; it took Reagan to bring it into the mainstream, "the Reagan Revolution" some call it, the unbridling of market forces that carried distinct racial overtones, the conservative hostility toward government displaying special animus for government's ongoing efforts to realize the promise of Emancipation.

The gross disparities not just of wealth but of opportunity—disparities that are even more pronounced for people of color—very arguably show that at this point in our history, the reaction is winning. Maybe it's a sign that we've lost all sense of the trauma that led to the first two reinventions. We don't remember, not in the visceral, experiential sense. The living memory of once-recent history has faded to abstraction; maybe this is the meaning of those eighty-year cycles of crisis and reinvention, that we have to live it all over again. And maybe nothing short of an existential crisis can trigger these profound acts of reinvention. Lincoln and Roosevelt had the vision and strength of will to lead the country out of two incarnations of hell. One wonders how close to hell we'll have to come in our own time before a similarly drastic act of reinvention is attempted. Either it succeeds, as has happened twice in our history, or America becomes a democracy in name only, a sham sustained by the props and gestures of representative democracy, as fake as the soundstage of the cheesiest Hollywood movie.

**MUCH OF THIS BOOK WAS WRITTEN OVER THE COURSE OF THE** 2016 presidential campaign. These essays attempt to bear witness to the events of an extraordinary election season, and to place those events in context, to decipher some meaning beyond the pileup of polls and speeches and news cycles. The scorched-earth tactics of the campaign, the wholesale retreat into fantasy, the daily outbreaks of absurd and disturbed behaviors, it seemed the only proper way to view these was as symptoms of tremendous stress. A fundamental break seemed to be building, a feeling that became more urgent with Trump's run to the nomination and election. Whatever the trajectory of the forces and stresses in play, it seemed certain he would deepen and accelerate their trajectory.

So this book may be read as the record of a developing crisis, one drastic enough to raise the possibility of a third reinvention, which, if attempted, will inevitably meet with vigorous, perhaps violent, resistance from stakeholders in the current order. In facing the crises of their own times, Lincoln and Roosevelt urged the country to a larger sense of itself, a broadening of Jefferson's principle of equality and what it means for humans to be truly free. The reinventions led by those two presidents can and should be viewed as moral actions, but they were supremely practical as well: the survival of the country as a genuine constitutional democracy was at stake. The beautiful country was burning: literally in the first instance, thankfully less so in the second. One wonders what manner of burning awaits us in the time of Trump.

# BOOK OF DAYS

## JANUARY

Otto Warmbier, a University of Virginia undergraduate, is arrested by North Korean officials at Pyongyang International Airport for an alleged "hostile act against the state." A Texas law takes effect allowing licensed gun owners to carry firearms, concealed or openly, into psychiatric hospitals. President Obama expands background checks for some forms of gun purchase, and requires anyone who makes a living by selling guns to register as a licensed gun dealer and conduct background checks. "Pretty soon you won't be able to get guns," Donald Trump says of the new rules, while a spokeswoman for the National Rifle Association comments, "This is it, really? They're not really doing anything." Immigration agents stage weekend raids that round up 121 people in Texas, Georgia, and North Carolina, and Sean Penn's interview with fugitive Mexican drug lord Joaquín Guzmán, a.k.a. "El Chapo," is published in *Rolling Stone*. "I supply more heroin, methamphetamine, cocaine, and marijuana than anybody else in the world," Guzmán, whose fortune is estimated at $1 billion, tells Penn. The French satirical magazine *Charlie Hebdo* marks the first anniversary of the terrorist attack on its office with a special edition whose cover features a caricature of a bloody God wielding an assault rifle. Obama delivers his final State of the Union address, saying, "The future we want is within our reach." The occupation of the Malheur National Wildlife Refuge in Oregon by armed militants continues; the group's leader, Ammon Bundy, who has said that his opposition to the federal government is divinely ordained, calls for "the federal government to give up its unconstitutional presence in this county." Iran captures two U.S. Navy patrol boats and ten American sailors in the Persian Gulf for alleged "snooping." Republican Party leaders express fears of a "hostile takeover" by so-called lunch-bucket conservatives, and Senator Lindsey Graham of South Carolina says the party is in a "demographic death spiral." Oil falls to $30.44 a barrel, its lowest level in twelve years, and the Powerball jackpot hits $1.5 billion, a sum that would fail to put the winner on the Forbes 400 list of wealthiest individuals. David Bowie dies at age sixty-nine. A suicide-bomb attack near the Blue Mosque in Istanbul's historic district kills ten tourists; ISIS claims responsibility. The Michigan National Guard is deployed to Flint to distribute bottled water, and rap artist Michael Render, better known as "Killer Mike," endorses Bernie Sanders. "I will gladly accept the mantle of anger," Trump says at a GOP debate in North Charleston, South Carolina, and Josh Holmes, former chief of staff for Mitch McConnell, tells *Politico*, "There are at least two candidates who could utterly destroy the Republican bench for a generation if they became the nominee." The ten U.S. sailors captured by Iran are released, along with their boats. Planned Parenthood sues the makers of "stealth videos" that purport to show the organization selling fetal tissue to researchers for profit; subsequent investigations by federal and state lawmakers revealed no wrongdoing by Planned Parenthood, and Republicans in Congress continue their efforts to cut off federal funding to the organization. U.S. and European nations lift sanctions on Iran after international inspectors conclude that Iran has followed through on its obligation to dismantle large parts of its nuclear program. Concurrent with the lifting of sanctions, Iran releases five American prisoners and the U.S. releases seven Iranians. The *New York Times* reports that death rates for whites in the U.S. are either rising or flattening for all adult age groups under sixty-five, and death rates for young whites are even higher, especially for those "less educated," that is, without a high school degree; drug overdoses are identified as the main driver behind the rise in mortality. Lena Dunham, creator of the HBO series *Girls,* campaigns in Iowa on behalf of Hillary Clinton, and Ted Cruz is revealed to have financed his 2012 Senate campaign with approximately $1 million in loans from Goldman Sachs and Citibank, which he failed to disclose in his filings with the Federal Election Commission. Two endangered whooping cranes are shot dead in Southeast Texas, and more than twenty whooping cranes have been shot and killed in the U.S. in the past five years, out of a worldwide population of approximately six hundred. Obama signs a federal emergency declaration for Flint, and Trump declares that if he is elected president, "American sailors will never be on their knees to a foreign country." Calls grow for a boycott of the Oscar ceremonies to protest the second straight year of all white actor nominees; Chris Rock, host for this year's ceremony, unveils a new promotion for the broadcast, calling it "the White BET Awards." ISIS confirms the death of notorious executioner "Jihadi John," Ted Cruz compares himself to Ronald Reagan, and some of the classified emails on Hillary Clinton's home computer server are found to be even more sensitive than "top secret." "I'll fix Flint," Michigan governor Rick Snyder promises, after requesting federal aid to meet an estimated $41 million in emergency costs. Sarah Palin endorses Trump at a rally in Ames, Iowa. "Media heads are spinning," Palin says as a smiling Trump looks on. "No more pussyfooting around . . . He's going rogue left and right. That's why he's doing so well." Ted Cruz questions whether Trump is "stable" and "calm" enough to lead the nation's military. El Chapo is captured in the Mexican state of Sinaloa, and Taiwan elects its first woman president. The UN reports that from January 2014 to October 2015, nearly nineteen thousand Iraqi civilians were killed, nearly double that number wounded, and three million fled their homes due to fighting among ISIS, Iraqi security forces, and pro-government militias. Eighteen die as a historic blizzard hits the eastern United States, and Glenn Beck endorses Ted Cruz for president. "I have prayed for the next George Washington, and I believe I have found him," Beck declares, after which he and Cruz take turns administering the presidential oath of office to one another. Abe Vigoda dies. Ammon Bundy and his fellow occupiers of the Malheur National Wildlife Refuge are arrested, and one—LaVoy Finicum, who once swore that he would die rather than go to jail—is shot dead by authorities after resisting arrest. U.S. military commanders discuss the necessity for a decades-long American commitment in Afghanistan, and the "Doomsday Clock" remains at three minutes till midnight, with geopolitical tensions and the lack of aggressive steps to combat climate change counteracting the positives of the Iran nuclear deal and the Paris climate accord. Trump, citing a "wise-guy press release" by Fox, says he will skip the final GOP debate before the Iowa caucuses after Fox refuses to drop Megyn Kelly from the panel of moderators. Senate Democrats propose $400 million in federal aid to help Michigan replace Flint's lead-contaminated pipes, about half of the estimated cost, and Senate Republicans refuse to commit without offsetting budget cuts. Braden Joplin, a Texas Tech University student and campaign volunteer for Ben Carson, is killed in a car accident on icy roads in Iowa, and Carson suspends his campaign to meet with Joplin's family. The World Health Organization says that Zika is "spreading explosively" in the Americas. Barbie dolls will soon be sold in three body types—curvy, tall, and petite—and will also come in seven different skin tones and twenty-two different eye colors. American film star Leonardo DiCaprio has a private audience with the Pope. Residents of Sebring, Ohio, learn that high levels of lead were found in their tap water during the previous summer, and the mayor is jeered at a council meeting when he tells the mother of a child who has elevated lead levels that it is "too early" to put all the blame on the town's water. Trump holds a "Special Event to Benefit Veterans Organizations" in Des Moines while the Fox-sponsored Republican debate takes place across town. A grand jury in Houston indicts two antiabortion activists for their roles in making the Planned Parenthood "stealth videos." The *Huffington Post* announces that its coverage of Donald Trump will move from the entertainment section to news, and that each Trump story will come with an addendum stating, "Donald Trump is a serial liar, rampant xenophobe, racist, birther, and bully who has repeatedly pledged to ban all Muslims— 1.6 billion members of an entire religion—from entering the U.S." Thirty-seven people—most believed to be Syrian refugees— drown when their boat capsizes while crossing from Turkey to Greece; at least ten children and babies are among the dead. More than two hundred fifty refugees have drowned during January while attempting to reach Greece.

# IOWA 2016
## RIDING THE ROADKILL EXPRESS

### 1. "SHE WAS NOT BLAH."

Is Hillary freaking? Has to be with all those '08 flashbacks frying the brainpan, that previous coronation spoiled by a grandiloquent rookie who nobody gave a chance, then he rolled her up like a Mafia hit in a cheap rug. Now it's a hectoring old geezer with scribby gray hair and suspiciously perfect teeth, the kind you slide in every morning and snap at the mirror, *clack clack*. Put a tan vest and a "Bernie" name tag on him and he could be one of those grizzled old guys down at the Home Depot, you ask him a perfectly reasonable question about sweat soldering, say, or flush valves, he just snorts and walks off. A career socialist no less. *And Hillary wailed unto the Lord: Why me?* Down fifty points in the polls a year ago, Sanders has clawed almost even just as the thing gets real.

Real as Iowa, the snows and throes of opening night, the first winnowing of contenders from the roadkill. Interstating it east from Des Moines with the sun at our back, the talk is mostly of *him,* not Bernie but the other one, the hair, the mouth, the Twitter king, the joke that stopped being funny sometime around Thanksgiving.

About the same time one noticed a kind of morbid countdown happening in the press. *With only two months before the Iowa caucuses . . . six weeks . . . a month . . . days . . .* Implicit here was rationalist disbelief at Trump's defiance of political physics, and the assumption, also implied, increasingly frayed, that he would crash long before actual votes were cast. In this his candidacy was supposed to be much like his hair, like a gas explosion or a mango soufflé, or any highly transient event involving lots of hot air and artificial volume. The pros, weren't they supposed to have a grip by now? The same machine that produced a reliable string of establishment nominees, the two Bushes, Dole, McCain, Romney, and now another Bush on deck, "the smart one," the one with the $100 million Super PAC. But something strange has happened. Is happening. In recent TV appearances, Reince Priebus, chair of the Republican National Committee, has had the thousand-yard stare of a mall cop whose Segway is in the shop.

But tonight is for Hillary, scheduled to rally in Davenport. The road runs ruler-straight for miles and miles. A bald eagle cruises the dome of severe-clear sky, flakes of cirrus dusting the bend of crystalline blue. Small towns and little commercial nodes heave up every few miles with their mix-n-match assortments of Subways, Exxons, Starbucks, Denny's. Apparently porn is one of the few non-franchised service industries left in America; there's the Lion's Den Adult Superstore outside Altoona, one of several such sui generis enterprises we'll see today. Barns are huge—full to bursting, one imagines, eyeing all this chocolatey earth—the houses big, solid, harbored in windbreaks of trees, everything fresh-painted and clean, and what's rare for farm country, hardly any junked machinery about. To keep a farm in this kind of spit-polish shape takes heroic physical effort. Hard enough to manage the main labor of farming, the work that has to be done this week, today, *right now*; niceties like structural maintenance and cleanup tend to slide for all but the most disciplined farmers, but here everyone seems bound to the strictest standards of neatness and order. There's something Puritan in it, an air of moral rigor, as if the tense self-discipline of early New England was moved two thousand miles and supersized for the huge proportions of the Midwest. One has a sense of blessings bestowed, of blessings vigorously earned. Of people who know they've landed in paradise and are determined not to blow it.

This is for a fact some of the most fertile soil on the planet. About a million years ago glaciers bulldozed the region, cutting off hilltops and dumping rich soil into the valleys. Eons of weather scooped and palmed the earth into low rolling hills, which today are a study in winter earth colors, brown and dun laced with patches of remnant snow, arctic blue where the ponds and creeks are iced over. The corduroy wales of plowed fields track the contour lines, such gentle curves as might be conjured in a meditation garden. It's beautiful country, pretty much heartbreaking in the golden afternoon light, and, as reported by Richard Manning in *Harper's*,[1] highly toxic. Massive concentrations of nitrates—from chemical fertilizers, and the shit of some twenty-one million Iowa hogs and fifty-two million Iowa chickens, most of them housed in animal factories—have rendered much of the state's drinking water unfit for human consumption. This is the same nitrate pollution that poisoned the water supply of Toledo, Ohio, in 2014, prompting Governor Kasich to call out the National Guard, and the same nitrates that are responsible for the vast (size of Connecticut) "dead zone" in the Gulf of Mexico. Large realities worm their way into daily life in odd ways. One Iowa sportsman told Manning that hunters now have to carry drinking water for their dogs out in the field, to keep them from being poisoned by algae blooms in the tainted streams and creeks.[2]

---

[1] "The Trouble with Iowa: Corn, Corruption, and the Presidential Caucuses," *Harper's*, February 2016.

[2] In a few weeks, Nicholas Kristof will report in the *New York Times* that 32 percent of Iowa children show elevated levels of lead in their bodies, compared to 4.9 percent of children testing positive for elevated lead in Flint, Michigan. "America Is Flint," the *New York Times*, February 7, 2016.

Manning notes that people have been growing crops and raising hogs in Iowa "ever since the Civil War," but it's only in the last twenty years that the practices of industrial agriculture have made Iowa water dangerous to drink. This span of time coincides with the unprecedented rise of obesity and associated illnesses in America, which Manning attributes to the crops—corn and soybeans, mostly—favored by Big Ag. It is, in other words, a food production model that gets you coming and going, and with Manning's report in mind the pleasure one gets from the beauties of the Iowa landscape is distinctly conflicted. And when you add the olfactory sense . . . the fact is, Iowa stinks. Literally, pervasively, far and wide and end to end. I grew up in the sticks and know from farm smells, but Iowa is of a different order altogether, its stench goes well beyond the localized funk of the barnyard, the ammoniac reek of summer shit in the stable and pen. Iowa is skunky like a pulp mill is skunky, like the sediment tanks of a big-city sewage treatment plant. It takes industrial-scale effort to create cosmic stinks like this.

People of Iowa, I apologize. No offense intended. The sun tips farther to the west, and the light softens, turns lavender as shadows crawl out from the ridges and hills. Near Iowa City there's a barn painted entirely as an American flag. Lopsided Vs of geese cut low overhead, and soon the terrain flattens out and all the snow has disappeared. We pass "the World's Largest Truck Stop—Iowa 80" and roll into Davenport at dusk, which features a not overly active downtown of 1950s bank and department-store architecture, red-brick warehouses, a smatter of low-rise office buildings. One hears the rumbling of trains in Davenport. The Mississippi River is rumored to be nearby. Where we're going the blocks turn scruffy, a dark run of empty storefronts and halfway houses that suddenly comes alive with people and cars, a pop-up traffic jam. Hillary! Hillary Appearing Tonight! An intersection near the Col presents a homiletic scene, it could be the stage set for a new American morality play—

```
          |       |
          |       |
          |       |
          |       |
          |       |
  VENUS NEWS      HARVEST
  ADULT MOVIES    KING MINISTRIES
          |       |
_____|       |_____
                  
  TIENDA MEXICAN   BAR (A BAR)
  RESTAURANT
          |       |
_____|       |_____
          |       |
          |       |
          |       |
          |       |
```

The line for the Col stretches far down the block. A few bundled-up protestors are stationed across the street, presumably the authors of the hand-scrawled banner hung from the building at their back. *Hillary Lied Americans Died.* Inside the Col the vibe is up, happy, fizzy, lots of bright young things are scurrying about, activist-organizer types psyched for a big night. A band is thumping out country tunes, *I'm lookin' for a good time,* the *djreowww djreowww* of the pedal steel soon giving way to the choo-choo chug of "Folsom Prison Blues." The Col, a.k.a. the Col Ballroom, the Coliseum, Saengerfest Halle, is a circa-1914 building with a barrel-vaulted main space and a brick exterior the color of Dentyne chewing gum, a product of civic pride and aspiration from a time when culture was local, or not at all. German immigrants brought the music to Davenport, liberal exiles fleeing the failed revolution of 1848, the same kaput grab at democracy that sent Karl Marx packing to London. The old country speaks in the Col's classical details, the arched proscenium and plaster reliefs, the stained-glass lyres wreathed in stylized vegetable matter. Modern touches include a disco ball over the dance floor, Christmas lights strung from the mezzanine's wrought-iron railing. Framed posters witness an impressive history, everyone from Sinatra to Chuck Berry has played here, Duke Ellington, Glenn Miller, the Beach Boys, Buddy Holly. Jimi Hendrix played the Col a month before Woodstock. The annual Bix Lives! festival celebrates the hometown boy who made good. All these threads of musical tradition are a happy thing to see; they do as all true culture does, encourage one's humanity.

Tonight's band keeps banging out tunes as the place fills up, the older folks in jeans and sneakers and puffy coats, the kids tatted and pierced, lightly misted in androgyny. Two middle-aged women here from Texas to volunteer for Hillary make the case to a guy with a notepad who says he's press. Time for a woman, they say. Hillary's earned it, *we've* earned it. She's pushed $18 million down ballot, Bernie zilch. The music stops and the crowd starts chanting *I'm with her! I'm with her!*, grinning, cheerfully raucous, nonchalantly diverse across the age-color-gender spectrum, though there's a notable lack of young white men. By the time Bill Clinton steps onto the stage the crowd is primed, maybe twelve hundred souls close-packed under the disco ball and another fifty or sixty standing on risers upstage, optics fodder for the news cameras.

The former president comes trailing his own story line tonight. News reports of the past few days have it that Bill has lost his mojo. He's seemed distracted, tired—*old,* in so many words, and maybe not all there? Tonight he's neatly turned out in a dark green flannel shirt buttoned to the neck, brown slacks, and a brown herringbone jacket, a country-weekend look for the good people of Davenport. His wiry hair—pure silver now, trimmed lower and tamer than in the old days—still sports that same sharp center-right part, the razorback ridge of it glinting with every turn. The slim-Bill version we've come to know these latter years has at last revealed the man without his baby fat. The face is narrower, longer, the bone structure clearly demarked, the jaw drops firm and clean down to the slightly cleft chin, but there's a fragility in his big face now, the blown-glass delicacy of elderly ladies and fine china. Bill got skinny to ease the strain on a problematic heart—now there's a brick of a metaphor for you, one you could argue either way. He loved too much? Too little? Or maybe both at once, a bipolar beast of the heart.

We can hardly look at skinny Bill these days without flashing on our own mortality, but he brings the fire tonight. "I was in awe of her when I met her forty-five years ago this month, and I'm STILL in awe of her," he booms, karate-chopping the air. He quotes John Wesley and the creed of the Methodist Church that Hillary was raised in—"Do all the good you can, for all the people you can, in all the ways you can, for as long as you can"—and the last line of Martin Luther King Jr.'s favorite hymn: "If I can do someone good then my journey is not in vain." Which brings us to the Hillary journey, starting with registering Hispanics to vote in South Texas during her student days, then "legal services for poor folks," and on to state and national levels and then into the stratosphere of global affairs. "BEST, CHANGE, MAKER, I, HAVE, EVER, KNOWN," Bill exhorts, arm chopping, finger wagging, eyes drilling the crowd. Then an anecdote: she saved the peace in Northern Ireland ("they love you guys over there"), she was the only, one, in, the WORLD who could have done it. "She dutton always agree with us, but she's always straight." Over and over Bill sticks the landing, as they say in gymnastics, every applause line hits via a potent combination of elder-statesman gravitas and gleeful good fun, he is a granddaddy lion romping with the cubs. We get the full treatment tonight, the twinkly eyes, the coyly bit lip, the curl of devilment in the grin, and so we're reminded that seduction is his basic unit of being, every transaction a form of charming the pants off someone. One has to say it worked out pretty well for him, a large life by any measure though not without its lumps and bumps, an impeachment here, humiliated wife there, not to mention the histrionic "values" backlash that brought us George W. Bush. But Bill Clinton's so smooth you might forget all that, for an evening at least.

Whoever said the man's lost it has rocks for brains. Perhaps he just needed a few days to strike the proper frame of mind, a trick of the Method actor's craft—he has to walk onstage pretending he's the candidate here. The cheering crowd has come out for *him*, not such a stretch considering he's the only president appearing at the Col tonight, and anyway where would Hillary be if not for him? Her eminence, however much she's worked and fought and suffered for it, began with the giant leg up of both feet firmly planted on Bill's shoulders. You can't help wondering how this fact plays out in the daily tug of marriage. Where would *you* be if it wasn't for *me*, babe? And Hillary: Right back at ya, bubba. If every marriage is un-knowable from the outside, theirs is the Mariana Trench of marital mystery.

Tonight she holds him extra long during the onstage hug, he has tried to make a quick self-effacing exit but she snares him in a boxer's clench and they confer for more than a token moment, murmuring, smiling eyeball to eyeball, a sweet show—is that what it is?—of conjugal harmony. What urgent thing could they possibly have to say to one another after all these years, all the thousands of similar moments? Though tonight maybe it's for real, something specific to the moment. *You've still got it, you big redneck bastard.*

"I brought a pretty good warm-up act!" she crows, finally releasing him. The crowd roars and Bill acknowledges the love with an aw-shucks grin. There's a high-octane oomph in the cheers; these Iowans know they're lucky, tonight they get two presidents (how can she lose?) for the price of one, and Hillary speaks the thought that's on everyone's mind. "And if I'm lucky enough to get this job I'm competing for, he'll be a really good adviser in the White House!" She ticks through Bill's stellar record: twenty-two million jobs created, 4 percent annual GDP growth, low inflation, budget surpluses. "As everyone knows," she says to roaring cheers, "the economy always does better when a Democrat's in the White House!" With her blond hair brushed back, the black slacks and peach blazer that hug her hips perhaps a bit more tightly than intended, Hillary could be a nicely aging country club matron, solid, well settled in life, the kind of comfortable-in-her-own-skin older woman whom thoughtful younger women pay attention to. Her earrings give off the occasional sparkle, a touch of money in the otherwise pared-down look. She uses her matronly chest to good effect, sourcing her words from deep in the diaphragm and a stout set of lungs: projects and never loses her breath, dials up the volume and never strains, her spiel humming along like a luxury import that's just hitting stride at 90 miles per hour.

Her voice has grown richer with the years, more sensuous and tougher at the same time. Gone is the nasal perkiness that infuriated millions, the bright alacrity of the born know-it-all. We get folksy Hillary tonight, lots of *ya knows* mixed with the policy, a down-home slackness on the tongue. *Crisscrossin' your state. Learnin' what's on folks' minds. I was at a little bowlin' alley in A-dell the other day* . . . "This is a job interview," she says, "I'm going to tell you what I want to do, and I want you to hold me to it," and for the next twenty minutes she delivers an entirely cogent talk on jobs and the economy, working in extended riffs on community colleges and Iowa's burgeoning clean-energy industry. This is Hillary at her strongest, and strange to say, her most relaxed and genuine, talking fact-based policy and programs, hawking the politics of grind-it-out incrementalism. She is, we've been told ad nauseam, the "pragmatic progressive" in the race, an obvious slam on the other guy, the old socialist, the not-even Democrat, and now that Sanders is surging her surrogates have been laying it on thick. "She quietly pulls people together and gets things done." She is "grounded in the realities of governance." Her "rational message" translates into greater "electability." This claim to the safe middle ground could be seen in the January 17 Democratic debate, when she characterized Sanders's plan for single-payer health care as an all-or-nothing gamble that would put Obamacare at risk. "We finally have a path to universal health care," she argued. "I don't want to see us start over again with a contentious debate . . . a whole new debate is something that would set us back."

A plainly false binary, one that assumes "contentious debate" ended with the passage of the ACA, Republicans sweetly conceding Obamacare as a settled fact. But the narrative preferred by the Clinton campaign is thuddingly obvious. She's the safe choice, the steady hand who will work within the system—she's always worked within the system—for the margin, the one step farther than the year before, the slow train to someplace better. No revolutions for Hillary; the freedom-profits-plunder equation will be fundamentally the same after her presidency as the day she takes office, and if it seems her bad luck to be running as a status quo candidate in a year of manifest outrage at the status quo, one might locate an element of personal responsibility here. It goes back, all the way back to early days in Arkansas, when Democrats throughout the country were searching for a viable identity to counter the Reagan Revolution. The economic populism of the New Deal seemed to have run its course, along with the notion that Wall Street and big business must be closely regulated in order to preserve the sovereignty of the democratic state. Starting in the early 1980s, a cohort of youngish Democrats—Bill and Hillary among them—began steering their party toward the faith-based free-market orthodoxy of the "Chicago school" of economics. Leaders of the faith such as Milton Friedman and Alan Greenspan preached an occult belief in markets' infallible ability to self-regulate, and the "New Democrats"—"The Neoliberal Club"[3] was the title of an early, prescient report on this rising subspecies of Democrat—developed their own marginally softer line of laissez-faire policies. The New Democrats became, in due course,

---

[3] By Randall Rothenberg, *Esquire*, February 1982.

the Democratic establishment, and would serve as the Republicans' handmaiden in deregulating banks and financial markets, gutting antimonopoly laws, and encouraging globalization through trade agreements such as NAFTA. This was the "New Covenant" that Bill Clinton ran on in 1992, and it promised old-fashioned Democratic social justice alongside a freewheeling, and highly profitable, corporate sector.

Over the short term neoliberalism seemed to work, at least on the economic side—that's the part of her husband's record Hillary can brag on. Long term, not so much: income inequality, stagnant wages, wholesale offshoring of American jobs, and massive concentrations of wealth—and the outsized political influence that comes with it—are some of the consequences we're living with now, in addition to a fiercely disillusioned and pissed-off electorate. The economic meltdown of 2008 is another; that big bang is still echoing in 2016, perhaps the prelude to an even bigger bang. Trump matches up well against Hillary in head-to-head polls. Substitute Bernie for Hillary, and the socialist, er, Democrat, handily beats the billionaire. Establishments of both parties would do well to consider that the rage may be more than a passing fad.[4]

But tonight in Davenport all is goodness and light. Hillary lays out a classic progressive agenda on jobs, education, infrastructure, the environment. Where will the money for all this excellence come from? "We'll get the money to pay for it all from where the money is, the wealthy!" she cries, the crowd bellowing approval. She calls for tax reform, to make the rich pay "their fair share." Penalties for companies that move jobs overseas: "They call it an *in*-version, I call it a *per*-version." And putting real teeth into financial reform: "No bank is too big to fail, no executive too big to jail." Mad cheers all around, but one becomes suddenly aware of an elephant in the room. This

---

[4] For more on the neoliberal transformation of the Democratic establishment, see "Hillary Doesn't Live Here Anymore," *infra*.

is interesting. This could get tricky if . . . and she does, and now the elephant turns its giant ass toward her as she rips into an anti–Wall Street riff that's a fair approximation of a proper stem-winder, facts and figures tumbling out in a white heat. Her text is the meltdown of 2008. The numbers, of course, are shocking, as the numbers tend to be in our modern era: so many billions for the gangs of Wall Street, foreclosures and layoffs for the little people. And none of the big shots went to jail! Hillary shows anger, she shows scorn. We're going to fix this! The elephant has backed its ass right up to the stage but Hillary is not fazed, she's giving a clinic in the essential political art of ignoring what's right in front of your face.

"You've received over six hundred thousand dollars in speaking fees from Goldman Sachs in one year," Sanders observed to Hillary in their January 17 debate. It was actually $675,000, in 2013, for three speeches to Goldman Sachs employees and guests; Bernie's intention, of course, was to question how strenuous Hillary's Wall Street fix would be given the comity implied by this gobsmacking pile of dough. Though it could be said Sanders was going easy on her. In the years 2013–2015, Hillary gave twelve speeches to Wall Street banks and investment firms, for which she received a total of $2,935,000. For her two Senate campaigns (2000 and 2006) she received contributions of more than $7 million from the banking and financial industry. For all of her campaigns, Senate and presidential, four of the top five donors thus far have been big banks, for a total of $712.4 million.[5] Since Bill left office, he and Hillary together have received more than $125 million in lecture fees, mostly from large corporations, banks, and investment firms. These amounts don't include the nearly $2 billion that outside donors—many of these same corporations and banks among them—have given the Clinton Foundation and its affiliates since 2001.[6]

---

[5] Citigroup, Goldman Sachs, JPMorgan Chase, and Morgan Stanley.

[6] See "The Clintons and Their Banker Friends," TomDispatch.com, May 7, 2015, http://tomdispatch.com/blog/175993/, and "Waking Up in Hillary Clinton's America,"

My fellow Americans, let us pause. A moment of reflection seems in order. The human mind wasn't built to comprehend moneys of this magnitude; we need time to behold and ponder, time for the vastness to seep into our brains like a cognitive vapor, and yet there remains an awesome abstraction to it all. American politics has become like an astronomers' conference where the experts speak of distance in terms of light-years. As if humans can really fathom that kind of scale—how far *light* travels in a *year*—and certainly not the nonexpert, whose idea of big distance is more like frequent-flier miles. And so the realm of political money is beyond the understanding of most of us. This many millions here, shit-tons more millions there . . . we numb out. Our synapses spaz and flicker. We resort to remedial math of the lowest sort. Suppose each dollar Hillary gets from Goldman Sachs is a Jimmy Dean sausage link, why then you'd have enough sausage to loop around the moon and back this many times!

God help us. $675,000 for three speeches, three hours of "work," more or less. It's not real. Money for nothing is not part of the natural order. The Clinton campaign, and the candidate herself, have voiced deep indignation at Sanders's suggestion that Hillary could be "bought," or the rather more rarefied "influenced." This is deemed "a personal attack," an attack on "character" of the sort that Sanders pledged not to do, a low blow, an ambush. It's all very arch and aggrieved, and basically hilarious. It's as if we're supposed to believe that the company one keeps, and how one makes her money, are somehow distinct from the personality that would be sitting in the Oval Office twelve or fifteen hours a day doing the work of governing.

*I found myself spending time with people of means—law firm*
*partners and investment bankers, hedge fund managers and*

TomDispatch.com, October 27, 2016, http://www.tomdispatch.com/blog/176203/, both by Nomi Prins.

*venture capitalists. As a rule, they were smart, interesting
people. But they reflected, almost uniformly, the perspectives
of their class: the top 1 percent or so of the income scale. I
know that as a consequence of my fund-raising I became more
like the wealthy donors I met. I spent more and more of my
time above the fray, outside the world of immediate hunger,
disappointment, fear, irrationality, and frequent hardship
of . . . the people that I'd entered public life to serve.*

BARACK OBAMA, *THE AUDACITY OF HOPE*

Well, sure, that's how it works. Face time, relationships, being
in the same rooms; the evolution of common points of view. Only
morons and fourth-raters do the straight-up bribe, the Rod Blago-
jeviches and Duke Cunninghams of the world. Chelsea Clinton
married a hedge fund manager, not a schoolteacher or a cop. Of
course there's nothing wrong with that. People fall in love with
who they will; usually it starts with being in the same rooms.[7] This is
the world the Clintons inhabited post-presidency, a world of rooms
populated by big-time CEOs and billionaires, a world where Bill
Clinton could pull down $15 million in five years as an "adviser" for
the investment firm Yucaipa Global, just one of the many corporate
glad-hander gigs he landed. It's no wonder that a collective howl rose
across the land when Hillary, pressed by Diane Sawyer on money
matters in a June 2014 interview, said, "We came out of the White
House not only dead broke but in debt . . . we struggled to piece
together the resources for mortgages for houses, for Chelsea's education. It was not easy." These comments were so transparently silly in
light of the facts—there was, for instance, the house purchased for
$2.85 million the last week of Bill's presidency, and the six-figure
lecture fees the former president immediately started pocketing, with

---

[7] "Propinquity and excitement," as my Southern aunts used to say. This is the primal impulse
underlying the grand tradition of the debutante ball. Herd all those birds of a feather into
one room, and let nature take its course.

blockbuster book deals and so much more to come—that the country couldn't help but call jerk on Hillary. She really thought we'd buy this bull? And where might we locate this feckless thought in what is clearly a very capable mind? The episode seemed not so much a matter of tone deafness, or of artless or awkward phrasing, as indicative of some fatal blind spot in her sensibility.

And so one wonders to what degree money underlies Hillary's "likability" problem, or more to the point, the deficits of "trust" and "trustworthiness" she regularly registers in the polls; whether her relentless hoovering of every dollar in sight counts for as much as Benghazi or the private email server. Obama brought a crucial measure of self-awareness to the money hustle, a capacity to detach and evaluate himself with a critical eye. The moral capacity, we could call it. It didn't stop him from scooping up wheelbarrows full of campaign money, but his ability to form and articulate a morally ambitious politics  one that had room for self-doubt—was surely part of why voters responded so strongly to him, at Hillary's expense. You sensed Obama hadn't stopped thinking, feeling, questioning; that he had it in him to become smarter and wiser over the years, to be better, because of that moral capacity. One sensed possibilities in Obama that simply weren't present in other politicians.

On this night in modest Davenport we won't hear the first word about those Goldman Sachs paydays. No explanation, nothing in the way of, Yeah, it sort of stinks but this is how the game works, or, No worries, people, okay, I took the money, I took gobs of it, sure, but my heart's with you. Soon, on February 3, to be exact—by then the Clinton campaign will have had several weeks to formulate a coherent response to this ongoing issue—CNN's Democratic Town Hall will give us this exchange:

ANDERSON COOPER: You were paid $675,000 for three speeches. Was that a mistake? I mean was that a bad error in judgment?

HILLARY CLINTON: Look, I made speeches to lots of groups.
I told them what I thought. I answered questions.
COOPER: But did you have to be paid $675,000?
CLINTON: Well, I don't know. That's what they offered, so—
you know, every secretary of state that I know has done that.
COOPER: But that's usually once they're out of office, they're
not running for office again.
CLINTON: Well, I didn't know—to be honest I wasn't—I
wasn't committed to running. I didn't know whether I
would run or not.

*That's what they offered.* It's the kind of answer a cornered adolescent might give. Someone watching that interview might find
himself wishing that just once somebody would be a hero and say no
to the money, say no for the wild-ass hell of it, an epic fuck-you to
the greedheads and the whole sorry racket. What a revolution in the
mind of America—you don't have to take the money! Such a world
of possibility opens up, so many ways to be besides Kardashian *luxe*
and the lifestyles of high-end real estate ads. Even ex-presidents and
their families might be allowed, might *choose,* to behave as more or
less regular citizens, to live reasonably well, in a reasonably comfortable house, on a reasonably safe and pleasant street. Modest mice,
moral giants. It used to happen, not so long ago. After leaving the
White House and moving back to Missouri, Harry and Bess Truman treated themselves to a cross-country road trip. They took the
family car, just the two of them. The former president drove. They
ate in restaurants, stayed at inns and motor courts, sometimes with
friends. Paid their own way, no junkets, no speaking fees.[8] Things
were different back then, back when America was great again.

But you have to give it to Hillary, she keeps a formidably straight

---

[8] Happily, there is a book on this heartening episode of ex-presidential life. See the charming
*Harry Truman's Excellent Adventure* by Matthew Algeo (Chicago Review Press, 2009, 2011).

face throughout the Wall Street rant. Mere mortals can't do this; we'd "crumb the play," in con-man lingo, betray ourselves with a skid of the eye, a slight shimmy in our voice. She moves on to a series of pithy briefs on abortion rights, *Citizens United,* gun control, drug prices, Obamacare. "We *will* get to universal health care." National defense: "I have a plan to defeat ISIS." She slams Republicans for demonizing Muslims. "We need to be unified in order to defeat terrorism." She's organized, vigorous, passionate, her policy points make such good common sense that you want to believe she can always be this fine—that perhaps the presidency would make it so, lift her above the careerist temporizing and compulsive money grab of the politician who aspires to ever higher. Can't go any higher than the White House, right? And so it's tempting to think that the best in her would be encouraged, and only the best. As if the history of the office didn't show how rare this is.

Oh Hillary, we wish we knew ye. She stays focused through the applause lines, often talking over the cheers, and this bracing absence of ingratiation serves to elevate the event, requires the crowd to come some distance toward meeting her. She's strong. The deep-lunged voice never falters. This is her third or fourth event of the day after weeks of such days, and one begins to appreciate all over again her matron's bulk. It suits her, the reserves implied by that broad chest, the solid grounding of those generous hips and thighs. With the years has come a kind of dreadnought presence, queen of the fleet, thick armor plating and heavy guns. She can take the hits—has anyone in American politics taken more these past thirty years?—and plow ahead, and surely that's one more reason for the right-wing to hate her, they've thrown everything they have at Hillary Clinton and she simply does not go away.

The evening finishes big. The crowd gives its loudest cheers of the night, the music cranks up, and you half expect confetti to come raining down, so festive is the mood. "She was not blah," a diminutive, bright-eyed elderly lady tells me. "She's a much stronger candidate than in 2008," says the lady's husband, and they confirm that, yes, they came out to see her then, right here in Davenport. We have to shout over the music, the driving *thunka thunka thunka* of a Kelly Clarkson anthem. *What doesn't kill you makes you **stronger,** stand a little **taller** . . .* The song selection's not lost on anyone. Up near the stage Hillary is working the crowd, we can't see her but her progress is marked by the density of the scrum, the aim of cell phones held aloft. Everywhere you look people are smiling and milling around, dazzled, reluctant to leave. Hillary made the troops happy tonight. The base has been "energized," as they say, it was all about rallying for the good true fight with never a mention of the socialist who's breathing down her neck. We leave the Col with a particular sense of her, awareness that she's fought countless battles, taken huge hits, suffered, been stupid, been brilliant, lost some and won some, put her head down and pushed no matter the result. Whatever else one might say of her record, she's earned the right to be judged on that. So let it be that; she's earned that much, at least. Which wouldn't seem like such a great deal to ask, in a democracy.

## 2. "THE CHISELS ARE READY."

Nine A.M. on a crisp Saturday morning in Hubbard, snow on the ground, that good Iowa funk in the air, and the sun so spanking bright it makes your eyes water. Tiny Hubbard (pop. 845) is a grain elevator town: the two beige silos and adjacent headhouse are the tallest things around, a few church steeples offering weak competition in the skyline department. The tree-lined streets proceed in an orderly grid. Every sidewalk is clean-swept, and tidy wood-frame houses project a somewhat dated air of middle-class comfort and modesty, that bygone America of home heating oil, asbestos shingles, Cream of Wheat on the breakfast table seven days a week. Aim your gaze down the length of any street, you're liable to see where town gives way to open fields.

We're standing outside South Hardin Middle School, "Home of the Tigers." It's not too intolerably cold in the sun, and sidling up to the candidate's bus with its rumbling engine, one imagines it to be a degree or two warmer. The bus is sleek, black, shiny, a rock-star touring number with dark-tinted windows for absolute privacy. CRUZIN' TO VICTORY runs in blazing red letters down each side, along with a tapering blob of a logo meant to evoke the flame of a candle, a near-copy of the logo of the United Methodist Church. The destination plaque in front reads CRUZ TO VICTORY. COURAGEOUS CRUZER is painted across the front bumper . . . okay okay, we get it already. A certain kind of smartass might be tempted to finger-scrawl CRUZIN' FOR A BRUISIN' into the dust of a dirty window, except all the windows are squeegee-clean and the Secret Service might tase you, but for a fact it's been a rough couple of weeks for Senator Ted Cruz, Republican of Texas, native of Calgary (Canada), BA Princeton, JD Harvard Law, Tea Party favorite, born-again Christian, and Most Likely To Be Wedgied by his congressional colleagues. Up ten points in the Iowa polls in early January, Cruz started sliding around the time Trump began hammering Birther II, as in: Cruz's Canadian birth potentially renders him ineligible for the presidency *per* the "natural born citizen" requirement of Article II of the Constitution. Not an issue, Cruz argued, I'm natural-born thanks to my American mom, and he released her Delaware birth certificate to prove it. Trump kept hammering. "This is a real problem for Ted, I can tell you," he informed the electorate in tones of seemingly genuine sorrow. Then Cruz's old constitutional law professor weighed in with an op-ed in the *Boston Globe*.

> *[T]he kind of judge Cruz says he admires and would appoint to the Supreme Court is an "originalist," one who claims to be*

*bound by the narrowly historical meaning of the Constitution's*
*terms at the time of their adoption. To his kind of judge, Cruz*
*ironically wouldn't be eligible, because the legal principles*
*that prevailed in the 1780s and '90s required that someone*
*actually be born on US soil to be a "natural born" citizen.*
*Even having two US parents wouldn't suffice. And having*
*just an American mother, as Cruz did, would have been*
*insufficient at a time that made patrilineal descent decisive.*[9]

As Trump warmed to the issue, he began playing "Born in the
USA" at his rallies. When asked to comment, Cruz suggested that
his rival play "New York, New York" instead, given that Trump
"embodies New York values." The line seemed to resonate. Cruz kept
using it, and at the Republican debate of January 14 he elaborated:

*[E]veryone understands that the values in New York City*
*are socially liberal or pro-abortion or pro–gay marriage,*
*focus around money and the media. And—and I would*
*note indeed, the reason I said that is I was asked—my friend*
*Donald has taken to playing Bruce Springsteen's "Born in the*
*USA," and I was asked what I thought of that. And I said,*
*"Well, if he wanted to play a song, maybe he could play 'New*
*York, New York'?" And . . . you know, the concept of New*
*York values is not that complicated to figure out . . . Not a lot*
*of conservatives come out of Manhattan. I'm just saying.*

One sensed that Cruz meant for this to be his big moment. He'd
obviously rehearsed the lines with much diligence, so smooth and
sparkling was the delivery, and in his manner there was an aspect of
easy confidence, as if he'd won the point (they were in South Caro-

[9] Lawrence Tribe, "Under Ted Cruz's Own Logic, He's Ineligible for the White House," *Boston Globe,* January 11, 2016.

lina) simply by trotting out that loaded phrase, *New York values.* Trump, for once, was patient. No interruptions, no talking-over, and there was fine drama in this, watching a consummate brawler bide his time. He heard out Cruz's spiel with his head cocked, a bulldog set to his face, then flipped the moment back on Cruz without breaking a sweat.

"Conservatives do come out of Manhattan, including William F. Buckley," Trump began, a little stick-and-jab as prelude to the full evisceration:

> *I've had more calls on that statement Ted made—New York is a great place. It's got great people, it's got loving people, wonderful people. When the World Trade Center came down, I saw something that no place on earth could have handled more beautifully, more humanely than New York . . . you had two hundred-and-ten-story buildings come crashing down. I saw them come down. Thousands of people killed, and the cleanup started the next day, and it was the most horrific cleanup, probably in the history of doing this . . . And the people of New York fought and fought and fought, and we saw more death, and even the smell of death—nobody understood it. And it was with us for months, the smell, the air. And we rebuilt downtown Manhattan, and everybody in the world watched and everybody in the world loved New York and loved New Yorkers. And I have to tell you, that was a very insulting statement that Ted made.*

The applause was like a glacier calving, the Holland Tunnel breaking open: that first hard crack, then the roar. Cruz, blushing, could only smile with a pants-around-his-ankles sort of squinch to his face. He had nothing. The big Ivy League debate champ, zilch. He seemed to have assumed one good stiff blow would do it, that there would be no counterpunch from Donald Trump, of all people, who famously learned at the knee of his mentor Roy Cohn that when somebody hits you, you hit back twice as hard.

"Drop Dead, Ted" was the next day's headline in the *New York Daily News*. He was having that kind of week. On January 13 the *New York Times* had broken the news that Cruz violated federal election laws during his 2012 Senate campaign by failing to disclose loans totaling more than $1 million. The bulk of the funds was borrowed from his wife's employer, Goldman Sachs (them again), and the rest from Citibank in the form of a line of credit, this at a time when Cruz was running a Tea Party–populist campaign that particularly targeted Wall Street bailouts and the predations of big banks. Later, once he was safely in the Senate, Cruz would list the loans in his annual Senate ethics report, though by then he was peddling a very different legend around his successful candidacy, that of a brave young couple who risked "all we had saved" on the husband's long-shot Senate campaign. "'Sweetheart,'" as Cruz told it to *New York Times* reporter Ashley Parker,[10] reenacting his pivotal conversation with Heidi, "'I'd like us to liquidate our entire net worth, liquid net worth, and put it into the campaign,'" to which the loyal Heidi readily agreed.

"It is an inadvertent filing question," Cruz said on the day the story broke. "And that is the end of that." The loans were the first question put to him at the following evening's debate. Cruz had the sublime gall to call the *Times* story a "really stunning hit piece" while simultaneously acknowledging his transgression, which he, the crack Harvard lawyer, characterized as "a paperwork error."

One began to get the impression of a candidate who wanted it both ways (don't they all) but wasn't up to the job of managing it. "Lyin' Ted" soon joined "Little Marco" and "Low-Energy Jeb" in Trump's repertoire of torments, with more blows to follow. On Jan-

---

[10] Ashley Parker, "A Wife Committed to Cruz's Ideals, but a Study in Contrasts to Him," *New York Times*, October 13, 2013.

uary 19, Trump received the semicoherent endorsement of longtime Cruz ally Sarah Palin, who wore for the occasion a spangly lamé number that seemed constructed from spare chandelier parts. On the same day, Terry Branstad, Iowa's popular Republican governor, broke protocol by specifically *not* endorsing a candidate, namely, Ted Cruz, whom Branstad, ever mindful of the Renewable Fuel Standard, slammed as "the candidate of big oil." On January 26, Trump was endorsed by Sheriff Joe Arpaio, the boss hog of Maricopa County, Arizona, and by Jerry Falwell Jr., president of Liberty University, "the world's largest Christian university"; it was at Liberty that Cruz had formally launched his presidential campaign in 2015, with a beaming Falwell presiding over the event. Then came the GOP debate of January 28, which Trump refused to show up for and won anyway.

Well, it's not a campaign if you aren't taking hits. After breathing bus fumes for a while we make our way into the school cafeteria, a sunny, surprisingly compact room with white cinder-block walls, big round tables painted blue, and a large school-days banner— RESPECT YOURSELF YOU ARE SPECIAL—amid the transient Cruz signage. Several moon-faced young men with severe expressions are holding placards that read "Don't Believe the Liberal Media." There is a black man in the audience. Everyone else is white, it's standing-room only with lots of whiskers and lumpy bedhead on display, body types tending toward the heavy, the low-centered, built for work not show. Eye contact with a stranger triggers discomfort, a kind of reflexive self-effacement; more than anything it reads as shyness, a not-unheard-of trait in farm communities, though a few of the more solitary-seeming men give off a Boo Radley vibe. Perhaps as many as a hundred of us have gathered as U.S. Congressman Steve King switches on his microphone and announces brightly, "We started on time!"

Representative King is a short, sturdy, personable man with a bit of starter paunch, balding, blue eyed, dressed today in a green shirt and green blazer, regular-guy khaki slacks. During his six terms in Congress he's become nationally known for spouting the sorts of unfiltered xenophobia that less extroverted bigots reserve for muttering at their television sets.[11] He is arguably the fiercest anti-immigration hawk in Congress, while his district, the Iowa Fourth, is a bastion of Big Ag, whose profitability depends on a compliant, low-wage labor force willing to do repugnant work under harsh conditions. Slaughterhouses, rendering plants, feed facilities and the like, these offer the sorts of jobs that people with few options tend to take, a group that broadly overlaps with the very same people King would like to round up and deport, yesterday. King's support of immigration policies that would, if enacted, wreck Big Ag's business model might make sense if he opposed the industry for its shameful commitment to inhumanely low wages, or the widespread destruction it wreaks on the environment, or its grotesque treatment of animals, or the fact that a great many of its products are, when consumed even in moderate quantities, harmful to human health; but he is, on the contrary, a zealous advocate for Big Ag. Which means either (1) he's a moral hypocrite and political cynic, rousing support for himself with nativist rhetoric he has no intention of acting on, or (2) he's too stupid to recognize the conflict in his positions.

---

[11] Perhaps his most famous comment to date was this July 2013 characterization of undocumented immigrants: "For every one who's a valedictorian, there's another hundred out there who weigh 130 pounds, and they've got calves the size of cantaloupes because they're hauling 75 pounds of marijuana across the desert." Responding to HUD secretary Julián Castro's comments on the Republican Party's difficulty in attracting Hispanic voters, King tweeted in July 2015: "What does Julian Castro know? Does he know that I'm as Hispanic and Latino as he?" (King is not Hispanic.) Of Barack Obama's candidacy for president, King remarked on March 7, 2008: "I will tell you that, if he is elected president, then the radical Islamists, the al-Qaeda, the radical Islamists and their supporters, will be dancing in the streets in greater numbers than they did on September 11." Obama's decision to include his middle name "Hussein" when swearing the presidential oath of office was described by King as "bizarre" and "a double standard." King has voiced support for racial profiling as "an important component of legitimate law enforcement." Even though Iowa was a stalwart Union state during the Civil War, King sees fit to display the Confederate battle flag on his desk.

So one watches Representative King with real interest, alert for clues that might solve this human mystery. He speaks easily, his manner casual but not condescending as he talks of the unique opportunity he's had the past few years to get to know each of the seventeen GOP candidates. In the end, he settled on Cruz—"an extraordinary candidate"—as the contender most in harmony with his own views. "You know my core principles," King says in his snappish, somewhat nasal voice, "and I can state it pretty clearly. I am a full-spectrum constitutional Christian conservative, and I think that fits probably most everybody in this room." That snap in his voice is put to good use as he rags on establishment Republicans who cut deals with K Street lobbyists and the likes of Nancy Pelosi and Harry Reid (the crowd groans at the names), but Cruz, King assures us, is not that kind of Republican. "This is a once-in-a-lifetime opportunity to vote for a man who checks all the boxes, so let's all get in this harness and pull together." A true conservative, a devout Christian, a candidate whom God will use to "restore the soul of America." And he's a very smart guy! Cruz has "an autographic memory," King tells us. Mention is made of our Judeo-Christian values and the threat of radical Islamist terrorism, followed by a flash of wit. "How about the right to keep your arms bare! ISIS wants to come in and take that away from us." What we need is a president who knows where to turn in times of crisis; who, after hearing out his advisers, "is gonna get down on his knees and ask God for that final counsel."

King has a short man's way of moving, his gestures curt, abrupt, his stubby arms punching the air like a wind-up toy. The audience is strangely inert, considering this is their own congressman making the pitch, a man who has presumably brought them honor by achieving some measure of national stature. Perhaps they're listless simply because he's a known quantity. Or maybe it's just too crowded and stuffy in here to get all worked up. But when King introduces the candidate's wife, there's real warmth in the applause, a flurry of cheers. Heidi Cruz brings a morning freshness to the room despite having spent most of the past two weeks on a bus. She is short, attractive, curvy, with a dramatically blown-out blond coif that would fit right in at the Dallas Junior League, and her ensemble too: designer jeans, form-fitting pastel sweater, floral scarf draped around her shoulders. Call it the grown-up Southern preppie look, high-end casual. A devout Christian, the daughter of Baptist missionaries—she grew up partly in Kenya and Nigeria—Heidi was, according to her father-in-law, Rafael Cruz (himself a freelance evangelical preacher), the vessel through which God conveyed his blessing on Ted Cruz's presidential run, as he recounted to Dr. Michael Brown:

> *My son Ted and his family spent six months in prayer seeking God's will for this decision. But the day the final green light came on, the whole family was together. It was a Sunday. We were all at his church, First Baptist Church in Houston, including his senior staff. After the church service, we all gathered at the pastor's office. We were on our knees for two hours seeking God's will. At the end of that time, a word came through his wife, Heidi. And the word came, just saying, "Seek God's face, not God's hand." And I'll tell you, it was as if there was a cloud of the holy spirit filling that place. Some of us were weeping, and Ted just looked up and said, "Lord, here am I, use me. I surrender to you, whatever you want." And he felt that was a green light to move forward.*[12]

We aren't told the specifics of how the word "came through" Heidi (was she bodily possessed by the holy spirit? she heard a voice

---

[12] See https://www.youtube.com/watch?v=EqiwUnxmfmc. See also David Corn, "Ted Cruz's Dad: My Son Ran for President After God Sent His Wife a Sign," *Mother Jones,* February 22, 2016.

in her head?) nor how this particular interpretation of a fairly general directive was arrived at—why seeking God's face would be seen as "a green light" to embark on a run for the presidency, as opposed to, for example, a call to withdraw from worldly affairs and instead pursue a life of prayer and contemplation—but the episode nevertheless offers a window into the Cruz decision-making process. A man who's getting his orders from God would seem to be above opposition or even questioning from his fellow mortals. This, at any rate, would naturally be the opinion of the man so privileged as to receive such orders, and recent history offers striking examples of such individuals in action—various ayatollahs, Osama bin Laden, Baruch Goldstein, certain clergy of the Catholic faith. People of a more skeptical cast of mind might detect strong whiffs of predetermination here, and so it is for those who have their doubts about Ted Cruz. One has the feeling that when Cruz falls to his knees for that final counsel, he's going to hear pretty much what he wants to hear.

Heidi embarks on a bullet-point summary of her husband's fine qualities, and it's quickly apparent that she's good at this. She is poised, polished, articulate; one has the impression of a supremely able and confident woman whose skill set includes not threatening men with her ability and confidence. Her firm but modulated voice steers clear of any note to which the dreaded word "shrill" could be applied. She hits her points, expertly wands the microphone from hand to hand. "Ted is a consistent conservative, not a campaign conservative." Applause. "Raised as a Christian, with the Bible at the center of his life." People nod, murmur approval. "Ted is always questioning the status quo." Amen to that. "He doesn't take instruction from the party leaders, he takes instruction from you." Cheers, big applause. Then a testament to his "loving and thoughtful nature," which might come as news to his colleagues on Capitol Hill, where he's widely regarded as a monster of personal ambition and insufferable self-regard.[13] But surely a wife would know! Though had the need arisen, Lady Macbeth could have probably dictated an entire treatise on her husband's kindly nature as she stood at the sink washing her hands.

The crowd is beaming by the time Heidi finishes. That she wins them over is no great surprise; Goldman Sachs, where she is a managing director, is one of the world's ultimate training grounds for how to sell a room. Interestingly, she and her husband keep their distance when the event transitions to him. They stand on opposite sides of the long "TRUSTED" banner at the front of the room and declare their love for one another from twenty paces. No hug and kiss, no whispered endearments in the clutch. This is good Christian modesty, perhaps. Or maybe all those days and nights on the bus are taking a toll.

The candidate begins with lavish props to Steve King. "Steve every day stands up and *fights* for the Constitution, he *fights* for freedom," Cruz intones in his righteous warble. "Every day Steve King crawls over broken glass with a knife between his teeth, *fighting* for the men and women of Iowa." This is a fair example of the Cruz rhetorical style, which tends toward the graphic, the violent, the overstimulated, a kind of Pee-wee's Playhouse of gaudy apocalypticism, the faithful ever at war with the armies of darkness. In Cruz World we are always *standing at the edge of the abyss,* we are charged with *pulling this nation back from the cliff,* and *the stakes have never been higher,* and we are perpetually *running out of time.* "We're here this morning for something a lot more important than politics," he

---

[13] Senator John Cornyn: "Ted Cruz has been running for president since the day he got here." Senator John McCain once called him a "wacko bird." Former senator Bob Dole: "Nobody likes him." Representative Tom Cole: "Classless, tasteless, and counterproductive." Former president George W. Bush: "I just don't like the guy." Former Speaker of the House John Boehner: "Lucifer in the flesh . . . I have never worked with a more miserable son of a bitch in my life." Representative Peter King: "I hate Ted Cruz. I'll take cyanide if he ever got the nomination." Senator Lindsey Graham: "If you killed Ted Cruz on the floor of the Senate, and the trial was in the Senate, nobody would convict you." And these are Republicans.

informs us in urgent, breathy tones of preacherly sanctimony, his voice dropping as it nears the end of every thought, digging for the tremble, the hushed vibrato of ultimate virtue. You'd think he gargles twice a day with a cocktail of high-fructose corn syrup and holy-roller snake oil. His tone and cadence take after the saccharine blather of the great Christian pitchmen of radio and TV, the hucksters who mastered the catch in the throat, the tremulous quaver and gulp, because as every pro knows that's where the money is. Cruz's sonic palette could be compared to the colors favored by another star of the evangelical right, the late bestselling artist Thomas Kinkade, a born-again Christian and the self-proclaimed "Painter of Light."[14] Kinkade's scenes of lighthouses, small-town Main Streets, and homey woodland bungalows skewed heavily toward what might be called stained-glass colors—cloying pinks and lavenders, buttery yellows, many-splendored shades of rose and purple, all infused with that sugary signature glow. Kinkade didn't paint people. His deliriously idealized images of the pastoral and bucolic suggest not nature so much as a five-star–bed-and-breakfast fantasy of heaven, well scrubbed of every trace of the human stain. Kinkade had his fair share of the demons that afflict us all, and he had talent, too— with guts and integrity he might have worked his way to making actual art, "actual art" presupposing an honest and bloody grappling with the hardest stuff of human existence. Instead he ramped up the treacle for mass production and had himself a winning racket, till the demons finally chased him down.

"Sentimentality," James Baldwin wrote in his essay "Everybody's Protest Novel,"

> *the ostentatious parading of excessive and spurious emotion, is the mark of dishonesty, the inability to feel; the wet eyes of the*

---

[14] He trademarked the phrase, and made millions through reproductions of his paintings sold in dedicated retail outlets and numerous licensing and merchandising deals.

> *sentimentalist betray his aversion to experience, his fear of life,*
> *his arid heart; and it is always, therefore, the signal of secret*
> *and violent humanity, the mask of cruelty.*[15]

A news photo from several weeks ago shows the Republican candidates lined up prior to one of their debates, each man—Carly Fiorina didn't make the cut—holding his hand over his heart. They're evidently singing "The Star-Spangled Banner," or perhaps reciting the Pledge of Allegiance. Cruz is posed like everyone else, right hand over his heart, except he's placed his hand *inside* his jacket, for it to be that much closer to his heart, one supposes; to signify that he is the most sincere, the most ardent, the most ferociously patriotic. Such are the reflexes of a man formed in an atmosphere of competitive piety, a species of evangelical Christianity that demands strenuous proofs of faith; where not parading your piety is to risk disapproval, reprimand, the bad opinion of peers and elders. You believe, but do you believe *enough*. To seem otherwise may not be as literally lethal as it was in Salem in 1692, but the principle is the same. To doubt, even seeming to doubt, is to risk losing your place in the world. The moral inquiry concluded a long time ago. Matters of faith, the cosmology of good and evil, are settled, the orthodoxy enforced by an authoritarian (and highly patriarchal) regime. And so you strive to sing the loudest, pray the longest, memorize the most Bible verses, every instinct and reflex develops to put yourself beyond reproach by being the indisputable best. In Stalin's Russia you could have been shot for being the first to stop clapping after one of the great leader's speeches. Ted Cruz is nothing if not competitive; he would have been the last man clapping every time.

This morning in Hubbard he describes his plan of action on assuming the presidency. First order of business, rescind all unconstitutional executive orders signed by Barack Obama. Number two:

---

[15] *Collected Essays* (Library of America, 1998), p. 12.

instruct the Department of Justice to investigate Planned Parenthood. Three: instruct the Department of Justice and the IRS to "stop the war on religion." And then: tear up the Iran nuclear deal. Move the U.S. embassy in Israel from Tel Aviv to Jerusalem, "the once and eternal capital of Israel." Repeal "every word" of Obamacare. Secure the border. Abolish weapons-free zones: "So the next time a jihadist goes into a marine recruiting center in Chattanooga, he'll meet the business end of the rifles of a dozen marines." And this, which whips up hoots and bellows: "I will take on the EPA and all the regulators that descend on good farmers and ranchers like locusts."

Stern-faced Cruz delivers each item with fire-and-brimstone ardor, then flips to a mealy-mouthed smile as he takes the applause. It's not what you'd call a winning smile. The Cruz happy face looks more like the pursed-mouth grimace of constipation, the top lip pulling a sort of widow's-peak hood over his front teeth while the rest of his mouth retracts to show rows of tiny possum teeth. And so it goes throughout the action-plan litany, stern face, smiley face, stern, smiley, stern, smiley, like a cheap lenticular toy you'd find in a box of Cracker Jack. In certain lights, from select angles, Cruz's unusual features add up to something close to handsomeness, and if the light falls just right he even has a touch of old-time Hollywood dash, the swoony, borderline effeminate prettiness of Rudolph Valentino, that same trace of Latin exoticism. It's most apt to happen on TV, Cruz showing up best in makeup and a sharp blue suit, all those high-tech studio lights aimed just so. In person there's a schlumpy fleshiness to him, a blurring of definition in his face and neck, the little knob of his chin dangling like a boiled quail egg. His skin reads soft, smooth, the skin of an avid indoorsman, and several inches of schlump are revealed at his waist when he's not buttoned up in a jacket.

Today he's wearing blue jeans, a blue button-down shirt rolled at the sleeves, no jacket. He recalls our country in the late 1970s, a sad time in America when, he tells us, "Russia and Iran were openly laughing at the president of the United States." But hapless Carter gave way to the Reagan Revolution, a revolution that "came from the people, not from Washington." Might the disaster of Obama lead to a similar redemption? Cruz invokes Reagan's "shining city on a hill," the return to "the Judeo-Christian values that built this great country." But we're running out of time, staring into the abyss, and "people of faith" must rise up before it's too late . . . This is Cruz doing what Cruz does best, perorating into the realms of absolute good and evil, which are, let's face it, so much more thrilling than all the drag-ass negotiating and compromising of functional politics. So much simpler to declare holy war on your opponent than to sit down and hammer out a compromise, and holy war is what the Cruz campaign is all about, a grand crusade against evil for the soul of the country, which places the Cruz firewall somewhere in the vicinity of the gates of heaven. Fifty years ago the political scientist Richard Hofstadter described the difference between traditional conservatism—the kind of conservatism that actually conserves—and the apocalyptic fevers of the right-wing ideologue. "The Paranoid Style in American Politics" gets most of the attention these days, but another of his essays, "Goldwater and Pseudo-Conservative Politics," probably brings us closer to the truth of a politician like Cruz, whose willingness to trash the basic mechanisms of American governance is always justified in the name of his divine mission. In October 2013 he went so far as to orchestrate a shutdown of the entire federal government for sixteen days in a failed attempt to defund Obamacare. He's regularly threatened similar shutdowns ever since: in November 2014, in response to Obama's executive action on immigration; in August–September 2015, over federal funding for Planned Parenthood; in September 2015, over "secret side deals" pertaining to the nuclear agreement with Iran; and in September 2016, over the domain-naming system for the internet.

At times it's hard to tell whether Cruz wants to prevent the apocalypse or hurry it along. "The final spiritual Armageddon of the fundamentalists, their overarching moral melodrama, the dream of millennial crusading and decisive conflict, plainly stirred his mind," Hofstadter wrote of Barry Goldwater, "but the hard realities of the current world seemed more remote."[16] What plainly stirs Cruz's mind are scary stories. When a lady asks him about the federal government's role in medical research—specifically, why aren't we doing more to cure cancer and other diseases—Cruz responds with a long disquisition on the threat of biological weapons in the age of terror. Someone asks about his plan for border security, and Cruz answers with a critique of Obama's lax border policies, which, among other evils, brought a "flood of minors into the U.S. with their ears and fingers cut off by the cartels." On the issue of Supreme Court appointments, Cruz goes full nightmare. When he tells us Hillary would like nothing better than to appoint Barack Obama to the Supreme Court, the crowd gasps, and a chorus of *noooo*s rings out. But even as it's currently composed,[17] this Supreme Court is "an activist, out-of-control court" that upheld Obamacare and "tore down traditional marriage" in a single twenty-four-hour period. "Lawless decisions," Cruz says through his teeth,[18] and he delivers a grave warning:

> *We are* one, justice, away, *from a leftist Supreme Court. We are* one, justice, away, *from the Supreme Court concluding*

---

[16] "Goldwater and Pseudo-Conservative Politics," in *The Paranoid Style in American Politics and Other Essays* (Knopf, 1965; Vintage, 2008), p. 130.

[17] Cruz made these remarks on January 30, 2016, several weeks before Antonin Scalia, arguably the most conservative of the court's conservative bloc, died.

[18] "Goldwater arrived at the decision, far from conservative in its implications, that the decisions of the Supreme Court are 'not necessarily' the law of the land. Of course, the decisions of the Court have always had political content and they have often been highly controversial; there is no reason why they should suddenly be regarded with whispered reverence. But it is only in our time, and only in the pseudo-conservative movement, that men have begun to hint that disobedience to the Court is not merely legitimate but is the essence of conservatism." Hofstadter, pp. 99–100.

*that nobody in this room and no American has an individual*
*right to keep and bear arms. We are one, justice, away,*
*from the Supreme Court striking down every restriction on*
*abortion, and mandating unlimited abortion on demand,*
*up until the time of birth, partial birth with taxpayer*
*funding, and no parental notification whatsoever. We are*
*one, justice, away, from the Supreme Court ordering veterans*
*memorials torn down all over this country if they contain any*
*acknowledgment of God Almighty.*

"The chisels are ready," he continues in rapturously dire tones, the little quail egg of his chin thrust forward. "We are one, justice, away, from the crosses and Stars of David being hacked off the headstones of dead veterans."

Are we scared yet? Cruz burns with the fervor of the righteous when speaking of absolutes, but a nuts-and-bolts question about health care trips him up. A middle-aged man sitting near the front—Mike Valde, we will learn later, sixty-three years old, of Coralville, Iowa—tells the story of his brother-in-law Mark, a barber, "a small-business man," who lived uninsured for years, then was finally able to afford health insurance because of Obamacare. "He had never been to a doctor for years," Valde says, and when he did go after getting insurance, the news was not good. "Multiple tumors behind his heart, his liver, his pancreas. And they said, 'We're sorry, sir, there's nothing we can do for you.' Mark never had health care until Obamacare," Valde continues, and then he puts his question to Cruz: "What are you going to replace it with?"

Cruz is nodding mournfully. Condolences are expressed. He's still nodding as he says "millions of Americans" have lost their coverage under Obamacare. People lost jobs, lost their doctors, saw their premiums "skyrocket." Then he brightens, and with a jocular little smile he refers to a proposition that he likes to put forward at campaign events. "Anyone whose premiums have dropped twenty-five hundred dollars, as President Obama promised, should vote for Hillary Clinton. I'll take everybody else."

Har. Cruz is smiling. There's a bit of laughter in the room. Valde, still standing, still respectful, clearly nervous—it's obvious this kind of thing isn't easy for him—persists.

"My question is, what are you going to replace it with?"

Abruptly the mood turns tense. The crowd is silent and very still; no one is laughing now. It's clearly a Cruz-friendly audience, but the moment has their attention. Cruz starts in again on the millions-of-Americans riff, all the people who'd been happy with their plans and lost them, lost their doctors, lost jobs, the burdens on employers, "all the millions of stories on the other side." Gradually, amid all the well-oiled verbiage, it becomes apparent that Cruz is talking as if the brother-in-law didn't have insurance because of Obamacare, inverting the question to its mirror opposite. The cheap dodge, the outright intellectual dishonesty of it, is, well, shocking. Shouldn't we expect more from our Harvard lawyers? Eventually Cruz offers a few words toward a replacement "plan": expand competition in the marketplace, allow people to buy insurance across state lines, which, according to Cruz, will bring down costs.[19] "Your father-in-law," he says, turning back to Mike Valde, "he couldn't afford it."

"Brother-in-law," Valde reminds him.

"Your brother-in-law couldn't afford it," Cruz amends.

"Right. But he could afford it. He finally got it under Obama."

Cruz reddens. For a second he's visibly flustered. Are we right to be shocked again? For how many years has health care been at

---

[19] Obamacare already allows cross-state sales by permitting two or more states to form "health care choice compacts." Georgia, Kentucky, Maine, Rhode Island, and Wyoming have passed laws allowing cross-state sales, but so far insurers have been unwilling to incur the substantial front-end costs of setting up multistate provider networks. Then there's the issue of pricing: insurance rates are based on local costs. If a resident of New York City buys Iowa insurance, then submits a claim for treatment incurred at New York City prices . . . it's the same kind of market disconnect that leads Manhattanites to fantasize about teleporting a brand-new 1,900-square-foot condo priced at $120,000 from Muncie, Illinois, into a prime Park Avenue address.

the forefront of our politics; for how many of those years has Ted Cruz been talking about it, arguing over it, campaigning on it, yet he can't handle a few basic questions from Mike Valde of Coralville, Iowa. So Cruz craps out on the issue, okay, he craps out, but he should at least have better bullshit than this.

"Sir, all I'm saying is *millions* have lost their coverage under Obamacare," Cruz answers, leaning harder than ever on that *millions*. "Your brother-in-law would have gotten it earlier if he could have afforded it earlier. But because of government regulations he couldn't."

Cruz looks past Valde and calls for the next question, and the moment passes with seemingly no great harm to the candidate, a speed bump in an otherwise smooth-running event. Easy enough to edit it out if you're disposed to like Cruz. There are more questions, more answers, and things proceed in a chummy way. Presently Cruz winds into his closing pitch.

"We are fifty-seven hours away from the Iowa caucuses," he says. "The time for the media nonsense is over. As the signs say"—he points at the reporters and TV cameras clustered at the back of the room—"don't believe the liberal media. *This,* is your time. *This,* is the time for the men and women of Iowa . . ."

The three fundamental acts of stump politics are the handshake, the baby kiss, and the ask.[20] A politician worthy of the name always asks for your vote, as Cruz does now, he asks for the vote of each person here, and more: "I want you to vote for me ten times!" This draws a laugh, but no, he's not encouraging voter fraud, "we aren't Democrats here," har, he's asking that you bring nine people—friends, family, colleagues from work—with you to caucus. And then one more ask, the third and final thing, which is to *pray*.

"Commit today," he urges in a fierce stage whisper, and the son-

---

[20] The politics of smoke-filled rooms is even more anatomically based, i.e., glad-handing, back-scratching, and ass-kicking.

ics of these final moments will play like an organ medley of classic church chords, from pleading exhortation to tremulous uplift to the throb of the heartfelt microphone croon, urgency guttering in the throat like a shot of Drano. "Commit each day," Cruz implores, "from now to election day to simply lift this country up in prayer. To say, *Father God!* Please continue this awakening. Con-*tin*-ue this spirit of revival, a-*way*-ken the body of Christ, that we might pull *back* from the abyss. You know"—and now for a second Cruz steps out of preacher mode, but just for a second, a gulp of earthly air—"you know, we're standing here today on the promises of Second Chronicles seven-fourteen," which he now recites, index finger pointed heavenward: *"'If my people which are called by my name shall humble themselves and pray and seek my face and turn from their wicked ways, then I will hear their prayers, and forgive their sins, and I will heal their land.'"*

The crowd applauds. Cruz returns a mild little smile. He resumes:

"Let me tell you a bit of history that our friends in the mainstream media"—he tips his palm at the press gang—"will never tell you. In January 1981, when Ronald Reagan took the oath of office"—Cruz's right hand goes up, acting it out—"his left hand was resting"—now the left hand does its part, flips palm-down—"on Second Chronicles seven-fourteen, a very *real* and *concrete* manifestation of that *promise* from the *word* of *God*. We *have* faced these challenges before"—Cruz softly punches the air—"we *have* faced the abyss before"—the punches keep coming—"and the American people came together, we rose up and we *pulled* this country *back*. We have *done* it before, and if we *stand* together, we can *do* it again. Thank you."

Big applause. The crowd comes to its feet. Is it a standing ovation? Hard to tell, because as soon as people stand they're moving, calling to friends, herding in a general drift toward the doors. In old-time Southern politics there was never a candidate who was not the most devout, ahem, of Christians, but you did hear of campaigns where one candidate had *out-Jesused* the other. It seems safe to say there's not a political animal alive who's going to out-Jesus Ted Cruz, a fact that would be less susceptible to cynicism if Cruz weren't such an utter dissembler and sneak. At the very moment of his Hubbard event, the Cruz campaign's "Voting Violation" mailers are landing in mailboxes across the state. Designed to look like an official government communication, the mailers feature the words *VOTING VIOLATION* in a bright red box at the top, and go on to assign the recipient and the recipient's neighbors a voting "score" and "grade," and warn that the recipient's neighbors will know his or her voting record as well. In response, Iowa's secretary of state will issue a statement condemning the Cruz mailer as "misrepresent[ing] the role of my office," "misrepresent[ing] Iowa election law," and "false representing of an official act." The reporter Ryan Lizza will later determine that the voting "scores" and "grades" assigned by the Cruz mailer to each recipient (everyone received a score of either 75 percent, 65 percent, or 55 percent, which translate to grades of C, D, and F, respectively) bore no relation to the recipient's actual voting record.[21]

In other words, the Cruz campaign made it all up. "I will apologize to no one for using every tool we can to encourage Iowa voters to come out and vote," Cruz will assert on Saturday evening—tools that include lies and intimidation, apparently. On Monday evening, moments before the caucuses begin, the Cruz campaign will spread the false rumor that Ben Carson—Cruz's main rival for evangelical votes—is dropping out of the race. A barrage of tweets, emails, and recorded phone messages will put out the word, all based on a CNN report that Carson plans to travel to his Florida home immediately following the caucuses. No matter that within moments of his origi-

---

[21] Ryan Lizza, "Ted Cruz's Iowa Mailers Are More Fraudulent Than Everyone Thinks," *New Yorker*, January 31, 2016.

nal report, the CNN reporter will tweet, "Ben Carson's campaign tells me he plans to stay in the race beyond Iowa no matter what the results are tonight," nor that the Carson campaign quickly sends out its own unequivocal statement that Carson, in the words of one senior staffer, is "not standing down." Throughout the evening the Cruz campaign will push the rumor, and at the end it will be Cruz, the candidate of skunk tactics and trickle-down Jesus, who stands before his happy warriors in downtown Des Moines and declares, "Let me say first—to God be the glory."

## 3. TRIUMPH OF THE SHRILL

One wonders how many tricks Trump poached from J. R. Ewing, another dashing jerk who crashed the scene in the late seventies and turned the common pieties on their pointy heads. No false modesty from these guys! And no piffle about giving back or serving others or the sacred public trust of the corporate sector, no apologies for having boatloads of money and always wanting more. The first episode of *Dallas* aired in 1978, precisely the time Trump was swinging his lowball deal for the old Commodore Hotel in New York City. This was the deal that put Trump on the map, and by the time the Commodore reopened in 1980 as the splendiferously flashy Grand Hyatt, Trump's TV soul brother was a mass-market American hero and international phenomenon.

Lorimar Productions intended for J. R. to be a secondary character. Bobby, the "good" brother, was supposed to be the star, a character the show's writers seemed to envision as an embodiment of the manly codes and virtues as set forth in *The Boy Scout Handbook*, 1957 edition. Bobby was loyal, trustworthy, kind, obedient, etc. Bobby was *nice*. J. R. was a snake and a bastard and cheated on his wife. Life has been imitating art for eons, but here was a twist on the old trope, art imitating life imitating art as J. R. hijacked

Lorimar's creative blueprint and made the show his own. Lots of winning for J. R., those early years. He liked the ladies. He worshipped his father, a rough-and-tumble striver who built the family fortune up from nothing. J. R. did big deals, lived large, crushed the competition, and gleefully shredded the illusions of idealistic young people. He had a master negotiator's knack for vibing out the vulnerabilities of the person across the table. Amid the show's weekly dose of clunking melodrama there was something in J. R. that felt vital and real, and ratings soared as his character moved front and center. He was the hero we didn't know we'd been looking for, an update on the frontier gunslinger who just happened to do his killing in the boardroom. The man truly did not give a shit about anyone else, though there was his son John Ross—basically an appendage of the J. R. ego—a wide-eyed, eager tyke on whom J. R. was always laying life wisdom with a social Darwinist slant, a perspective that could be summarized as: Screw others before they screw unto you. Which rang true, out here in the real world. J. R. lied, cheated, and swindled, but no more than the system itself, and he was authentic in the sense that he hardly tried to hide it. His honesty was thrilling. One of the sublime cheap pleasures of television in those years was tuning in each week to see what new havoc J. R. would inflict on the hypocrites and chumps. He enacted perhaps the oldest of the founding American fantasies, the honky version of paradise where a white man is free to take what he wants. Nobody seemed to notice—it certainly didn't hurt the ratings—that we never saw the Ewings in church.

One can imagine Donald Trump studying the J. R. phenomenon and thinking, I can work with this. Just be myself, only more so. Larry Hagman tapped into the pagan id at the heart of good Christian America and found the role of a lifetime. For Trump the challenge was to take Method acting to its extreme, cultivating the raw material of his personality into an ever more authentic performance of himself. At this he seems to have worked very hard. Nobody has ever described Donald Trump as lazy. His artistry seemed to culminate in the fourteen seasons of *The Apprentice* and *The Celebrity Apprentice*, in which he starred as Himself, the celebrity billionaire Donald Trump. For fourteen seasons of prime-time network TV this was how non–*Wall Street Journal*[22]–reading America came to know him, as the brusque, cut-the-bullshit guy at the head of the conference table whom everyone, celebrities included, reverently addressed as "Mr. Trump." In a world where power seems so distant and abstract—where the mysterious things that happen in Washington and New York and Beijing filter down through intricate channels to the rest of us, usually changing our lives for the worse—here was a rare glimpse, however staged and hokey, into the guts of the system. If there was more than a touch of farce in the presentation—if the shtick got awfully aggressive at times—the core truth of the show could not be denied, for there was Trump in all his real-life glory with the planes and helicopters, the gilded office suites, the glam lifestyle, not to mention his own hit TV show. Art imitating life imitating art imitating life *ad infinitum*, one thing affirming the other in an endless loop.

There's a theory floating around Iowa these days, that showbiz is all there is. Trump's crowds, the whoops and hollers, the fizz and fury wherever he goes, this is, according to the theory, just folks coming out for the circus, wanting to see for themselves the boy with two heads, the man who can stop a cannonball with his abs of steel. Once we get down to the actual business of voting, that deadly serious business, foundation of our democracy, scourge of tyrants and so forth, reasonable people will forget the Trump nonsense and vote for a real candidate. But the theory fails to account for the fact that Trump is more about art than politics. For millions of Americans there is nothing so real as Trump's performance of himself, this spectacle of a billionaire businessman–reality TV star

---

[22] Or the *New York Post*, for that matter.

whose very offensiveness—the bragging, the gutter insults, the lying and whining, the blatantly racist and sexist riffs that would doom a conventional candidate—only makes him more authentic. No phony would dare do such things, just as no conventional candidate would so self-consciously ham it up for the cover of his campaign biography, as Trump did for *Crippled America*. It's a mug worthy of Mussolini: thrust chin, glowering eyes, operatic scowl enacting a tough-guy schtick of sternness and strength. For it to work requires buy-in by the audience, an understanding of performance as the ultimate authenticity. "It's a terrible, horrible, nasty picture," Trump said of the cover on the day of the book's release. And, as described in the same report, one book buyer "admired Mr. Trump for the candor of his facial expression, adding: 'It's just a nice scowl. It's a very well-composed picture.'"[23]

If that photo makes some of us think of Trump as a clown and buffoon, then maybe we're the clowns and buffoons for thinking we know what's going on. There might be three or four candidates who could inspire a crowd to wait two hours in ten-degree weather, as fifteen hundred souls did for Trump on a recent night in Claremont, New Hampshire, but how many could draw thirty thousand to an open-air football stadium on a blistering summer day in Alabama, as happened for Trump last August 21 in Mobile? Thirty thousand Alabamans sweating it out for a New Yorker!

Hitler had his beer hall; Trump had his TV boardroom, fourteen seasons' worth. He leads by significant margins in all of the national polls. He weathered a surge by Carson in November—petulant Trump called the people of Iowa "stupid" when Carson's poll numbers briefly surpassed his own—and the past few weeks he's been stronger than ever on the stump, loose, commanding, jolly, enjoining abuse both verbal and physical on protestors at his rallies.

---

[23] Michael Barbaro, "Donald Trump Employs a Scowl to Help Sell His New Book," *New York Times*, November 4, 2015.

Perhaps his finest moment came in the January 14 debate, when he crushed Cruz's "New York values" line with presidential cool. No histrionics, no insults, but rather a sober, measured, quietly passionate takedown that left Cruz standing in a puddle of his own sweat. At that moment Trump seemed to contain dizzying potential. Perhaps we'd grossly underestimated him. Perhaps this is the most elaborate performance in the history of American politics, by a master of the psyche who knows better, who *is* better, than the troll he seems to be—perhaps he really is putting on an act, an act within an act such as double agents perform. Could a genuine wing nut do all the serious things he's done in his career? Building skyscrapers in New York is about as serious as it gets. I heard the legendary Dallas developer Trammell Crow speak once, shortly after he'd finished the Anatole hotel complex. "I'll never do it again," said Crow, who was a formidable person, built like a lineman of the Bronko Nagurski era. "A project like that is just too much for one man." This is the world where Trump has survived and often thrived, a world of labor unions, architects, bankers, lawyers, the mob, community activists, endless thickets of government regulation, acts of God, heavy equipment, materials science, plumbing and HVAC on the biblical scale. Compared to construction, flapping your mouth on the floor of the Senate is a Sunday sleep-in.

Trump's spasms of normalcy, the real achievements in his bio, there's just enough of this to keep us guessing. Meanwhile the Republican establishment is in meltdown mode, and Jeb, its anointed candidate, is still phoning it in like a guy who doesn't know his cell phone's dead. The papers run such headlines as "For Republicans, Fears of a Lasting Split"[24] and "In Iowa, Battle for GOP Soul,"[25] and the *National Review* devoted an entire issue to the theme "Against Trump." One would think that Trump threatens a radical departure

---

[24] *New York Times,* January 10, 2016.
[25] *Dallas Morning News,* January 24, 2016.

from the Republican politics we've come to know and love—that he's a force for tolerance and liberalism in the party, as opposed to a virtuoso of the very politics of paranoid rhetoric, cultural resentment, xenophobia, and racism on which the GOP has prospered for the past fifty years. To further confuse the issue, there's this, from the *Times:* "Manners Fit Jeb Bush, If Not an Uncouth Race,"[26] in which Jeb's flailings are interpreted "as perhaps the last, wheezing gasp of the WASP power structure," with its political tradition, according to the *Times* writer, "of cordial restraint, of civil discourse, of earnest public service." Which is insane, in addition to being herniatingly funny: the WASP is as ruthless as a Comanche when his prerogative is threatened.[27] It seems to have escaped the *Times*'s notice that heathen Trump, destroyer of the allegedly genteel WASP, is himself as pink-cheeked WASPy as they come: Ivy League, Presbyterian, born and raised rich, made richer by plying the same world of power and privilege that's been so good to the Bushes. A Trump presidency may differ from Jeb's in matters of style and speech— there is the Bush family tradition of "kinder, gentler" verbiage, and the "compassionate conservatism" that started two wars and gutted the net worth of America's working and middle classes—but when it comes to the root politics of who holds the power, who gets the wealth?

Meet the new boss. Same as the old boss.

IT'S A COLD AFTERNOON IN CLINTON, MIDWINTER BLEAKNESS prevailing over the land like nature has the flu. Gray sky, bare trees, soggy slug-brown earth streaked with old snow; hard weather on a mood. Driving west to east across the middle of the state we see two

---

[26] *New York Times,* January 17, 2016.
[27] Two examples from the Bush family readily come to mind: the Willie Horton ad in 1988, and in 2000, the South Carolina push poll implying that John McCain had fathered an illegitimate biracial child.

Iowa. Courtesy of David Taylor

bald eagles, and outside of Belle Plaine, a barn on which some genu-
inely gifted artist has painted a blimp-sized copy of Grant Wood's
*American Gothic*.

The interstate routes us through Cedar Rapids, its huge Archer
Daniels Midland complex belching smoke like the pits of Mordor;
Cedar Rapids, where residents joke there's a fifth season of the year,
thanks to the weather produced by ADM. Farther east the farms
become smaller, scrubbier, more evidently hardscrabble. Shabbi-
ness begins to leak in around the edges: peeling paint on the houses
and barns, flotsam in the yards, spavined trailer homes with all the
curtains drawn. The terrain is choppy, rocky; glaciers barely grazed
this part of the state. It seems reasonable to wonder if meth is the
area's main cash crop.

Clinton is a river town, neither overly prosperous nor immediately distinctive, the kind of place where a visitor might decide the

best bet for lunch is the Subway tucked into a corner of the massive Walmart. But the venue for Trump's rally—the gymnasium of Clinton Middle School—is modern, bright, themed in the signature scarlet red of the school's colors. Smells of varnished hardwood and vulcanized rubber summon up nostalgic blips of good and horrible memories from one's own school days. The basketball goals have been swung up toward the rafters, and a small stage sits center court, topped by a lectern and surrounded by steel crowd barriers, then row upon row of black folding chairs. A sociable buzz comes off the crowd, uptempo'ed by the Trump playlist booming over the sound system. These people look more town than country, and comfortably suburban at that. There's money in the clothes, a cared-for sheen to hair and skin that's more naturally associated with golf courses and Caribbean cruises than the physical grind of farming. The crowd numbers some two thousand, the *Washington Post* will later report, which sounds about right. And white faces as far as the eye can see, a fact not noted in the *Post*'s report.

People are happy, there's much milling and moving about, a church-assembly sort of cheer in the air. The playlist—personally curated by Trump himself, according to the campaign website—runs mostly to classic rock. There's Elton John, "Tiny Dancer." The Stones' "You Can't Always Get What You Want." Then "Hey Jude," then Elton again, "Rocket Man." Then a blast of opera, Pavarotti belting out "Nessun Dorma." Heads are lifted, cocked; it takes a moment to adjust to this new sound, then everyone's back to talking. I'm standing behind the last row of chairs, and the two middle-aged couples seated in front of me are exclaiming over the image on someone's smartphone. Perched as I am at their shoulders, I have no choice but to look. The screen shows a clumsily shopped photo of Barack Obama locked in a passionate kiss with another man. Oprah Winfrey stands on the right, smiling her approval, while Michelle Obama can be seen in the background left, face warped in shock and revulsion.

Wife: "Is that real? That can't be real."

Husband: "It is, [so-and-so] sent it to me this morning!"

The wife studies the photo. "He is so gross," she says, and hands the phone back to her husband, though whether it's Obama who's gross or the friend who sent the photo is unclear. Next to me a reporter from the *Guardian* is interviewing another foursome, everyone strong for Trump. Why?

"He'll take care of the rabies."

Rabies?

There are smiles, sideways chuckles.

"The Arabs."

I expected to have to work somewhat harder to find the cliché Trump supporter. We wait a long time, long enough for the playlist to cycle through and the fannies to find their seats, then rise and roam again. I talk to a slender, well-tanned gentleman on my left, Dan, a retired river-tug captain. He's wearing khakis, a plaid button-down shirt, a handsome jacket of chestnut-brown suede. His full head of graying brown hair is parted neatly on the side.

"Texas," he echoes when I tell him where I live. "I've been to Texas."

He says it with a sweet, almost childlike wonder. Lackland Air Force Base, he continues, he was a jet engine mechanic during Vietnam, deployed to Thailand '71–'72. "We were still bombing," he says with that same soft declarative wonder. He seems too bashful and gentle to have captained a working boat, but there's that deep tan. We talk. He's still shopping around for a candidate, and that's how he puts it, "shopping around." He likes Trump—"with all his business experience he could fix the economy"—and Bernie. "I like some of the things he says." Such as? "What he says on free college tuition." And? "Like raising the minimum wage. My son's a graphic designer, he had to go to school for it, he was just making minimum wage for a long time. Now he's doing a little better than that, but it still doesn't seem right. Go to school to learn that and he still can't make a living."

We talk about the long wait. "I've been standing here over an hour," he says, smiling, not meaning to complain. "And I walked a bunch of miles this morning." At the far corner of the gym there's a stir, a sudden burst of energy that instantly lifts everyone to their feet, cell phones flashing, "TRUMP" signs waggled aloft, Adele's "Rolling in the Deep" surfing the crowd roar like a spray-can topping of whipped cream. It is Himself. In the Flesh. He is making his way to the stage and taking his time about it, as ponderous, as ceremonial and stately as fat Elvis making the entrance for one of his gruesome late-life arena shows. He turns, pivots, waves here, waves there, like the most conscientious of tanners he is determined to soak up the glow on every side, and I wonder if I've ever witnessed such contentment as Trump seems to be experiencing now, he is beatific, his smile as transcendently serene as the Buddha's, or that of a sultan who's just enjoyed an afternoon of great sex. His security detail moves with him in a loose phalanx, a flying wedge of five or six Men in Black who peel off as he ascends the several stairs to the stage. A vast roar bangs forth as Trump presents himself, grinning, arms spread, suit jacket swinging wide to show a slice of ample

Trumpian gut. More security take up position around the perimeter of steel barriers. They are dressed in nearly identical blue-gray suits, and there they will stand for the entirety of Trump's remarks, facing the crowd with their feet planted at parade rest, backs straight, faces blank, hands clutching their lapels (for fast access to their shoulder holsters, one presumes), a totally gratuitous bit of theatrics. The strongman and his security goons: won't small minds be impressed! It's a fascist visual worthy of Mussolini's Blackshirts, or a bleached-out version of the Fruit of Islam.

Trump is already talking as he steps up to the microphone. "It's crunch time, folks, it's crunch time, and we're gonna make America great again . . ." This inspires a great cheer from the crowd. He orders everyone to sit, sit, c'mon take a seat, and promptly launches into his poll numbers, which are "uh-mazing," and the people of Iowa who are "uh-mazing," and "I'm even leading in all of the polls in Iowa now. Some big ones are coming out I guess—but they don't even matter anymore to be honest, because we're so close to the end what difference does it make," and "By the way this is some crowd, this is your record crowd out here, a great crowd and amazing people." The audience happily applauds itself. "We had to drive an hour and a half to get here! I said isn't there a closer airport, and they said yeah but your plane's too big, you can't land at their airport. Well . . ." He flaps his hand in a *whatever* sort of gesture, he's laughing, the crowd is laughing and right away they've gotten what they came for, a big dose of the Trump treatment up close and personal, the compulsive casual boasting and self-congratulation, and that "well," the dismissive little flick of the hand that puts them on the inside of the joke. Oh never mind, who cares if my plane's too big for your pokey little airport, forget I even mentioned it, but, hey, it really is such a great big plane, I can't help it, that's just how I roll!

He riffs on last Thursday's Fox debate, the one he skipped ("sometimes you have to take a stand") because of his feud with Megyn Kelly, choosing instead to hold a fund-raiser for wounded veterans. "So amazing what took place . . . we raised six million in one hour . . . people lined up around the block . . . turned away THOU-sunz and THOU-sunz . . ." And what about the young veteran who spoke, who lost a leg in combat, "an amazing story from a great young man," then he's on to the "mess" in the Middle East, the "fantastic" company he built, his record as a job creator, the terrible deals our government makes, bad deals with China, bad deals everywhere, then he's back to the Middle East. "We'll kick ISIS's ass." War whoops, big applause. And Iran! What a terrible deal that was! "They were taunting us, calling us dummies . . . John Kerry an idiot . . . they put our sailors in a begging position . . . a total disgrace and horrible . . . they were rough and nasty and no good and horrible."

"Iraq and Iran, for thousands of years they've been fighting over the same ten feet of ground, THOU-sunz of years, and they kept each other in check. I said, Look, if we take out Saddam the Iranians are gonna come in and take the oil, I said it at the time! And that's exactly what happened!"

Of course he said nothing of the sort, but facts stopped mattering some time ago; our most successful politicians have all become fantasy novelists. Trump goes on, mugging and shrugging, goggling his eyes, jutting his chin, he is a one-man special effects shop spewing the junky nonstop patter of a telethon host, a vaporous chum of *I love you, you're beautiful, amazing,* and everything is *fantastic gorgeous huge* when it isn't being *crazy* or *ridiculous* or *horrible* or just *not good,* though sometimes it's everything all at once. "I don't care about endorsements from politicians, look, I hate politicians, okay, I don't hate 'em, I love everybody, I get along with everybody . . ." There's more than a touch of the mafioso here, the whipsawing from scorn to laughs to threat to cajolery. It's the bully's classic line: if you're with me, great, I love you, everything's beautiful with us, otherwise you're dead to me. If Trump internalized J. R. Ewing he clearly lifted just as much from Tony Soprano, the histrionics, the

Jersey slosh in the mouth as the words come fast and hot and the voice cracks high, jumping an octave like a ventriloquist's trick or a kick in the balls, such weird squeakings from these human water buffaloes. "Why would I denounce Putin for saying I'm a genius?" The eyes widen, arms and shoulders lift in stagey disbelief, and the North Jersey skronk flows thick. "Why would I do that fah? What fah? Whah fah? Whah th' hell is this?"

People clap and cheer on cue, eager to please this remarkable man. The intimacy he creates is astonishing, the word jumbles and jump cuts that force us to listen, the confiding stream-of-consciousness slurry like the boss's arm draped over your shoulder, trusting you above all others. Trump is a master of the casual aside, the conversational sidebar that seals the deal. "Hey, I'm a *big* customer of John Deere." (There's a factory down the road.) And Paris, the Bataclan attacks, "if some of you had been there, those of you with guns strapped to your ankles, your hips, there woulda been bullets going the other way, and that changes everything." The crowd seems as nearly dazed as if witnessing a miracle, and in a way they are. TV is such a liar. It's engineered to overpromise and underdeliver (e.g., car commercials, celebrity skin tones, electronic thingamajigs that cure baldness), but after all these weeks and months of watching Trump on the tube and wondering, hoping, wishing, with surely many a literal prayer thrown in, here he is every bit as good as advertised, no, *better,* for once that lying suckhole of the TV screen has soft-sold the product. The crowd is seduced, and who among us isn't happy to be seduced when it's done so expertly, with such sincerity. True love makes it more than just a one-off fuck, and how many times in the course of the hour will Trump declare his love for us?

He's back to bad deals and why we don't win anymore, because "we don't send our best negotiators, we send *idiots,* government *hacks*" (booooo), which becomes a random riff on repealing Common Core (Yay! Yay!), which somehow leads to creating "*borders,* and the borders are gonna be *real* borders, and"—the chin juts, the arms go up and out—"*aaannnd, aaaannnnd*"—he's conducting, leading us on—"and we are going to build a *waaaaallll*"—yay! yay!—"and who's gonna *pay* for the wall?" He points at the crowd, which musters a raggedy "MEXICO!!!" "Mexico," he echoes, chuckling, looking down at his notes, then more softly, almost like he's marveling to himself: "Everyone, *ehhhh-ver-ee-one* knows."

It's an odd little moment, hardly a hitch in the rolling thunder of Trump's sound-and-fury revue. Was it even anything? Months later we will come across a clue dropped by Trump himself, in a conversation with the editors of the *New York Times*:

> *If my speeches ever get a little off I just go: "We will build a wall!" You know, if it gets a little boring, if I see people starting to sort of maybe thinking about leaving—I can sort of tell the audience—I just say, "We will build the wall," and they go nuts. "And Mexico will pay for the wall!" But—ah, but I mean it. But I mean it.*[28]

Trump is, in the final analysis, a realtor. He sells. He knows how to sell all kinds of things—condos, dreams, himself. With his bag of tricks he could probably sell a '79 Pinto to Elon Musk. Now he embarks on an imaginary colloquy with his primary opponents who insist, and here he goes into *opéra bouffe* mode, furrowing his brow, jerking side to side as he blusters, "'You'll never build a *waaaall*, it's *too tough* to build a *waaaall*,'" to which Trump answers as himself, incredulous, arms outstretched, voice breaking Soprano-style, "Really? Two thousand years ago China built a wall that's thirteen thousand miles long, the Great Wall of China, and we can't do it today? We could do it so easy, *I* could do it, to me it's a simple project, you use plank, prefab, gimme a break, you guys know, I mean come on, half this audience knows construction, it's simple, you do the footings and put it up and it's gonna be beautiful, and you have a nice little design, Trump-Trump-Trump," he playfully lilts, and the laughter rises, he shakes his head as the applause powers up for this new idea, "no, I don't want my name up there, I don't want it named for me, I just want it to *work,* and it will work . . . Walls work, you can ask Israel by the way, walls work if you do it right."[29]

"'But Don'"—now he's back to the blustering skeptic—"'whaddeya mean Mexico's gonna *pay,* why do you keep sayin' that, you know they won't *pay.*'" But of course they'll pay, "only a businessman would understand this" and "there are five different ways to make them pay," though neither details nor even the broadest outlines of any one of these five ways are mentioned. Soon he moves on to Cruz (lusty *boooo*s at the name) and the issue of his Canadian birth. "It's a serious problem for Ted," Trump says with devastating offhandedness, it's as if we're sitting across the table from him, this is the chummy postprandial talk that happens after the plates are cleared, frank, confiding, a touch philosophical. Is "Ted" a natural-born citizen as required by the Constitution? Even the experts, the lawyers and law professors, they can't say one way or the other, which means it will have to go to the courts, which means if Cruz gets the nomination (*booooooo*) he could be disqualified at any moment. Even the day before the election. Even the day *after* the election. Why would we nominate someone like that? Why would Ted do that to our party? Then Trump looks down, smiles coyly as he brings out the knife.

"I called him Anchor Baby the other day, did you hear about that?" A razzing laughter rises from the crowd, it could be hundreds

---

[29] Trump: "By the way, if you want to know if a wall works, just ask Israel. Israel built a wall and it works."
*New York Times:* "And they heave rockets over it."
Trump: "Yeah, I know. Well, no. Now they're doing the rockets, yeah. That's a—they have a—they have a different—they probably have a bigger—they have a different kind of problem. You have to build a real wall. They don't have a real wall right now. They don't have a wall that works . . ." *Ibid.*

of tiny trombones sputtering off-key. "Before I was calling him Wall Street Ted, but now I don't know, maybe I like Anchor Baby better. Whaddeya think, Wall Street Ted or Anchor Baby, Wall Street Ted, Anchor Baby . . ." He pretends to muse amid the laughter, the shout-outs from the crowd for one or the other. "How about this, you help me decide," and now he's laughing, everybody is laughing as he solicits applause first for Wall Street Ted, then Anchor Baby, and back and forth it goes for several rounds to great hilarity, the noise louder, more raucous with each new round; this is audience participation at its finest. When was the last time these sober Midwesterners enjoyed themselves so much? And it's the best kind of fun, the catty, cozy, us-against-them kind with its tribal threads that reach all the way back to the earliest safety of the clan and the cave. Either you're with us or against us, and God help those too cucked and soft to scream allegiance at the top of their lungs.

"We can't be great again until we're rich again . . . nineteen trillion in debt . . . the stupid deal they made, your politicians that you sent to Washington . . . gonna add two trillion more . . ." And how about *this* for a stupid deal: three billion for the new Air Force One! Come on! "Do you think I can make a better deal than that?" The big cheer testifies they do. "I call Boeing"—now he's acting it out, he's got an invisible phone to his ear—"I say, 'Boeing, we love you, you know what, do it as a contribution to our country'"—now he's wheedling, coaxing, it's the classic Mafia squeeze from a guy who should know, who's bought many millions of cubic yards of overpriced concrete from the Gambino and Genovese crime families—"'make a *con-tri-buuuu-shun*'"—he's really leaning into it now—"'like I got the *con-tri-bu-shunzzz* for the vets the other day!'"

About those *con-tri-bu-shunzzz*. Among them were $1 million that Trump claimed on the night of the fund-raiser he "gave" (past tense) out of his own pocket, although nearly four months later he will have yet to write a check, which he will do, finally, testily,

with much bitching and moaning at the media for the intense public scrutiny they brought to bear on the matter.[30] By then a fuller
picture of Trump's philanthropic career will be emerging, and like
most everything having to do with Trump—think of Pig Pen in
*Peanuts,* the dirt cloud that swirls around him wherever he goes—
patterns of sleaze and self-dealing quickly assert themselves. A lot
of it is funny, sloppy funny, twisted-sitcom funny, as if, say, we're
watching a television satire of a fictional reality TV show about a
megalomaniacal business mogul who decides to run for president.
The gags are so cheap and broad, so over-the-top, as to hardly be
credible, but who cares—it's TV! There are, for instance, the two
large oil portraits of himself that Mogul purchased with funds from
the Mogul Charitable Foundation, one of which ended up on the
wall of the sports bar at one of his golf courses; the legal disputes
involving Mogul's for-profit enterprises that he settled using Mogul
Charitable Foundation funds; the $100 two-person membership to
the Metropolitan Museum of Art, paid for with Mogul Charitable
Foundation funds; the $7 from the Mogul Charitable Foundation
that went to the Boy Scouts in 1989, when it cost $7 to register a
new Scout, and Mogul Jr. just happened to be eleven years old at the
time, prime Tenderfoot age; the illegal campaign contribution made
from the Mogul Charitable Foundation to the attorney general of
Florida, who shortly thereafter announced that her office would not
launch a formal fraud investigation into Mogul University; and the
$100,000 given in the 1990s to the "National Museum of Catho-
lic Art and History," a now-defunct nonprofit housed in the former headquarters of Anthony "Fat Tony" Salerno of the Genovese
crime family, the museum's collection consisting of a photograph
of the Pope, some nun dolls purchased from the Home Shopping

---

[30] "When asked Tuesday whether he had given the money this week only because reporters
had been asking about it, Trump responded: 'You know, you're a nasty guy. You're really a
nasty guy.'" David A. Fahrenthold, "Four Months After Fundraiser, Trump Says He Gave $1
Million to Veterans Group," *Washington Post,* May 24, 2016.

Network, and a black Jacuzzi decorated with gold-plated soap dishes and angel figurines. Then there's Mogul's colorful history of grandstanding at charity events to which he's contributed only nominally or not at all, and his promises—no evidence indicates they were ever fulfilled—to give away his profits from Mogul University; his salary from the TV show *Mogul Apprentice;* unspecified sums to charities selected by contestants on his other TV show, *Celebrity Mogul Apprentice;* and $250,000 to a charity serving Israeli soldiers and veterans.[31]

There's more,[32] but nobody would believe it, not that believing or disbelieving has anything to do with it. Reality has been irrelevant for many months now. "We're gonna win again," Trump promises the crowd at Clinton Middle School, "we're gonna make, America, great, again," he says to rising applause, and "really, really" as the cheers drown him out, and he waits for the noise to settle before making the closing pitch.

"I'm leading every single poll nationally. I'm leading every single poll of the states." In fact, Iowa is the only state where it's even close! "Wouldn't it be terrible," he says with a smile, "if I lost in Iowa and won everywhere else? And, I don't know, I'd be very angry"—he's still smiling, almost playful, it's Tony Soprano very nicely warning you to toe the line—"but only for a day, I'd still love you."

Everyone is laughing, clapping, but a seed has been planted. Just supposing he were to be elected president without Iowa's help . . . the record shows he's a vindictive son of a bitch, no bones about it. Easy to imagine his presidency being guided less by reason and calculation than by grudge, favor, whim, boredom, fear, vanity, all the classic animating emotions of tyrants down through the ages, from half-mad kings to Mafia dons to lunatic African dictators. Best

---

[31] David A. Fahrenthold, "Trump Boasts About His Philanthropy. But His Giving Falls Short of His Words," *Washington Post,* October 29, 2016.

[32] Such as the fake million-dollar bill he gave to the Bronx high school chess team that was trying to raise funds to travel to an out-of-town tournament. *Ibid.*

be on the Trump train when it leaves the station, something to think about as he urges us to get on board and caucus! caucus! go out and caucus! Even if you're lying in bed with a fever of 104 and the doctor's telling you to stay in bed—get out of bed! Caucus!

"You will be so proud and you will be so happy that you went out and did it," Trump assures us. "We're gonna be so good, you're gonna love me as president and I love you anyway. I love you! I love you! Thank you!" he cries, and he could be the most gallant sort of philanderer, that final flourish of love and thanks as he zips up his pants and leaves. He has screwed this crowd cross-eyed and they wanted nothing less. "Rolling in the Deep" booms through the speakers as they come to their feet with a roar like a forest going up in flames, and for long moments everyone holds their place and claps and cheers, it's a no-doubt standing O that Trump receives with blushing gratitude, he beams at them with the fondness of a man beholding his newborn grandchild for the first time.

Many won't leave the building until he does (once again we're in Elvis territory). He has brought them joy on this somber dead-of-winter afternoon, and so they linger, it's as if the home team just won the biggest game of the year and they're going to soak up every speck of glow. Trump steps outside the steel barriers and starts working the edge of the crowd, a praetorian guard of security guys moving with him. They are tense, coiled, very busy with their eyes, ready to pounce at the first false move; pity the poor schmuck who goes fishing in his pockets for his phone as the candidate draws near, but Trump himself is as loose as his security guys are tight. He works the crowd with relish, signing hats, signing "TRUMP" placards, jawing, laughing, he's happy as a glutton turned loose on a hundred-foot buffet. Seen up close, his body mass impresses: big bones, generous slathers of meat on those bones, big face, head large and square as a toaster, it is a Terminator style of battering-ram head, though how much of it is hair is open to question. There's something primal in that bulk, a kind of infantilizing reassurance, patriarchy expressed as physical presence: godfather knows best and swings the weight to back it up. One expects this is a worldview that few of his supporters have a problem with. His coloring, to state the obvious, is unique, kiln colors of brick red, hot pink, burnt orange, a palette keyed to his flamethrower lick of hair. His eyebrows and lashes are light sand, almost white, his complexion so ruddy you're tempted to think he's a lush, or scrubs with a pumice stone every day. Vitiligo—loss of pigment—has given him reverse raccoon eyes, circles of white around his orbital sockets like a pair of headlights stuck on high beam.

His looks are nearly as singular as the middle-aged Michael Jackson's, but right now it's Theodore Roosevelt he's channeling, his smile as toothy-wide as TR posing with a slaughtered animal. He sucks up the free-floating energy of the crowd, what's static in them becomes kinetic in him and he'll be riding high for the next rally, a man like this won't run out of gas till the day he dies. He leaves with his entourage through a roped-off door, turning around for last good-byes, a flurry of farewell waves. *Good-bye! Good-bye!* the people call back, a piping chorus as sweet and trusting as Munchkins crying out to the great and powerful Oz.

The playlist is still going as the gym empties out. For about the sixth time today the Stones are telling us what we think we already know about wanting and getting, getting and needing, and going to the Chelsea drugstore to stand in line with Mr. Jimmy and get a certain prescription filled. Gazing down the row I'm delivered a vision of Mr. Jimmy himself, a dazed-looking elderly man sitting on the aisle, much too thin, with an open sore the size of a biscuit on one cheek. He's sick—perhaps terminally—but sits there with the timeless patience of the mercifully doped, waiting, we assume, for someone, a friend or family member, to return and help him to the door.

How long will he wait? Mr. Jimmy, give our regards to Mr. Godot. He's still sitting there after we've zipped up our coats, pulled on our hats, and stepped outside into the leaden half-light, it's been dusk and not-dusk all afternoon. The cold announces itself in the parking lot, the hard slap of our shoes on frozen asphalt. One has the sense of having just witnessed a genuine phenomenon. Trump's absolute ease, the seamless weave of silk and steel in his pitch, and charisma like the unstoppable Blob, absorbing everything in its path. Trump is good, so good that I half expect myself to be taken with him, to feel some glimmer of inclination toward the optimistic view, but the prevailing mood is dread, dread bordering on depression. Then the thought arrives fully formed, without effort, without joy or pleasure either, just this final, crude certainty like a hammer coming down: Donald Trump, plainly and simply, is full of shit.

## 4. REV-O-LU-TION:

A sudden political overthrow or seizure of power brought about from within a given system; activities directed toward bringing about basic changes in socioeconomic structure.

Ballparking the median age of the crowd on this Saturday night at the barnlike, venerable (1927) Field House on the campus of the University of Iowa, you might guess nineteen? Twenty? Though so much depends on the age of the guesser; the older you get, the younger the young inexorably seem. They are, in any case, young, these four or five thousand kids bouncing shoulder to shoulder on the Field House floor and a few hundred more lining the mezzanine, bright-eyed, humming with hamster energy, a genial seethe and surge of all colors and shapes of bodies out to the walls and up to the literal rafters. Looks like teen spirit! Though so lithe and smooth cheeked they seem closer to childhood than majority, but no point trying to tell them that. Who among us didn't think in our late teens that we had, at last, *arrived,* that the ass-from-elbow sorts of problems were behind us, which of course turned out to be yet one more station on the endless highway of self-delusion. It's a wonder anybody makes it to thirty.

The house lights are dim, as for a concert. It *is* a concert. Glow sticks and fluorescent twirly things leave strobe streaks on the eye like slow-drying stains. Smoke clouds of weed drift past the platform erected for the press, who have the grim, let's-get-this-over-with air of campers near the end of a cold and rainy weekend. An all-woman acoustic trio is performing onstage. The Awful Purdies, they call themselves, and they are tall and slender, they have blue streaks in their hair, and their wardrobe bespeaks thrift-shop cool. Enormous American and Iowa flags flank the stage, centered by a large "Future To Believe In" banner. Winking amid the crowd are dozens of campaign placards with "Bernie" outlined in soft pink lights, some with small American flags poking out of the top. *What's so funny about peace love and understanding,* the Awful Purdies croon, and looking down from the press platform one feels a surge of tenderness for the kids. They seem so open and easy with one another, flash-scenes erupting everywhere of hugs, gentle moshing, discrete little scrums of spontaneous dance. It moves you, seeing them happy this way. It turns your mind to hopeful thoughts. Fifty years ago practically to the day, Allen Ginsberg was traveling these same regions, writing these lines—

So, tender lipt adolescent girl, pale youth,
                              give me back my soft kiss
Hold me in your innocent arms,
              accept my tears as yours to harvest
              equal in nature to the Wheat
              that made your bodies' muscular bones
                     broad shouldered, boy bicept—
       from leaning on cows & drinking Milk
                            in Midwest Solitude—
No more fear of tenderness, much delight in weeping, ecstasy
       in singing, laughter rises that confounds
              staring Idiot mayors
                     and stony politicians eyeing
                     Thy breast,
                            O Man of America, be born![33]

Someone looking to colonize space could hardly do better than
this frisky crew. They cheer as the lights go all the way down and a
giant video screen unfurls. The latest Bernie commercial is played,
a sunny *e pluribus unum* collage of citizen diversity soundtracked to
Simon & Garfunkel's "America." Every image is crisp, glossy, satu-
rated with color and light, it's a sterling example of the advertiser's
art, and the high production values send a message: Bernie's for real.
No amateur hour here, the guy's raising serious money and getting
much bang for his bucks.

Mad cheers for the ad. The screen rolls up and two young black

---

[33] "Wichita Vortex Sutra," composed February 14, 1966, in *Allen Ginsberg, Collected Poems 1947–1980* (Harper & Row, 1984), p. 395.

comedians take the stage, identical twins—they flip a coin every night to see who's straight man?—then a twentysomething star from *The Hunger Games* who talks in that punch-drunk California way of being super-amazed at everything. "Wow, Iowa is crazy, man!" he marvels in genial stoner style. He achieves a mighty roar for his critique of student debt, and for good reason: undergraduate student debt—a relatively recent phenomenon in American life—will warp and stunt the entire trajectory of many of these lives. I invariably think about my father at such moments. He had a PhD in education from Chapel Hill and spent most of his career running community colleges; when asked his profession, his answer tended to be the matter-of-fact, "I'm a school man." In the late 1970s he served on a state commission studying proposals for the latest innovation in higher education, government-guaranteed student loans offered by private companies. He arrived at a negative view of such loans. Tuition would skyrocket, he predicted, while public funding for higher education would shrink, and the gap would be filled by students taking on unconscionable levels of debt. His analysis was not a popular one, and he was dropped from a second iteration of the commission. Some thirty years and $1.2 trillion of outstanding student debt later, he'd grown disgusted by higher ed's chirping insistence on "investing in yourself" as justification for piling mountains of debt onto eighteen-year-olds. "We've got it backwards," he'd say. "Should be the other way around. Society's supposed to be investing in the students, turning out the doctors and lawyers and engineers who are going to keep it moving forward." His point—that education is a collective, as well as an individual, good; that it's a value multiplier for society, returning benefits far in excess of the public cost—is borne out by decades of research and study. There is, for example, "the Solow residual," which attributes most of the rise in productivity in modern societies to "technological progress in the broadest sense," namely, the advance, transmission, and application of knowledge. Another example: "the Flynn effect"—the generation-by-generation rise in IQ scores in modern societies—and the crucial role that formal education plays in developing our capacity for higher-level cognitive tasks.[34]

Further to Dad's point: nobody *gives* you an education. Even if she doesn't pay a dime in tuition, the student is making a momentous investment in terms of the time, talent, and energy she devotes to her education, as well as the wages she forgoes during her years of study. The student is doing her part. It seems only fair—rational and fair, given all it stands to gain—that society make a no less equal investment in her education. Applied broadly, this anthropological equation has a name, the social contract, and history shows that by upholding its side of the bargain in education—by investing lavishly in public education over the course of a century or more, especially in the decades immediately following World War II—America made itself rich, and did so without condemning its youth to debtor hell.[35]

Anyone baffled by a recent YouGov poll—43 percent of respondents under the age of thirty have a favorable view of socialism, compared to 32 percent in the same age group who view capitalism favorably—hasn't been paying attention. Here's a modest notion for the country: a society structured in such a way that the economics of higher education and health care don't ruin the lives of millions of its citizens. Are we at least allowed to dream? We are, even Americans in hard-core capitalist America are allowed to dream of a life in which the costs of college and health care are less than ruinous threats. How much energy, practical and psychic, do we burn each day stressing over, dealing with, the dollar cost of these two areas of life? And how much energy would be freed for pursuits of excellent happiness if we were relieved of worst-case scenarios, if these goods

---

[34] See Jacob S. Hacker and Paul Pierson, *American Amnesia: How the War on Government Led Us to Forget What Made America Prosper* (Simon & Schuster, 2016), pp. 58–65.

[35] For a discussion of this history that's as eloquent as it is clear-eyed, see Marilynne Robinson, "Save Our Public Universities: In Defense of America's Best Idea," *Harper's,* March 2016.

weren't even necessarily free or nominal, but manageable. Afford-able according to our honest means. So much that wasn't possible before now would be, practically a paradise of possibility. Take your education as far as you will without wrecking your future with debt; change jobs, change professions, strike out on your own with-out exiling yourself from the mercies of modern medicine. Yes, the mind boggles. We're just dreaming, of course, not making policy, but it's a useful exercise nonetheless. A certain kind of politician is always gassing about *Freedoms! American Freedoms! Best and Freest in the World!,* but it's in trying to imagine a life in which education and health care come with the citizen package—a life a bit closer to that of your average Spaniard or Swede—that we confront just how stingy and cramped our poor American notion of freedom has become.

Up there on the stage the program rambles from act to act like a hipster version of *Prairie Home Companion.* We get a fifteen-minute set from Mark Foster, a rangy singer-songwriter in a bright red suit whose soulful, wincingly earnest compositions come across as a sort of secular Christian rock. Between songs he asks, "Who's plan-ning to caucus on Monday?" *Yaaaaaaay,* many thousands respond. "Okay, who knows where they're supposed to caucus?" A querulous *thuuuuhhhhpt* comes back, flat as a back-of-the-fridge beer being opened. Presently the lights go down again and the screen un-furls for another campaign ad, Sanders's distinctive Brooklynese ("brrringing people togethah") talking over a dice-and-splice reel of everyday faces. More cheers when it's done, *yaaaaaaay.* Until now the action's been happening on the big stage, a broad cutout in the Field House wall with proper wings, curtains, and backstage. A much smaller portable stage sits in the middle of the Field House floor, and it's this stage, essentially an island surrounded by thousands of people, where the lights come up on Dr. Cornel West, BA Harvard, PhD Princeton, former tenured professor at Harvard (he quit after knocking heads with its then-president, that ultimate establish-mentarian Larry Summers), currently professor of philosophy and religion at Union Theological Seminary, and a rare crossover hit in American culture, working from academe (author of over twenty books) into the wider world of hip-hop and spoken-word records (former MTV Artist of the Week), movies (as "Councillor West" in *The Matrix Reloaded* and *The Matrix Revolutions*), and TV (a frequent guest on news and talk shows; portrayed by Kenan Thompson on *Saturday Night Live*). Tonight he is dressed in his trademark three-piece black suit with dark scarf, white shirt, and black tie, the French cuffs of his shirt sticking out so far and bright they might as well be sodium flares. In that suit, with his gray-streaked Afro and facial hair like Spanish moss, he looks less like a man of the twenty-first century than a fire-and-brimstone preacher and part-time potion doctor hurled out of the 1890s. A prophet, a cloud splitter and atom smasher, certainly a conjurer of explosive verbal alchemies that he turned on Barack Obama several years ago for what he regarded as the president's tragic squandering of a once-in-a-generation opportunity, the historical moment pissed away in back-bending compromise and conflict-averse finickiness. "A black mascot of Wall Street oligarchs," West called the president. "A black Muppet of corporate plutocrats." And a "Rockefeller Republican in blackface." Standing before us now, West drapes himself over the lectern like a giant spider and brings the word.

"Brothers and sisters of all colors in Iowa are you ready to make history on Monday n-i-i-i-i-i-i-ght!" he thunders like God's own MC. The scratchy bob-and-weave of his voice, that bombs-away fade on "niiiiiight," light the fuse on five thousand Roman candles. The kids go nuts.

"Are you ready," he declaims in one long rush, "are you ready for the rebirth of democracy *tired* of Wall Street domination *ready* for those *yessss* are you ready for those slash *stone-cold* everyday people and James Cleveland called *ordinary* people to be the center of *policy,* center of *vision,* this is a new day in America as of Monday n-i-i-i-i-i-ight," that fade again and the roar this time is levitatory, the kids have never seen anything like Cornel West with his flailing arms and incandescent French cuffs and the rock-drill delivery of his voice, every syllable banging home with the hard ratta-tatta of a speed bag or a Gatling gun. He could be Great-Granddaddy Hip-Hop, the original guy up there in the pulpit from whom everything and everybody flowed, blues, jazz, soul, skiffle, R & B, rock & roll, funk, punk, rap, ska, and whatever comes next. The root of it all. Cornel West is teacher and class is now in session.

"And it's nothing *alien* to America, this is the *legacy* of Martin, Luther, King, Junior, this is the *legacy* of Rabbi Abraham, Joshua, Heschel, it's the *legacy* of Dorothy, Day, the *legacy* of Fannie, Lou, Hamer, the *legacy* of Grace, Bowles, black-white-red-yellow-brown all together concerned about something bigger than u-s-s-s-s-s-sssssss!"

Bombs away. He stands up straight while the cheers explode, then hunches low to the lectern, throbbing like a human tuning fork that's just been whanged by the great cosmic spoon. The words come in an urgent rush.

"This is not just a campaign this is a *moral* and *spiritual* transfor-MA-tion of the NA-tion fundamentally committed to unarmed *truth* and the condition of *truth* is always to allow suffering to *speak* it's about unapologetic *love* and *justice* is what love looks like in puh-bli-i-i-i-i-i-i-c!"

He straightens, stands back for the avalanche roar, pounces again.

"So the Bernie Sanders campaign is an attempt to convince all of us to get, *on,* the **love, train,** to get, *on,* the **justice, train,** to keep track of the poor children of *any* color, working people of *any* color, gay brothers, lesbian sisters, bisexual transgender of *any* color, elderly of *any* color"—now he steps back and gathers himself, returns to the lectern with extra heat—"*allll-ways* mindful of how the vicious legacy of white supremacy has been used to divide us we *won't allow it to do it this t-i-i-i-i-i-ime!*"[36]

We won't? We'll need all of Professor West's incantatory mojo magic to repel this *vicious legacy that has been used to divide us,* which deserves a full lecture of its own, no, an entire semester's intensive seminar to elaborate in all its rancid realpolitik gutter-wallowing glory, expertly plied these past fifty years by successive Republican Party brain trusts and "New Democrats" as the notorious (but not to them) Southern Strategy. May God save the United States! from itself. Much of the modern screwover of the working and middle classes should be laid at the feet of the Southern Strategy, which gave cover to the biggest redistribution of wealth in human history. Racism provided the essential political leverage: the GOP and a certain kind of Democrat claimed to have the backs of racially aggrieved white voters, then busily filled those backs with knives when it came to money matters.[37]

"And we see it in our artists, oh my God," West is saying, "from James Baldwin to Nina Simone to Bruce Springsteen, to Gil Scott-Heron, to Carole King . . ." He graciously welcomes Vampire Weekend into the pantheon, and the lights shift to the big stage where this same Vampire Weekend is set to play, joined by the Dirty Projectors and the University of Iowa Hawkapellas. Ten minutes of tunes and political patter follow. The press on its platform shifts and stirs like cows in a holding pen. When Sanders at last steps onto the small stage—wife Jane at his side, Springsteen on the speakers—the roar of the crowd rolls out to the walls and up to the ceiling and reverbs

---

[36] "Slaveholders do not allow their slaves to compare notes: American slavery, until this hour, prevents any meaningful dialogue between the poor white and the black, in order to prevent the poor white from recognizing that he, too, is a slave. The contempt with which American leaders treat American blacks is very obvious; what is not so obvious is that they treat the bulk of the American people with the very same contempt. But it will be sub-zero weather in a very distant August when the American people find the guts to recognize this fact." James Baldwin, "Malcolm and Martin," *Esquire,* April 1972.

[37] Explored further in "American Crossroads: Reagan, Trump, and the Devil Down South," "Hillary Doesn't Live Here Anymore," and "A Familiar Spirit," *infra.*

back, noise crashing into noise and more noise. This is what being in a gravel crusher must feel like, and so you marvel at the incongruity of all these cheers not for LeBron or Beyoncé but for Grandpa over there, the old white guy you see at every CVS you ever walked into badgering the poor pharmacist tech at the pickup counter. Clunker eyeglasses, woke-up-like-this hair (what's left of it), a voice whose natural register tends toward hector and harangue. He moves well, give him that, without the doddering premeditation of someone over the hill, and he steps up to the lectern with a grin nearly as wide as Barack Obama's. The roar tails off for a brief moment, then comes back louder, laced with war chants of Bernie! Bernie! Bernie!, and he waves, smiles, waves some more. "Whoa!" he cries into the mike, "there's a lotta people heah!" The volume climbs another notch and he grins, ducks his head as if both pleased and embarrassed. Such fearsome racket, a crowd of thousands packed right up to the stage, and the only security in sight is a lone gentleman in a suit standing behind the stage, earbudded, wired, professionally calm amid the storm. Trumpian displays of thug muscle aren't the Sanders style.

He begins with ritual thanks to the evening's musicians and speakers, with special thanks to "my brothah, Cohnel West." He knows better than to try for West's blood-thumping oratory, and pitches his opening in a different key altogether, sober, measured, not squelching the energy so much as easing it down to sustainable altitude. "What this campaign is about," he says slowly, working through some hoarseness, "is something that is very, very serious business. What it is about"—he picks his words like stepping over puddles—"is not just electing a president of the United States, as important as that is. It is about"—the volume picks up, the hoarseness recedes—"it is about a political revolution and transforming America"—the cheers are coming and he quickens the pace—"it is about creating a *nation* that all of us *know we can become!*"

The applause is such that you'd think he just launched a battleship, but Bernie's oratory exists on much the same level as his clothes:

nothing fancy, but they get the job done. Tonight he's dressed like an emeritus econ professor, in a dark gray blazer, navy V-neck sweater, blue button-down Oxford shirt open at the collar. Reason and explanation are his default mode, along with a bricklike tendency toward enunciatory emphasis. "*End* institutional racism." "*Climate* change is *real.*" "What we *must* do from a *moral* perspective . . ." As with the old econ professor lecturing at the front of the hall, you feel obliged to write down everything he says because it all sounds important, and yes you will be responsible for it on the exam.

"Given the realities of American political and economic life . . . only way we can bring about change . . . only way we can take on the powers that be in America . . . Wall Street . . . corporate America . . . the corporate media . . . huge financial institutions that make hundreds of millions of dollahs in campaign donations . . . only way we can bring real change to this country is when *millions* of people, *young* people, *working* people, *black* people, *white* people, *Latino* people, *gay* people, *straight* people, women, men, when all of us stand togethah and very loudly and clearly say"—the kids know what's coming, they cheerfully woof it with him—"ENOUGH, IS, ENOUGH!"

Big cheers. Everybody agrees. Stand together, sounds good. It is the old progressive dream of solidarity across racial lines, black-white-brown prying loose their fair share from the bosses and bankers. Hard to pull off, and near impossible in the South. *That vicious legacy of white supremacy that has been used to divide us.* "In America today," Sanders continues, but his Brooklynese mugs him and it comes out thus: "In Americur today we have more income and wealth inequality than at any time since 1928, and it is worse than almost any major country on earth."

*Boooooo.*

"What America has historically been about is the concept of fairness"—*faohness*—"but it is not *faoh* when the top one-tenth of One Percent today owns almost as much wealth as the bottom ninety percent." And the numbers come, the familiar litany of inequality statistics that, in those moments when we choose to listen, can't help but disturb and unsettle us, the ground shifting beneath this shining city on a hill that we seem to have built on an active fault line. *It is not faoh:* the twenty richest individuals in America own more than the entire bottom fifty percent. *It is not faoh:* one family, the Waltons of Walmart, owns more than the bottom 40 percent. *It is not faoh:* people having to work two or three jobs just to survive, while 58 percent of all new income goes to the top One Percent.

The Field House crowd is dead silent. You reach a point in life, your late teens or early twenties, when it gets real and you find yourself looking for answers. Why are things the way they are? Is there a place for me? How do I live a decent life, and what does that even mean, "a decent life"? The daily discourse of America gives precious little guidance, but tonight Sanders is offering hard numbers, statements of verifiable fact, clues a person might use to begin to understand something about her prospects in life.

"Are you guys ready for a radical ideer?" Sanders bellows, rousing the kids to cheers. "Togethah we are going to create an economy that works for *all* of us, not just the One Percent!"

Big whoops, *yaaaaaaay.* He doesn't say we've already lost. He doesn't say, not in so many words, that the One Percent already owns American democracy, and now the battle is getting it back. For proof we have the crash of 2008, a trauma so profound that it prompted the country to take the extraordinary step of electing a black man president. Obama promised change. He embodied change in his very person, but the system that brought about the crash would remain fundamentally the same. As things turned out, it didn't matter much who had the power in Washington, Democrat or Republican in the White House, Democrats or Republicans running Congress. The big banks got bailed out. The big banks got bigger. One (1) medium-fry trader went to jail, meanwhile the CEOs and the One Percent kept getting richer and working people were stuck in the same place, working too hard for too little and hoping for a break.

People were looking for justice, looking for *faohness,* and they also wanted some relief, but by the time 2010 rolled into 2011—Tea Party time, Occupy time—it had begun to sink in that change of the fundamental sort would not be forthcoming. We could vote, hold marches and rallies, write Congress, post our views on Facebook and Twitter, join movements, sign petitions, support this or that candidate—it hardly mattered. Something had gone wrong with the American democracy; or, rather, what was happening only looked like democracy but in fact was something different altogether. A few people understood this. When the Occupy kids went down to Wall Street in 2011 and set up camp in Zuccotti Park, they showed by their tactics, their bewildering refusal to follow the script, that this is a different kind of fight. Occupy declined to designate leaders. Nor would Occupy articulate a specific program, furnish a "list of demands," or declare a particular orthodoxy beyond "We are the 99%." The movement's stubborn amorphousness caused broad conceptual meltdown in mainstream culture, much old-fart conniption and sputtering addlement. Who are these clowns? What do they want? Why don't they say what they want? Occupy was dumb. Occupy needed to get with the program, which, as described by the movement's many critics, seemed directed toward bringing Occupy in line with modern corporate models of organization and efficiency, the culture of bullet-point summaries, action plans, dynamic interface. How dutifully dull and obedient the American mind has become. That this might be one of the points Occupy was making would, naturally, be lost on a number of those minds.

Occupy was after bigger game than platforms and ten-point plans. By its presence in Manhattan's financial district, with its simple and insistent message of protest *in that place,* Occupy was demanding awareness of the state of things: the vast majority of Americans had lost meaningful agency over our lives. Our economic struggles were proof, the truth borne out in the enduring freedom-profits-plunder equation: profit proportionate to freedom, plunder correlative to subjugation. We still had our political rights—to vote, to assemble, to speak freely and so forth—but real power resided elsewhere. Political science has a name for this condition of ersatz democracy, "nautonomy," defined as

> the asymmetrical production and distribution of life chances which limit and erode the possibilities of political participation . . . *To the extent that nautonomy exists, a common structure of political action is not possible, and democracy becomes a privileged domain operating in favor of those with significant resources. In such circumstances, people can be formally free and equal, but they will not enjoy rights which shape and facilitate a common structure of political action and safeguard their capacities.*[38]

In modern industrial society, political rights alone can't prevent this *asymmetrical production and distribution of life chances.* Franklin Roosevelt explicitly acknowledged this truth when he proposed an "economic bill of rights" in 1944.[39] Martin Luther King Jr. did as well when he elevated economic equality to the same level of importance as political equality,[40] and Bobby Kennedy too during his 1968 presidential campaign, which he envisioned as a "black and blue" coalition that would unite the economically and politically dispossessed across racial lines.

---

[38] David Held, *Democracy and the Global Order* (Stanford University Press, 1995), pp. 171–72 (emphasis in the original).

[39] See "Prologue: The Third Reinvention," *supra,* and "Two American Dreams," *infra.*

[40] "I'm concerned about white poverty as much as I'm concerned about Negro poverty"—1965. "If a man doesn't have a job or an income he has neither life nor liberty nor the possibility for the pursuit of happiness. He merely exists"—1968. "Now our struggle is for genuine equality, which means economic equality"—1968. The Poor People's Campaign of 1968, which he conceived but didn't live to see, was intended to pressure Congress to pass a five-point economic bill of rights.

Occupy Wall Street was as much an economic protest ("We are the 99%") as it was a political protest. It was a protest against nautonomy, until the billionaire mayor of New York ("those with significant resources") decided he'd had enough and shut it down. Whether a state of nautonomy is, or ever has been, the conscious policy of the One Percent toward the rest of us,[41] it certainly makes for a situation they can work with. Profit proportionate to freedom; plunder correlative to subjugation. So much easier for *those with significant resources* to keep their foot on the neck of a citizen if she's working a low-wage job or two or three with no health insurance, no sick days, no vacation, she's always scrambling for good, affordable day care for her kids (the impossible dream!), medicine and visits to the doctor have to be strictly rationed, leaded water might be coming out of her pipes, and getting a form of ID that would enable her to vote involves not only a pain-load of logistical hassles but taking several or more hours—unpaid, of course—off from work.[42] And we can easily conjure a middle-class version of nautonomy, where you have health insurance but high deductibles and always-rising premiums, the day care problem, the private-school-tuition problem, the still-paying-off-your-old-student-loans problem, the mortgage that takes two incomes to support, with college tuition for the kids and retirement still to be determined, and one thing, *one thing*, can crash the whole house of cards: loss of a job, cut in pay, serious illness, the economy tanks. But, hey, you can vote—knock yourself out! You might even find the time and energy to get involved a bit, to paddle your little dinghy out into the oceans of dark money that cover the political landscape, but when Sanders tells the Field House

---

[41] *Dark Money* by Jane Mayer (Doubleday, 2016) and *Democracy in Chains* by Nancy MacLean (Viking, 2017) make the case that it is.

[42] "'I wanted people like me to be cared about. People don't realize there's nothing without a blue-collar worker.' She regretted that she did not have a deeper grasp of public affairs. 'No one that's voting knows all the facts,' she said. 'It's a shame. They keep us so fucking busy and poor that we don't have the time.'" Alec MacGillis, "Revenge of the Forgotten Class," ProPublica, November 10, 2016.

crowd, "This government belongs to *all* of us, not just a handful of *billionaehz,*" he is making an aspirational, as opposed to factual, statement.

But the kids take it on faith. *Yaaaaay! Yaaaaay!* they cry, and it's not like they have it wrong, exactly. The American project has always been in large part aspiration.

"But now we are living in a country wheah as a result of this disastrous *Citizens United* Supreme Court decision, billionaehz are able to buy elections."

Booooooo.

"Maybe I'm an old-fashioned guy, but I believe that democracy is about one person, one vote . . ."

Yaaaaaay!

". . . what is *not* a good thing is when people like the Koch brothahs and a handful of billionaehz are able to spend *nine hundred million* dollahs in this election cycle to elect candidates who represent the wealthy and the powerful."

Boooooo.

"When you have a handful of billionaehz spending more money on a campaign than either the Democratic or Republican parties, that is *not* democracy, that is *oligarchy,* and togethah *we're gonna change that!*"

More aspiration, and mountains of trouble to climb. Yaaaay! Yaaaay! the kids cheer happily, but it's going to be so much harder than we imagine. The self-reinforcing cycle of money and power makes it so; or, as the Nobel Prize–winning economist Joseph Stiglitz put it, "Wealth begets power, which begets more wealth."[43] Which begets still more power, Stiglitz might have continued, and more wealth on top of that, and yet more power and on and on to the point—are we there already?—where nautonomy is the lived reality of all but a tiny sliver of Americans. One begins to suspect that

---

[43] "Of the 1%, by the 1%, for the 1%," *Vanity Fair,* May 2011.

in the era of *Citizens United,* Super PACs, the Koch brothers and their posse, a Forbes 400 list stuffed with multibillionaires, vast inequality of opportunity as well as of income, a well-financed movement aimed at suppressing the popular vote, and roughly twenty registered lobbyists for every lawmaker on Capitol Hill—one suspects that the system as it stands in 2016 is beyond curing itself. And so if anything is going to change, everything has to change. Sanders isn't blowing smoke when he calls for a political revolution. It's not merely a cue for applause, a battle cry to jazz the troops. This is a man following his political logic to its only possible conclusion.

Presently he turns to a discussion of pot, playing it deadpan. "Now, I know that none of you know anything about marijuana." Waves of conspiratorial laughter wash forward, then roaring applause when he cracks a smile. Bernie is the cool old prof you can imagine having had a toke or two back in the day—who might, at the end of the semester at the off-campus party, out there in the dark backyard where the cool kids gather and the real party happens, reminisce in a general way about some righteous weed he and his crew might have encountered on a cross-country road trip back in '65. Bernie gets it, whereas Cruz or Fiorina would narc you out in a second. "Pot should not be a federal crime," he states plainly, and points out the idiocy of a system that saddles a kid with a permanent criminal record for possessing marijuana, whereas the bankers of Goldman Sachs can defraud investors, game the financial system, and help drive the economy to the brink of collapse—malfeasance so self-evident that they paid $5 billion (*billion!*) to the federal government to settle charges related to the 2008 crash—then go on about their lucrative lives without the baggage of a rap sheet. The cheers get louder and deeper as he ticks through the liberal checklist on abortion rights, gay marriage, climate change, and clean energy. "What this campaign is about is asking you to think big, not small." The big thoughts: A Medicare-for-all, single-payer health care system. Tuition-free public universities and colleges, and relief on student debt. Billionaires paying "their fair share" of taxes. Tonight he omits—surely an oversight—his standard plug for a $15 minimum wage.

The polls are virtually tied, he reminds us. It will all depend on turnout, and whether his supporters are committed enough to go out and caucus. "I know many of your friends are going to say"—and here he slows it down, slides into the lilting, high-in-the-sky elisions of Cheech and Chong—"'You went to a *political meeting*? Wow, that's pretty *lame*.'" Everyone laughs—Bernie said *lame*! Which in itself would be lame if he hadn't said it with such knowing nerdness, fully aware that he can't own the word except ironically. One thinks back to George McGovern, another liberal, bald senator from the boonies who was dearly beloved by the kids; who, like Sanders, offered to remake the country, and for his trouble got creamed by Richard Nixon in the worst rout in the history of the Electoral College. This is history as aversion therapy: to say the election of 1972 scarred the Democratic Party is roughly the same as saying the chicken is scarred by being cooked and served for dinner. Many of the "New Democrats" who would make their careers determinedly pulling the party toward the right cut their teeth on the McGovern campaign, Bill and Hillary among them. Walter Mondale was the last "Old Democrat" to get the party's nomination, in 1984, and he got thrashed nearly as badly as McGovern. Does the trauma ever really go away? Probably not for Democrats of a certain age, and even those excited by Sanders's rise are surely feeling the squirm, those first tremors and tinglings of the McGovern cold sweats. Easy to lose your nerve, at such moments; to view Hillary in a safe, maternal light. At least she won't wreck the brand, put it that way. No wonder the party establishment is digging in its heels for her.

"Democracy is not a spectatah sport," Sanders declares, and he closes with a homily: football is for watching and politics is for doing, otherwise you're letting a bunch of billionaires run your life. "On Monday night we are poised to make history!" he cries. "Help us do that! Join the political revolution!"

Chants of Bernie! Bernie! Bernie! follow him up the runway into darkness. The lights rise on the big stage, where Vampire Weekend is set for the send-off. "We gotta play one more for Bernie," says the front man, and they launch into a twangy acoustic rendering of "This Land Is Your Land." The guitars and vocals don't quite sync up, and the tune wanders a bit, but it's a jam—the Dirty Projectors and Hawkapellas are up there too—and the ramshackle sound feels right anyway, lots of dust and tumbleweed blowing through it. Soon Sanders has materialized onstage, he's happy to stand in the background and sing along, nodding, dipping his knees, doing the Grandpa Bop, occasionally clapping the beat but more often clasping his hands in front of his crotch, sincere and awkward. And there he stands, representing what may be the biggest gamble in American politics since the New Deal. Universal health care, tuition-free college, living wages for all, a robust social safety net—surely few would object to such a society in the abstract, but do the numbers add up? The numbers themselves pure vapor, all those billions and trillions of dollars that exist in our heads as a branch of metaphysics, so far from our daily experience of earning and spending. Yet this is our task, to fathom budgets on the order of $4 trillion, a national debt of $19 trillion, and the seismic changes Sanders proposes for this surreal realm. We could, of course, look to the economists for guidance—and in a few weeks there will be a firestorm of economists debating the merits of Sanders's plan—but homegrown analyses are too easily tainted by the charge of political bias. So perhaps our best option, and in keeping with the new American tradition, is to outsource. Appoint a panel of brilliant, disinterested economists from, for instance, Canada, Germany, India, Malaysia, and Peru, and task them with evaluating the Sanders program; maybe then we'd have some notion of whether he's pointing us toward the promised land or the cliff of no return. Or maybe, as Adam Davidson will write later this spring,[44] the mainstream economics of the past eighty years are inadequate for the task. The Keynesians, the disciples of the Chicago and Austrian schools, they all start from the basic premise that market forces determine the distribution of goods in a society. For a clearer perspective on Sanders, perhaps we should look to the fringy "institutionalists" inspired by Thorstein Veblen's *The Theory of the Leisure Class* (1899), who believe that a society's institutions count more than markets for determining how wealth is distributed. By these lights, the changes that Sanders is proposing— single-payer health care, free college, raising the minimum wage, spending $1 trillion on infrastructure—will transform the structure of the American economy so fundamentally that the Keynesian and Chicago models are largely irrelevant.

"[F]or many people who support Sanders," Davidson will note, "the fact that his ideas run counter to decades of established economics is exactly the point." Well, yes; for many people who support Sanders, revolution is exactly the point. Jane Sanders joins her husband, and soon the entire evening's lineup has gathered onstage, the Awful Purdies, the comedy twins, Rob Foster, Cornel West, it becomes a motley, we-are-the-world singalong, everyone swaying and holding hands like it's the sixties again, a good dose of the old lefty touchy-feely to tide us through evil times. The night ends on this mellow but rousing note—such is the power of a good folk song—and with a last, laconic exhortation from Vampire Weekend: "Good night, guys, go vote." The lights come up, and Bowie booms from the sound system, singing of a star man up there in the sky who wants to meet us, but he's afraid he'll blow our minds.

---

44 "On Money," *New York Times Magazine*, April 17, 2016.

The vast Field House floor slowly clears, leaving scattered clusters of kids doing the Deadhead thing, Iowa dervishes off in their own whirling ether. Was there ever a revolution without at least a few lightning bolts of ecstasy? The One Percent has the money, the pros, the organization and networks, the high-dollar behavioral-science gurus, and the latest in algorithmic clickbait magics. They've won, and their grip is such that they'll probably keep winning for a good while longer, distinctions of Democrat and Republican quite to the side. But you wonder, and you wonder if they ever wonder, what ratio of young capitalists to "other" their system is creating. Socialists, Communists, anarchists, nihilists, skinheads, discontents by any name who feel no great loyalty to the capitalist system—are they gaining? And so one wonders how long the center will hold, that critical mass of the 99 percent who maintain the short end of what becomes, with every passing year, an increasingly lopsided bargain.

# BOOK OF DAYS
## FEBRUARY

**IOWA CAUCUSES**
> Democratic
>> Clinton: 50%
>>
>> Sanders. 50%
>
> Republican
>> Cruz: 28%
>>
>> Trump: 24%
>>
>> Rubio: 23%
>>
>> Carson: 9%
>>
>> Paul: 4%
>>
>> J. Bush: 3%
>>
>> Fiorina: 2%
>>
>> Kasich: 2%
>>
>> Huckabee: 2%
>>
>> Christie: 2%
>>
>> Santorum: 1%

"This is the moment they said would never happen," Marco Rubio says of his third-place finish in Iowa. Punxsutawney Phil fails to see his shadow, indicating an early spring, and the British government gives scientists approval to conduct gene-editing experiments on human embryos. The annual report of the National Registry of Exonerations reveals that a record-setting 149 men and women were exonerated in 2015 after spending an average of 14.5 years in prison for crimes they did not commit. Obama proposes quadrupling the military budget for troops and training in Europe in order to deter Russian aggression. Americans spent an estimated $5.4 billion on legal marijuana in 2015, and $4.9 billion on Cheetos, Funyuns, and Doritos. The Sanders campaign reports that it raised $20 million in January, $5 million more than Clinton, and Clinton supporters worry about her campaign's "muddled message." In a YouTube video, singer Alicia Keys offers to be House Speaker Paul Ryan's "Valentine" if the House acts on criminal justice reform. North Korea launches the Kwangmyongsong, or "Shining Star," rocket, whose potential range of seventy-four hundred miles would enable it to reach the U.S. West Coast. Campaigning in New Hampshire, Cruz cracks that if Trump is elected, "we're liable to wake up one day and Donald, as president, will have nuked Denmark." In a Democratic debate in Durham, New Hampshire, Clinton calls Sanders's criticism of her Wall Street campaign contributions and speaking fees "an artful smear," and most New Hampshire newspapers, along with the *Boston Globe* and the *New York Times,* endorse Kasich. "I'm tired of angry men," says one New Hampshire voter, a retired Air Force officer, explaining his support for Kasich. Former president George W. Bush appears in a campaign commercial for his brother Jeb, saying that the former Florida governor's "good heart and strong backbone" will unite the country and the world in the fight against terrorism. "CHOKE!" reads the front-page headline of the *Boston Herald,* referring to Marco Rubio's performance in the previous night's GOP debate, at which he repeated four times, virtually word for word, the same twenty-five-second talking point, which brought on the ridicule of New Jersey governor Chris Christie and jeers from the audience.

**NEW HAMPSHIRE PRIMARY**

Democrat

Sanders: 60%

Clinton: 39%

Republican

Trump: 35%

Kasich: 16%

Cruz: 12%

J. Bush: 11%

Rubio: 11%

Christie: 8%

Fiorina: 4%

Carson: 2%

Chris Christie suspends his presidential campaign. The Obama administration sends a proposed $4.1 trillion budget to Congress; breaking a forty-one-year tradition, the Republican chairmen of the House and Senate budget committees announce they will not allow the administration's budget director to testify in committee hearings. In Palm Beach County, Florida, Joshua James is arrested and charged with assault with a deadly weapon for throwing a three-and-a-half-foot-long alligator through a Wendy's drive-thru window. Director of National Intelligence James Clapper delivers a "litany of doom" at the annual "worldwide threats" hearing of the Senate Armed Services Committee, citing, among other dangers, ISIS's determination to attack the U.S., and cyberattacks sponsored by China and Russia. Antonin Scalia, the current longest-serving Supreme Court justice, dies in bed at age seventy-nine at the Cibolo Creek Ranch, a luxury hunting resort forty miles south of Marfa,

Texas, after a day of hunting blue quail. Presidio County judge Cinderela Guevara pronounces Scalia dead of natural causes without seeing the body, and within hours of the news of Scalia's death, Senate majority leader Mitch McConnell releases a statement declaring that the newly vacant seat should not be filled by an Obama nominee. In a debate that takes place a few hours after Scalia's death is reported, Trump articulates his strategy on any Supreme Court nominee put forward by Obama—"Delay, delay, delay"—and draws boos for pointing out that 9/11 happened while George W. Bush was president. At the same debate, Cruz repeatedly and incorrectly asserts that "we have eighty years of precedent of not confirming Supreme Court justices in an election year," ignoring the fact that Justice Anthony Kennedy, a Reagan appointee, was confirmed in February 1988, an election year. A 5.1-magnitude earthquake hits northwest Oklahoma, the third-strongest ever recorded in that state, where temblors linked to oil and gas production have increased dramatically in recent years. Pope Francis holds a "bi-national mass" in Ciudad Juárez, Mexico, on the United States border, calling for greater Christian ethics in business and declaring: "God will hold the slave drivers of our day accountable . . . The flow of capital cannot decide the flow and life of people." Cruz dares Trump to sue him for defamation for an ad claiming that Trump supports abortion rights and gun control, and an NBC/*Wall Street Journal* poll shows Cruz leading Trump nationwide for the first time, 28 percent to 26 percent. A car bomb attack on a bus convoy of Turkish soldiers in Ankara kills twenty-nine. The Southern Poverty Law Center reports that the number of hate groups in the U.S. grew by 14 percent in 2015, and the IRS rules that Karl Rove's political organization Crossroads GPS is a nonprofit "social welfare group" under 501(c)(4), allowing it to receive unlimited donations from individuals and corporations and to spend unlimited money on political activities without revealing the identities of its donors. OpenSecrets.org reports that $100 million in "dark money" was spent on elections in the period 2000–2010, and $300 million was spent during the 2012 election cycle alone. Pope Francis, when asked by a reporter about Trump's vow to build the wall, answers: "A person who thinks only about building walls, wherever they may be, and not building bridges, is not Christian . . . I say only that this man is not a Christian, if he has said things like that." Trump responds from Kiawah Island, South Carolina: "For a religious leader to question a person's faith is disgraceful . . . If and when the Vatican is attacked by ISIS, which, as everyone knows, is ISIS's ultimate trophy, I can promise you that the pope would have only wished and prayed that Donald Trump would have been president." Jerry Falwell Jr., the president of Liberty University and a longtime advocate for basing public policy on Christian principles, says in Trump's defense: "Jesus never intended to give instructions to political leaders on how to run a country." California's OSHA board rejects a proposal requiring porn actors to wear condoms. Harper Lee dies at age eighty-nine. Five more earthquakes hit Oklahoma.

**NEVADA DEMOCRATIC CAUCUS**
Clinton: 53%
Sanders: 47%

**SOUTH CAROLINA REPUBLICAN PRIMARY**
Trump: 32.5%
Rubio: 22.5%
Cruz: 22.3%
Jeb Bush: 7.8%
Kasich: 7.6%
Carson: 7.2%

Jeb Bush suspends his campaign. Explaining why she supports Sanders over Clinton, actress Susan Sarandon tweets, "I don't vote with my vagina." U.S. air strikes on an ISIS training camp in Libya kill two Serbian hostages, and the Afghan government pulls its troops out of the Musa Qala district of southern Helmand Province after Taliban forces overrun the area. Samuel Willenberg, the last of the sixty-seven known survivors of the Nazis' Treblinka death camp, dies at age ninety-three in Israel.

## NEVADA REPUBLICAN CAUCUS
    Trump: 45.9%
    Rubio: 23.9%
    Cruz: 21.4%
    Carson: 4.8%
    Kasich: 3.6%

Senate Republican leaders say there will be no confirmation hearings, no vote, and no courtesy meetings for any Supreme Court nominee put forward by Obama, and predict that they'll face no election fallout from their position. Republican House leaders take legal steps to block Obama's plan to close the U.S. prison at Guantánamo Bay and move the remaining detainees to the U.S. China surpasses the U.S. in number of billionaires, 568 to 535, and Beijing, with 100 billionaires, replaces New York (95) as the "billionaire capital of the world." News reports show that Trump's Mar-a-Lago resort has pursued more than 500 visas for foreign workers while hundreds of domestic applicants fail to get the same jobs, and Chris Christie endorses Trump.

## SOUTH CAROLINA DEMOCRATIC PRIMARY
    Clinton: 73%
    Sanders: 26%

Day one of a heavily negotiated cease-fire in Syria brings a significant decrease in violence. Suicide bombings kill at least twenty-six in Afghanistan. Rubio says that Trump requires a "Hair Force

One," has the nation's worst spray-tan, is a con artist, calls to mind "the lunatic in North Korea," and would be "selling watches" on the streets of Manhattan if not for his father's wealth. "Donald Trump likes to sue people," Rubio tells an audience in Kennesaw, Georgia. "He should sue whoever did that to his face." Trump asserts that Rubio lacks "the capacity" to have attended Trump's Ivy League alma mater, and relies on his big ears to protect against "flop sweat," an allegation that causes widespread bafflement. "I'm so non-litigious, it's amazing," Trump says of himself at an Arkansas rally, while John Kasich, appearing in Nashville, remarks: "Frankly, we need to have an adult as president." Jean-Marie Le Pen, the founder of France's far-right National Front Party, endorses Trump, and on CNN's *State of the Union,* two days before six Southern states vote in the Super Tuesday primaries, Trump refuses to disavow the support of former KKK grand dragon David Duke, saying, "Well, just so you understand, I don't know anything about David Duke, okay? I don't know anything about what you're even talking about with white supremacy or white supremacists." That same day, Trump retweets a quote from Benito Mussolini—"It is better to live one day as a lion than 100 years as a sheep"—and is endorsed by Alabama senator Jeff Sessions, whose 1986 nomination to the federal court of appeals was blocked because of racist statements. Chris Rock hosts the black-boycotted Oscar ceremonies, declaring, "If they nominated hosts, I wouldn't be here," and speculating that blacks didn't boycott the Oscars in the fifties and sixties because "we had real things to protest at the time. We were too busy being raped and lynched to care about who won best cinematographer. When your grandmother is swinging from a tree, it's hard to care about best documentary foreign short." The Syrian cease-fire is shaky but for the most part holding. Democrats predict that Republican obstruction of Obama's Supreme Court nominee will galvanize African-American voters. At a press conference in Pyongyang, Otto Warmbier reads a prepared statement in which he confesses to attempting to steal a propaganda poster from the Yanggakdo International Hotel at the request of a Methodist church in his hometown as well as of the Z Society, a secret society at the University of Virginia, both of which he says are affiliated with the CIA; Western experts suspect that Warmbier's "confession" was made under duress. ISIS bombings kill fifty-nine in Baghdad, and a video appears on YouTube of a drone-mounted handgun firing into the Connecticut woods, as well as a second video of a flying flamethrower igniting a spit-roasting Thanksgiving turkey, both posted by a Central Connecticut State University sophomore.

# THE PHONY IN
# AMERICAN POLITICS

For most of history we had an excuse. Emperors, pharaohs, kings, queens, czars, sultans, sheiks, they lorded over us via peremptory power structures and the vagaries of genetics. If the king was a war-mongering dolt or half-mad egomaniac, it wasn't our, the people's, fault. The best we could do was keep our heads down and suffer as God almighty seemed to want us to. Occasionally there was re-gime change, a new family of dolts and psychotics in charge, but for the mud-dwellers of the 99 percent, life was largely a cowering slog through the nether regions of obedience.

American democracy was supposed to change all that. No more twits or hysterics ruling us, no more beef-fed murderers in ermine robes; we would choose for ourselves, a system that assumes some skill for discernment on the part of the chooser. A quite neces-sary skill, we should note. Rare is the candidate for high office who announces he intends to screw the common folk to the wall. Policy is always put forth in the name of the greater good, to be judged as better or worse, sound or flawed based on reasoned analysis and experience, but beyond policy a more instinctive, earthier judgment is taking place about truth, character, authenticity, all in search of the straight talkers who mean what they say and intend to carry through. Americans care a lot about authenticity, rightly so. Every election is a quest for the genuine article. This is precisely what makes the long con of American politics such a rich and mystifying study.

As Trump, Cruz, Clinton, Sanders, and the rest of the 2016 crew tackle the snows and insults of February in pursuit of votes, all the theatrics of authenticity are on display. The furrowed brows. The throbbing voices. The feel-your-pain hugs. Then they move on to the next town and do it all over again. Americans like to think of ourselves as a savvy and skeptical people, but in the gyms of Iowa, the Rotary Clubs of South Carolina, and all the coffee shops and civic halls to come, our perennial gullibility is there for the plucking.

Let the record reflect: The American people are a bunch of suckers. "Weapons of mass destruction." "I did not have sexual relations with that woman." "Read my lips." "I am not a crook." "We still seek no wider war." And these whoppers are merely a sampling from a handful of recent presidents. To strike the broad pure vein of American credulity one only has to dig a bit deeper to turn up such regional gems as Wilbert Lee "Pappy" O'Daniel, a Depression-era salesman for the Burrus Mill and Elevator Company of Fort Worth, Texas, producer of Light Crust Flour.[1] In the early thirties O'Daniel began hosting a radio show featuring the soon-to-be-famous Bob

---

[1] In telling O'Daniel's story I have relied on George Norris Green's classic *The Establishment in Texas Politics* (University of Oklahoma Press, 1979), particularly chapters 3 and 4, "The O'Daniel Era" and "Rebellion Against the New Deal, 1944," respectively; Gene Fowler and Bill Crawford's *Border Radio: Quacks, Yodelers, Pitchmen, Psychics, and Other Amazing Broadcasters of the American Airwaves* (Texas Monthly Press, 1987), especially chapter 5, "Please Pass the Tamales, Pappy"; and the first volume of Robert Caro's biography of Lyndon Johnson, *The Path to Power* (Knopf, 1990), chapter 34, "'Pass the Biscuits, Pappy,'" pp. 695–703 in particular.

Wills and the Light Crust Doughboys, though O'Daniel's soothing, fatherly voice and easily digestible patter quickly became the
main draw of the show. At twelve thirty each weekday the broadcast opened with a country matron's request to "please pass the biscuits, Pappy." For the next fifteen minutes, listeners—many of them
housewives taking a midday break—were treated to juicy renditions
of gospel and hillbilly tunes interspersed with Pappy reading scripture, ad copy for Light Crust Flour, sentimental poems, and tributes
to motherhood, Texas heroes, and good Christian living. His pop-
ularity grew to the point that he left Burrus Mill and started his
own company, Hillbilly Flour, and began blasting his show over the
hundred thousand watts of XEPN, a pirate radio station across the
border in Mexico.

Flour sales boomed, and Pappy himself was a star, the biggest
mass-media celebrity in the Southwest and a man with his eye on
the next big thing. On the regular Hillbilly Flour program of May 1,
1938, he announced that as the result of a letter-writing campaign
from "thousands" of listeners, he would humbly bow to popular demand and run for governor. His platform consisted of the Ten Com-
mandments, no sales tax, and a guaranteed pension of $30 a month
for every Texan over the age of sixty-five. His campaign theme was
"Pass the Biscuits, Pappy," his motto the Golden Rule. He avowed
that his business experience would enable him to manage the state's
affairs in a businesslike manner, and with his wife, three kids, and
the Hillbilly Band (Wills had left years ago, disgusted with Pappy's
skinflint ways), the flour salesman began a barnstorming tour across
Texas.

The effect was electric. O'Daniel was a "brand," as we say these
days; he had huge "name recognition." Everyone had heard, or at
least heard of, Pappy. Crowds of twenty thousand or more turned out
for his rallies, and mobs of fans forced his caravan to unscheduled
stops so they could hear the "Common Citizen's Candidate" rail on
professional politicians, recite scripture, and plug Hillbilly Flour. An

evangelical fervor was present from the start, fanned by the candidate's Christian oratory and old-timey gospel music. The prominent Baptist minister J. Frank Norris compared Pappy to Moses, predicting he would lead the country back to its Christian roots. One historian has explained O'Daniel's appeal this way:

> *The O'Daniel rallies appealed to the same deep human instinct and provided the same emotional outlets which the camp meeting formerly offered. Here again was the chance to enjoy the thrill and glory of a martial movement without risking any physical bloodshed. Christ was still the hero and Satan still the enemy, but . . . Christ's good, which had previously radiated from the camp-meeting preacher, was now represented by the flour-salesman. Satan's evil, previously attached to that abhorred aristocracy which had been the pioneer's European superior, was now found to reside in the professional politician.*

In Texas, this sort of raw emotional appeal is known as "the glandular technique."[2] When attacked by establishment candidates, O'Daniel responded with scripture: "Blessed are ye when men shall revile you and shall say all manner of evil falsely against you for My sake." He countered objections to his Yankee origins (he was born in Ohio, reared in Kansas) with a characteristically schmaltzy story about his name: one of his uncles, a Union soldier in the Civil War, had been mortally wounded in combat, but was nursed so tenderly on his deathbed by a Southern family that he sent word to his sister saying if she should ever have a son, he should be named after the great Confederate general Robert E. Lee. In answer to charges of being secretly backed by big business, he replied, "How can you say I'm against the working man when I buried my daddy in overalls?"

---

[2] This memorable phrase was coined by Billy Lee Brammer in his *Texas Observer* column of May 2, 1955.

If you're looking for the phony in American politics, just follow the money. O'Daniel was being backed by a cabal of Texas's richest oilmen and bankers, ultraconservatives all, and his campaign was directed by a sharp PR man out of Dallas. O'Daniel himself had grown wealthy in business and real estate, which didn't keep him from sending his pretty daughter out at rallies with a small barrel labeled "Flour Not Pork," appealing for supposedly much-needed campaign funds. Sales of Hillbilly Flour doubled over the course of the campaign; running for governor, O'Daniel admitted, was "sure good for business," and he never denied that boosting the brand was one of his goals from the start. When Election Day came he won more than twice the number of votes of his nearest competitor, and the only counties he didn't win—23 out of 254—were hundreds of miles from radio stations that carried his program. Once in office, he set up a studio in the governor's mansion in Austin and began broadcasting every Sunday morning, pledging, "This administration is going to be me, God, and the people, thanks to the radio."

O'Daniel had found a medium as effective for his day as Twitter is now. No filters, no media bracketing, no third-party commentary, just the Leader communicating directly with his people. In answer to a reporter's question—"What are you going to do about delivering the goods?"—O'Daniel cupped his hand as if holding a microphone and answered, "I've got my own machine. This little microphone." Listening to tapes of O'Daniel's broadcasts today is to be treated to the rankest sort of huckster charm, along with a primer in the shamelessly pandering arts of political suasion. Christian homilies, dogtrot poetry, and treacly moralizing are delivered in a smooth, slightly formal country voice that goes down like lemonade with all the sting sugared out of it. Did he believe his own schtick? He was, one longtime acquaintance said, "a born actor. He may not believe it, but he feels it at the time." Once, with his eyes tearing up as the studio band played "The Old Rugged Cross," Pappy leaned over to a visitor and whispered, "That's what brings 'em in, boy.

That's what really brings 'em in!" In person he was a different man altogether: aloof, awkward, insular, reluctant to engage the legislative leaders with whom he had to work, loath to meet even the adoring constituents who traveled to Austin in hopes of meeting their hero and telling him their troubles. But with a microphone to his lips, O'Daniel, as they say in showbiz, killed. "Son," one longtime listener explained to her skeptical offspring, "I've been having breakfast with Lee O'Daniel on the radio . . . for the past eight years, and I know he's a good man."

A man who delivered virtually nothing to the working people who gave him their votes. These voters had every reason to be fed up with the "professional politicians" whom O'Daniel was constantly railing against. Perhaps the richest state in the union in natural resources, Texas consistently ranked among the lowest by any measure of its citizens' quality of life—education, public health, the social safety net. But once in office, O'Daniel immediately set to work serving the interests of "the big lobby." He pushed the legislature for a regressive 1.6 percent sales tax, as well as for a constitutional amendment that would freeze state taxes on oil, gas, and sulfur at laughably low rates. He sabotaged his campaign pledge of an old-age pension by refusing to consider new taxes to pay for it. Instead of addressing the state's dire finances or its anemic public schools, he hammered on Communist infiltrators and Nazi sympathizers. As one contemporary recalled, "He'd just drum, drum, drum with his little catch phrases: 'professional politicians,' 'pussy-footing politicians,' 'labor leader racketeers,' 'Communist labor leader racketeers'—you wouldn't think there would be that many ways to get 'labor leader racketeers' into a sentence. He just got up at his rallies, and said, in effect, 'I'm going to protect you from everything.'"

His talents were such that in the span of four years he won four statewide elections for high office, including a 1941 special election for the U.S. Senate in which he beat a young congressman named Lyndon Johnson. Even as his allegiance to big business and special interests became increasingly apparent, Pappy's rural and blue-collar base kept faith with their hero. "Just because he's a Christian man." "Because he's honest, mister, and because he ain't no politician." "He's almost a preacher. He knows how to catch up with them Congressmen and tell us about them."

In the arsenal of the phony, the politics of God is one of the deadliest punches to the sweet spot of the American mind. Citizens capable of the most astute analysis in other areas of their lives—in personal finance, say, or consumer technology, or the infinitely complex variables of fantasy sports leagues—are reduced to blithering dupes when exposed to the Christian pitch. Trot out a few verses of scripture, a little Jesus lip service, and something spooky happens to the excellent American mind that gave us moon landings and the silicon chip. No matter if the candidate has had three or four wives, fired thousands of workers, or dropped biblical plagues of bombs on rice farmers and sheepherders, merely saying the magic words makes it so. Christian values. Strong for Jesus. In God we trust, and all the rest. Incantations that render large chunks of the electorate as dazed and pliable as precontact tribesmen hearing a radio for the first time.

O'Daniel incarnated in one person several styles of the American political phony: media celebrity, master of branding, man of God. His eventual colleague in the Senate, Joe McCarthy of Wisconsin, embodied that other avatar of American phoniness, the national security bully.[3] Even as he became a hero to many Americans for his anti-Communist crusade, McCarthy had throughout his career what would now be called "high negatives." This is normal: high negatives are the bully's stock-in-trade.

---

[3] For McCarthy's story, I have relied on David M. Oshinsky, *A Conspiracy So Immense: The World of Joe McCarthy* (Oxford University Press, 2005); Eric Alterman and Kevin Mattson, *The Cause* (Viking, 2012), especially chapter 6, "The Two Joes"; Arthur M. Schlesinger Jr., *Robert Kennedy and His Times* (Houghton Mifflin, 1978), especially chapter 6, "The First Investigating Committee: Joe McCarthy"; Don E. Carleton, *Red Scare!* (Texas Monthly Press, 1985); and Sam Tanenhaus, "Un-American Activities," *New York Review of Books*, November 30, 2000.

Later it would be known as the McCarthy Era, though it has other names as well. The Red Scare. The Scoundrel Time. The Time of the Toad. But early in his career McCarthy was a run-of-the-mill Senate mediocrity known mainly for fighting price controls on sugar, work that earned him the nickname "the Pepsi-Cola Kid" for a $20,000 personal loan he received from a Pepsi executive. He was disliked by his fellow senators, who regarded him as a crude, quick-tempered jerk; the Senate press corps voted him "worst senator" one year. But he became a literal overnight sensation with his February 1950 Lincoln Day speech to the Republican Women's Club of Wheeling, West Virginia, in which he claimed the State Department was "infested" with Communist spies. Holding up a piece of paper—he had that dramatic flair—McCarthy declared, "I have here in my hand a list of two hundred and five—a list of names that were made known to the secretary of state as being members of the Communist Party and who nevertheless are still working and shaping policy in the State Department." The ensuing media firestorm surprised even the senator himself. Over the next few days the number of names on his alleged list dropped to fifty-seven, then rose to eighty-one; it seems that McCarthy, an alcoholic, couldn't remember the number from one day to the next, and he later admitted to J. Edgar Hoover that he made up the numbers as he went along.

But no matter, McCarthy had struck the mother lode. Riding high on his sudden fame, he embarked on a national speaking tour after confiding to a friend that he had "a sockful of shit—and knew how to use it." His luck was to stumble onto a legitimate national security issue; his genius was the way he exploited it for partisan advantage and personal gain. In 1950 America was ripe for the kind of paranoia McCarthy was peddling. The Soviet Union had successfully tested a nuclear weapon the year before, and was aggressively consolidating its control over Eastern Europe. Communists had triumphed in the Chinese Civil War, and within months of the Lincoln Day speech, North Korea would invade South Korea.

The Alger Hiss–Whittaker Chambers affair was fresh in Americans' minds, and a young Richard Nixon was making a name for himself with allegations of far-reaching Communist conspiracies in the government. McCarthy entered the scene like a blowtorch touched to a gas leak. Returning to Washington from his speaking tour, he made a five-hour speech on the floor of the Senate describing the "loyalty risks" of eighty-one State Department employees. The resulting Senate investigation into his allegations previewed the techniques he would use for the next four years to terrorize the political class and the press. He was big on exaggeration, innuendo, and alarmist rhetoric, short on evidence, fast and loose with facts. The Senate report ultimately concluded that McCarthy's charges were "a fraud and a hoax." McCarthy responded by accusing the Democratic chairman of the committee that produced the report, Millard Tydings of Maryland, of "protecting Communists" and "shielding traitors." McCarthy campaigned for Tydings's opponent that fall, and Tydings's defeat marked McCarthy's arrival as a force in national politics.

Like every political phony before him and all the rest to come, McCarthy was a headline hog. The painstaking work of an actual investigation—basic research, paper trails, questioning witnesses—these didn't interest McCarthy or his young chief counsel, Roy Cohn. The senator's specialty was the spectacle, the big show with himself in the starring role, and as chairman of the Senate Permanent Subcommittee on Investigations he occupied center stage in American life for the better part of five years. In hearings that were often televised and always packed with print journalists, he went after alleged Commies at the Voice of America, ruining careers and hounding VOA personnel so mercilessly that one engineer committed suicide. But the end result of all this sound and fury was: zero indictments, zero convictions. He came up double zeros again with his investigation into that nefarious nest of spies at the U.S. Information Agency, namely, the librarians who staffed the libraries at U.S. embassies. And double zeros again when he investigated alleged Communists at the Army Signal Corps laboratory at Fort Monmouth, New Jersey.

He had lots of tricks, among them holding hearings in closed session, then going out to give reporters a grossly slanted version of the testimony that had just transpired. Another favorite tactic was scheduling announcements for late afternoon, when reporters would have scant time to check facts or get a response from McCarthy's victim of the day. For their part, reporters and editors usually gave the senator the benefit of the doubt. They were scared of him, and more than that he was good for the bottom line. The man sold newspapers. He glued eyes to the tube. He put on grand inquisitorial shows and had a gift for the snappy insult. When Senator Margaret Chase Smith, Republican of Maine, and six more GOP senators called for an end to the smear tactics, McCarthy tagged them as "Snow White and the six dwarfs."

God, or at least his anointed mouthpieces here on earth, stood firm with McCarthy. New York's Francis Cardinal Spellman declared, "Only the batblind can fail to be aware of the Communist invasion." The Reverend Billy Graham, spiritual consigliere to a succession of warmongering presidents, termed Communism a "tool of Satan" and pledged support for the senator's crusade to hunt down spies. For hard-line right-wingers, especially foes of Franklin Roosevelt's New Deal and Harry Truman's Fair Deal, McCarthy was the hero with a thousand uses, a handy stick for flaying political enemies and serving private interests. Archconservative Texas oilman Clint Murchison Sr. lavished support on the Wisconsin senator, acknowledging that McCarthy's red-baiting tactics helped keep "the albatross hung about the neck of the New and Fair Deals." Governor Allan Shivers of Texas, another big-business conservative who knew a good thing when he saw it, bestowed honorary Texas citizenship on McCarthy, along with a brand-new $6,000 Cadillac.

McCarthy habitually referred to the Roosevelt and Truman administrations as "twenty years of treason." When Eisenhower's first year as president failed to deliver wholesale purges of alleged Communists, McCarthy amended the catchphrase to "twenty-one years of treason," though he'd already taken aim at Eisenhower's army mentor, General George C. Marshall. Marshall was U.S. Army chief of staff during World War II, and had served as secretary of defense and secretary of state under Truman. As secretary of state, he'd been the driving force for Europe's postwar reconstruction, better known as "the Marshall Plan," for which he received the Nobel Peace Prize in 1953. But in a speech later published as the book *America's Retreat from Victory: The Story of George Catlett Marshall,* McCarthy alleged that Marshall was a foreign agent and traitor, and accused him, in words that have yet to fade from the paranoiac echo chamber of the American mind, of being part of "a conspiracy so immense, and an infamy so black, as to dwarf any previous venture in the history of man."

*Any previous venture.* In the history of man, no less. Let it be said the senator always dreamed big. The irony, if you want to call it that, is the fact that there were scores of Soviet agents in the U.S. government at the time, as would eventually be shown by the VENONA program's intercepts of Soviet communications.[4] But for all his grandstanding and all the lives he wrecked, McCarthy didn't catch a single spy. No indictments, no convictions, but there was a small war's worth of collateral damage, and a general poisoning of national politics and culture. To oppose McCarthy, or even to identify oneself on the liberal side of the political mainstream, was to risk having your life destroyed. For him, it was apocalypse or nothing: he transformed good-faith differences about methods and policies into moral absolutes, leveraging hysteria to a level of unchecked power that's rarely been seen in American politics. Edward R.

---

[4] See, among others, Ronald Kessler, "The Real Story on Joe McCarthy," *Newsmax,* April 7, 2008; John Earl Haynes and Harvey Klehr, *Venona: Decoding Soviet Espionage in America* (Yale University Press, 2000).

Murrow, one of the few journalists willing to confront him head-on, is worth quoting at length:

> *[McCarthy's] primary achievement has been in confusing the public mind as between the internal and external threats of Communism. We must not confuse dissent with disloyalty. We must remember always that accusation is not proof and that conviction depends upon evidence and due process of law. We will not walk in fear, one of another. We will not be driven by fear into an age of unreason, if we dig deep in our history and our doctrine, and remember that we are not descended from fearful men . . .*
>
> *The actions of the junior Senator of Wisconsin have caused alarm and dismay amongst our allies abroad, and given considerable comfort to our enemies. And whose fault is that? Not really his. He didn't create this situation of fear; he merely exploited it . . .*

Fear, as Yoda said, and as Dick Cheney tacitly acknowledged back in 2001, leads to the dark side. One might put a finer gloss on that and say *unhinged* fear is the active agent of our doom. Fear is a natural part of life. Hysterics, not necessarily so.

How easy it is, how satisfying for us, to despise demagogues like McCarthy and Pappy O'Daniel, two of the great phonies and con artists of American politics. But as any confidence man or woman will tell you, the con can't work without willing buy-in by the mark. "It is not intelligence but integrity which determines whether or not a man is a good mark," David Maurer tells us in his classic *The Big Con.*[5] More precisely, it's *lack* of integrity that makes a good mark, the man with larceny in his veins: "If a man with money has this trait, he is all that any con man could wish."

---

[5] Anchor Books/Doubleday, 1999; originally published in 1940. See pp. 104, 117.

Easy to despise the political phony, at least in retrospect. The harder work is plumbing the truth of an electorate that allows the phony to succeed. *He didn't create this situation of fear; he merely exploited it.* What is it about the American character that allows the long con of our politics to go on and on, electing crooks, racists, bullies, hate-mongering preachers, corporate bagmen, and bald-faced liars? Not always, but often. The history is damning. We must, on some level, want what they're offering.

# BOOK OF DAYS

MARCH

"We have expanded the Republican Party. I am a unifier," Trump says after his Super Tuesday primary wins across the South, as well as in Massachusetts and Vermont. During a postelection press conference in which he largely avoids insulting his opponents, he observes, "I'm becoming diplomatic." Of his second-place finish in Virginia, Marco Rubio comments, "If I didn't have to share the ballot with two or three other people, I would have won." Clinton wins seven out of ten Super Tuesday Democratic primaries, and Trump mocks the Clinton campaign's new slogan of "Make America Whole Again." Japan's government issues ten-year bonds with negative yields, and Germany's top court opens hearings on whether to outlaw the extreme-right National Democratic Party, which police suspect is behind a recent surge in racist violence against immigrants. French authorities begin razing the migrant shantytown known as "the Jungle" outside of Calais, home to an estimated four thousand people. TSA authorities bar a woman from boarding a flight while wearing gun-shaped stiletto heels, warm weather forces organizers to ship in tons of snow for the start of Alaska's Iditarod Trail sled dog race, and a study reveals that 99 percent of the top

One Percent wealthiest Americans voted in 2008, while only 49 percent of people making less than $10,000 a year voted. A group of Republican business leaders, led by Hewlett-Packard CEO Meg Whitman and Chicago Cubs co-owner Todd Ricketts, hold a conference call to raise funds for an anti-Trump Super PAC called Our Principles PAC. Ben Carson suspends his campaign, and CNN reports that top GOP officials will soon urge him to run for the U.S. Senate in Florida. The departing commander of U.S. and NATO forces in Afghanistan, General John Campbell, warns of a Taliban resurgence, while nine Republican congressmen vote against naming a post office in Winston-Salem, North Carolina, in honor of Maya Angelou. She was "a communist sympathizer" says the press secretary for one of the congressmen opposing the measure, which passes 371–9. The Trump campaign issues a press release saying the candidate will campaign over the weekend in "Witchita, Kanasas." Rob Morrow, who previously accused former Texas governor Rick Perry of being "a rampaging bisexual adulterer," has said members of the Bush family "are criminals and should be in lockdown in federal prison," and has said that LBJ and the CIA conspired to assassinate President John F. Kennedy, wins election as the new chairman of the Travis County, Texas, GOP. Also in Texas, retired kindergarten teacher Mary Lou Bruner faces a runoff after coming within two percentage points of winning a seat on the state Board of Education. Bruner, who says she "stands for Texas values," has accused Obama of being a male prostitute to support his drug addiction and said he "is not really a black man" and "is not even an American," among other statements; she has also asserted that the Grand Canyon was created by the biblical Great Flood, sex education is a method to indoctrinate kids to be gay, and the dinosaurs brought onto the ark by Noah were too young to reproduce, which explains the absence of dinosaurs in modern times. At the March 3 Republican debate, Rubio indirectly comments on the size of Trump's penis, saying that Trump's "small hands" imply that "something else must be small."

Trump responds: "I guarantee you there is no problem." Spain seizes twenty thousand military uniforms that were to be shipped from Spanish ports to ISIS fighters. Mitt Romney and John McCain, the Republican Party's two most recent presidential nominees, denounce Trump. "His [Trump's] personal qualities would mean that America would cease to be a shining city on a hill," says Romney, while Steve Forbes, heir to the magazine fortune and two-time candidate for the GOP presidential nomination, comments: "Political parties don't usually commit suicide." Hip-hop impresario Russell Simmons endorses Clinton. Turkish authorities seize *Zaman*, the country's most widely circulated newspaper, as part of a continuing crackdown by President Recep Erdoğan on freedom of the press. Pat Conroy dies at age seventy. Nancy Reagan, age ninety-four, dies. William Kristol, editor of the *Weekly Standard* and a crucial early supporter of Dan Quayle and Sarah Palin, as well as of the Iraq War, solicits suggestions for the name of the new party that he says Republicans will have to start if Trump wins the GOP nomination. Maureen Dowd, columnist for the *New York Times,* suggests "Losers." The third massive suicide bombing in a little over a week in Baghdad claims at least forty-seven lives. Marco Rubio wins the Republican primary in Puerto Rico. On International Women's Day, Texas state representative Myra Crownover says that the best way for college students to avoid rape is to stay sober.

**MICHIGAN PRIMARIES**
  Democratic
    Sanders: 50%
    Clinton: 48%
  Republican
    Trump: 48%
    Cruz: 36%
    Kasich: 9%
    Rubio: 5%

Former star of *Walker, Texas Ranger* Chuck Norris endorses Ted Cruz. "I think they will bear some resemblance to a piñata," Texas senator John Cornyn says of any Supreme Court nominee put forward by Obama to replace the late Antonin Scalia. A man drives his snowmobile into the teams of two mushers competing in the Iditarod, killing one dog and injuring several others. NASCAR chairman Brian France endorses Trump, while Rubio rejects the possibility of teaming up with Cruz on a single ticket to stop Trump. Elevated levels of lead prompt the Newark Public Schools to shut off water fountains at thirty school buildings. Calling poverty "one of the most widespread and persistent health risks facing children," the American Academy of Pediatrics issues new recommendations urging pediatricians to ask at checkups if families are able to make ends meet. Iran test-launches two ballistic missiles bearing the phrase "Israel must be wiped out" in Hebrew. Trump's rally at the University of Illinois at Chicago Pavilion is canceled amid widespread scuffles between protestors and Trump supporters inside the pavilion. Carson endorses Trump, Chuck Norris says that he hasn't endorsed Cruz or anyone else, and two girls, ages fifteen and seventeen, are arrested in France on suspicion of plotting a terrorist attack on a Parisian concert hall. Russia bans the National Democratic Institute, a nonprofit pro-democracy group. At a Trump rally in Fayetteville, North Carolina, a white man, John McGraw, sucker-punches a black protestor, Rakeem Jones, as security guards are leading Jones to an exit, and Jones is then instantly tackled and pinned down by the security guards, who ignore McGraw. Later, McGraw, age seventy-eight, admits to punching Jones, and tells the CBS program *Inside Edition,* "You bet I liked it," and "We don't know if he [Jones] is ISIS. We don't know who he is, but we know he's not acting like an American and cussing me . . . and sticking his face in my head. He deserved it. The next time we see him, we might have to kill him. We don't know who he is. He might be with a terrorist organization." At previous rallies, Trump's comments regarding protestors have included

"I'd like to punch him in the face," "In the old days" they would be "carried out on a stretcher," "Maybe he should be roughed up," and "Get him out. Try not to hurt him. If you do, I'll defend you in court." Clinton defeats Sanders in Ohio, North Carolina, and Florida. Kasich wins his home state of Ohio, Trump wins Florida, and Rubio drops out, stating, "The politics of resentment against other people are not going to just leave us as a fractured party. They're going to leave us as a fractured nation." Pope Francis approves Mother Teresa, "the saint of the gutters," for sainthood, and air strikes by the military coalition led by Saudi Arabia kill at least ninety at a restaurant and crowded market in northern Yemen. Obama becomes the first U.S. president since Calvin Coolidge to visit Cuba, and in North Korea Otto Warmbier is tried and convicted for the theft of a propaganda poster in an hourlong trial that Human Rights Watch calls a "kangaroo court." He is sentenced to fifteen years of hard labor. Establishment Republicans mobilize to run an intensive hundred-day campaign to deny Trump the nomination, and discuss plans to field an independent candidate "to defend Republican principles" in the event of a Trump nomination. The European Union and Turkey agree to a deal that will send Middle East war refugees in Greece back to Turkey, and two Americans are killed in a suicide bombing at a popular tourist area of Istanbul. ISIS attacks on the Brussels airport and subway kill at least 34 and injure more than 230 in the worst terrorist assault in Europe since the Paris attacks in November, and Ted Cruz calls for a security crackdown in the U.S. on "Muslim neighborhoods." Rush Limbaugh criticizes Obama for flamenco dancing and "doing the tango with women not even his wife" while visiting Cuba and Argentina. Trump and Clinton win decisive victories in Arizona, Jeb Bush endorses Cruz, and NPR gives its political reporters hostile environment awareness training. ISIS's second-in-command is killed by U.S. Special Forces inside Syria, and an ISIS suicide blast at a soccer game near Baghdad kills thirty-one and injures thirty. Obama nominates Merrick

Garland, chief judge of the federal appeals court in Washington, for the Supreme Court. Sanders trounces Clinton in the Alaska and Washington state caucuses, and San Francisco bans city employees from traveling to North Carolina on official business after North Carolina passes a law limiting transgender rights. Islamic militants kill at least sixty-five and wound three hundred in Lahore, Pakistan, in an Easter suicide-bomb attack that specifically targets Christians. Cruz accuses Trump of being behind a "tabloid smear" alleging that Cruz had affairs with multiple women in recent years; a week earlier, in an effort to encourage "values voters" in Utah to vote for Cruz, an anti-Trump Super PAC publicized a years-old photo of Trump's wife, Melania, posing seminude for *GQ* magazine. "He started it," Trump said of Cruz. "I didn't start it." Trump's campaign manager, Corey Lewandowski, is charged with battery for grabbing Michelle Fields, a reporter for Breitbart News, as she tried to ask Trump a question. David Brooks, columnist for the *New York Times,* writes, "This is a wonderful moment to be a conservative."

# AMERICAN CROSSROADS

## REAGAN, TRUMP, AND THE DEVIL DOWN SOUTH

*I went to the crossroad, fell down on my knees.*
*I went to the crossroad, fell down on my knees.*
*Asked the Lord above, "Have mercy now,*
*Save poor Bob, if you please."*

ROBERT JOHNSON, "CROSS ROAD BLUES"

How did it get to Trump?

To put it in Trump terms, you could say it started with a deal. Or more precisely, a big deal with various side deals attached, all amounting to one grand, dark bargain whose payment may be coming due at last. If one was inclined to reach for metaphor, you could say it was a deal with the devil. Or you could say it started with this, a plank adopted by the Democratic National Convention of 1948:

*The Democratic Party commits itself to continuing efforts to eradicate all racial, religious, and economic discrimination.*

That was enough to bring the devil howling out of his hole, that foot-on-the-neck-of-the-black-man devil of the Jim Crow, hookworm, lynch-prone South, "the solid South" that reliably delivered its votes to the Democratic Party every four years. 1948 was a flash that led to a slow burn, a simmering fuse that wouldn't erupt again for sixteen years. The flash was the breakaway States' Rights Democratic Party, a.k.a. the Dixiecrats (motto: "Segregation Forever"), who recoiled from the regular Democrats' spasm of conscience and put up their own candidate for president, South Carolina governor Strom Thurmond. Thurmond campaigned on a platform that decried civil rights as "infamous and iniquitous," "totalitarian," and an attempt by the federal government to impose "a Police Nation" on the land of the free. That fall the Dixiecrats took four Deep South states and thirty-nine electoral votes from Harry Truman, a rippling of racist muscle that cowed the Democratic establishment and squelched the party's egalitarian impulses throughout the 1950s.[1]

That decade was the slow burn, but the blaze was coming. Occasional aberrations aside, the South stayed solid for the Democrats after 1948, though the devil felt the cracks beneath his feet, roamed uneasy over the land. *Brown v. Board of Education* was a temblor. Montgomery and Little Rock, more temblors. Devil stamped his feet, sniffed the air. At the Democrats' 1960 convention, African-American delegates walked out in protest over John F. Kennedy's concessions to the Southern segs, this at a time when the Republican Party, the party of Lincoln and Emancipation, and thus a ninety-pound weakling in most of the South, was welcoming civil rights advocates to its convention. Across the South people were marching and sometimes dying for civil rights, though you didn't have to march or even reach the age of majority to qualify for murder, as happened with the 1963 bombing deaths of four young African-

---

[1]  See Kari A. Frederickson, *The Dixiecrat Revolt and the End of the Solid South, 1932–1968* (UNC Press, 2001).

American girls, on a Sunday morning, *at church,* in Birmingham, Alabama. After Kennedy's assassination, Lyndon Johnson, Democrat of Texas and son of the hardscrabble South, seized on JFK's cautious civil rights agenda and turned it into a juggernaut. "If you get in my way I'm going to run you down," Johnson told his old Senate mentor, Richard Russell of Georgia,[2] and it's surely one of the great mysteries not just of American politics but of human nature in general that Lyndon Johnson, a man born and formed in one of America's most enduring sinkholes of racism, would be the crucial force multiplier for civil rights.

He knew better than anyone the political risk. "I think we just gave the South to the Republicans for a long time to come," he told his staff after ramming the Civil Rights Act of 1964 through Congress.[3] His aide Bill Moyers recalled the moment in more drastic terms: Johnson feared he'd delivered the South to Republicans "for your lifetime and mine," a prediction whose proof, while not yet conclusive—we are happy that Mr. Moyers is still with us—has trended ever since toward prophecy.[4] The first evidence was soon coming. In the presidential election that fall, Johnson's landslide victory over Barry Goldwater saw only Arizona (Goldwater's home state) and the old hard-line Dixiecrat states, plus Georgia, go Republican. Goldwater had been one of only a handful of Republican senators to vote against the Civil Rights Act, and his nominating convention turned into a raucous, racially animated revolt against the party's eastern establishment. Nelson Rockefeller, millionaire governor of New York and avatar of what's now known as the country club Republican, was roundly booed, hooted, and dissed. Goldwater delegates berated and shook their fists at the press, and

---

[2] Rick Perlstein, *Before the Storm: Barry Goldwater and the Unmaking of the American Consensus* (Hill and Wang, 2001), p. 306.

[3] Robert Dallek, *Lyndon Johnson: Portrait of a President* (Oxford University Press, 2005), p. 170.

[4] Robert David Johnson, *All the Way with LBJ: The 1964 Presidential Election* (Cambridge University Press, 2009), p. 128; Taylor Branch, *Pillar of Fire: America in the King Years, 1963–1965* (Simon & Schuster, 1998), p. 404.

African-American delegates were "shoved, pushed, spat on, and cursed with a liberal sprinkling of racial epithets." Something new and nasty was afoot; Republicans were acting like a bunch of Dixiecrats. One black delegate had his suit jacket set on fire. The Southern Caucus at the convention named its hotel headquarters "Fort Sumter." Jackie Robinson spent several "unbelievable hours" on the convention floor, and summed up his experience with, "I now believe I know how it felt to be a Jew in Hitler's Germany."[5]

Ex-Dixiecrat Strom Thurmond, now a Democratic U.S. senator and as fiercely segregationist as ever, broke party ranks and declared support for the Republican nominee, not only campaigning with Goldwater in the South but switching his party affiliation from Democrat to Republican in the middle of the race.[6] Goldwater ended up capturing 55 percent of the white Southern vote, the first Republican ever to win a majority of white Southerners,[7] and the party of Lincoln was transformed, for one election at least, into the party of Southern racism.

The transformative chemistry went by various names. "White backlash." "Racial conservatism." Or the old standby "states' rights," a political term of art that presumed wide latitude on the part of individual states to regulate provincial society, which included, it hardly need be said, though plenty of hot-blooded segs shrieked it anyway, the power to grind black citizens down to the legal and economic equivalent of inmates on a Louisiana prison farm. As channeled by Goldwater, this new force in the Republican Party was a disaster. He may have won white Southerners, but he was drubbed in the overall popular vote, and Republicans lost over forty seats in the House. His support from Wall Street was tepid at best, and he was deserted by establishment Republican constituencies throughout the Northeast and Midwest.

---

[5] Branch, *Pillar of Fire,* pp. 401–4.
[6] *Ibid.,* pp. 492–93.
[7] Earl Black and Merle Black, *The Rise of Southern Republicans* (Belknap Press/Harvard University Press, 2002), p. 209.

Clearly, the situation called for serious soul-searching in the GOP. One might have expected the party to reject Goldwater's white-backlash strategy and return to establishment Republican conservatism, but party pros, and in particular that political genius Richard Nixon, saw in Goldwater's defeat the makings of an extraordinary coalition. A compact. A combination. A deal.

> *Mmmm, standin' at the crossroad, I tried to flag a ride.*
> *Standin' at the crossroad, I tried to flag a ride.*
> *Didn't nobody seem to know me,*
> *Everybody pass me by.*

What was needed was white backlash with a kinder, gentler face. Years later, the Republican strategist Lee Atwater, by then an operative in the Reagan White House, would explain the essence of the "Southern Strategy" to an academic researcher:

> *You start out in 1954 by saying, "Nigger, nigger, nigger."*
> *By 1968 you can't say "nigger"—that hurts you. Backfires.*
> *So you say stuff like, uh, forced busing, states' rights and all*
> *that stuff. You're getting so abstract now you're talking about*
> *cutting taxes, and all these things you're talking about are*
> *totally economic things and a byproduct of them is blacks get*
> *hurt worse than whites. And subconsciously maybe that is part*
> *of it. I'm not saying that. But I'm saying that if it is getting*
> *that abstract, and that coded, that we are doing away with the*
> *racial problem one way or the other. You follow me—because*
> *obviously sitting around saying, "We want to cut this," is*
> *much more abstract than even the busing thing, and a hell of*
> *a lot more abstract than "Nigger, nigger."*[8]

---

[8] See Rick Perlstein, "Lee Atwater's Infamous 1981 Interview on the Southern Strategy," *Nation*, November 13, 2012.

Thus the problem was mainly one of marketing: how to make racism suitable for prime time. It was Atwater's mentor and fellow South Carolinian Harry Dent Sr.,[9] a former adviser to Strom Thurmond, who helped Nixon perfect the Southern Strategy, tutoring the future president in the kinder, gentler vocabulary of the new racial politics, a politics that would deliver the White House to Republicans in five of the next six presidential elections.

It wasn't an accident. It took planning and work. As made plain in the 1969 book *The Emerging Republican Majority* by Nixon adviser Kevin Phillips, the Southern Strategy was a considered, premeditated, highly disciplined appeal to Southern whites, and more generally to the deep-seated racism of America. In a 1970 interview published in the *New York Times,* Phillips put it this way:

> *From now on, the Republicans are never going to get more than 10 to 20 percent of the Negro vote and they don't need any more than that . . . but Republicans would be shortsighted if they weakened enforcement of the Voting Rights Act. The more Negroes who register as Democrats in the South, the sooner the Negrophobe whites will quit the Democrats and become Republicans. That's where the votes are. Without that prodding from blacks, the whites will backslide into their old comfortable arrangement with the local Democrats.*[10]

Well if *that's where the votes are,* then by God we gotta get down in that hog wallow and root 'em out! And so the Grand Old Party, the party of New York bankers, thrifty New Englanders, and wholesome Midwesterners whose ancestors fought and defeated the

---

[9] Described as "a Southern-fried Rasputin" in "Uncle Strom's cabin" by adversaries. See Patricia Sullivan, "Harry Dent: Advised Key Republicans," *Washington Post,* October 3, 2007. Late in life, Dent would offer a mea culpa: "When I look back, my biggest regret now is anything I did that stood in the way of the rights of black people. Or any people."

[10] James Boyd, "Nixon's Southern Strategy: It's All in the Charts," *New York Times,* May 17, 1970.

Confederacy and its slave-based economy, made a deal with the South. It had taken the better part of forty years, but Republicans finally found their answer to the New Deal.

Goldwater discovered it; Nixon refined it; and Reagan perfected it into the darkest of the modern political arts. Where does Trump come in? We're getting there. It may seem hard to reconcile so congenial a presence as Ronald Reagan with the violent racism behind the Southern Strategy, but Reagan knew that devil well; knew him and paid him court on his home turf. In early August of 1980, for his first speech as the Republican Party's newly minted nominee, Reagan traveled to the Neshoba County Fair near Philadelphia, Mississippi, and spoke the following words:

> *I believe in states' rights. I believe in people doing as much as they can for themselves at the community level and at the private level. And I believe that we've distorted the balance of our government today by giving powers that were never intended in the Constitution to be given to that federal establishment. And if I do get the job I'm looking for, I'm going to devote myself to trying to reorder those priorities and to restore to the states and local communities those functions which properly belong there.*[11]

The Neshoba County speech is a remarkable moment in American history. It is nothing less than the crystallization of an existential struggle in this country whose outcome is still very much in doubt. Why would Reagan, fresh off the Republican Convention with his party's nomination, travel to a remote, rural county in a poor Southern state that possessed all of seven piddly electoral votes? Devil knows why, indeed. It's in the history, and in particular an

---

[11] "Transcript of Ronald Reagan's 1980 Neshoba County Fair Speech," *Neshoba Democrat*, November 15, 2007.

episode from the summer of 1964, the "Mississippi Freedom Summer" when scores of civil rights workers traveled to Mississippi to organize and register African-Americans to vote. On June 21, three of these activists—Michael Schwerner, age twenty-four; James Chaney, age twenty-two; and Andrew Goodman, age twenty: kids, basically—drove from their base in Meridian to Neshoba County to investigate the burning of tiny Mount Zion AME Church, whose congregation had recently agreed to host a "Freedom School" on its premises. That afternoon, the three young men were arrested on a speeding charge by Neshoba County sheriff Lawrence Rainey, held in jail for six hours, then released around ten thirty in the evening. They drove off in the direction of Meridian and disappeared.

> *Mmm, the sun goin' down, boy,*
> *Dark gon' catch me here.*
> *Ooo ooee eeee, boy,*
> *Dark gon' catch me here.*
> *I haven't got no lovin' sweet woman*
> *That love and feel my care.*

For the next six weeks—a span of time that included Johnson's signing of the Civil Rights Act, and Barry Goldwater's nomination at the Republican National Convention—the country watched as more than a hundred FBI agents fanned out across Mississippi in search of the three young men. Walter Cronkite did a special report on their disappearance for CBS; the national press had dozens of reporters on the ground. Mississippi officials insisted that the whole thing was a hoax, a publicity stunt to drum up support for the civil rights movement. Mississippi senator James Eastland alleged that the movement's Meridian office had reported the three men missing *in advance* of their disappearance, and he called on President Johnson to launch an investigation into "civil rights fraud." Leaders of the Mississippi Sovereignty Commission, a state government entity charged with maintaining white supremacy, asserted that the young men were regularly being sighted alive and well, most reliably in Alabama. One of the more feverish claims had the three men hiding out in Cuba, "with Fidel Castro and the communists."

The FBI found plenty of murdered bodies during those weeks,[12] but not the ones they were looking for. Eventually the search homed in on an earthen dam on the farm of one Olen Burrage, about five miles southwest of the small Mississippi burg of Philadelphia, and on a 106-degree day in August, with FBI agents fighting off swarms of blowflies and a stench so bad that some of the men puffed strong cigars to mask the smell, the bodies of Chaney, Schwerner, and Goodman were dug out of the Burrage dam.

In the months and years to follow, the story of their deaths would gradually come to light: their abduction by a Ku Klux Klan posse; the vigorous collusion of local law enforcement; the point-blank execution of the three young men in a clearing in the woods, though one of the three wasn't dead when they buried him in the Burrage dam—his clawed hands were filled with dirt, evidence that he'd tried to dig himself out. Far from being the work of a few vigilantes, a quite distinct picture emerged of a brutal, highly organized power structure procuring the murders of the three young men, then spinning hard to keep the truth from coming to light. Elected officials were in on it. As well as local Citizens' Councils. The Sovereignty Commission. Law enforcement. The "community."[13]

And that's where Reagan went to speak the words "I believe in states' rights," in his first appearance as the Republican nominee. These days we know it as dog-whistle politics, that coded language Lee Atwater was talking about. Reagan did not, by the way, mention Chaney, Schwerner, or Goodman, whose bodies had been found a

---

[12] No fewer than eight. See Stanley Nelson, *Devils Walking: Klan Murders Along the Mississippi in the 1960s* (Louisiana State University Press, 2016).

[13] For a thorough account of the murders of Michael Schwerner, James Chaney, and Andrew Goodman, see Branch, *Pillar of Fire*, pp. 351–74, 387–400, 427–42, 498–509, 529.

mere handful of miles away. That screaming silence, that was a dog whistle too, and to think that Reagan didn't know what he was doing is to consign him to the ranks of the epically stupid. He'd campaigned for Goldwater. He was a two-term governor of California, a veteran of national politics, and had been running for president since 1968. The Neshoba County speech stands as one of the true masterpieces of the Southern Strategy, a dog whistle that blew out the eardrums of every racist reactionary within three thousand miles. That fall, Reagan was elected president in a landslide.[14]

THE STORY GOES THAT ROBERT JOHNSON MET THE DEVIL AT A crossroads one night, and bargained away his soul in exchange for ungodly musical chops.[15] "Who's the other guy playing with him?" Keith Richards is supposed to have asked the first time he heard a Robert Johnson record, but it was just Johnson and his guitar, one man playing fast and strong enough for two. Literal-minded blues fans have burned a lot of gas over the years roving the Mississippi Delta in search of the crossroads where the deal went down, but that crossroads belongs more to myth than any actual place. The devil standing at the crossroads, waiting to make a deal: it's an archetype, a trope of folklore and myth that repeats in cultures all over the world. Something powerful is being expressed here, a deep dive into conscience and compromise that goes to the heart of human nature. Republican guru Karl Rove, a protégé of Lee Atwater and himself a grand wizard of the Southern Strategy, chose "American Crossroads" for the name of his Super PAC. It's an apt choice, even

---

[14] For additional commentary on Reagan's Neshoba County speech, see David Greenberg, "Dog-Whistling Dixie," *Slate*, November 20, 2007; Paul Krugman, "Republicans and Race," *New York Times*, November 19, 2007; Bob Herbert, "Righting Reagan's Wrongs?," *New York Times*, November 13, 2007; Joseph Crespino, "Did David Brooks Tell the Full Story About Reagan's Neshoba County Fair Visit?," *History News Network*, November 11, 2007; David Brooks, "History and Calumny," *New York Times*, November 9, 2007.

[15] There are almost as many books and articles on Robert Johnson as on Che Guevara. See, for example, Tom Graves, *Crossroads: The Life and Afterlife of Blues Legend Robert Johnson* (DeMers Books, 2008), and Peter Guralnick, *Searching for Robert Johnson* (Dutton, 1998).

if Rove might not be fully aware of the implications. His political instincts are perhaps even sharper than he knows.

In Johnson's case, the devil didn't have to wait long to collect his due. The bluesman died at age twenty-seven, poisoned, according to lore, by the jealous husband of a woman he'd been flirting with. The Republican Party's pact with the South has had a much longer run, going on fifty years now, though the deal is looking shaky. It won't come as a news flash to anyone that the Tea Party, the true believers, "the base"— the core of which is all those white Southerners who gave an estimated 70 percent of their votes to Romney in 2012—is fed up with the party establishment, the country club Republicans who have prospered beyond imagining these past few decades. And how has the base been doing? Lousy, by pretty much every measure—income, life expectancy, drug addiction, job security, health care, education, and social mobility.[16] "Take the bureaucratic shackles off" was Goldwater's war cry back in 1964, and his laissez-faire economic gospel has echoed down through the years, from Nixon to Reagan to the Bushes and all the way through Romney. Cut taxes and regulation, roll up the social safety net, squash organized labor to nil. It's worked out wonderfully for the job creators, but not so great for the job doers. While the true believers in the base were fighting that Kenyan in the White House over prayer in the schools and the hetero sanctity of marriage, tidal waves of money have been flowing upstream to their bosses.

No wonder people are pissed off. The South's been suckered, along with all the other blue-collar and middle-class "Reagan Democrats" who put their faith in the GOP. The deal at the heart of the Southern Strategy might be falling apart, and with it the modern Republican Party. At this point it seems only a preternaturally gifted dealmaker could save the situation. Boehner couldn't do it; now he's

---

[16] See Jacob S. Hacker and Paul Pierson, *American Amnesia: How the War on Government Led Us to Forget What Made America Prosper* (Simon & Schuster, 2016), pp. 23–44.

off someplace playing golf. McConnell can't do it; it's all he can manage to keep the Senate from sinking into a cesspool of dysfunction. So just when it looks like the deal is beyond saving—

Lo, unto us a Trump is given. It's no fluke that the loudest and most persistent of the Obama birthers took the Deep South states on Super Tuesday. While the other Republican contenders keep their xenophobia within the bounds of acceptably cruel discourse, Trump blows it out. His racist rants play like full-fledged operas compared to the dog-whistle stuff, rupturing the finely honed code that's worked so long and so well for the GOP establishment. But that's why the base loves him; he feels their rage. Even better, he's beyond the establishment's control. Nobody is the boss of Trump, not the Kochs, not Sheldon Adelson, and certainly not Reince Priebus, chief dogsbody of the Republican National Committee.

If Bernie Sanders has caused more than a few McGovern flashbacks for the Democrats, then surely Trump is giving the Goldwater jitters to plenty of old heads in the Republican Party. But if Trump is the guy, the South looks solid for at least one more election. At what long-term cost to the party, we shall see. The country grows more colorful, less like that white Southern man with each passing year.

> *You can run, you can run*
> *Tell my friend-boy Willie Brown,*
> *You can run, you can run,*
> *Tell my friend-boy Willie Brown,*
> *Lord, that I'm standin' at the crossroad, babe,*
> *I believe I'm sinkin' down.*

# BOOK OF DAYS

## APRIL

'Trump says that women should face "some sort of punishment" for getting abortions if the procedure is made illegal, then backtracks and says that doctors, not women, would need to be punished. Cruz, Trump, and Kasich all abandon their long-standing pledges to support the eventual Republican nominee, and Trump complains that he's being treated "unfairly" by his opponents. The city of Philadelphia issues an apology to the late Jackie Robinson for the racist abuse he experienced in that city when his team, the Brooklyn Dodgers, played in Philadelphia in 1947. Polling indicates that Trump would be hard-pressed to win more than two hundred electoral votes in the general election, citing his two-to-one unfavorable rating among women, nonwhites, Hispanics, voters under thirty, and those with college degrees. "The math just doesn't work" for Trump, said Stanley Greenberg, longtime Democratic pollster. Brussels Airport reopens. Revelations in "the Panama Papers" of financial self-dealing and conflicts of interest lead Iceland's prime minister to resign, and prompt calls for a government inquiry into the finances of British prime minister David Cameron.

**WISCONSIN PRIMARIES**
Democratic
Sanders: 56%
Clinton: 43%
Republican
Cruz: 49%
Trump: 35%
Kasich: 14%

"Tonight, Wisconsin has lit a candle guiding the way forward," Cruz says of his primary win, and predicts that he will take the nomination. Global military spending reached almost $1.7 trillion in 2015, according to the Stockholm International Peace Research Institute, led by the U.S. at $596 billion, followed by China at $215 billion and Saudi Arabia at $87.2 billion. Four people allege that former U.S. House Speaker Dennis Hastert sexually abused them when he was their high school wrestling coach in Yorkville, Illinois. FBI director James Comey resists calls to speed up the investigation into Clinton's email server: "The urgency is to do it well and promptly. And 'well' comes first." Trump says he will force Mexico to pay for the wall by blocking wire transfers of money from the U.S. to Mexico. London mayor Boris Johnson backs the campaign for Britain to leave the European Union. Pope Francis visits the Moria refugee camp on the Greek island of Lesbos and brings twelve Syrian refugees back to Rome with him on the papal plane. Michigan governor Rick Snyder announces that he will drink Flint water at home and at work for at least a month to show it is safe, with the use of a faucet filter.

**NEW YORK PRIMARIES**
Democratic
Clinton: 57.6%
Sanders: 42.4%

Republican
>    Trump: 60.1%
>    Kasich: 25.2%
>    Cruz: 14.7%

NASA, the National Oceanic and Atmospheric Administration, and the Japan Meteorological Agency all predict that 2016 will set a third consecutive annual record for heat, and trend lines on Arctic sea ice, floods, drought, and carbon dioxide levels indicate that the Earth is warming even faster than climate scientists predicted. Taliban militants storm a government security agency in central Kabul, killing at least twenty-eight and wounding hundreds. In an attempt to prove that same-sex marriage is absurd, a Texas man sues for the right to marry his computer. The Treasury Department announces that Harriet Tubman will replace Andrew Jackson on the $20 bill. Two state regulators and a city employee are charged with official misconduct, evidence tampering, and other offenses in connection with the Flint water crisis. Prince dies at age fifty-seven. Representatives of one hundred seventy-five countries gather at the UN to sign the Paris climate accord, and Queen Elizabeth II of England celebrates her ninetieth birthday. The Centers for Disease Control and Prevention report that middle-aged white people now account for a third of U.S. suicides, up from about a quarter in 1999. When a focus group of Republican women in Pittsburgh is asked what animal best describes Ted Cruz, the answers include "mosquito" and "hornet." "You just want to bat it away," says one woman. New Trump senior adviser Paul Manafort, a Washington lobbyist, assures a group of Republican insiders that Trump is ready to tone down his persona. "He's been projecting an image," Manafort reportedly says at the meeting. "The part that he's been playing is now evolving." Syrian peace talks break down amid repeated violations of the February cease-fire, and the UN accuses the Syrian government of blocking humanitarian aid. The Associated Press reports that almost all of the eighty-two corporations, trade associations, and other groups that paid for or sponsored Hillary Clinton's speeches between 2013 and 2015 have lobbied federal agencies, bid on government contracts, or otherwise sought to influence public policy. Conservative billionaire activist Charles Koch says in an interview on ABC's *This Week with George Stephanopoulos* that "it's possible" Hillary Clinton would be a better president than Cruz or Trump. The city of Cleveland agrees to a $6 million settlement in a lawsuit over the death of Tamir Rice, age twelve, shot to death last year by a white police officer. Trump wins primaries in Connecticut, Delaware, Maryland, Pennsylvania, and Rhode Island, and Clinton wins four out of five as Sanders takes only Rhode Island. Cruz names former rival Carly Fiorina as his vice presidential running mate "after a great deal of consideration and prayer," and is blasted on social media for referring to a basketball hoop as a "basketball ring." Aleppo plunges into "all-out war," and more than sixty people, most of them civilians, are killed in air strikes and mortar attacks, among them one of the last pediatricians in the city. "If Hillary Clinton were a man," says Trump, "I don't think she'd get five percent of the vote. The only thing she has going is the woman card."

# AMERICAN EXCEPTIONALISM AND THE GREAT GAME

## AT PLAY IN THE FIELDS OF THE LORD

*The game of ball is glorious.*

WALT WHITMAN

*. . . His almost chosen people . . .*

ABRAHAM LINCOLN

If you want to see a bunch of happy Americans, go to opening day at any baseball stadium in the land. Pretty much any day is a good day to go to the ballpark, but that first day of the season is special. It's spring. The grass is green. Pessimism is impossible, at least until the other team scores. The promise of the season sits before us with all the pristine shine of a new car, the latest vehicle for the secret aspirations we all hold for ourselves. Life will be better, this time. *We* will be better: smarter, richer, funnier, and absolutely better-looking, all in magical correspondence with the home team's pennant drive. Deep down we know what's going to happen to our fine new car, all those dingers and scrapes that lie in wait, the hailstorms, the exploding batteries, and yet, and yet . . . Opening day is "the triumph of hope over experience," as a wise man once said, though he was talking about second marriages, not baseball.

On this opening day at Globe Life Park in Arlington, Texas—formerly "the Ballpark in Arlington," then "Ameriquest Field in Arlington" until the subprime-mortgage bubble burst, then "Rangers Ballpark in Arlington" for a while before Globe Life plunked down a reported $50 million for name rights—the weather is, to state it plainly, perfect. Literally not a cloud in the sky, which is the brilliant turquoise of a well-chlorinated pool. The temperature is a summery 84 degrees, and while the pollen count is high—not unusual for North Texas, which is a Pandora's box of seasonal allergens—the Air Quality Index is in the healthy-for-children-and-old-folks range. The outfield grass is a cow's or pro golfer's dream—lush, smooth, preternaturally green, with crisscross stripes laid down by artisanal mowings. Curated grass. Heavenly grass. It brings out the dog in me, I want to take off all my clothes and roll around on it.

Globe Life is an earnest, determinedly fan-friendly park, eager to please with its historically referenced quirks—home-run porch in right field, whimsically jiggered outfield wall—and cozy red-brick and forest-green color scheme. Cognoscenti describe it as "retro jewel-box," in the highly specialized nomenclature of baseball stadia. (Thanks to generations of brainy, obsessive fans, everything about baseball is highly specialized.) Players and coaches assemble along the baselines for the pregame ritual, the Rangers in crisp white uniforms with blue and red trim, the Seattle Mariners somewhat baggier in their subdued blue-gray. Makes a body look fast, those Ranger whites. Dozens of scurrying workers unfurl the largest American flag I have ever seen, we're talking flag *acreage* here, it practically covers the entire outfield, then country singer Neal McCoy stands near the pitcher's mound and belts out "The Star-Spangled Banner."

"Now there's a snappy tune," Senator Thomas Gore of Oklahoma, "blind Senator Gore," used to say to his young grandson Gore Vidal whenever the national anthem was rendered, and Neal McCoy does a creditable job with the song, managing the devilish stadium acoustics like the pro he is. Everyone cheers as the final notes fade away, and a pair of F-16 fighter jets banks low overhead, creasing the air with a mighty roar.

America, America. The ceremony encourages us, if not to think about the country, at least to be aware of it for a couple of moments, to experience a fluttering uplift of national spirit. Land of the free, home of the brave, the "shining city on a hill" as Ronald Reagan loved to put it, a formulation that reaches back to the Puritan pioneers, with echoes from the Sermon on the Mount. Transiting from England to the New World on the *Arbella* in 1630, the Puritan leader John Winthrop preached it thus:

> We shall find the God of Israel is among us when ten of us
> shall be able to resist a thousand of our enemies, when He shall
> make us a praise and glory, that men shall say of succeeding
> plantations: "The Lord make it like that of New England."
> For we must consider that we shall be as a city upon a hill, the
> eyes of all people are upon us.[1]

To this day that Puritan sense of divine mission remains a defining characteristic of the American self-image. The Puritans were miliasts, die-hard believers in the millennial prophecies of the Bible: the coming of the Antichrist, the Second Advent, Armageddon, the works. It's worth noting that Winthrop situates his city in a war context, God's chosen ten resisting a thousand enemies, and the Puritans

---

[1] As quoted in "Lincoln's Black Theology," in Garry Wills, *Under God: Religion and American Politics* (Simon & Schuster, 1990), pp. 207–8.

viewed their settlements in just such militant terms, absolute good purging the wilderness of absolute evil, clearing the way for God's kingdom in the New World. And, eventually, beyond. Preaching in Boston some sixty years after Winthrop, Cotton Mather urged his congregation to consider the "great increase" of the colonies, "the blessings of land and sea" bestowed on them in the New World:

*Indeed, if we cast up the account and lay all things together,*
*God hath been doing the same thing here that he prophesied*
*of Jacob's remnant . . . And we may conclude that he intended*
*some great thing when he planted these heavens, and laid the*
*foundations of this earth. And what should that be if not a*
*scripture-pattern that shall in due time be accomplished the*
*whole world throughout?*[2]

America was the chosen land, specially blessed and purposed with a world-changing mission. Thanks to several centuries of refinement and accretion, the doctrine has come down to us with a name, American Exceptionalism, and a remarkably bellicose history. The millennial aspect has waxed and waned according to the temper of the times, but it's coded in even the more secular varieties of Exceptionalism. America's missionary zeal to remake the world always tends toward the quasi-religious tone: Woodrow Wilson, son of a Presbyterian minister, urged U.S. Naval Academy graduates to go forth "onto the seas like adventurers enlisted for the elevation of the spirit of the human race."[3] John F. Kennedy often hit similar notes, at times explicitly invoking the "city upon a hill." "I have been guided by the standard John Winthrop set before his ship-mates on the flagship *Arbella*," Kennedy said in a 1961 speech. "'We must always consider . . . that we shall be as a city upon a hill—

[2] As quoted in Wills, "Lincoln's Black Theology," p. 208.
[3] Woodrow Wilson, "Annapolis Commencement Address," June 5, 1914, American Presidency Project, http://www.presidency.ucsb.edu./ws/?pid=65380.

the eyes of all people are upon us.' Today the eyes of all people are truly upon us—and our governments . . . must be as a city upon a hill, constructed and inhabited by men aware of their great trust and their great responsibilities."[4] George W. Bush famously termed the war on terror a "crusade," a descriptor loaded with white-hot millennial connotations,[5] and in his acceptance speech to the 2004 Republican National Convention he declared that Americans "have a calling from beyond the stars to stand for freedom." Reagan, of course, was a master of the quasi-religious tone. Christian fundamentalists were a crucial part of his base, and Reagan himself was raised in the millennial worldview of the Disciples of Christ. "I have quoted John Winthrop's words more than once on the campaign trail this year—for I believe that Americans in 1980 are every bit as committed to that vision of a shining 'city on a hill' as were those long ago settlers," he said on the eve of the 1980 election.[6] And he was striking deep millennial chords when he described the Soviet Union as "the evil empire" and "the focus of all evil in the world."[7]

Election season in the U.S. is pure carnival for this sort of stuff, candidates beating each other bloody with the American Exceptionalism stick. It's the I-Love-America-More-Than-You smackdown: America is and always has been the greatest, ever, at everything, and anyone who disagrees just doesn't love America enough. Which is political discourse as fairy tale, a made-up story for children. Instead

---

[4] "Address of President-Elect John F. Kennedy Delivered to a Joint Convention of the General Court of the Commonwealth of Massachusetts," January 9, 1961, John F. Kennedy Presidential Library and Museum, https://www.jfklibrary.org/Asset-Viewer /ohJztSnpV06qFJUT9etUZQ.aspx.

[5] Peter Waldman and Hugh Pope, "'Crusade' Reference Reinforces Fears War on Terrorism Is Against Muslims," *Wall Street Journal,* September 21, 2001.

[6] Ronald Reagan, "Election Eve Address 'A Vision for America,'" November 3, 1980, American Presidency Project, http://www.presidency.ucsb.edu./ws/?pid=85199.

[7] As quoted in "Reagan and 'the Prophecies,'" in Wills, *Under God,* p. 150. Some miliasts saw in USSR president Mikhail Gorbachev's birthmark (clearly visible on his bald pate) the "mark of the Beast" as prophesied in the Book of Revelation.

of fantasy, how about this for a more adult, and more useful, for-mulation: America has done very many great and noble things. America has also done many shocking and terrible things, always—always—in the name of doing good. Am I about to be critical of my country? I am, and by the way the United States was founded on dissent, contrariness, critical thinking; if not for independent thought, we might still be carrying water for the Brits.

Even a cursory run through American history shows Exception-alism has been used to justify monumental bloodshed, oppression, and profit. Cotton Mather saw "the evident hand of God" in the colonists' wholesale slaughter of Native Americans in King Philip's War, a genocide that would eventually roll all the way to the Pacific under the quasi-religious doctrine of Manifest Destiny.[8] Over three hundred years of slavery were justified on biblical grounds, as, vari-ously, a means of saving African souls, or adherence to a divinely ordained natural order. For invasion and conquest in the name of lib-erty and democracy, we have the land grabs in Mexico in 1846–48, the Philippines in 1899–1902, and Panama in 1903. For the softer sorts of grabs—i.e., imperialism—in the early twentieth century, the career of Major General Smedley Butler (1881–1940) provides a use-ful guide to U.S. adventures in Mexico (again), Central America, Haiti, the Dominican Republic, Cuba, and China.[9] A partial list of U.S.-sponsored or actively supported interventions, regime changes, and coups d'état for the latter half of the twentieth century would include Iran (coup, 1953), Guatemala (coup, 1954), Vietnam (coup, 1963; the war, 1965[?]–1973[?]), the Dominican Republic (interven-tion, 1965), Chile (coup, 1973), Argentina (coup, 1976), Nicaragua (war, 1980s), El Salvador (war, 1980s), Panama (invasion, 1989), and Haiti (coup, 1991; invasion, 1994; coup, 2004). Underneath all the high-minded missionary rhetoric, you will usually find the throb-

[8] As quoted in "America's Miliast Founders," collected in Wills, *Under God*, p. 143.
[9] See Hans Schmidt, *Maverick Marine: General Smedley Butler and the Contradictions of American Military History* (University Press of Kentucky, 1998).

bing heart of the profit motive. Reflecting on his military career, General Butler wrote, "I spent most of my time being a high-class muscle man for Big Business, for Wall Street and the bankers. In short, I was a racketeer, a gangster for capitalism."[10] For anyone who cares to look, a survey of just three U.S. industries—oil, finance, and bananas—will more than prove out Butler's gangster claim.

All this by way of saying: America is complicated. American history is not clean. Blood and bullshit run through it every bit as robustly as high-minded Puritan principles, the invasion of Iraq being just the latest example. Americans are chronically vulnerable to appeals to our goodness and innocence, as generations of pols and con men have found to their benefit. Exceptionalism is an easy sell in the land of the free, and yet the country does contain much that can be called, well, exceptional. The founding of the American republic was truly something new under the sun, a remarkable achievement that can bear the weight of shining-city aspirations. So how about this for a working theory of American Exceptionalism: it is a real and volatile phenomenon in the world, with as much potential for doing good as wreaking havoc.

Donald Trump named one president, just one out of the entire field of forty-four, who he felt he couldn't match for excellence in presidential demeanor—Abraham Lincoln, who also happened to be the most dogged champion of American Exceptionalism ever to hold the office. And it's Lincoln who may well be our best guide to what's truly exceptional in the American project.

**WALT WHITMAN, THE *BROOKLYN EAGLE*, JULY 23, 1846:**

> *In our sundown perambulations of late through the outer parts of Brooklyn, we have observed several parties of youngsters playing "base," a certain game of ball. We wish such sights were more common among us. In the practice of athletic and*

---

[10] Smedley Butler, *War Is a Racket* (Skyhorse Publishing, 2013), p. 4.

> *manly sports, the young men of nearly all our American cities*
> *are very deficient . . . Clerks are shut up from early morning*
> *till nine or ten o'clock at night—apprentices, after their days'*
> *work, either go to bed or lounge about in places where they*
> *benefit neither body nor mind—and all classes seem to act as*
> *though there were no commendable objects of pursuit in the*
> *world except making money . . .*[11]

Even then we were exceptional workaholics! It speaks to Whitman's genius that he was quick to seize on both the American game and American drudgery, just as he predicted Lincoln long before the obscure, one-term former congressman was elected president; before he even knew the flesh-and-blood Lincoln existed. In his 1856 essay "The Eighteenth Presidency!" Whitman got a load of democratic angst off his chest by describing the current political class as "robbers, pimps . . . malignants, conspirators, murderers . . . infidels, disunionists, terrorists, mail-riflers, slave-catchers . . . monte-dealers, duelists, carriers of concealed weapons, blind men, deaf men, pimpled men, scarred inside with the vile disorder, gaudy outside with gold chains . . ." He believed our only hope against this mob was a rough-hewn "Redeemer President" from the West who, in Whitman's conjury, bears a striking resemblance to Lincoln: "some heroic, shrewd, fully-informed, healthy-bodied, middle-aged, beard-faced American blacksmith or boatman . . . with the tan all over his face, breast, and arms."[12]

Lincoln's supporters at the 1860 Republican Convention presented him as "the rail-splitter," a man of the people who'd done his share of sweat-hog work. But well before he rose to national prominence, Lincoln was proclaiming—*preaching* would be closer to the mark—the gospel of American Exceptionalism. He based his ver-

---

[11] See https://ourgame.mlblogs.com/opening-day-e5f9021c5dda.
[12] Justin Kaplan, ed., *Walt Whitman, Complete Poetry and Collected Prose* (Library of America, 1982), pp. 1307–25.

sion of the gospel on the Declaration of Independence, specifically the clause stating the "self-evident" truth "that all men are created equal." Later, at the Gettysburg battlefield, he would employ a consciously biblical idiom in stating his case—*Fourscore and seven years ago our fathers brought forth on this continent a new nation, conceived in liberty, dedicated to the proposition that all men are created equal*— but he'd been hammering the "proposition" for years, usually stirring the same biblical echoes as Winthrop and Mather. And the "proposition" wasn't limited to the U.S., as he emphasized in a speech en route to Washington in 1861 to take the oath of office:

> *It [the Revolution] was not the mere matter of separation*
> *of the colonies from the motherland, but [of] that sentiment*
> *in the Declaration of Independence, which gave liberty not*
> *alone to the people of this country, but hope to all the world,*
> *for all future time. It was that which gave promise that in due*
> *time the weights would be lifted from the shoulders of all men,*
> *and that all should have an equal chance.*[13]

Lincoln's Exceptionalism gospel was as vehement as that of any blowhard politician in 2016, but several essential qualities in the Lincoln version are worth pointing out. Immigrants were included in the American proposition with just as much right as if they'd arrived in America by accident of birth. Speaking in 1857, Lincoln said:

> *. . . when they [immigrants] look through that old Declaration*
> *of Independence they find that those old men say that "We*
> *hold these truths to be self-evident, that all men are created*
> *equal," and then they feel that the moral sentiment taught in*

---

[13] Speech at Independence Hall, Philadelphia, Pennsylvania, February 22, 1861, in *Lincoln, Speeches and Writings, 1859–1865,* ed. Don E. Fehrenbacher (Library of America, 1989), pp. 213–14.

*that day evidences their relation to those men, that it is the*
*father of all moral principle in them, and that they have a*
*right to claim it as though they were blood of the blood, and*
*flesh of the flesh of the men who wrote that Declaration, and*
*so they are.*[14]

Even more striking is the insistent *humility* of Lincoln's Exceptionalism. His was very much a searching, self-doubting, self-examining Exceptionalism: he believed in the American mission with religious fervor but maintained a healthy skepticism toward its mortal agents. Throughout his presidency, Lincoln stressed human fallibility, both individual and collective, and even in the midst of a horrifically bloody civil war—in the midst of what we might call *partisanship run amok*—he refused to vilify or demonize the South. Slavery was a national, not exclusively Southern, sin, and he was insistent about reminding the North of its complicity and profit in the slave economy. Even the Gettysburg Address, delivered at the site of the North's greatest victory, is about as far from triumphant as one can imagine.[15] No "Mission Accomplished" banners for Lincoln. No military swagger, no thumping chants of "U-S-A! U-S-A!"

In our age of relentlessly upbeat branding, Lincoln's humility and chastened tone wouldn't get much traction in the public sphere. "Manic-depressive Lincoln, national hero!" as Delmore Schwartz described him in a poem from the 1950s.[16] One might venture to construct a metaphysical argument that Lincoln's private suffering was crucial to making him a genuine hero—that this suffering was key to the self-doubt and self-examination that led him to distrust all claims of earthly exceptionalism. He understood pain, loss, guilt; in the Bible he found the language to express the dark side of human

---

[14] As quoted in Wills, "Lincoln's Black Theology," *Under God*, p. 212.
[15] As emphasized by Wills, *ibid.*, pp. 212, 214, 217.
[16] *Summer Knowledge: New and Selected Poems, 1938–1958* (Doubleday & Company, 1959), p. 236. The poem is titled "Lincoln."

experience and bring it into the public realm. It was the language of reflection; the language of atonement. Lincoln's gospel of American Exceptionalism depended to a large degree on acknowledging just how flawed and morally suspect are the human vessels charged with fulfilling the mission.[17] The Declaration may have stated the "proposition" of equality, "the standard maxim for a free society," as Lincoln put it, but "enforcement" of the maxim would be an endless, and endlessly messy, process, "constantly looked to, constantly labored for, and even though never perfectly attained, constantly approximated . . ."[18]

How was this "maxim" of equality to be enforced, however imperfectly? Through the laws of the land: the Constitution, judicial decisions, statutory and common law. The goal, "constantly labored for," was (and surely continues to be) just laws, justly and fairly applied. And as early in his career as 1838 Lincoln was preaching "reverence for the laws" as "the *political religion* of the nation."[19] Equality would be possible only if no individual, group, or entity was above the law. Even the state itself, the government, must be subordinate to the law.

Which explains why the "American Exemptionalism" championed by the Bush-Cheney administration, and continued in many respects by Obama, was so corrupting, so blatantly *un*-American. You could call Exemptionalism the doppelgänger of Exceptionalism:[20] it's the belief that America is so unique, so righteous, so divinely inspired and guided that it's exempt from the law whenever its government deems fit. If America—God's chosen country! that shining city on

---

[17] Wills, "Lincoln's Black Theology," *Under God*, pp. 217–21.

[18] *Ibid.*, p. 213.

[19] *Ibid.*, p. 209 (emphasis in Lincoln's original). "Address to the Young Men's Lyceum of Springfield, Illinois," January 27, 1838, in *Lincoln, Speeches and Writings, 1832–1858*, ed. Don E. Fehrenbacher (Library of America, 1989), pp. 32–33.

[20] See D. Robert Worley, "American Exceptionalism and Other Isms," Huffington Post, December 4, 2012, and Michael Ignatieff, ed., *American Exceptionalism and Human Rights* (Princeton University Press, 2005), especially chapter 11, "American Exceptionalism, Exemptionalism, and Global Governance," by John Gerard Ruggie, pp. 304–38.

a hill!—does it, then it must be right, and to hell with the law. It's a tautology that verges on madness, and leads straight back to all those marauding kings and despots in the old country who cited "reason of state" as justification to act as they wished, in disregard of the law, in order to serve an alleged national interest. By virtue of which, the ruler becomes the law, in effect, which is no law at all, but raw personality acting under color of law.

"Our strength as a nation-state will continue to be challenged by those who employ a strategy of the weak using international *fora,* judicial processes and terrorism." This arresting sentence, found in the 2003 edition of the National Security Strategy of the United States, could be said to sum up the attitude of our executive branch, and a good bit of the legislative as well, toward the law since 9/11. We are told that our national integrity is under threat from *international fora* (the UN and similar organizations, along with the conventions and treaties—as ratified in accordance with the Constitution—that establish their authority), *judicial processes* (the law and the courts, both domestic and international), and, finally, *terrorism.* An odd threesome to lump together, "judicial processes" characterized as threats commensurate with terrorism.[21] These are strange, most peculiar days indeed. A quick survey of the past fifteen years shows just what Exemptionalism, our American version of "reason of state," has wrought: undeclared wars that go on and on, torture, indefinite detention, wholesale surveillance and spying, and extrajudicial executions of American citizens, all in the name of national security, all of which tend to render the objects of their attentions rather less than equal. We have laws against these sorts of things, and it's our laws that distinguish the U.S. from the old monarchies, not to mention dictatorships, drug cartels, and military juntas. That make the U.S. *exceptional,* in other words. The

---

[21] See Mark Danner, "Words in a Time of War," TomDispatch.com, May 31, 2007, www .tomdispatch.com/blog/174791/. This fine essay led me to the relevant passage in the National Security Strategy, and also flagged the sheer weirdness of the "strategy of the weak" construct.

law does provide for making a person "less equal"—for depriving him or her of property, liberty, even life. It's called due process of law, and it's required by the Constitution.

For Lincoln, it wasn't enough to save the Union—it had to be worth saving, true to the "Declaration principle" of equality. "If this country cannot be saved without giving up that principle—I was about to say I would rather be assassinated on this spot"—he was in Philadelphia, en route to his inauguration, when assassination was a very real and present threat—"than to surrender it."[22] Post-9/11 American leadership has proved all too ready to surrender the "Declaration principle" in the name of national security, and no 2016 presidential candidate has been louder or more emphatic than Donald Trump in stating their willingness to continue the trend. Trump, admirer of Lincoln. "He was very presidential, right?"

Delmore Schwartz on Lincoln, again:

**Later they made him out a prairie Christ**
**To sate the need coarse in the national heart.**

**THIS OPENING DAY AT GLOBE LIFE PARK IN ARLINGTON IS A** happy one for the home team. The weather stays fair, nobody gets hurt, and the Rangers squeak out a 3–2 win on the strength of Prince Fielder's mighty bloop single. The *Dallas Morning News* will report tomorrow that history was made on this opening day. According to the Elias Sports Bureau, the Rangers are the only team since 1900 to win its season opener with fewer than two hits, a statistic that is perhaps less amazing for itself than for the fact that it exists, a nugget sieved from all the stats of all the opening-day games ever played.

"Well—it's our game; that's the chief fact in connection with it," Walt Whitman observed of baseball. "America's game: has the snap,

---

[22] As quoted in Wills, "Lincoln's Black Theology," *Under God*, p. 220.

go, fling of the American atmosphere . . ."[23] Whitman took great pleasure in the sight of Americans doing things together, especially outdoor things, muscular things. "America, her athletic Democracy," he called it, and he urged us to aspire to "adhesiveness," the generous affection between citizens that's the crucial binding agent of democracy.

> Whoever degrades another degrades me . . .
> I speak the password primeval . . . I give the sign of democracy;
> By God! I will accept nothing which all cannot have their counterpart of on the same terms.[24]

In 2016, it seems fair to say that baseball in America is alive and well. As for adhesiveness, it remains to be seen whether affection will endure amid vast inequalities of income and opportunity, and a political culture so toxic with partisan flatulence that poor Flint still drinks its water from trucked-in bottles, the Supreme Court soldiers on with an empty seat, and trolls roam the internet in search of better angels to slay.

---

[23] Horace Traubel, *With Walt Whitman in Camden*, ed. Sculley Bradley (University of Pennsylvania Press, 1953), Vol. 4, p. 508.
[24] "Song of Myself," in *Walt Whitman: Complete Poetry and Collected Prose*, ed. Justin Kaplan (Library of America, 1982), p. 50.

# BOOK OF DAYS

MAY

When asked if they would consider being Trump's vice presidential running mate, prominent Republicans offer responses ranging from "Never" (spokesman for John Kasich) to "That's like buying a ticket on the *Titanic*" (Lindsey Graham) to "I'm not ruling myself in" (Senator Tim Scott) to "Hahahahahahahah" (senior adviser to Jeb Bush). Hundreds of protestors storm Baghdad's Green Zone and force their way into parliament, waving flags, breaking furniture, and demanding an end to government corruption. The Reverend Daniel Berrigan dies at age ninety-four. Bobby Knight, former Indiana basketball coach, says, "There has never been a more honest politician than Donald Trump." Larry Wilmore concludes his remarks at the annual White House Correspondents' Dinner with a tribute to Obama, pounding his chest and exclaiming, "Yo, Barry, you did it, my nigga!" Obama responds with a chest pound and dap for Wilmore. Hillary Clinton embraces Trump's "woman card" comment, and over the last three days of April raises a record-setting $2.4 million by offering a bright pink "Hillary for America Woman Card" to each contributor to her campaign. "Deal Me In" T-shirts and a deck of cards with statistics such as "Only 5 percent of Fortune 500 CEOs are women" are also soon offered. In Germany, the nationalist Alternative for Germany party calls for a ban on minarets, muezzin calls, and head scarves for women and girls. An unsubstantiated story appears in the *National Enquirer* alleging that Rafael Cruz, the father of Ted Cruz, can be seen in a photo with Lee Harvey Oswald taken three months before the assassination of President John F. Kennedy. "His father was with Lee Harvey Oswald prior to Oswald's being—you know, shot," Trump tells *Fox & Friends* on the day of the Indiana primary. "What was he doing—what was he doing with Lee Harvey Oswald shortly before the death—before the shooting? It's horrible." Cruz, in response, calls Trump "a pathological liar."

**INDIANA PRIMARIES**
  Democratic
    Sanders: 52.5%
    Clinton: 47.5%
  Republican
    Trump: 53.3%
    Cruz: 36.6%
    Kasich: 7.6%

Cruz suspends his campaign, and Kasich does the same a day later. "Donald Trump spells big trouble for the Republican Party," says one Democratic strategist, commenting on Democrats' hopes of taking control of the Senate and House. In Austria, a far-right nationalist candidate comes within three-tenths of a percentage point of being elected head of state. The World Bank releases a report asserting that water shortages due to climate change could result in "sustained negative growth" in some parts of the world by 2050. In a letter to Governor Pat McCrory, the U.S. Department of Justice warns that North Carolina's new law limiting restroom access violates the civil rights of transgender people. Mary Matalin, veteran strategist for the Republican Party and former president George H. W. Bush's campaign director in 1992, switches her party registration from Republican to Libertarian, and tells Bloomberg Politics that she is a Republican in the "Jeffersonian, Madisonian sense," and that her move has nothing to do with Trump being the presumptive Republican nominee. House Speaker Paul Ryan says he's "not ready" to endorse Trump, and that there is no point in trying to "fake" party unity. Former Texas governor Rick Perry, who once called Trump's candidacy "a cancer on conservatism," endorses Trump and says he would consider being Trump's running mate. Cruz returns to the Senate and refuses to endorse Trump. A Public Policy Polling survey finds that 72 percent of Republicans are comfortable with Trump as the GOP nominee, that two-thirds of voters with a favorable opinion of Trump believe that Obama is a Muslim, and that a quarter believe that Supreme Court justice Antonin Scalia was murdered. Sadiq Khan, the son of a bus driver from Pakistan, is elected mayor of London, making him the first Muslim to lead a major Western capital city. Despite earlier assurances that he would release them, Trump tells the Associated Press that he doesn't expect to release his tax returns before the election, and says "there's nothing to learn from them." Three ISIS car bombings in three different neighborhoods kill ninety-three in Baghdad. George Zimmerman attempts to sell in an online auction the gun he used to kill Trayvon Martin, saying that a portion of the proceeds would go toward fighting what Zimmerman calls violence by the Black Lives Matter movement against law enforcement officers, and combating the anti gun rhetoric of Hillary Clinton. Mitt Romney, William Kristol, and Erick Erickson are among a group of Republicans plotting to run an independent presidential candidate as an alternative to Trump; potential recruits include John Kasich, Condoleezza Rice, Stanley McChrystal, and Dallas Mavericks owner and *Shark Tank* costar Mark Cuban. As of May 6, Obama has been at war longer than any U.S. president in history. Four ISIS car bomb attacks kill at least sixty-nine in Shiite neighborhoods of Baghdad. The Earth's average temperature for April was 56.7 degrees, setting a heat record for an unprecedented twelfth straight month. Sanders supporters disrupt the Nevada State Democratic Convention, shouting down Clinton delegates and threatening the state party chairwoman. An EgyptAir flight from Paris to Cairo crashes into the Mediterranean Sea after making a series of abrupt turns; Egypt's aviation minister says the possibility of a terrorist attack is "higher than the possibility" of a technical failure. Protestors storm Baghdad's Green Zone for a second time, and are repelled by security forces firing live ammunition and tear gas, killing four protestors and injuring ninety. Jesse Oliveri of Ashland, Pennsylvania, is shot and wounded by Secret Service agents after he approaches a checkpoint outside the White House and refuses to drop his gun. Mark Cuban says that he would consider offers from both Hillary Clinton and Donald Trump to be their vice presidential running mate. Seven closely coordinated blasts kill at least eighty people in the Syrian coastal towns of Tartus and Jableh, both pro-government strongholds; ISIS claims responsibility. Former Whitewater independent counsel Kenneth Starr bemoans the loss of civility in contemporary politics, and regrets "the unpleasantness" that led to the impeachment of former president Bill Clinton for lying about his sexual relationship with Monica Lewinsky. Three days after these comments, Starr is ousted as president of Baylor University over his handling of sexual assault cases involving Baylor students. In a report delivered to Congress, the State Department's inspector general strongly criticizes Hillary Clinton's use of a private email server while she was secretary of state, saying that she had not sought permission for the server and would not have received it if she had. The attorneys general of Texas and nine other states sue the federal government over the Obama administration's order to public schools to let transgender students use restrooms that match their gender identity. With pledges of support from a handful of unbound delegates, Trump's delegate total reaches 1,239, two more than the 1,237 needed to win the Republican nomination. In a letter to the World Health Organization, more than one hundred physicians, bioethicists, and scientists urge moving or delaying the Rio de Janeiro Olympic Games because of the Zika outbreak. An estimated seven hundred migrants and asylum seekers drown while attempting to reach Italy from Libya. "Sometimes you get the feeling they're in a professional boxing match," the Reverend Al Sharpton says of Clinton's campaign team, "and he [Trump] is in a street fight, and they're coming in with their gloves on. This is a street fight with a guy with a razor and a broken Coca-Cola bottle, and you've got to fight him like that." Former Massachusetts governor William Weld compares Trump's immigration plan to Kristallnacht, and the *Washington Post* publishes an op-ed on Trump titled "This Is How Fascism Comes to America." "There is nobody less of a fascist than Donald Trump," says Donald Trump. At the Cincinnati Zoo, a four-hundred-pound male lowland gorilla named Harambe is shot and killed after a four-year-old boy falls into the animal's exhibit, and on his radio show Rush Limbaugh argues that the existence of gorillas disproves the theory of evolution: "A lot of people think that all of us used to be gorillas, and they're looking for the missing link out there. The evolution crowd. They think we were originally apes. I've always had a question: if we were the original apes, then how come Harambe is still an ape, and how come he didn't become one of us?" Former House Speaker Newt Gingrich, a possible Trump vice presidential pick, says he is "deeply offended" by analogies comparing Trump to twentieth-century fascist leaders. "He [Trump] doesn't have the sort of ideology that they did. He has nobody who resembles the brownshirts. This is all just garbage." Iranian military advisers and intelligence officers assume leading roles in the Iraqi army's attempt to retake Fallujah from ISIS. President Obama visits Hiroshima's Peace Memorial Park and calls for "a moral revolution." Sanders wins caucuses and primaries in Wyoming, Oregon, and West Virginia, and attempts to win over superdelegates with polls that show him performing substantially better than Clinton in a general-election matchup with Trump. "I will be the nominee for my party," Clinton tells CNN. "That is already done, in effect. There is no way that I won't be." Vice President Joe Biden tells *Good Morning America,* "I think I would have been the best president."

# DOING THE CHICKENHAWK WITH TRUMP

## TALKING FAST AND LOOSE IN THE TIME OF ENDLESS WAR

*Jack Satan's the greatest of gods*
*And Hell is the best of abodes.*
*'Tis reached through the Valley of Clods*
*By seventy beautiful roads.*

AMBROSE BIERCE, "A SOLE SURVIVOR"

Memorial Day is upon us, our fourteenth since the dawning of the Era of the AUMF, and you'd think smart people would have learned a few things by now. Is it a war yet? Or still the same damn movie that's been playing since 2001, that revenge-and-war-porn fantasy where the USA kicks terrorist ass. Afghanistan, Iraq, Pakistan, Somalia, Yemen, Libya, Syria, and on it rolls like a fifteen-year-old beater with two hundred thousand miles on the engine and balding tires, "it" being the AUMF, the Authorization to Use Military Force, passed by the U.S. Congress on September 14, 2001. All these years later it's worth revisiting the document, this act of Congress whereby President George W. Bush was empowered

> *to use all necessary and appropriate force against those nations,*
> *organizations, or persons he determines planned, authorized,*
> *committed, or aided the terrorist attacks that occurred on*
> *September 11, 2001, or harbored such organizations or*
> *persons, in order to prevent any future acts of international*
> *terrorism against the United States by such nations,*
> *organizations, or persons.*

What a long, strange trip it's been, and all on the same set of wheels. Granted, we did get an upgrade with AUMF 2.0, the Iraq invasion authorization of 2002, but they're basically one and the same. How many of us are still driving the same car we had in the early aughts? But like siblings handing down the family junker, Bush drove that AUMF hard for eight years and passed it on to Obama, who promised to end two wars and will probably leave us with three. Come next January he'll be handing over the keys to the next in line, and off we'll go with a brand-new driver at the wheel.

This trip we're on, a while back it started looking more like a circle than progress from Point A to Point B. Invasions, occupations, air campaigns, and blizzards of drones have led to levels of chaos that only madmen and prophets could have imagined when all this started. Just two of this season's presidential candidates—Bernie Sanders and Rand Paul—have seriously questioned the hard-military tactics of the past fifteen years. Everyone else seems to be stuck in a 2002 time warp, back when deploying the world's most powerful military was supposed to bring peace and democracy to an insanely complex region. Gas on the fire. It failed, and a lot of people died. In this, the fourth presidential election in the Era of the AUMF, the debate hasn't been about war per se—whether it's necessary, whether it's an effective means to a plausible end—but rather, a difference of degree: will we have more of the same, or much, much more of the same?

The times are such that fantasy warmongering is solidly mainstream. We've seen candidates call for carpet-bombing and making the desert glow (Cruz),[1] for "bomb[ing] the shit out of them" (Trump),[2] for "bringing back waterboarding and a hell of a lot worse than waterboarding" (Trump again).[3] One candidate purchased a handgun as "the last line of defense between ISIS and my family" (Rubio),[4] and the likely Democratic nominee includes "the nail-eaters—McChrystal, Petraeus, Keane" among her preferred military advisers, and supports "intensification and acceleration" of U.S. military efforts in Iraq and Syria.[5] Yes, America has many enemies who heartily hate our guts and would do us every harm they could, but the failures of hard power over the past fifteen years seem utterly lost on our political class. After the Paris attacks last December, William Kristol of the *Weekly Standard* suggested that a force of fifty thousand U.S. troops deployed to Syria, supported by air power, would crush ISIS in short order, leading to the liberation of Fallujah, Mosul, and other ISIS strongholds. "I don't think there's much in the way of unanticipated side effects that are going to be bad there," opined Kristol—*funny guy!*—who back in 2002 said that removing Saddam Hussein "could start a chain reaction in the Arab world that would be very healthy."[6]

It makes you wonder: Are these people stupid? Are *we*? Is this

1  Katie Glueck, "Cruz Pledges Relentless Bombing to Destroy ISIL," *Politico*, December 5, 2015.
2  Tim Haines, "Trump's Updated ISIS Plan: 'Bomb the Shit Out of Them,' Send in Exxon to Rebuild," RealClearPolitics, November 13, 2015.
3  Tom McCarthy, "Donald Trump: I'd Bring Back 'a Hell of a Lot Worse Than Waterboarding,'" *Guardian*, February 7, 2016.
4  Rebecca Kaplan, "Marco Rubio: My Gun a 'Last Line of Defense' Against ISIS," *Face the Nation*, CBSNews.com, January 17, 2016.
5  Mark Landler, "How Hillary Clinton Became a Hawk," *New York Times Magazine*, April 24, 2016.
6  Matt Welch, "Before You Read Bill Kristol About 'What to Do in Iraq,' Read Bill Kristol in February 2002 About What to Do in Iraq," Reason.com/blog, June 16, 2014.

the politics we deserve? "Stupidity is the American disease," said Norman Mailer, though maybe it's not so much stupidity as fantasy, a determinedly infantile notion of what it means to go to war. Americans like the idea of breaking heads and drawing blood, but the burden of actual war? Not so much. And so the politicians pander, and we're more than willing to be pandered to. Throughout fifteen years of war there's been no appreciable rise in the tax rate, no mass mobilization, no call for sacrifice from the general population. Even our vocabulary slides toward the soothing and anodyne. *Collateral damage, alternative set of procedures, detainees*—these are practically mental pillows by now. *Extraordinary rendition* instead of kidnapping; *targeted killings* for presidentially ordered assassinations; *intensification* for escalation. The term *base* is out, and *counter fire complex* in—that's the name for the physical place where all those U.S. troops who don't constitute *boots on the ground* are currently quartered in Iraq.

"I would listen to the generals," Trump said in debate as he called for deploying thirty thousand troops to Syria. I would say: Screw that. How about we listen to the sergeants, lieutenants, and captains who wore those boots on the ground the past fifteen years. The ones who've left the military, who are free to speak their minds and have no stake in the business-as-usual business of American war. No sergeant or junior officer is angling for a lucrative post-military career sitting on defense industry boards or yakking for cable news. On a fall night in Austin last year I sat in a bar and listened to one of these former sergeants—infantry, two tours in Iraq—tell me, Sure, we can invade Syria and whip ISIS's butt. Just make sure we go in with four or five hundred thousand troops, and plan on keeping at least two hundred thousand there for the next, say, fifteen or twenty years. And we'd better commit to a massive investment in infrastructure, schools, the legal system, to keep ISIS or something like it from coming back. Oh, and we'll have to bring back the draft, that's what it'll take to keep an army that big over there. And raise taxes to pay for it, including health care for all the fucked-up people who'll be coming home. We can beat ISIS, sure. But not the way *those* guys—he nodded at the TV, where one of the circus-style debates was going on—are talking about.

IN THE BEGINNING IT WAS KNOWN AS "DECORATION DAY." THE call went out in May 1868 to decorate the graves of the Civil War dead "with the choicest flowers of springtime," formalizing a practice that had cropped up locally in the North and South even as the war was being fought. But the scale of death was such that scattered local gestures no longer sufficed. A national observance was needed, a collective acknowledgment of just how profoundly devastating the war had been. Over time, as the tradition took hold across the country, the holiday came to be known as Memorial Day.[7]

Back in April 1861, eighteen-year-old Ambrose Bierce was the second man in Elkhart County, Indiana, to enlist in the Union army.[8] Eventually he would be known as "Bitter Bierce," famous for such insights as "War is God's way of teaching Americans geography," but in 1861 he was just an aloof, touchy kid with some smatters of education and not a clue that the country was about to turn into a charnel house. Then again, no one did; the industrial slaughter of the Civil War was something new under the sun, and Bierce survived some of the worst of it. He fought at Shiloh, where more Americans died in two days of battle than in the Revolutionary War, the War of 1812, and the Mexican War combined. At Stones River, he and his company fought for a crucial three-foot rise of ground so bloody it became known as Hell's Half Acre. Chickamauga was bloodier still; after the first day of battle, thousands of

---

[7] See, for instance, "Memorial Day History," United States Department of Veterans Affairs, May 27, 2010, https://www.va.gov/opa/speceven/memday/history.asp, and Campbell Robertson, "Birthplace of Memorial Day? That Depends Where You're From," *New York Times*, May 26, 2012.

[8] For Ambrose Bierce's life I have largely relied on Roy Morris Jr., *Ambrose Bierce: Alone in Bad Company* (Crown Publishers, 1995).

wounded soldiers stranded between the lines either died of exposure in the freezing cold or roasted alive in the brushfires that sprang up across the battlefield, their screams and wails carrying far in the frigid mountain air.

"A night of waking," Bierce tersely described it years later.[9] The sheer volume and accuracy of ordnance made this a new kind of war, a machine for pulping metric tons of human flesh. Regardless of who was winning or losing, shock-and-awe was the common experience of both sides; Confederate and Union soldiers alike could hardly believe the things they were doing and having done to them, and when Bierce turned to the writer's trade after the war, some fundamental rigor or just plain contrariness wouldn't let him portray his war in conventionally heroic terms. In his hands, sentimentality and melodrama became foils for twisted jokes. Glory was ambiguous at best, a stale notion that barely hinted at the suicidal nature of valor in this kind of war. His wicked gift for honesty served up the eternal clash between duty and the survival instinct, as when, early in the war, he and his fellow rookies come across a group of Union dead:

> *How repulsive they looked with their blood-smears, their*
> *blank, staring eyes, their teeth uncovered by contraction of*
> *the lips! The frost had begun already to whiten their deranged*
> *clothing. We were as patriotic as ever, but we did not wish to*
> *be that way.*[10]

And again, when he encounters a woman on the boat ferrying him and his platoon to the Shiloh killing fields:

> *She was a fine creature, this woman; somebody's wife. Her*
> *mission, as she understood it, was to inspire the failing heart*

---

[9] *Ibid.*, p. 57.
[10] "On a Mountain," *Ambrose Bierce: The Devil's Dictionary, Tales, & Memoirs*, ed. S. T. Joshi (Library of America, 2011) (hereinafter, *Bierce*), p. 659.

*with courage; and when she selected mine I felt less flattered*
*by her preference than astonished by her penetration. How did*
*she learn?*[11]

Black humor sits alongside mordantly cool accounts of battles, wounds, horrors, absurd and tragic turns of luck. We encounter lots of ghosts in Bierce's work, a menagerie of spirits and bugaboos as well as hauntings of the more prosaic sort, people detached one way or another from themselves—amnesiacs, hallucinators, somnambulists, time trippers. People missing some part of their souls. Often Bierce writes of the fatal, or nearly so, shock, the twist that flips conventional wisdom on its back and shows reality to be much darker and crueler than we'd like to believe. It's hard not to read the war into Bierce's writing, even when the subject is ostensibly otherwise. He was the first American writer of talent to experience modern warfare, war as mass-produced death, and to try for words that would be true to the experience. He charted this new terrain, and it's in Bierce that we find the original experience that all subsequent American war writers would grapple with. Hemingway and Dos Passos in the First World War; Mailer, Heller, Jones, and Vonnegut in World War II; O'Brien, Herr, Caputo, and Marlantes in Vietnam: they're all descendants of Bierce.

It's not decorative, what these writers were going for. They weren't trying to write fancy, or entertain, or preach a sermon; they weren't writing to serve a political cause, at least not in any immediate sense. One suspects that on some level they had no choice but to write as they did—that they realized they would never have any peace in themselves unless they found a way of writing that, if it couldn't make sense of their war, at least respected it. Words that described the experience for what it was, without illusion or fantasy. Words that would resist the eternal American genius for cheapening and dumbing down.

---

[11] "What I Saw of Shiloh," *Bierce*, p. 665.

Donald Trump has said he "will be so good at the military, your head will spin." Sure, how hard can it be? This rich man's son who was never in the military, who in fact used student deferments (four) and a diagnosis of heel spurs to avoid Vietnam. He did, however, attend a military-style prep school in his teens, and therefore "always felt that I was in the military." He has said that sleeping around in New York during his bachelor days, risking venereal disease, was "scary, like Vietnam," and "my personal Vietnam," a comparison so bizarre, so clearly the product of a disturbed mind, that this alone should disqualify him from public office. Senator John McCain, a former naval aviator who nearly died in combat and was a prisoner of war in North Vietnam for over five years, repeatedly refusing offers of early release in order to stay with his fellow POWs, is not, according to Trump, much of a soldier, whereas he, Trump, according to Trump, is the "most militaristic man in the room" whose as-yet-unspecified plans for taking on ISIS would draw the approval of such military lions as General Douglas MacArthur and General George Patton.[12]

And so on, a nonstop ream of pure and abject bullshit such as has never transpired in presidential politics. Somehow, remarkably, he gets away with it, and the fact that he does is one of the central mysteries of this election season. Could it be that Trump is giving voice to the inner life of a large portion of the U.S. male population (and how much of the female as well)? Which might explain the mystery: he is the bog monster of the American id, rising out of the masturbatory muck of our military fantasies in which the

---

[12] See Steve Eder and Dave Philipps, "Donald Trump's Draft Deferments: Four for College, One for Bad Feet," *New York Times,* August 1, 2016; Dana Milbank, "Donald Trump's War with the U.S. Military," *Washington Post,* September 9, 2016; Tim Mak, "Draft-Dodger Trump Said Sleeping Around Was My 'Personal Vietnam,'" *Daily Beast,* February 16, 2016; Ginger Adams Otis, Reuven Blau, and Nancy Dillion, "Photos Show Donald Trump in Military Uniform, with Athletic Teams Before Dodging the Vietnam Draft with 'Bull–t' Injury," *New York Daily News,* July 21, 2015; James Fallows, "Donald Trump and the Generals," *Atlantic,* October 10, 2016; Emily Flitter, "Trump's Obsession with WW2 Generals Strikes Sour Note with Historians," Reuters, February 25, 2016.

manly man slays his enemies and laughs at the lamentations of their women. So easy to be the hero in your wet dreams, your shooter games, your securely located war rooms stocked with emergency rations and, in Dick Cheney's case, the ever-present defibrillator. This sort of unhinged fantasizing[13] has been the defining feature of the Era of the AUMF, in which people—old men, for the most part, a good number of them rich—who never experienced war—who in their youth ran as fast from it as they could—send young men and women—most of them middle- and working-class kids—across oceans to fight wars based on half-facts, cherry-picked intelligence, and magical thinking on the grand geopolitical scale. Surely it's no coincidence that the Era of the AUMF, the Era of Endless War, is also the Golden Era of the Chickenhawk. We keep electing leaders who, on the most basic experiential level, literally have no idea what they're doing.

Maybe they get away with it because we the people who keep electing them don't know anything about war ourselves. We know the fantasy version, the movie version, but only that 1 percent of the nation—and their families—who have fought the wars truly know the costs involved. For the rest of us, no sacrifice has been called for: none. No draft. No war tax (but huge deficits), and here it bears noting that the top tax rate during World War II was 90 percent. No rationing, the very mention of which is good for a laugh. *Rationing?* That never entered the discussion. But those years when U.S. soldiers were piling sandbags into their thin-skinned Humvees and welding scrap metal onto the sides in hopes of deflecting enemy ordnance also happened to coincide with the heyday of the Hummer here at home. Where I live in Dallas, you could hardly drive a couple of blocks without passing one of those beasts, eighty-six hundred hulking pounds of chrome and steel. Or for a really good laugh,

---

[13] For more on the national talent for fantasizing, and on our mighty Fantasy Industrial Complex, see "Two American Dreams," *infra*.

how about this: gas rationing. If it's really about the oil, shouldn't we support the troops by driving less, walking more? Or suppose it's not about the oil at all, but about our freedoms, our values, our very way of life—that it's truly "a clash of civilizations," in the words of Marco Rubio.[14] If that's the case, if this is what we truly believe, then our politicians should call for, and we should accept no less than, full-scale mobilization: a military draft, confiscatory tax rates, rationing of gas and other war-critical resources.

Some 3.5 million Americans fought in the Civil War, out of a population of 31 million. For years the number of killed in action was estimated at 620,000, although recent scholarship suggests a significantly higher figure, from a low of 650,000 to a high of 850,000. Whatever the exact number, it's clear that the vast majority of American families had, as we say these days, skin in the game. The war was real; having loved ones at mortal risk made it real. Many endured battles being fought in their literal backyards. Lincoln himself watched the fighting from behind the DC ramparts, poking his head up far enough to see men die in combat.[15] The lived reality of the thing was so brutally direct that it would be more than fifty years before the U.S. embarked on another major war. To be sure, there was the brief Spanish-American War in 1898, and a three-year native insurgency in the Philippines, and various forays around the Caribbean and Central America, but the trauma of the Civil War cut so deep and raw that the generation that fought it was largely cured of belligerence. Our own generation's appetite seems steadily robust even as we approach the fifteenth anniversary of the AUMF, which, given the circumstances, makes sense. As long as we're cocooned in our comfortable homeland fantasy of war, one

[14] Theodoric Meyer, "Rubio Sees a 'Clash of Civilizations,'" *Politico*, November 15, 2015.
[15] "Get down, you damn fool, before you get shot!" Captain Oliver Wendell Holmes Jr., age twenty-three, barked at Lincoln as bullets whizzed past the commander in chief's head. Shelby Foote, *The Civil War: A Narrative (Red River to Appomattox)* (Random House, 1974), pp. 458–59.

can safely predict a long and successful run for the Era of the Chicken-hawk.

BIERCE SURVIVED HIS OWN WAR, BARELY. TWO WEEKS AFTER writing to a friend "my turn will come," and one day before his twenty-second birthday, he was shot in the head near Kennesaw Mountain, Georgia. The sniper's ball broke his skull "like a walnut," penetrating the left temple, fracturing the temporal lobe, and dog-legging down and around behind his left ear, where it stayed. Head shots in that era were almost always fatal, but Bierce survived not only the initial wound, but an awful two-day train ride on an open flatcar, in the rain, to an army hospital in Chattanooga.[16]

He recovered, more or less. Not the easiest personality to begin with, Bierce showed no appreciable mellowing from his war experi-ence. His postwar life is an ugly litany of feuds, ruptures, lawsuits, friends betrayed or abandoned, epic temper tantrums and equally epic funks. He was a lousy husband—cold, critical, philandering—and essentially abandoned his wife after seventeen years of marriage. His older son shot himself dead at age sixteen, and the younger drank himself to death in his twenties; for his own part, Bierce maintained a lifelong obsession with suicide. In October 1913, after a distinguished, contentious fifty-year literary career that had made him one of the most famous and hated men in America, Bierce left Washington, DC, and headed for Mexico, intending to join, or report on—it was never quite clear—Pancho Villa's revolutionary army. Along the way, dressing every day entirely in black, he visited the battlefields of his youth, trekking for miles in the Indian summer heat around Orchard Knob, Missionary Ridge, Hell's Half Acre. For a whole day he sat by himself at Shiloh, in the blazing sun, in his black suit, silent. In November he crossed from Laredo into Mexico and disappeared, an exit dramatic enough to inspire a bestselling

---

[16] Morris, *Ambrose Bierce*, pp. 88–89.

novel by Carlos Fuentes, *The Old Gringo,* and a movie adaptation of the same name starring Gregory Peck.[17]

Late in life, Bierce described his military service in these terms:

> *It was once my fortune to command a company of soldiers—*
> *real soldiers. Not professional life-long fighters, the product*
> *of European militarism—just plain, ordinary American*
> *volunteer soldiers, who loved their country and fought for*
> *it with never a thought of grabbing it for themselves; that is*
> *a trick which the survivors were taught later by gentlemen*
> *desiring their votes.*[18]

About those *gentlemen desiring votes*—since when did it become not just acceptable but expected that politicians orate on Memorial Day? Who gave them permission to speak for the violently dead? Come Monday we'll be up to our ears in some of the emptiest, most self-serving dreck ever to ripple the atmosphere, the standard war-fantasy talk of American politics, complete with sentimentalist purlings about heroes, freedoms, the supreme sacrifice. Trump will tell us how much he loves the veterans, and how much they love him back. Down-ticket pols will re-terrorize and titillate voters with tough talk about ISIS. Hemingway, for one, despised this kind of cant, his disgust borne out in a famous passage from *A Farewell to Arms,* in which the wounded veteran Frederic Henry reflects:

> *There were many words that you could not stand to hear*
> *and finally only the names of the places had dignity. Certain*
> *numbers were the same way and certain dates and these with*
> *the names of the places were all you could say and have them*

---

[17] *Ibid.,* pp. 247–68. See also Jake Silverstein, "The Devil and Ambrose Bierce," in *Nothing Happened and Then It Did* (Norton, 2011), exploring the possibility that Bierce died and was buried in Marfa, Texas.

[18] Morris, *Ambrose Bierce,* p. 97.

*mean anything. Abstract words such as glory, honor, courage, or hallow were obscene beside the concrete names of villages, the numbers of roads, the names of rivers, the numbers of regiments and the dates.*

Here's a proposition: We stand a better chance of understanding something about ourselves and our wars if we tune out the politicians, for one day at least, and turn our attention to a certain kind of writer: namely, the man or woman who experiences war firsthand, then devotes heart and soul to finding the correct words, the true words, for describing the reality of the thing. Crazy, right? Maybe you think I've been smoking that good Texas dope? The very idea, ignoring Hillary and Trump and instead reading a poem by Brian Turner or Kevin Powers, or a passage from *Youngblood* or *Fobbit* or *Green on Blue*. But a country going on its fifteenth year of war would seem obliged to use every available tool for making sense of its situation. And if looking at poems and novels seems like a radical act, that in itself might be a clue to our problem.

Or how about silence. In an era where language has been so mangled and abused, maybe the sanest thing we can do is reserve some space for silence. The National Moment of Remembrance Act puts this notion into law, encouraging a minute of silence at three P.M. local time on Memorial Day. At least then we would be spared someone trying to sell us something—cars, appliances, political agendas, war—for as long as the silence lasted, and that alone seems like a mercy. It's hard to hijack silence, and maybe that's the point. One thinks of Ambrose Bierce sitting alone all day at Shiloh, an old man, his war long past, biding silently with his ghosts.

# BOOK OF DAYS

## JUNE

In testimony in a California fraud lawsuit against Trump University, a former Trump U. salesman describes the company's high-pressure sales tactics and deceptive marketing, and bluntly states, "I believe that Trump University was a fraudulent scheme, and that it preyed upon the elderly and uneducated to separate them from their money." Amnesty International reports that the number of people internally displaced by the war in Afghanistan has doubled since 2012. Two opinion polls for the *Guardian* indicate growing support for a British exit from the European Union, and the British pound falls sharply. Water in Flint is declared safe for bathing but not drinking. After attempting to recruit, among others, Senator Tom Cotton, Senator Ben Sasse, and 2012 Republican nominee Mitt Romney, *Weekly Standard* editor William Kristol announces that his choice for a conservative independent candidate for the presidency is David A. French, a constitutional lawyer and blogger for the *National Review* who lives in Tennessee. A second baby with Zika defects is born in the U.S. House Speaker Paul Ryan quietly endorses Trump in an article he writes for his hometown newspaper in Janesville, Wisconsin. Hillary Clinton calls Trump "unprepared" and "temperamentally unfit" to be president, and Trump immediately tweets of her speech: "Reading poorly from the teleprompter! She doesn't even look presidential!" Muhammad Ali, age seventy-four, dies. Trump calls on the federal judge in the Trump University fraud case, Gonzalo Curiel, to recuse himself, because he "happens to be, we believe, Mexican," and is therefore biased against Trump because of Trump's plan to build a wall between Mexico and the U.S. Curiel, a native of Indiana, once lived under threat of assassination by a Mexican drug cartel while he was assistant U.S. attorney for the Southern District of California. John McCain endorses Trump, and Sanders predicts a contested Democratic convention. Trump says his remarks regarding Judge Curiel have been "misconstrued." House Speaker Paul Ryan denounces Trump's remarks on Judge Curiel as "racist," and urges his fellow Republicans to unite behind Trump.

**CALIFORNIA DEMOCRATIC PRIMARY**
Clinton: 55.8%
Sanders: 43.2%

**NEW JERSEY DEMOCRATIC PRIMARY**
Clinton: 63.3%
Sanders: 36.6%

Obama endorses Clinton, and soon afterward meets with Sanders at the White House to appeal for unity. Vice President Joe Biden and Senator Elizabeth Warren endorse Clinton, while Sanders goes home to Vermont without conceding defeat. Mitt Romney says Trump is promoting "trickle-down racism," and Trump responds that Romney is bitter because he is a failed presidential candidate who "choked like a dog." The hip-hop musical *Hamilton* wins eleven Tonys, including best new musical, best score, best book, best direction, and best featured actor and actress. Omar Mateen, a twenty-nine-year-old native New Yorker, kills forty-nine people and wounds fifty-three at Pulse, a gay nightclub in Orlando, Florida, in the deadliest mass shooting in U.S. history. During the three-hour standoff with police, Mateen, the son of Afghan immigrants, calls 911 to declare his allegiance to ISIS. Trump and Cruz condemn President Obama for omitting the phrase "radical Islamic terrorism" in his remarks on the attack, and Trump later calls for a ban on immigrants from any part of the world with "a proven history of terrorism" against the U.S. or its allies. Gun sales spike, and stock prices of gun manufacturers gain on Wall Street. Without mentioning Trump by name, President Obama blasts "language that singles out immigrants and suggests entire religious communities are complicit in violence." On *Fox & Friends,* Trump suggests President Obama is sympathetic to ISIS: "Look, we're led by a man that either is not tough, not smart, or he's got something else in mind. And the something else in mind—you know, people can't believe it . . . There's something going on. It's inconceivable." The *Washington Post* reports that two groups of hackers affiliated with the Russian government accessed the computer systems of the Democratic National Committee in the summer of 2015, and had full access to the party's communications and research materials for approximately one year. Hillary Clinton's campaign was also targeted, although it's unclear whether that hack was successful. Rupert Murdoch's *Sun* tabloid, the most popular in Britain, comes out in favor of a British exit from the EU. Clinton wins the District of Columbia, the final primary of 2016, and meets with Sanders that evening. The American Medical Association calls gun violence a public health crisis, and announces plans to lobby Congress to overturn legislation that prohibits the Centers for Disease Control and Prevention from conducting large-scale epidemiological studies on the crisis. The AMA also notes that approximately thirty thousand men, women, and children die of gun violence each year in the United States. The Trump campaign refuses to issue press credentials to reporters whose coverage

Trump dislikes, including reporters from the *Washington Post,* and the Cleveland Cavaliers' playoff run impedes preparations for the Republican National Convention scheduled there for next month. Mark Cuban donates $1 million to the Dallas Police Department in response to the Pulse shooting; the money will be used for sixteen thousand hours of overtime pay for a stronger police presence in Dallas's Oak Lawn neighborhood, which has a substantial gay community. A *Washington Post*/ABC News poll finds that 70 percent of Americans view Trump negatively, compared to 55 percent for Hillary Clinton. Obama calls on Congress to tighten gun-control laws, and Donald Trump calls the nation's current leadership weak and ineffective, and vows to protect America against terrorism by controlling the country's flow of immigrants. Jo Cox, the mother of two young children and a Labour Party member of Parliament known for her advocacy on behalf of refugees and civilians in Syria, is attacked and killed by an assailant shouting, "Britain First!," the name of a far-right group that stages provocative anti-Muslim demonstrations. The IAAF bans the entire Russian track and field team from the Rio Olympic Games because of doping. Eight days after the Pulse shootings, the Senate fails to pass legislation to tighten gun-control laws, including a proposal to prohibit the sale of guns to anyone on the terrorism watch list. Trump fires his campaign manager, Corey Lewandowski, and replaces him with senior adviser and Washington lobbyist Paul Manafort. Meeting with conservative religious leaders, Trump asks that they pray for the success of his candidacy, and declares that "we've got to spiritize this country." "I know a lot of people who are holding their nose," one meeting participant said afterward. House Democrats stage a twenty-five-hour sit-in on the House floor to demand a vote on tightening gun laws, chanting, "No bill! No break!" and "Shame! Shame! Shame!" at Paul Ryan as he exits the Speaker's chair. Marco Rubio announces that he will seek reelection to the Senate, reversing the position he took during his presidential campaign, and former House Speaker Dennis

Hastert reports to prison in Minnesota. The state of Rio de Janeiro declares a "state of public calamity" fifty days before the start of the Olympic Games, citing a financial crisis so severe that it could bring about "a total collapse in public security, health, education, mobility, and environmental management." Defying polls, the political establishment, and foreign allies, Great Britain votes to leave the European Union, rattling global financial markets and casting the future of the seventy-year-old EU into doubt. Trump, in Scotland to publicize the opening of a Trump golf course, praises the vote. The Supreme Court deadlocks 4–4 on a lower court's ruling that strikes down Obama's executive order shielding millions of undocumented immigrants from deportation, thereby leaving the lower court's ruling intact. Volkswagen agrees to spend $10.2 billion in fines and remedies to settle claims from its diesel emissions cheating scandal, and ISIS abducts nine hundred Kurdish civilians and forces them to build fortifications in Manbij, Syria. A *Washington Post*/ABC News poll shows Clinton leading Trump, 51 percent to 39 percent. Fallujah is declared to be "fully liberated" from ISIS after five weeks of fighting. Dr. James Dobson, founder of Focus on the Family and a leading evangelical, says that Trump has recently come "to accept a relationship with Christ" and is now "a baby Christian." Senate Democrats balk at advancing a $1.1 billion anti-Zika spending measure when Republicans include amendments to cut funding for Obamacare and Planned Parenthood, to exempt pesticide spraying for mosquito control from Clean Water Act standards, and to strike down a ban on flying the Confederate battle flag in military cemeteries. Suicide bombers attack Istanbul's Ataturk International Airport, killing more than forty and wounding more than one hundred forty; Turkish authorities blame ISIS, although the terrorist group does not claim responsibility. The House Select Committee on Benghazi issues a final eight-hundred-page report that finds no evidence of culpability or wrongdoing by Hillary Clinton. European Council president Donald Tusk tells Great Britain that "Europe is ready to start the divorce process, even today"; Rio de Janeiro's cash-strapped security forces beg for supplies as basic as pens, cleaning materials, and toilet paper; and a member of the British Parliament complains in the House of Commons that his fellow lawmakers are being bombarded with fund-raising appeals from "somebody called Donald Trump."

# CHEERLEADERS OF THE STAR-SPANGLED APOCALYPSE

## FEAR AND LOATHING WITH THE NRA IN LOUISVILLE, KENTUCKY

*A frightened population is obedient.*

HUNTER S. THOMPSON

*I'm not scared about going to jail. Somebody's got to do something to knock the fear out of these Negroes.*

MUHAMMAD ALI

At the 145th National Rifle Association annual convention you could see and purchase replica flintlock muskets like Daniel Boone's, "wardrobe" handguns the size of a cell phone, a carriage-mounted 1883 Gatling gun, historic firearms from the Renaissance down through the latest surge, bullet-splat jewelry, deep-concealment holsters, triple-barrel shotguns, and camo everything—coolers, flasks, four-wheelers, deer blinds, lingerie, infant-wear. There was a motor-cycle with a .50-caliber machine gun mounted on the handlebar (sorry, not for sale), all manner of scopes, optics, and laser-sighting technologies (how do the animals stand a chance?), "shelf-stable" food products, bulk ammo, precision ammo, make-your-own-ammo ammo, historical exhibits, mom-and-pop purveyors of cleaning fluids and swabs, and corporate icons with slick, multilevel sales areas worthy of luxury car showrooms. And the flag, everywhere, all the time, the stars and stripes popping from pistol grips, knives, banners, T-shirts, shawls, bandannas, sunglasses, product brochures, and shopping bags. America, America, sweet land that we love. A photo spread for a well-known gun manufacturer featured a whiskery, camo-clad, Viagra-aged Caucasian male standing in ankle-deep marsh with a dog by his side, shotgun slung to his back, and a large U.S. flag in one hand, the pole planted in the muck, as if staking a claim.

A country, a product, a lifestyle. That word shows up a lot in firearms ad copy, as in, "We find peace in the solitude of this lifestyle, and we thrive on all the great outdoors has to offer." But on this rainy opening day of the NRA convention all the action was indoors, "Eleven Acres of Guns & Gear" promised the banner draped outside the Kentucky Exposition Center, a stunningly nondescript complex of enormous beige boxes that inhaled thousands of humans without so much as a belch. How big is eleven acres? Felt like a hundred, which isn't to say that this conventioneer was the least bit bored.

Mingling with a crowd striking for its nearly uniform whiteness, I did lapse into a kind of fugue state from time to time, a retail trance brought on by sheer sensory overload, but with all this American ingenuity and weirdness on display, actual boredom was out of the question. Old people and those less old but morbidly obese trundled about on motorized scooters, their baskets overflowing with corporate swag. The crowd buzz was punctuated by promotional videos, impromptu live briefings on subjects such as "target acquisition" skills, and music, mostly country or guitar-skronk, though I did pass a booth where "Lido Shuffle" was playing. A guy dressed like Zorro was wandering around, and another guy done up as a frontier sheriff, with a badge on his vest and six-shooters on his hips. Eddie Eagle was here, the NRA's kid-outreach and gun-safety mascot, a flightless bipedal cousin of Big Bird. Glossy signage pushed a steady visual diet of Americana—cowboys and pioneers, war heroes, the family, Founding Fathers, rugged outdoors individualism, our freedoms and the defense of same, all embodied by photogenic white people, not a brown or black face to be seen. Celebrities signed posters and flacked merchandise, among them stars of cable-TV hunting shows, NASCAR drivers, pro wrestlers, decorated veterans. More flags. History. Freedoms. America and her guns, cultural icons embedded in the brain like saints in the stained-glass windows of a church, Colt, Remington, Winchester, Smith & Wesson, all curated at the Kentucky Exposition Center with the solemnity of high holy relics.

What gun culture lacks in wit—for grown-up delinquent fun and sly-dog subversion you can't beat a custom-car rally—it more than makes up for in design genius, precision tooling, and a long and honorable tradition of craftsmanship. But something's happened in the past several decades, a kind of hyper-consumerist fetishizing where categories divide, then subdivide into ever narrower specialties that have little to do with utility. How many variations on the AR-15 "platform"—the civilian version of the military's M16 assault rifle—can there be? Many. More than many. To infinity and beyond. The AR-15 was used in the San Bernardino and Sandy Hook Elementary School mass shootings, and was featured in a January 20, 2016, post on the NRA's website titled "Why the AR-15 Is America's Most Popular Rifle." "The AR-15s [sic] ability to be modified to your own personal taste is one of the things that makes it so unique," reads the post, and indeed, walking the floor of the

exhibition hall I ended up cross-eyed at all the polymers, alloys, finishes, calibers, stock and barrel configurations, buffer systems, trigger systems, muzzle brakes, and so on, to, truly, infinity and beyond.

I had entered the realms of style; that is to say, the dark swamps
of consumer psychology where desire, identity, and aspiration are
always bubbling in a subterranean psychic stew. What kind of AR
man do you want to be? Or woman, for that matter—take yours
in solid pink or "Muddy Girl" camo? There's agency in a purchase.
Most of our buying these days has less to do with need than with
serving fantasies and tamping down fears. Clothes do it for us. Vehicles too, profoundly; in my neighborhood in Dallas you can see
plenty of gleaming pickup trucks "hauling air," as the saying goes,
driven by men with soft hands and closets full of business suits.
But in our terrorized, polarized, ferociously tribalized times it's hard
to think of a more charged consumer item, one as psychologically
fraught, as a gun. For relatively not much money we can buy ourselves a piece of rugged individualism and triumphant history ("For
nostalgic hunting or cowboy type shooting the 1886 Classic Car-
bine or Standard Rifle are perfect") and raise a big middle finger
to ISIS, the feds, the liberals, feminists, whoever we think is messing with us. A gun keeps us in character, the American character,
as helpfully illustrated by all those fancy marketing visuals, which
might as well be movie stills from the reel of greatest hits playing
in every American's mind. With a century's worth of Hollywood
puffing your product, not to mention the explicit blessing of the
U.S. Constitution, gun marketing has to be one of the pig-laziest
gigs around. What other consumer item is sanctioned by the Bill of
Rights? And by God if the NRA has anything to do about it this
market shall not be infringed upon in any shape, form, or fashion,
even if a reading of the Second Amendment happens to turn up
the words *well regulated*. Maybe that inconvenient phrase explains
why the NRA's extensive website neglects to include the actual text
of the Second Amendment.

At the Exposition Center I kept seeing the word *tactical*—tactical gear, tactical clothes, tactical categories of guns. What did it mean? "Tactical" as opposed to, uh, strategic? Then I watched a fantastically violent, Tarantino-style promotional video of a "tactical" semiautomatic shotgun in action. A guy in a ghillie suit—he looked like a half-grown Chewbacca—blasted his way through a series of targets that included watermelons, glass globes filled with red liquid, and fully clothed anthropomorphic mannequins, *bam bam bam,* stuff exploding faster than you can snap your fingers. That's when I got it, or at least I think I did. This wasn't a hunting firearm. Not for game, no. *Tactical* denotes human. The intraspecies encounter.

**"IT'S JUST NOT THE WAY IT WAS," DONALD TRUMP SAID THAT** day to thousands of NRA faithful gathered in Freedom Hall. "It's just not the way it was, and we're gonna bring it back, and we're gonna bring it back to a real place to where we don't have to be so frightened, we don't have to be so afraid."

At that instant I felt a kink in the air, which was possibly the **gckh!** of hundreds of sales reps choking on their Cheetos. *Not . . . be . . . frightened?* What the hell! Who does Trump think we're going to sell all these guns to?

Those sales reps needn't worry. Fear is the herpes of American politics: the symptoms bloom and fade, but the virus never dies. That the world is full of dangers is beyond dispute. Peril is the air we humans have always breathed, a fact of life that demands of us open eyes, a clear head, and some degree of self-control. Otherwise we're doomed to live like scampering mice, or, as one authoritative text put it long ago:

> [T]he sound of a driven leaf shall put them to flight, and they
> shall flee as one flees from the sword, and they shall fall when
> none pursues. They shall stumble over one another, as if to

*escape a sword, though none pursues; and you shall have no*
*power to stand before your enemies.*

LEVITICUS 26:36–37

Your true enemies, as opposed to the imagined, the inflated, the convenient. In his classic 1964 essay "The Paranoid Style in American Politics," Richard Hofstadter did the nation a great service by analyzing our gift for phobia,[1] but I was thinking of another writer when I arrived in Louisville, a native son of the city, life member of the NRA, and author of such latter-day classics as *Hell's Angels* and *Fear and Loathing in Las Vegas*. Hunter Stockton Thompson (1937–2005) was the wild-child son of an insurance salesman father and librarian mother, his formative years marked by mischief and petty crime that progressed, by the time he was a senior in high school, to stealing cars and robbing liquor stores. "I was cursed with a dark sense of humor," he later wrote (much too modestly) of his youth, "that made many adults afraid of me, for reasons they couldn't quite put their fingers on."[2] These days the young Hunter would likely earn himself a diagnosis of ADD, along with IQ scores well in the genius range. Add to these a taste for risk, an acute and easily offended sense of justice, and a congenital contempt for authority, and what you have is a prime example of a distinctly American strain of outlawry, the same wildness that drove Huck Finn to light out for the territory, and Diane Arbus into the precincts of the damned and deformed.

"There is no human being within 500 miles to whom I can communicate anything—much less the fear and loathing that is on me after today's murder."[3] Thompson wrote these words to a friend on

---

[1] *The Paranoid Style in American Politics and Other Essays* (Vintage, 2008; originally printed in 1965).

[2] Hunter S. Thompson, *Kingdom of Fear* (Simon & Schuster, 2003), p. 10.

[3] Hunter S. Thompson, *The Proud Highway: The Fear and Loathing Letters, Volume I*, ed. Douglas Brinkley (Villard, 1997), p. 420.

the day of John F. Kennedy's assassination, and thus the fear-and-loathing franchise was born, out of a cold rage that would develop over time into a tool for analyzing the country's soul and psyche. Years later he elaborated in an interview:

> *People accused me of stealing "fear and loathing" [from Søren Kierkegaard]—fuck no, that came straight out of what I felt. If I had seen it, I probably would have stolen it. Yeah, I just remember thinking about Kennedy, that this is so bad I need new words for it. And "fear and loathing"—yeah, it defines a certain state, an attitude.[4]*

It was a state and attitude that any number of phenomena could provoke in him—Richard Nixon, Bill Clinton, Iran-Contra, the marketing of Z28 Camaros, or the death of the American Dream. *Fear,* for the damage a particular horror might do to body and soul; *loathing,* for its affront to justice, love, mercy, and the spirit of fun. For Thompson fun included enthusiastic and knowledgeable gun ownership. Lots of boys like messing around with things that go boom, and some never stop liking them. Thompson, who once gave a firecracker bomb to David Letterman on the air, was one of those boys, his passion going hand in glove with his famous appetite for drugs, alcohol, and other adult activities, including politics and the Book of Revelation. At times his own prophecies show biblical big-league vision, as in this piece titled "September 11, 2001" (dated the day after) from his book *Kingdom of Fear:*

> *The towers are gone now, reduced to bloody rubble along with all hopes for Peace in Our Time, in the United States or any other country. Make no mistake about it: We are At War*

---

[4] Beef Torrey and Kevin Simonson, eds., *Conversations with Hunter S. Thompson* (University Press of Mississippi, 2008), p. 125.

*now—with somebody—and we will stay At War with that*
*mysterious Enemy for the rest of our lives.*

*It will be a Religious War, a sort of Christian Jihad,*
*fueled by religious hatred and led by merciless fanatics on both*
*sides. It will be guerrilla warfare on a global scale, with no*
*front lines and no identifiable enemy . . . This is going to be a*
*very expensive war, and Victory is not guaranteed.*[5]

Hunter Thompson, American genius. The synchronicity seemed perfect: I would go to Louisville and hang out with the NRA, and in my downtime seek out traces of America's prose laureate of fear, loathing, and firearms. One morning, a very generous retired *Courier-Journal* editor drove me around the Cherokee Park neighborhood where Hunter Thompson grew up, a pleasant area of rolling hills, comfortable houses, and woody urban parks. Another day Thompson's extremely awesome grand-niece fetched me from my motel and drove me to meet one of his childhood friends, an old-school Southern gentleman who observed that for all his alleged madness, Thompson was scrupulously careful with guns. Check out the photos, he told me. In nearly every photo of Thompson with guns—and there are many—the gun is "safe" when not in actual use, i.e., bolt actions with the bolt open, shotguns broken, revolvers with the cylinders out.

"A lot of people shouldn't own guns," Thompson said once. "I should. I have a safety record."[6]

I'd come to Louisville for guns, but around town I began seeing

---

[5] Pages 161–62.

[6] Anita Thompson, ed., *Ancient Gonzo Wisdom: Interviews with Hunter S. Thompson* (Da Capo Press, 2009), p. 218. Though in July 2000 Thompson accidentally shot his assistant Deborah Fuller while trying to scare a bear off his property. Several shotgun pellets ricocheted off the ground and struck Fuller in the arm and leg. "I screamed, 'You son of a bitch, you shot me.' And poor Hunter, I don't think I had ever seen him run so fast. He felt horrible," Fuller later said about the incident. See also Meko Haze, "A Brief Look into the Life of the Father of Gonzo Journalism, Hunter S. Thompson," *The Daily Haze,* July 18, 2017.

Louisville, Kentucky. Mural by Carol McLeod, Evan Leibowitz, Alexander King, and Andy Cook. Photo courtesy of the author

banners for something called the Festival of Faiths, this year's edition billed as "Pathways to Nonviolence." Synchronicity + Serendipity = Karma, or at least a trail that seemed worth following. Friends of friends led to cocktails with some amiable Louisvillians, which led to dinner, which led to a Festival concert presided over by Teddy Abrams, the twentysomething *wunderkind* conductor of the Louisville Orchestra, which ended with all of the evening's performers— Abrams, a Pakistani rock group, a thirteen-piece salsa band, an angelic South African vocalist, and Ricky Skaggs and his bluegrass band—jamming like a musical UN while dozens of people who evidently don't dance very much (I was one) happily danced below the stage.

America is various. It refuses to be all one thing or all the other. The next day I was back at the Festival of Faiths to hear a panel discussion, "Face to Face with Islamophobia," moderated by Tori

Murden McClure, MDiv (Harvard), president of Spalding University, author, and the first woman to row solo across the Atlantic Ocean (America is various!). She began with a series of thoughtful, measured remarks about Islam, the global war on terror, and the abiding power of the military-industrial complex in the life of the country. She discussed "terrorism in context," and offered numerical markers such as these:

US deaths from terrorism, 2001–2015 (all numbers estimated high end and rounded up):
9/11: 3,000
Military personnel KIA, Afghanistan and Iraq: 7,000
Military contractors KIA, Afghanistan and Iraq: 7,200
Military personnel, postwar trauma (pegged to KIA in the absence of reliable figures): 7,000
Civilians, domestic terrorism: 87
Civilians, overseas terrorism: 350
Total: 24,637

And this:

US deaths in non-terror incidents involving firearms, 2001–2015: 404,496

Also this:

Estimated civilian deaths from GWOT in Iraq, Afghanistan, and Pakistan, 2001–2015 (from neutral sources, low-end estimate): 1,170,000

The numbers added up to something quite different from the dominant narrative of the past fifteen years about whom and what we should fear and loathe. Another Islamophobia speaker, Dr. Ingrid Mattson, former president of the Islamic Society of North America, talked about the "great closing of the American mind" since 9/11 and its emotional corollary, as performed by people in airports flipping out at the sight of her head scarf. What's the deal with all these Americans scared out of their wits? Dr. Mattson had a clue: "Follow the money." Track it through to the books, the think tanks, the TV pundits. Fearmongering can be a great career move for a politician or talking head. It's exciting. It draws attention. It moves product and boosts sales. There's big profit to be made in plowing the fertile ground of American fear.

"This country depends on war as a primary industry," Hunter Thompson said in a 2003 interview, but he might have just as easily said "fear" as "war." Later in the same interview he commented:

> *This country has been having a nationwide nervous breakdown since 9/11. A nation of people suddenly broke, the market economy goes to shit, and they're threatened on every side by an unknown, sinister enemy. But I don't think fear is a very effective way of dealing with things—of responding to reality. Fear is just another word for ignorance.*[7]

So it was that fear and loathing, war and terror, ignorance, body counts, and *money-money-money* were all banging around in my head when I walked into the Kentucky Exposition Center and confronted those eleven acres of guns. I had found the money, lip-smacking gobs of it, but so what? This is America and this is what Americans do, we sell stuff and make dough, but something in me resisted this soothing reduction to ordinary mercantilism, to the ho-hum everyday. I wandered around arguing with myself in this vein for a while, then decided that what was confusing me was the *marketing*, for lack of a better, less anodyne word. The casual mashup of stone-cold lethality and sleek retail culture, a Mall of Death sort of upbeat

---

[7] Torrey and Simonson, *Conversations with Hunter S. Thompson*, pp. 191, 193.

perkiness, with thick dollops of belligerence and bravado. "[O]ur high-performance Brass Jacket Hollow Point rounds deliver massive expansion and deep penetration for ultimate stopping power." "Shoulder Bones Are Mere Speed Bumps." "[O]ptimal penetration and expansion through even heavy clothing." "One-shot confidence." "Cutting petals." "Deadly downrange stopping power." "[E]xpands rapidly to 2X the diameter to carve massive wound channels."

Should the fact that living bodies are the ultimate subject here give us pause? Yet this kind of verbiage makes perfect sense, once we accept the basic premise. Guns are tools for inflicting deadly force—what's the point of the damn thing if it shoots marshmallows? It's easy to envision a scenario where you would want a firearm; where you would feel very much a fool for not having one. The world is indeed a dangerous place. Lots of disturbed people out there, damaged people, fanatics, shitbirds, and scumbags with all the conscience of a starved rat. But here's the rub: we're much more likely to shoot our families, our lovers, ourselves than we are that marauding stranger. The numbers bear this out: you bring a gun into your house, the chances of you or a family member being killed by a gun are far greater than the chance you'll use it for self-defense.[8]

Which could be viewed as statistical proof—as if it were needed—that human beings are flawed. We're creatures of passion, impulse, mood, and pitifully fragile ego, with barely the patience to drive a mile in our cars without wanting to kill someone. Four hundred four thousand four hundred ninety-six dead in fourteen years, not by war, not by terrorism or at the hands of foreign enemies, but among ourselves. Four hundred four thousand four hundred ninety-six dead, approximately the equivalent of twenty to twenty-five army divisions, or the population of Cleveland, Ohio. Shall we consider this normal. Shall we consider it normal that women's mortal-

---

[8] "Risks of Having a Gun in the Home," Brady Center to Prevent Gun Violence, https://www.bradycampaign.org/risks-of-having-a-gun-in-the-home.

ity rises dramatically when guns are around. Or that suicide risk goes up by a factor of something like three to five when a gun is kept in the house. Or that drivers with guns in their cars are more likely to drive aggressively and more prone to road rage.[9] I thought about all this as I sat in Freedom Hall listening to Wayne LaPierre, the NRA's longtime CEO, deliver a phrase so familiar to the membership that they recited it with him:

*The surest way to stop a bad guy with a gun is a good guy with a gun.*

Good guys versus bad guys, just like the movies. Sometimes it really is as pure as that, pure as white hats and black hats, Clint Eastwood or John Wayne running the dirtbags out of town. But then there's all the mess and confusion of the rest of life, with our soft and tender egos in the middle of it. Human nature being what it is, most of us contain sufficient good and bad in ourselves that we can recall a crisis in our lives and be grateful that there wasn't a gun nearby. Or remember to our everlasting regret that there was. Just as I can imagine scenarios where I'd feel foolish and reckless for not having a gun, I can conceive of just as many where I'd be the world's biggest fool for having one.

But in NRA Land the lines are always bright and clear: us against them, good versus bad, American versus villain. "We, in this room, we ARE America," insisted Wayne, whose gulpy, cat-coughing-up-a-hairball delivery belied the clench of a man in drastic need of breathing lessons. A listener hoping for nuance or even coherence would be disappointed with his speech, which hacked out a steady drumbeat of fear and alarm. He warned of those "other rooms" where "political and media elites at the highest levels" are conspiring to destroy the Second Amendment, and with it "our core

---

[9] *Ibid.* See also "Statistics on the Dangers of Gun Use for Self-Defense," Giffords Law Center to Prevent Gun Violence, posted May 11, 2015, http://lawcenter.giffords.org/dangers-of-gun-use-for-self-defense-statistics/; Evan DeFilippis and Devin Hughes, "The Myth of the Good Guy with a Gun," Slate, January 25, 2015; Christopher Mele, "Firearms and Drivers, a Lethal Combination," *New York Times,* May 26, 2017; Eli Gottlieb, "The Guns That Won," *New Republic,* April 2016.

values, our freedom." "A Clinton White House would be a cesspool for NBC, ABC, and CBS elitists to plan programming and orchestrate interviews to bombard the airwaves against our freedom." Elitists are "shredding the very fabric of our country," "seizing and destroying all the freedoms and values we care about most," and planning to "put the full weight of a weaponized IRS, ATF, EPA, Interior Department, and every other federal agency behind attacks against groups and people they don't like . . ." If Hillary wins, "it's *game over* for everyone in this room, and everything that we all care about."

It seems safe to say that the paranoid style in American politics is alive and well. All of the classic elements that Hofstadter described in his 1964 essay were on full and florid display at Louisville's Freedom Hall: conspiracy, persecution, apocalypticism, the characterization of political difference not as a matter of good-faith give-and-take, but a final showdown between absolute good and absolute evil. "We will save freedom!" Wayne shouted in closing. "And America truly will be America again!" He ceded the podium to Chris Cox, executive director of the NRA's Institute for Legislative Action, who, after slamming Hillary for "defending violent felons and crack dealers against law-abiding citizens"—clearly a man born to dog-whistle, is young Chris Cox—announced the NRA's official endorsement of Donald Trump for president, and Trump himself sauntered onto the stage to thunderous cheers.

In that long-ago essay, Hofstadter took pains to point out that the U.S. has never had a monopoly on the paranoid style. As proof, he cited the one instance in modern history of the paranoid style's "consummatory triumph," a distinction that belongs to Germany in the era of the Third Reich.[10] "Voice or no voice, the people can always be brought to the bidding of the leaders," Hermann Goering, the number two man in the Reich, once observed. "That is easy. All

---

[10] Hofstadter, *The Paranoid Style in American Politics*, p. 7.

you have to do is tell them they are being attacked, and denounce the pacifists for lack of patriotism and exposing the country to danger. It works the same in every country."[11]

**IN LOUISVILLE I SOUGHT OUT TRACES OF ANOTHER NATIVE SON** of the city, a near contemporary of Hunter Thompson's. I went to this Louisvillian's childhood home on Grand Avenue, a neat, modest, one-story pink house with a historical marker out front. I saw the gym where he trained as a youth, and toured the museum and cultural center that bears his name. Two weeks later I would turn on the TV and see these places swamped with crowds mourning a good man's death, and would feel the faint tingle of the uncanny running up my neck. The little house and the fine modern museum had become, for the moment, and perhaps for all time, pilgrimage sites. I'd gone not to mourn—two weeks ago there was no death to mourn—but to come a little closer to the personification of a genuine ideal. For a real-life demonstration of independence of mind, the courage of convictions, and rugged American individualism, you would be hard-pressed to find a better example than Muhammad Ali, né Cassius Marcellus Clay Jr.[12]

As a loud, proud black man in the early 1960s Ali blew out the hottest circuits in America's paranoid wiring. "The Louisville Lip" was one of the nicknames the press tagged him with, and the day after taking the heavyweight championship from Sonny Liston— the consensus going in was that Liston would destroy him—a reporter asked Clay, "Are you a card-carrying member of the Black Muslims?" "Card-carrying, what does that mean?" Clay answered. "I know where I'm going and I know the truth, and I don't have to be what you want me to be." Then he announced he was renouncing

---

[11] Gustave M. Gilbert, *Nuremberg Diary* (Farrar, Straus and Company, 1947), pp. 278–79.
[12] See Thomas Hauser, *Muhammad Ali: His Life and Times* (Simon & Schuster, 2006); Mike Marqusee, *Redemption Song: Muhammad Ali and the Spirit of the Sixties* (Verso, 1999); David Remnick, *King of the World* (Vintage Books, 1999).

his last name, the name that his ancestors may have taken from the white people who once owned them. "I will be known as Cassius X."

Which would soon become Muhammad Ali. White America, mainstream America, freaked. The lip, the pride, the swagger, the refusal to talk nice and stay down, the association with a strange and radical-seeming faith—Ali wasn't acting like a black man was supposed to act. Eventually his Muslim faith would lead him to decline to participate in the latest venture of that "primary industry" that Hunter Thompson talked about, otherwise known as the Vietnam War. At a time when paranoid delusions were driving the U.S. into a criminal and monumentally catastrophic war, Ali saw the thing for the fraud it was. His was a mind free of unreasoning fear, which isn't to say that he had nothing to fear. By refusing to serve in the wartime military, Ali faced the loss of pretty much everything a person can hold dear: freedom, livelihood, hard-earned renown. Within an hour of his formal refusal to be inducted into the army, he was stripped of his world championship title and his boxing license—thus his means of making a living—and would face criminal charges that eventually led to conviction and the maximum penalty allowed by law: a $10,000 fine and five years in federal prison.

"I strongly object," he said on the day he was stripped of his title, "to the fact that so many newspapers have given the American public and the world the impression that I have only two alternatives in taking this stand—either I go to jail or go to the Army. There is another alternative, and that alternative is justice."

He could have taken the easy way out. The Louisville businessmen who'd sponsored his start in professional boxing had arranged for him to serve in the National Guard. Mort Susman, the U.S. attorney whose office prosecuted Ali, had gotten a "strong indication" from the army that Ali could serve in a noncombat role; he would be assigned to "Special Services," where his duty would consist of visiting troops and putting on exhibition matches. Ali refused. His lawyers advised him that he would likely go to jail, and it was almost certain that his boxing career was over. He had to surrender his passport, which denied him the chance to box overseas. He was under surveillance by the FBI and U.S. Army Intelligence. He was denounced by the sports media, the mainstream news media, Jackie Robinson, U.S. senators and congressmen, and an official proclamation passed by the Kentucky state senate. People called his house to say they hoped he'd die. After his conviction, during the years when his case was winding through appeals to the Supreme Court, he continued to speak vigorously against the war, white supremacy, injustice of every kind. "I wanted America to be America," as he explained it years later.

He lost much. For a while it looked like he might lose everything. What did he gain? Bill Russell, one of the African-American sports stars who counseled Ali as his trial date approached, told us what years later:

> *Philosophically, Ali was a free man. Besides being probably the greatest boxer ever he was free. And he was free at a time when historically it was very difficult to be free no matter who you were or what you were. Ali was one of the first truly free people in America.*[13]

---

[13] Hauser, *Muhammad Ali*, pp. 178–79.

# BOOK OF DAYS

JULY

Taliban insurgents bomb a convoy of police cadets outside of Kabul, killing thirty-three. Elie Wiesel dies at age eighty-seven. Accompanied by five lawyers, Hillary Clinton undergoes a voluntary three-and-a-half-hour interview at FBI headquarters as part of the agency's investigation into her private email server. ISIS militants kill twenty-eight during an eleven-hour standoff in Dhaka, Bangladesh, targeting foreigners while taking care not to harm their Bangladeshi hostages. A minivan packed with explosives blows up during Ramadan celebrations in central Baghdad, killing more than two hundred, and ISIS claims responsibility; when Iraqi prime minister Haider al-Abadi visits the devastated neighborhood, residents pelt his convoy with rocks, shoes, and buckets. Trump calls the Clinton campaign "ridiculous" for characterizing as anti-Semitic Trump's retweet of an anti-Clinton meme depicting the Star of David atop a pile of cash, an image that previously appeared on a white-supremacist message board filled with anti-Semitic messages. FBI director James Comey announces that the FBI will not recommend criminal charges against Clinton regarding her use of a private email server to handle classified information. In an unusually detailed public accounting of the investigation, Comey states, "Although we did not find clear evidence that Secretary Clinton or her colleagues intended to violate laws governing the handling of classified information, there is evidence that they were extremely careless in their handling of very sensitive, highly classified information." In response to Comey's announcement, Trump says, "Today is the best evidence ever that we've seen that our system is absolutely, totally rigged." Israel authorizes the construction of hundreds of new homes in Jewish settlements in the West Bank and East Jerusalem, ISIS is using apps to sell sex slaves, and an ISIS suicide bomber on a bike kills ten people outside a bakery in Lebanon. A gun shop in Illinois announces that it will auction off an AR-15 rifle and donate the proceeds to victims of the Pulse nightclub shooting. The White House pledges to increase a $30 billion military aid package to Israel, and Clinton announces a proposal to eliminate in-state tuition at public colleges and universities for families with annual incomes under $125,000. Police in Baton Rouge shoot a black man, Alton Sterling, whom they had tasered and pinned to the ground, later alleging that he was reaching for the gun in his pocket; protests erupt across the city as authorities plead for calm, and federal law enforcement is asked to take over the investigation. The Justice Department formally closes its investigation into Clinton's emails. House Speaker Paul Ryan says that it appears Clinton got "special treatment," Senator Cornyn of Texas promotes legislation to strip Clinton of her security clearance, and FBI director Comey is called to appear before the House Oversight and Government Reform Committee. Media report that Clinton's campaign aired over twenty-two thousand commercials in battleground states during June while the Trump campaign aired none. Senators Bob Corker and Joni Ernst withdraw from consideration for Trump's VP pick. "A lot of people are calling me that you wouldn't even think about," Trump says of his VP contenders. "They want to have their names thrown into the hat." Philando Castile, a black man, is shot and killed during a traffic stop in Falcon Heights, Minnesota, and his girlfriend Diamond Reynolds uses Facebook to live-stream the immediate aftermath of the shooting, in which she can be heard saying calmly to the police officer, "You just shot four bullets into him, sir. He was just getting his license and registration, sir," and "He was reaching for his wallet and the officer just shot him," and "The police just shot my boyfriend for no apparent reason." During a Black Lives Matter march in downtown Dallas, five white and Hispanic police officers are shot dead and seven are wounded, along with two civilians; the lone shooter, Micah Johnson, a black man and army veteran described as having a hatred of white people, is killed by a robot-deployed bomb. Vigils, protests, and prayer services are held throughout the country. "We have broken into tribes," says Charlie Beck, police chief of Los Angeles. Black Lives Matter is "a terrorist group committing hate crimes," says Rush Limbaugh. "White people need to understand how African-Americans feel every day," says Hillary Clinton. "Black people are getting to a boiling point," says Ja'Mal Green, a Black Lives Matter activist. "We are tired of watching police kill our brothers and sisters. We are tired of being tired . . . [there] comes a time when black people will snap." A "vicious, calculated and despicable attack," says President Obama of the shootings. "An attack on our country," says Trump. "We must stand in solidarity with law enforcement, which we must remember is the force between civilization and total chaos. Every American has the right to live in safety and peace. We will make America safe again." Trump asks to address afternoon roll call at a midtown Manhattan police precinct to show solidarity with law enforcement, a request that the NYPD denies. "Our interest is in staying out of the politics of the moment, not to provide photo-ops," explains NYPD commissioner William Bratton. "Ark Encounter" opens in Williamstown, Kentucky, to promote "young Earth" Christian fundamentalism, and features a wooden ark one and a half football fields long and seven stories high, with an animatronic Noah and paired models of some of the animals that Noah may have taken aboard, such as bears, giraffes, and Tyrannosaurus rexes. Clinton proposes increased federal money for community health centers and outlines steps toward providing universal health care, and Trump is reported to be "increasingly intrigued" by the idea of having retired lieutenant general Michael Flynn as his running mate. Flynn does not deny that he is under consideration, and adds: "I've been a soldier too long to refuse to entertain any request from a potential commander in chief." North Korea fires what appears to be a submarine-launched ballistic missile, Iraqi government forces retake a key air base from ISIS, and the U.S. says it has cut ISIS's Twitter traffic by half in the past two years. The UK government's Chilcot inquiry releases a 2.6-million-word report on the Iraq War, concluding that the invasion was based on fabricated intelligence that might have been inspired by the 1996 action film *The Rock*. Osama bin Laden's son threatens revenge against the U.S. for killing his father. Snoop Dogg addresses graduating cadets at Los Angeles Police Department headquarters, and later explains: "This is how you make moves. You make it happen. You get some dialogue, some understanding with the new recruits before they hit the streets, so that way they know we're just like them and we're trying to live and go home and get some understanding." At least 100 Black Lives Matter protestors are arrested in St. Paul, and 120 are arrested in Baton Rouge. President Obama deploys an additional 560 U.S. troops to aid Iraq in retaking Mosul, Iraq's second-largest city, from ISIS. Anti-Trump forces within the GOP mount a "Free the Delegates" effort, hoping to change party rules to allow convention delegates to vote for the nominee of their choice regardless of their state's primary results. Sanders endorses Clinton in a joint appearance in Portsmouth, New Hampshire, where some Sanders supporters jeer and display signs reading, "Won't Vote Hillary." Gun-control advocates begin a forty-nine-hour sit-in near Senator Marco Rubio's Orlando office, and Brazil provides $24 million in additional funds to boost security for the Olympics. Joined onstage by George and Laura Bush, Michelle Obama, Joe Biden, Senators Cornyn and Cruz, Dallas mayor Mike Rawlings, Dallas police chief David Brown, and numerous others, President Obama speaks at an interfaith service in Dallas: "The deepest fault lines of our democracy have suddenly been exposed, perhaps even widened . . . Faced with this violence, we wonder if the divides of race in America can ever be bridged . . . I'm here to insist that we are not as divided as we seem." Supreme Court justice Ruth Bader Ginsburg calls Trump a "faker" who "really has an ego" in a CNN interview, arguably violating canon 5 of the Code of Judicial Conduct prohibiting federal judges from endorsing or opposing a candidate for public office. In advance of the Republican National Convention, Cleveland announces plans to triple its sixteen-hundred-member police force by recruiting police from Ohio and other states. Congress adjourns for a seven-week recess after failing to pass routine budget bills and legislation to combat the Zika virus. In Nice, France, a nineteen-ton truck driven by Tunisian native Mohamed Lahouaiej Bouhlel plows through a crowd celebrating Bastille Day, killing at least eighty-four and injuring over three hundred. Bouhlel also opens fire on the crowd before being shot to death by police. "The terrorist nature of the attack cannot be denied," says French president François Hollande. Trump picks Indiana governor Mike Pence to be his running mate. Newt Gingrich calls for a program to "test every person here who is of Muslim background" and to deport those who "believe in sharia." An estimated 265 soldiers and civilians are killed and over 1,400 injured in Turkey as pro-government forces thwart a nighttime coup d'état attempt against President Recep Erdoğan in which fighter jets bomb tanks on the streets of Ankara, and a military helicopter used by the coup plotters is blown up in midair. Thousands of military personnel accused of taking part in the coup attempt are arrested, and 2,745 judges are dismissed. "I must say it does not appear to be a very brilliantly planned or executed event," comments Secretary of State John Kerry amid speculation that the coup attempt was a hoax to enable Erdoğan to consolidate power. ISIS issues a statement claiming that Mohamed Bouhlel was an ISIS "soldier." Gavin Long, a black man and marine veteran, shoots six law enforcement officers in Baton Rouge, killing three, before being shot and killed himself. The day after Micah Johnson killed five police officers in Dallas, Long posted a video on YouTube calling the shootings "justice" and endorsing violence. "If you all want to keep protesting, do that, but for the real ones, the alpha ones, we know what it's gonna take. It's only fighting back or money. That's all they care about. Revenue and blood." The day before the start of the Republican National Convention, one hundred women are photographed standing naked on the banks of Cleveland's Cuyahoga River to protest "the hateful repressive rhetoric of many in the Republican Party towards women and minorities," in the words of the photographer, Spencer Tunick. Of the nineteen RNC speakers listed as "headliners," six are named Trump. Other speakers include former navy SEAL Marcus Luttrell, 1980s sitcom actor Scott Baio, pro golfer Natalie Gulbis, PayPal founder Peter Thiel, and Dana White, president of the Ultimate Fighting Championship. A former U.S. intelligence official reveals that pornography comprises 80 percent of the material on jihadists' captured laptops. Melania Trump delivers a speech on the opening night of the Republican Convention in which substantial passages match word for word the speech given by Michelle Obama at the 2008 Democratic Convention. George W. Bush tells a gathering of former staffers in Dallas that he fears he'll be the last Republican president. Turkey's government fires tens of thousands of teachers, university deans, and others accused of having ties to the U.S.-based Muslim cleric Fethullah Gulen, whom President Erdoğan accuses of masterminding the attempted coup. Trump receives the Republican Party's nomination for president, Ted Cruz is booed and given the finger by convention delegates for telling his supporters to "vote your conscience," and Breitbart News technology editor Milo Yiannopoulos is banned from Twitter for "participating in or inciting targeted abuse of individuals." Roger Ailes, who began his media career as a cue-card holder for *The Mike Douglas Show,* who was instrumental in resurrecting Richard Nixon's political career in 1968, who taught a long line of political clients the art of speaking in "kickers," who studied the Nazi propaganda films of Leni Riefenstahl, who advised Ronald Reagan, George H. W. Bush, Rudolph Giuliani, and Donald Trump, who kept guns and ammunition hidden in the thick wooden door of his office, who ordered the removal of all the trees around his Garrison, New York, house in order to have a clear view of "any leftist assault teams preparing to rush the house," who reportedly called a fellow executive a "little fucking Jew prick" while working at NBC, and who as head of Fox News directed the most influential force in American conservatism for the past twenty years, is forced to resign from Fox two weeks after former Fox News anchor Gretchen Carlson sues him for sexual harassment. Donald Trump delivers an acceptance speech to the Republican National Convention in which he speaks the phrase "law and order" no fewer than five times, and promises that "the crime and violence that today afflicts [sic] our country will soon come to an end." In North Miami, Florida, Charles Kinsey, a therapist and an African-American, is shot by police while trying to coax his autistic patient back to the facility from which he'd wandered. Video shows Kinsey lying flat on his back with his hands in the air, calling to police officers, "All he [the patient] has is a toy truck in his hand. That's all it is. There's no need for guns." Seconds later an officer fires three times, hitting Kinsey in the leg. "Sir, why did you shoot me?" Kinsey later recalls asking the officer, who, according to Kinsey, answered, "I don't know." Hillary Clinton selects Senator Tim Kaine as her running mate, and Wikileaks releases twenty thousand Democratic Party emails that include discussions amid ostensibly impartial party officials on how to undermine Bernie Sanders's primary campaign. An eighteen-year-old gunman with both German and Iranian citizenship kills nine people at a mall in Munich, Germany, then kills himself. Democratic Party chairwoman Debbie Wasserman Schultz resigns on the eve of the party's convention. The FBI investigation into possible state-sponsored Russian hacking of the Democratic Party's computer networks expands to determine whether aides and organizations close to Hillary Clinton were also attacked. Trump is dismissive of the idea that Russia may be aiding his campaign, and on CNN, Paul Manafort calls it "crazy," saying, "I don't even know what you're talking about." Hillary Clinton becomes the first woman to be nominated for president by a major political party as advisers debate whether to change her campaign slogan from "I'm With Her" to "She's With Us." "Russia, if you're listening, I hope you're able to find the thirty thousand emails that are missing," Trump says during a press conference in Doral, Florida, referring to Clinton's deleted emails. "I think you will be mightily rewarded by our press." At the same press conference Trump indicates a willingness to recognize Crimea as Russian territory and to lift economic sanctions imposed by the Obama administration in response to Russia's annexation of Crimea. Directly addressing Trump from the podium of the Democratic Convention, Khizr Khan, an American lawyer whose son, an army captain, was killed in Iraq in 2004, says: "You have sacrificed nothing and no one." Two French teenagers of Algerian ancestry stab to death an eighty-five-year-old priest as he celebrates Mass in St.-Étienne-du-Rouvray; ISIS releases videos in which the two young men pledge allegiance to the group. Wearing a suit of brilliant white, Hillary Clinton accepts the Democratic Party's nomination for president in a speech that the Trump campaign instructs its supporters not to watch, telling them to send money to Trump's campaign instead, and during which Bill Clinton falls asleep. "We," Hillary Clinton tells the convention, "begin a new chapter tonight."

# CLEVELAND FEAR
# FACTORY

### 1.

So after a miserable couple of months for everyone who gives a damn
about peace, love, and understanding, and with more bad news soon
on the way from Baton Rouge, the word came down from Cleveland: no tennis balls. For the sake of public safety and national security, no tennis balls would be allowed in the *cordon sanitaire* around
the Quicken Loans Arena, "the Q," site of the Republican National
Convention. Same for water guns, toy guns, knives, rope, tape, metal-
tipped umbrellas, lightbulbs, gas masks, and several dozen other
items. Guns, however, were authorized. A week after five police
officers were shot dead in Dallas at a Black Lives Matter march,
Cleveland was duty-bound to follow Ohio's open-carry statute.

"Our intent is to follow the law," said a stiff-lipped Mayor Jackson. "And the law says you can have open carry, that's what it says.
Whether I agree with it or not is another issue."

Guns allowed, but *no tennis balls.* Let the word go forth: America has lost its mind! Walking down Euclid Avenue on the second
day of the convention, along a raucous city block of bars and tourist

joints and sidewalk peddlers pushing T-shirts and Trump-related campaign junk, I came upon a skinny, stringy-haired street preacher raging at the heathen through the amplifier rigged to his God-truck, an apocalypse-mobile decorated with photos of aborted fetuses, starving Africans, scrawl-painted Bible verses, and other visual aids. But that wasn't God talking back at him from above, but a large black woman leaning out her window hollering, "Preach love! Preach love! Preach love!" and "You don't know *nothin'* about being a woman in this world!" A debate between prophets, while right around the corner MSNBC was broadcasting live from a pop-up studio, political blather booming up and down Fourth Street.

What is it about America, that every public happening becomes a carnival of the sordid and sublime, and discourse has degraded to the point where basic decency counts as sublime. When the Art of Rap concert in Dallas was canceled after the police shootings, Chuck D, front man for Public Enemy, had this to say to the *Dallas Morning News:*

> "It's understandable," said the man who wrote "Fight the Power" in 1989. "Those officers were out there securing a Black Lives Matter protest."
>
> He paused.
>
> "There's nothing can be said here. We have to let it rest for a while . . . To go in there Saturday? That would be inappropriate."

But America can't shut up or slow down for a second, and so we rolled past Dallas, past Black Lives and Blue Lives and Baton Rouge on Sunday morning with three cops dead and three more wounded, this only days after Philando Castile was shot dead in St. Paul and Alton Sterling in Baton Rouge, and eighty killed in Nice, France, by a terrorist in a truck, and bombings in Baghdad, ISIS attacks in Bangladesh, and a failed coup in Turkey with hundreds of casualties.

Where would the hammer fall next? Maybe Cleveland was next. So we took a deep breath, and . . . welcome to Cleveland! Where the Trump movement arrived on a rumbling tidal surge (nothing so crisp or cleansing as an actual *wave*), a molasses-thick swash carrying all manner of bottom sludge, including 37 primary and caucus wins, 1,543 delegates amassed, gazillions of dollars' worth of "free media coverage," and the shattered wreckage and random personal effects of what was once the GOP establishment. It all washed up on the shores of Lake Erie and backed into the channel of the Cuyahoga River that so famously burned in 1969, emblem of Rust Belt decline when Cleveland was the butt of a thousand jokes.

Nobody laughs at Cleveland now. It has a spiff downtown, a happening hipster scene, and royalty—and an NBA championship—to its name. King James lives here, James as in LeBron, and now an aspirant to the biggest throne of all was squalling into town. Trump, one suspected, didn't really want to be president; only monarch

Another normal day in Cleveland. Courtesy of the author

would do, and so we tried to imagine His American Majesty's style, the *ne plus ultra* plumage of a Trump presidency with its slathers of gold gilt and reflective glass, the aesthetic of, say, a 1970s mid-level mobster from Buffalo, with Real Housewives updates of high tech and glitz. Richard Nixon, raised a Quaker, went hard for royal pomp, with the presidential seal stamped on everything from cufflinks to golf carts, and trumpeters in livery announcing his entrance and exit. Nixon came within a whisker of madness—is imperial style a marker of mental instability? Safe to say Trump's would not be a modest presidency.

"How many law enforcement and people have to die because of a lack of leadership in our country?" Trump posted on Facebook that afternoon. He burned hotter on Twitter. The country was "divided and out of control." Obama "doesn't have a clue." "Our country is a divided crime scene, and it will only get worse!" And on this mild, sunny Sunday afternoon in Cleveland, sniper teams were visible on downtown rooftops, concrete barriers in the streets made cabbies gnash their teeth, and a small plane circled lazily overhead, dragging a "Hillary For Prison 2016" banner. Police were everywhere, in massive force: on foot, on horseback, cruising the streets in bike packs à la the Tour de France, and private cops nervous as cats manned security checkpoints. Clumps of honey-colored horse shit decorated the asphalt. Conventioneers wandered about getting the lay of the land, many sporting "Don't Trust the Liberal Media" buttons. Stephen Loomis, president of Cleveland's police union, called on Governor Kasich to suspend Ohio's open-carry gun laws, telling CNN he didn't care if it was constitutional or not. The governor demurred.

**2.**

At five P.M., some two hundred of the media gathered in Meeting Room 1 of the Cleveland Convention Center, a square, windowless room done up in neutral grays and blues, as antiseptic as an archival box. The big-screen TV in front was tuned to live coverage of Obama's press conference on the Baton Rouge shootings. As people entered and saw the TV, their voices dropped to whispers. Many in the media had received, or been offered, "civil unrest" training by our employers, which included instruction on situational awareness, crowd dynamics, riot police tactics, and personal protective gear. A number of avowedly militant groups with conflicting agendas were expected in Cleveland this week. "I think you'd have riots," Trump had answered some weeks ago when asked what would happen if the convention denied him the nomination, and many thousands of his supporters had vowed to converge on Cleveland, ready to raise hell should the need arise.

Obama concluded his remarks. The TV was switched off, and several white men took their seats at the table in front. "Our thoughts and prayers go out to Baton Rouge," said Jeff Larson, CEO of the 2016 Republican National Convention, a jowly, unconfident, middle-aged man with a hedgehog ruff of hair down the center of his skull. Thoughts, prayers, hope, healing, this is the theater of atrocity aftermath that plays with numbing regularity in America, a chloroforming of the soul that is its own horror show. Larson moved from expressions of grief and condolence to name-checking tomorrow's featured speakers, then to a description of the stage at the Q, the seventeen hundred panels that comprised the onstage electronic screen. "We're very proud," Larson said of the high-tech stage, a hint of beseeching in his voice. Paul Manafort, the campaign's chairman and chief strategist, sat next to Larson with his hands folded neatly on the table, his face tuned to the studiously bland expression of a sharper with a thousand tricks up his sleeve. A big, broad-shouldered guy, Manafort looked a bit of the lug with his thick neck and blocky linebacker's head, his moose face topped by flawless bourbon brown hair. As a longtime K Street lobbyist and Republican operative he would seem to embody the very Washington establishment that

Trump was promising to take down, and there was in fact an insider's diffidence to Manafort, the reserved, selectively confiding manner of a pro who does his best work in luxury hotel bars and the private back rooms of fine-dining restaurants. Tomorrow, when Manafort calls Governor Kasich "dumb" for not endorsing Trump, Kasich aide John Weaver will respond in an email to reporters:

> *Manafort's problem after all those years on the lam with thugs and autocrats, is that he can't recognize principle and integrity. I do congratulate him, though, on a great pivot at the start of the convention after such a successful vice-presidential launch [i.e., Trump's rambling introduction of Mike Pence as his vice presidential running mate]. He has brought great professionalism, direct from Kiev, to Trump world.*

One did not get the warm and fuzzies from Paul Manafort. He was all business when it came his turn to speak, borderline Jersey brusque as he informed us "this is a Trump convention, the party is united," and the "Super PAC–funded" anti-Trump forces had been "crushed" in Rules Committee. His voice was throaty, street-rough, and his *the*s kept slumping toward the Rocky Balboa *duh*. And so, "We will be getting to know Trump the man" was almost "Trump duh man." "The/duh historic nature of the/duh convention will be in the/duh family members appearing to talk about Trump." "The/duh failed policies of the/duh Obama-Clinton administration." He fielded questions dutifully, parried with impatience. "Donald Trump will be Donald Trump. To say he'll be scripted, I mean . . ." He finished with a snort. *I mean, only a moron would even ask.*

Manafort came across as a work in progress, a classic behind-the-scenes guy who had yet to adjust to the light, and it was at this Sunday briefing that he made the first of several curious slips. The convention's theme for Monday night, he told us, was "make the company safe again," then he instantly amended, "make the *country* safe again," plowing straight-faced through the giggles and titters of the press. At Monday morning's briefing, the slip was even weirder. The convention was "an opportunity to present Donald Trump to a broader spectrum of the American people," Manafort said, "to present parts of his bad personality—of his biography, that people might not be aware of." The press gasped, laughed. Heads swiveled. Did he really just . . . ? Manafort acknowledged his goof with the briefest of smiles and pattered on, soon to misspeak again when he called Jeff Larson "John Larson," a garden-variety goof, admittedly, but still; presumably Manafort and Larson had been working together for months.

It served no purpose to speculate on Manafort's slips of the tongue, though their precision, their breathtaking aptness to the moment, smacked of the uncanny. Were Freudian slips back in fashion? This was information as vapor, effluent rising from the bogs of the subconscious, off-limits even to a reporter with a fiction habit. But those vapors would take on form and substance in the coming months as we discovered the sorts of high-end bottom feeding that were Manafort's bread and butter. "Off the books" payouts from Ukraine, labyrinthine corporate structures and money flows, the client list that included authoritarian torturers and police-state oligarchs— clients that might charitably be called "bad personalities"—this was the world where Manafort plied his lobbyist's trade. And so we can hardly imagine the contempt with which a player like Manafort must view our mainstream world of "I VOTED" stickers and civics-class flow charts on how a bill becomes a law. What a bunch of chumps we must seem with our elections and democratic institutions, our cherished rule of law. We think those things matter, that *we* matter. My God, a nation of idiots. How could Manafort *not* hold us in the deepest contempt, but it was his job, at least for the moment, to play to the chumps. But what a strain, even for a seasoned pro. Those pinpoint slips of the tongue could be read as flashes of Manafort's truth slipping out, spasms of scorn for this joke election he'd signed on for.

John Weaver sent up a flare, *direct from Kiev.* Manafort's Ukraine connections were generally no great secret, but one wonders how much Weaver, and by extension the professional Republican class, knew of specifics. That Trump had spent the primary season promising to drain the Washington swamp hadn't exactly sent the influence industry running for cover. "Reluctant Lobbyists Descend on Cleveland," the *Hill* reported in its July 18 convention issue, an article that suggested the industry's "lightened social calendar" had more to do with Trump's poor general-election prospects than the possibility of swamp-draining in Washington. "Half the people running the thing [Trump's campaign] are lobbyists," one member of the tribe told the *Hill,* "so I don't know that they have to stay low."

In this light, the militantly populist Trump rally I attended at Settler's Landing Park on Monday seemed as quaint as a whistle-stop campaign from the 1940s. This was the "America First Unity Rally" on the banks of the Cuyahoga, cohosted by the political provocateurs Roger Stone and Alex Jones, and sponsored by, among others, Tea Partiers for Trump, Bikers for Trump, Christians for Trump, Women United for Trump, Vets for Trump, Truckers for Trump, and so on, the true believers, their faith in Trump undisturbed by thoughts of what might be happening at the "Private Top Investors Brunch" at the Cleveland Botanical Garden, say, or the "Red, White and Blue Western Whiskey and BBQ Reception," where "invited guests" got to mingle with members of Congress. More than once this year I'd heard the Trump phenomenon described as a peasants' revolt. Well, here they were, and they were mightily pissed off, their anger, however much of it justified—and much was—matched by their evident inability to manage even the most basic vocabulary of American politics. The mistress of ceremonies, one Tricia Cunningham, a blond, florid woman in a short-short orange dress who was described as the "godmother of the Pennsylvania Tea Party," seemed not to understand the difference between a state senator and the U.S. kind, but by God she never left her house without a gun, a copy of the Constitution, and her voter registration card in her purse. The national anthem suffered the absolute worst mangling I have ever heard, the soloist flubbing about every third word ("the rockets' red flare," "through the perilous night," etc.). One of the speakers, a New Hampshire state rep and former first sergeant in the marines, insisted in his best boot-camp snarl that this year the GOP would "take back the hill," by which I think he meant, Capitol Hill? Congress? Where the Republicans currently held majorities in both houses.

There on the grassy slopes of Settler's Landing Park I was informed by my fellow rally-goers that 9/11 was "false," that Israel "arranged" Barack Obama's election, that "we've got to take our country back," and that "the liberal media is portraying Trump as a racist for wanting to secure our borders, and it's not right and totally unfair." Onstage, Ken Crow, a talk-radio personality with a genial, down-home Midwestern drawl and a big black Stetson on his head, told the assembled, "You are Hillary Clinton's and Barack Obama's worst nightmare. You carry Bibles. You cling to your guns." Trump's diversity director, a slightly hysterical African-American man with conked-straight hair, passionately slammed the African-American Democratic congressman Elijah Cummings. Kelli Ward, Tea Party candidate for the U.S. Senate seat currently held by John McCain ("the maverick of mediocrity," "the ultimate insider"), told us "constitutional isn't optional," and she was "ready to mix the mortar to secure the border." "And as a family doctor I have to say," she continued, "we need to make America healthy again, and the first step is *full repeal* of Obamacare!"

Big whoops for full repeal of Obamacare. A stiff breeze kept the flags snapping prettily, a battalion's worth of stars and stripes and almost as many of the "Don't Tread On Me" variety. Every other person seemed to be wearing a "Hillary For Prison" T-shirt. The place was a bazaar of overpriced political merchandise, hats, shirts, flags, buttons, posters, yard signs. People wore pistols on their hips. They had knives strapped to their belts. A scuffle near the stage turned out to have Geraldo Rivera and his cameraman at the center. "Be nice," Ken Crow urged the restless crowd. A shirtless kayaker paddled up behind the stage and observed for a while, orienting his boat so that the sun could tan his belly. "Need Prayer? The Knee-Party" read someone's T-shirt. "Tyranny Response Team" said another, and someone else carried a sign, "Donald Trump Has Been Delivered From Hell Now He Wants To Deliver America From Hillary Clinton." A man dragged a big wooden cross through the crowd and no one batted an eye. Then Alex Jones took the stage, and suddenly we weren't in Cleveland anymore.

We were . . . where were we? Imagine you go to an amusement park. Imagine you eat some magic mushrooms. Imagine you board one of those little boats that takes you into the tunnel of frights, and maybe you're just naturally a little bit paranoid to begin with? And your gondolier for the trip is a chesty fellow with a booming depth charge of a voice reminiscent of the pro-wrestling school of public speaking, and he's wearing Ray-Bans, frat-bro khakis, and a navy blue blazer, and with his girth and receding hairline and potato-plain face he could be the long-lost brother of Jim and John Belushi. He is a boat-rocker—*hold tight!* He might even be out of his mind. "The Mad Gondolier" could be the name of this ride, and off you go into a lurid underground world filled with "RE-ANIMATED POLITICAL CORPSES POSING AS LIBERALS," creatures who are "ANTI-FREE SPEECH, ANTI-FREEDOM **SCUM** WHO NEED TO TAKE THEIR **ASS** BACK TO **NORTH KOREA!!!!!!!**" We have entered a world where the mainstream media "ARE TRYING TO GET A RACE WAR GOING," and "GEORGE SOROS IS TRYING TO OVERTHROW UKRAINE AND EVERYWHERE ELSE," and "ANY COUNTRY THAT TRIES TO BE FREE THESE **GLOBALISTS** COME IN AND

THEY CAUSE A BUNCH OF **DIVISION** AND THEY STIR UP A BUNCH OF **RACISM** AND THEY GET EVERYBODY **FIGHTING** WITH EACH OTHER!!!!!"

The gondolier is really going now, and the crowd is roaring, and off to the side some young men put shofars to their lips and emit a *hnneee*-woooo sort of tuba hoot.

"THESE ARE THE PEOPLE WHO ARE CONQUERING US!!!!!!" the gondolier screams, the same people who are "FUNDING GUN CONTROL DOMESTICALLY AND OPEN BORDERS!!!!!" He steps back, has a huff and a puff. Easily winded is our mad gondolier, he blows hot and hard. "Well," he growls, regrouping, "you know what," the voice rises, "IT ISN'T WORKING, ALL THIS GARBAGE HAS **BROUGHT AMERICA TOGETHER!!!!!**" He squares his shoulders, huffs, puffs. *Hnnneee*-woooo go the horns. "DONALD TRUMP IS SURGING IN **EVERY MAJOR POLL** ACROSS THE **COUNTRY!!!!** NATIONALISM, SOVEREIGNTY, TRUE FREE-MARKET CAPITALISM IS **RISING** WORLDWIDE AS THE GLOBALISTS TRY TO IMPLEMENT THEIR WORLD GOVERNMENT WELL, IT IS **DEAD ON ARRIVAL!!!!!!!!**"

*Hnneee*-woooo. The crowd is bonkers. They're getting just what they came for, a massive wingdinger of an InfoWars smackdown. Alex Jones is undefeated at one-on-none.

"HAVE WE NOT DEFEATED THE PEOPLE WHO THOUGHT THEY'D SHUT DOWN OUR FREE SPEECH?" he thunders. "HAVE WE NOT GIVEN THEM A BIG GIANT RED WHITE AND BLUE **MIDDLE FINGER**!!!!!!" A mighty roar rises from the slopes of Settler's Landing Park, and Jones, a man who claims that 9/11 was an inside job, that the massacre of twenty first graders and six adults at Sandy Hook Elementary School was a hoax intended to usher in strict gun-control laws, and on whose show Trump has been a featured guest multiple times, leads the crowd in a gleeful chant:

*HIL-LA-REE FOR PRISON!*
*HIL-LA-REE FOR PRISON!*

People know when they've been screwed. Not right away, maybe, and maybe they don't know exactly how, or by whom, or on which end, but sooner or later the sensory signal tickles the spinal cord and makes its way up to the brain. For thirty years the Republican base dutifully nominated every establishment candidate the party leaders put before them. They resisted the lush temptations of a Pat Buchanan, a Rick Santorum, a Michele Bachmann, and in return lost ground by virtually every measure of economic and social well-being. Screwed? Royally and to the wall. Three decades of supply-side economics, gung-ho globalization, and the biggest redistribution of wealth in history—not trickle-down, but vacuum-up—had at last brought about a reaction. Establishment be damned, the base was going its own way, and in their populist wisdom they were about to nominate a career globalist whose signature clothing line was manufactured overseas, who depended on Deutsche Bank and Russia for much of his financing, who had extensive business and personal ties to the oligarchs of the Russian police state, who imported foreigners to staff his Mar-a-Lago resort, and whose campaign, for the moment at least, was being run by a globalist tool with his own extensive network of thug oligarchs and a K Street résumé as long as a landing strip.

The peasants had picked up their pitchforks—about time!—and now they were busily stabbing themselves in the eye. It was as stupid and tragic as that. As depressing. As hopeless. How much trouble the American people might save themselves with only a modest exercise of intelligence at the ballot box. On Monday afternoon we watched the last of the last-ditch anti-Trump efforts die a loud and sloppy death on the convention floor, but first Pastor Mark Burns of South Carolina offered the opening benediction. "Republicans, we've got to be united," the good pastor admonished the delegates, "because our enemy is not other Republicans, but is Hillary Clinton and the

Democratic Party." *Enemy?* Peace to you too, brother! Several hours into the session, a voice vote on the rules package got the delegates acting like a bunch of Democrats, erupting in catcalls, standing on chairs and booing and jeering with such primal gusto that the presiding officer, Representative Steve Womack of Arkansas, simply walked away from the podium and disappeared backstage.

"ROLL-CALL VOTE! ROLL-CALL VOTE!" the anti-Trump delegates chanted. "NO!" they chanted, and "SHAME!" and "POINT OF ORDER!"

"WE WANT TRUMP!" the pro-Trumpers chanted back, along with the mindless standby that sprang to life at some long-ago Olympics and has been with us ever since, "U-S-A! U-S-A!"

At issue was the anti-Trump delegates' effort to force a roll-call vote on the motion to approve the convention rules. Seven states were needed to trigger a roll-call vote, as opposed to the regular procedure of a voice vote. Eleven states, according to Senator Mike Lee of Utah, one of the anti-Trump leaders, had signed the roll-call petition. At the root of it all was the anti-Trumpers' goal of inserting a "conscience clause" into the rules that would release the delegates from voting according to their state's primary results, a crucial change given that some 44 percent of the delegates had expressed their preference for a nominee other than Trump. At this point, the conscience clause was a dead issue; what the anti-Trumpers wanted now was a lengthy roll-call vote that would embarrass Trump and eat into the convention's evening schedule.

"The podium has been abandoned!" Senator Lee marveled to reporters on the convention floor. Amid all the racket he seemed to be speaking from a mine collapse. "This is unprecedented," he went on, milking the moment for all it was worth. "I have never seen the chair abandon his post. Maybe there was a medical emergency. Maybe his mom called with bad news from home, I don't know."

"ROLL-CALL VOTE!" chanted the anti-Trumpers.

"WE WANT TRUMP!" chanted the pro-Trumpers.

TV showed repeated shots of the forlorn and empty stage. Down on the floor there was some jostling, some hugger-mugger as tempers flared. It was the kind of rumpus that used to break out all the time at conventions, when real stuff actually happened. A demonstration that was loud enough, prolonged enough, could inspire sufficient mania to sweep the floor and change votes, but with the advent of the strictly choreographed, TV-friendly convention, this mode of democratic expression has been largely lost.

After ten minutes Womack returned to the podium, presumably having gotten his marching orders. And march he would: with his kempt silver hair, his pointy WASP looks, and the fine blue suit that might have stepped out of the pages of a Brooks Brothers catalogue, Womack was the company man from central casting. He called for "a voice vote de novo" on approving the rules. AYEs and NAYs were bellowed; to this innocent bystander they sounded basically even, but Womack called it for the AYEs, and it seemed the roof would blow off. The anti-Trumpers were back on their chairs screaming and booing. "POINT OF ORDER! POINT OF ORDER!" they cried. Womack coolly surveyed the seething floor. "Is anyone seeking recognition from the chair?" he asked with a straight face, and, oh, that really set them off. Howling and screaming, shrieks from the pits of hell it sounded like. Eventually Utah was recognized, and moved for a roll-call vote. Womack refused. Nine states had submitted petitions for the roll-call vote, he explained over the din, but three states had subsequently withdrawn their petitions. Later we would hear rumors of strong-arm tactics on the floor, of delegates physically menaced in the restrooms, but right now the convention was a howling mess. Members of the Colorado and Iowa delegations walked out. Utah and Virginia had their mics cut off, but still they cried POINT OF ORDER! POINT OF ORDER! John Barrasso, senator of Wyoming and chairman of the rules committee, stepped up to the podium amid the cheeping calls of POINT OF ORDER!

"Who's proud to be an American?" he boomed, words that

worked a kind of Manchurian-candidate magic on the Republican brain. A huge cheer went up, YAY!, and *point of order* was heard no more. The senator made a soothing, self-congratulatory speech about the excellence of the rules package, how hard and well the committee had worked, the party was unified blah blah blah. Then Barrasso's cochair, Governor Fallin of Oklahoma, spoke, and she, too, opened with the Pavlovian cue. "I have one question," she twanged from the podium. "Who out there is an American patriot that's willing to stand up and fight to make our country great again?"

A great cheer bosomed forth. When Barrasso called for a final vote on adopting the rules, the AYEs had it, hands down. If there was a single NAY from the floor, I didn't hear it.

### 3.

The rules fight sealed the deal for Trump. Short of being found in a closet with a dead boy or a live goat he would be the party's nominee, the culmination (*so far!*) of a new kind of politics in America, one that had its beginnings, coincidentally, right here in Cleveland some fifty years ago. Even as Trump was riding this politics to stupefying heights, the man who'd conceived and engineered this momentous force—indeed, the great magus of the convention itself, unseen, unheard, but everywhere at once, his genius and the herpetarium of his id alive in every berserko chant of *Build that wall!*, every roaring *Lock her up!*—was fighting for his professional life in faraway New York.

And losing; Roger Ailes was going down. Sex, and specifically, years of relentless sexual harassment, would undo this man who possessed, in photographs at least, all the sex appeal of a manatee. "The most powerful man in the world," President Obama once called him, joking, sort of. On Thursday, mere hours before Trump took the stage in Cleveland to accept the party's nomination, Ailes would resign as chairman of the media phenomenon he'd founded and built into the epically transformative force known as Fox News. But it was in Cleveland that Ailes learned his media chops, first as a prop boy and then as producer for KYW-TV's *The Mike Douglas Show,* and it was here he came to believe that TV was the most persuasive medium ever invented. In January of 1968, presidential candidate Richard Nixon was a guest on the Douglas show. Ailes got the candidate into his office before the show and said:

"Mr. Nixon, you need a media adviser."

"What's a media adviser?"

"I am."[1]

Ailes applied the techniques of middle-American daytime TV to Nixon, repackaging the fatally dour and slippery "Tricky Dick" into the reassuringly humanoid "New Nixon." At that year's convention, Nixon pitched hard to "the forgotten Americans," "the non-shouters, the non-demonstrators," the "decent people" who "work and save" and "pay their taxes," and who—Nixon aimed his "law and order" drumbeat directly at them—were mortally freaked out by the widening cracks in the established order. For Ailes, TV was all about entertainment; viewers wanted emotion, drama, conflict, and if they weren't getting it on one channel they'd switch to another. He turned politics into entertainment by putting Nixon in carefully orchestrated settings and having him pound the same few simple themes. The result was that Nixon—plodding *Nixon* of all people—became the hero that a slim majority of Americans decided they were searching for.

"The next guys up will have to be performers," Ailes confided to a friend on the eve of Nixon's election. Soon he would go even farther: someday television would effectively take the place of party politics. "The skeletons of political parties will remain," he predicted.

---

[1] See Gabriel Sherman's excellent, thoroughly sourced biography of Ailes, *The Loudest Voice in the Room* (Random House, 2017). Ailes's version of the origin story is recounted on pp. 32–33.

"But television will accelerate the breaking down of mass registration by party."[2]

If Ailes was the invisible maestro of the 2016 convention, Richard Nixon was its surprise-guest revenant. At a breakfast hosted by Bloomberg News, Paul Manafort announced that the template for Trump's acceptance speech would be Nixon's from 1968. The *New York Times* was sufficiently cloistered to view this as "a startling disclosure."[3] "It was an instructive speech," the *Times* quoted Manafort as saying. "If you go back and read, that speech is pretty much on line with a lot of the issues that are going on today." But Nixon was a disciplined political operator and undeniably brilliant man with twenty years' experience at the highest levels of politics. Trump was a realtor/developer with a checkered business record and a gaudy soap opera of a TV show. The Republican Party of 1968 would have bum-rushed Trump like a sideshow lunatic, but forty going on fifty years of Roger Ailes, the last twenty as head of the driving force in American conservatism, had transformed conservative politics into an entertainment machine. Drama + Emotion + Conflict = Entertainment = $$$ = Power. Ailes was a master practitioner of the Southern Strategy. He was the brain behind the Willie Horton ad. He launched Rush Limbaugh into TV, and helped Dan Quayle and Mitch McConnell win their Senate seats. Under Ailes's direction, Fox not only made Whitewater, Monica Lewinsky, and Swift Boat Veterans for Truth daily news, but itself played crucial roles in encouraging the underlying events. Morbidly paranoid himself, Ailes stoked the dominant right-wing phobias of the day, xeno, homo, Islamo, and, regular as the equinox, he peddled "the war on Christmas" every holiday season. He debuted Glenn Beck's show the day before Obama's first inauguration, and when Beck declared that the

---

[2] *Ibid.*, pp. 58, 71. See also p. 156: "This [TV] is the most powerful force in the world. Politics is nothing compared to this."

[3] Michael Barbaro and Alexander Burns, "In Trump's Voice, It's a New New Nixon," *New York Times*, July 19, 2016.

president had a "deep-seated hatred of white people," Ailes said of his new star, "I think he's right." Starting in 2011, Ailes gave Trump a weekly call-in segment on *Fox & Friends,* where the future candidate could ramble and weasel-word to his heart's content about Obama's birth certificate.[4]

"Fox did not have viewers. It had fans . . . To watch Fox was to belong to a tribe."[5] Which could be viewed as the fulfillment of Ailes's prophecy that TV would someday overtake political parties. By 2010, one out of every four Americans got their news from Fox. Profits were running upwards of $1 billion a year. Drama, emotion, conflict; the thrills never stopped. Politics-as-entertainment was a bestseller, and a big chunk of America was eager to be sold to. "I think what Nixon understood," Trump said shortly before Cleveland, "is that when the world is falling apart, people want a strong leader whose highest priority is protecting America first. The sixties were really bad. And it's really bad right now. Americans feel like it's chaos again."

No doubt. Dallas was bad. Baton Rouge was bad. So were Ferguson, Baltimore, St. Paul, and Staten Island. But let's be clear. A simmering civil war was being fought in America during the 1960s. Entire districts in multiple cities went up in flames, and hundreds of people died violent deaths. What we have now is bad, yes, but not "falling apart." Not "chaos." Or to put a finer point on it: the street chaos that we saw in Baltimore and Ferguson is dwarfed by the much quieter, more systematic chaos inflicted on those same streets by American institutions. Redlining, shitty schools, and a malign justice system are every bit as violent in their effects as corrupt policing and riots, but in the industry of politics-as-entertainment, riots play so much better to the target audience.

On "Make America Safe Again" night at the convention, exactly

---

[4] In addition to Sherman's *The Loudest Voice in the Room,* see Jill Lepore, "Bad News: The Reputation of Roger Ailes," *New Yorker,* January 20, 2014, and David Remnick, "Sirens in the Night," *New Yorker,* August 1, 2016.
[5] Sherman, *The Loudest Voice in the Room,* p. 291.

one (1) law enforcement officer spoke, and the issue most often cited by law enforcement across the land as their chief policy concern—enactment of meaningful gun-control laws—was hardly mentioned, and then only to skewer Hillary Clinton. The speakers presented a four-hour litany of fear, grievance, outrage, and death. There were stories of Americans killed in Benghazi, Iraq, Afghanistan; of Americans killed—some tortured first—by undocumented immigrants; of ISIS terrorists operating "in all fifty states"; of police killed by Black Lives Matter "supporters" and "a collapse of the social order." Some droned per the teleprompter, others delivered their remarks with bitter, lashing passion. Representative Mike McCaul: "Our own city streets have become the battleground." Rudy Giuliani: "Fear of being politically incorrect" resulted in "San Bernardino" and "Major Nidal." Lieutenant General Mike Flynn: "These next four years will be consumed by the perils we face." Flynn, a man practically cockeyed with spleen—surely I wasn't the only one that night to be reminded of General Jack Ripper, the rogue wingnut of *Dr. Strangelove*—vigorously led the delegates in chants of *Lock her up!* "Damn right," he said, clapping in time with the chants, "Exactly right. Nothing wrong with that."

Melania provided the only real uplift of the evening, with a performance that could be described as "understated dazzle." She wore an elegant form-fitting dress of brilliant white that she'd reportedly bought herself—no wardrobe advisers—off of Net-a-Porter. She managed to be simultaneously reserved and forthright, and spoke warmly, convincingly of her adopted country, a testimonial that couldn't help but flatter every American Exceptionalist within earshot. Listening to her praise America in her agreeable Slavic accent, it was easy to think, Yes, how true, our country is strong and good; why else does everyone want to come here? She spoke nicely of motherhood and family values. She seemed entirely poised and comfortable in herself, in the manner of a woman who knows her worth. She witnessed her husband's character in clusters of abstractions, kind, fair, caring, loyal, and so forth. She offered no stories, no anecdotes that might give life to the strings of adjectives, and the Trump children's speeches over the next several nights would have this same static quality, as if the thinking of the entire Trump camp had been formed by the verbiage of luxury real estate marketing materials. But Melania's affect was of a higher order than the text of her speech, perfectly adequate though it was. The steel wasn't just in those world-class cheekbones. She would, one sensed, emerge intact from trials that would shred the rest of the Trump clan, and she'd bring young Barron with her. If it was her fate to be the first third wife to serve as First Lady, she gave assurance that she would not dishonor the country.

### 4.

So one couldn't help groaning at the next morning's news that entire passages of her speech had been lifted from Michelle Obama's convention speech eight years ago. Somebody had screwed up, bigly, whoever's job it was to translate Melania's thoughts and feelings into public speech. This is how it works: there are sit-downs with the principal where ideas are discussed, notes taken, piths and gists absorbed, then the speechwriter goes off and writes the speech. What they'd done with Melania's speech was stupid, sloppy, lazy, childish, feckless, and stupid some more. They thought no one would *notice*? With half the world watching? Clearly, a higher power than competence had made this the winning campaign.

At the morning press briefing Manafort was understandably testy on the subject. Man was steamed. Bigly. And of course it was the first thing the press wanted to talk about.

"I'm not acknowledging any of it," Manafort huffed. "We think Melania gave a great speech. The American people responded very warmly to her speech."

But when you look at the two speeches side by side—

"These words are used by a lot of people. Look, you all are trying to distort her words, you're talking about maybe fifty words including *and*s and *but*s. Certainly these are words that many people would use in talking about family values."

The press snickered. Manafort set his jaw and glared.

"Excuse me," said a polite German lady in the row behind me, "maybe my English is not so good? But I look at those sentences and it is word for word—"

"There were fourteen hundred words in that speech and you're telling me it was word for word? Look, this is what happens time after time, as soon as Hillary Clinton is confronted with a strong female she attacks and tries to destroy that person."

The press laughed out loud at this. Manafort glowered.

Do you think Melania is being treated unfairly?

"YES I absolutely do think Melania is being treated unfairly. I don't want to discuss this anymore."

Does Donald Trump have any plans at the convention to apologize for the comments he has made about Hispanics?

"I have no idea what you're talking about," Manafort ripped. He didn't so much dodge questions as assassinate them. "He was planning to give two speeches to Hispanic groups before the convention, but these had to be canceled because of the police shootings. Those speeches have been rescheduled for after the convention."

Do you have any comment on reports of a Utah delegate being threatened in the bathroom during yesterday's roll-call fight?

Manafort might have almost smiled. "I think I have a pretty good idea of what's happening at this convention. But I haven't been checking out the bathrooms."

**POLICE KEPT ARRIVING FROM DISTANT PLACES. TEXAS. GEORGIA.** California. Many went out of their way to be friendly. Walking outside, I found myself looking up to the rooftops to check out the sniper teams, as automatic as scanning the sky for weather. Helicopters buzzed around downtown day and night. There was one particularly obnoxious unit for which I conceived a special distaste, a spidery, bone-white, clattering thing that would hover menacingly in one spot for several minutes, then streak off with great urgency toward the horizon, only to reappear a few minutes later in a different spot, hovering.

Tuesday night Trump was officially nominated, a night on which Mitch McConnell was booed when he stepped onstage, and Chris Christie led a mock prosecution of Hillary Clinton. "GUILTY!" the delegates joyfully roared to every charge. GUILTY! GUILTY! GUILTY! LOCK HER UP! LOCK HER UP! This was also the night we were instructed in life wisdom by Donald Trump Jr., who appeared at the podium looking as natty and tanned as a Palm Springs concierge. He tended to snap and bite his words, fighting the language in his mouth as he told us about "the dignity of hard work" and the values he'd learned from working with "the guys and gals" on his father's construction sites, as opposed to "the guys from Harvard and Wharton locked away in their offices from the real work." He made a serious play for blue-collar cred for himself and his siblings, saying, "We didn't learn from MBAs, we learned from people with degrees in common sense." He talked about "pouring Sheetrock," which he quickly corrected to "pouring concrete," and lauded the workers "who taught us how to drive heavy equipment, operate tractors and chain saws." That Poppa Trump "would trust his own children's formative years to these men and women says all you need to know about Donald Trump."

There are useful lessons to be learned from the sweat-hog life, that's true, though listening to Trump Jr. one wondered: Did it occur to him that the hardhats never for a second forgot he was the boss's son? And that the more typical rookie experience is having a borderline-sadistic asshole of a boss who rides you just because he can, and whatever you do you are an idiot, a moron, a dumb ass, a butthead, a worthless piece of crap and punk-ass little shit that doesn't have the brains God gave a weed?[6] Work has dignity, sure, and for those not born to the One Percent it delivers plenty of humiliation as well.

That was "Make America Work Again" night. The theme for the following evening was "Make America First Again." On this night Newt Gingrich warned of a coming apocalypse, and the giant screen behind the podium kept fritzing out, and Ted Cruz, after urging us to "cast aside anger for love," so enraged his fellow Republicans that his wife, Heidi, had to be escorted off the convention floor for her safety. Then it was Thursday, the final day, with "Make America One Again" as the climactic theme. It was also the day on which the *New York Post* reported that male prostitutes were having a banner week in Cleveland. "When it comes to anything people aren't supposed to be doing, they like to do it," one escort told the *Post*. "The Republicans have a lot of delegates in the closet, let's put it that way."[7]

The streets were more crowded and raucous than ever, and yet the vibe felt more Mardi Gras than impending doom, a weirdly jolly bounce to all the bitter politics. Young men strolled about exercising their open-carry rights, as determinedly nonchalant as the most popular girl in school showing up with a new hairstyle. Other rights were being exercised too, such as the right to stomp about Public Square with an American flag on a pole while being filmed by a hundred news cameras, and the right to carry a sign that says "Another Chump Against Trump," and the right to pull around a little wagon with a sign that says "FOOD NOT BOMBS!" and hand out free sandwiches and bottled water. Sidewalk peddlers were hawking a nasty new T-shirt, advertising the goods at the tops of

---

[6] It was in the midst of such encouragements that I learned how to back a trailer, among other arts.

[7] Alexandra Klausner, "Male Escorts Are Making Crazy Money at the RNC," *New York Post*, July 21, 2016. Female escorts reported that business was slow.

their lungs: "Hillary sucks but Monica does it better!" Pelotons of bicycle cops whooshed by, and a sly, smiling fellow walked around with a sign that read, "My Arms Are Tired of Holding Up This Sign." On Fourth Street, Alex Jones and Roger Stone were rolling out their latest product, a T-shirt with a Shepard Fairey–style portrait of Bill Clinton, and below his face, the word RAPE. *Lock her up!* the crowd chanted as Jones and Stone did their thing and the news cameras swarmed. The weather was beautiful; it had been beautiful all week. The flags were still at half-mast. Across the street from the shirt ceremony, a yoga group sat chanting *ommmm* next to a sign that offered "Trump Therapy."

EVERY NARCISSIST IS THE SUN OF HIS OWN LIFE, THE SOURCE and sum of light around which all things revolve. The dream of the narcissist, the hunger, the ultimate fulfillment, is to feel the light enlarged and reflected back on him from a justly adoring world. That final night of the convention, we witnessed the apotheosis of the narcissist's dream: the grand entrance to the soaring theme music of the action movie *Air Force One,* the crowd of thousands on their feet chanting the name, thousands of signs with the name, the name burning in giant letters on the giant video screen. TRUMP. TRUMP. TRUMP. It was happening. It was real. The fantasy, the wildest fantasy but one, had come to life, an order of transcendence that seemed to awe even Trump himself. His eyes swept the crowd as he took charge of the podium, he smiled, he shook his head several times as if saying to himself, Unbelievable. Unbelievable.

"Friends," he began, his voice ponderous, solemn, stately. For how many years, how many tens of thousands of times had he rehearsed this moment in the Q Arena of his mind?

"Friends; delegates; and fellow Americans. I humbly"—and no one had ever uttered *humbly* greater than Trump—"and gratefully"—ditto *gratefully*—"accept, your nomination, for the presidency of the United States!"

The delegates answered with a suitably frothy ruckus of applause and cheers and manic sign-wiggling, and U-S-A! U-S-A! could be heard inside the roar, and TRUMP! TRUMP! TRUMP!, and Trump looked down on it all and found it good. Thus the speech commenced, and what followed for the next seventy-seven minutes was the rhetorical equivalent of suburban sprawl. ISIS was here, murderous migrants over there, political correctness, the rigged system, and "international humiliation" plunked down there there and there like strip malls scattered about a mishmash of housing developments. You could have moved chunks of the speech around like so many interchangeable parts or even reversed the order entirely with no noticeable effect. It was a speech of serial culs-de-sac, quick spins around successive dead ends with no center, no organizing logic that might lead us to a new, and newly adequate, vision of ourselves. "Make America great again" was the ultimate dead end, a stunted vision of the future that bent back toward a mythical past whose realest incarnation might have existed in Ronald Reagan's brain, a well-scrubbed America of hardworking white people, small towns, tidy streets, and the occasional appearance by a jolly, well-mannered member of a dark-skinned minority. A social order that must have appealed quite nicely to white males of authoritarian inclination. And as for everyone else—women, "the Negroes," "Mexicans," "Indians"—well, wasn't it all very nice for them too?

Not that anybody at the convention was asking. "We can't afford to be so politically correct anymore," Trump declared. He spoke of terrorist attacks, attacks on police, chaos in our communities. "Illegals roaming free to threaten us, released by the thousands . . ." The applause shuffled forth as dutifully as traffic when the light turns green, but the magic was missing tonight, the holy-roller thunder of all those rallies that had made him the year's unstoppable force. Tonight he spoke like a man slowly suffocating, his words came from the top of his throat instead of deep in the lungs and so his voice

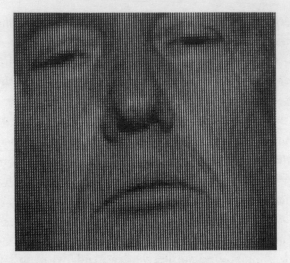

**Jumbotron, Quicken Loans Arena. Courtesy of
David Taylor**

kept guttering out in the clutch. It didn't help that he leaned so hard
on the teleprompter. Maybe it was the crutch itself that crippled
him, the script, the perceived need, for one night at least, to "act
presidential." Nixon's iconic 1968 convention speech made cut-and-
paste cameos. We heard it in "the forgotten men and women" and
"these wounded American families," and in the "law and order" re-
frain whose racist freight is always sourced to Nixon, practically
his signature phrase, second only to *I am not a crook.* "I will restore
law and order," Trump proclaimed. "I am the law-and-order candidate." "Crime and violence will soon, and I mean very soon, come
to an end."

Things perked up whenever he whaled on Hillary. "This is
the legacy of Hillary Clinton—death, destruction, terrorism, and
weakness." *Lock her up!* "Her terrible, terrible crimes." *Lock her
up!* "Corruption has reached a level like never, ever before." A large
claim. "Nobody knows the system better than me, which is why I

alone can fix it." Talk of "illegals" and "open borders" brought forth the inevitable *Build that wall!*, but it felt rote, dutiful, lacked the righteous malice that had made his rallies red zones for minorities. At thirty-five minutes we could see him sweating, the glint of a silver mustache tracking his upper lip. How much longer would he go? "Make life safe for all our citizens." "There can be no prosperity without law and order." "She is their puppet, and they pull the strings." That consummate pro Richard Nixon thought the ideal length for a political speech was twenty minutes. The '68 convention speech, the most important of his life, clocked in at thirty two min utes, but that included long, raucous ovations that frequently forced him to pause.[8] Trump's only surprise showstopper came shortly after the hour mark, when he promised to eliminate *wasteful government spending.* A thin shout-out from a few delegates down front got a smile and finger-point from Trump, and within moments the entire convention was on its feet chanting, YES YOU WILL! YES YOU WILL! YES YOU WILL!

"Wasteful government spending," now there's a cry to stoke the fires of the Republican heart! On he went, his cheeks and upper lip shiny with sweat, his poor dry mouth pooching and pursing, dredging up moisture from the depths. The rhetoric continued in cul-de-sac mode. "Repeal and replace disastrous Obamacare." "Completely rebuild our depleted military." "The replacement of our beloved Justice Scalia." "My opponent wants to essentially abolish the Second Amendment." He had to shout to get his applause lines across, and by the end he was practically lockjawed with fatigue, punched out, a runner staggering toward the finish. He'd overestimated himself, the narcissist's eternal curse. "We are going to start winning again," he bellowed. And, "History is watching us," a profundity that would do any D student proud. "I will fight for you. I will win for you."

---

[8] See Rick Perlstein, "Mr. Trump, You're No Richard Nixon," *New Republic,* July 22, 2016.

And at last, the finish line in sight. "We will make America *strong* again. We will make America *proud* again. We will make America *safe* again. And we will make America *great* again."

Again! Again! Again! Back to the future, a hard reverse into dead-end regression, the white tribe walled into the ultimate gated community: this was the vision Trump offered us. One would wager he was soaked with sweat by the end, his shirt and underwear sopping, the waist of his pants a clambake. His smile was ghastly, dry lips snagging on dry teeth. His face had the dull sheen of junkyard chrome. One wondered what Roger Ailes thought of it all, Ailes the maestro of TV optics, the guru whose Fox News spared no expense when it came to resourcing the makeup department.[9] Had we witnessed the second coming of Nixon, Ailes's original creation? But which Nixon; which future were we backing into? Trump aimed to resurrect the New Nixon of 1968, but perhaps he'd channeled the broken Nixon of 1974 instead, the Nixon who perspired so heavily during his resignation speech that when his wife and daughters went to hug him afterward, they found he'd sweated all the way through his suit jacket.

# BOOK OF DAYS

AUGUST

Tests find that levels of contamination in the waters off Rio de Janeiro in which swimmers, sailors, and windsurfers will be competing are far higher than previously suspected, and include pathogens
ranging from rotaviruses that cause diarrhea and vomiting to drug-
resistant superbacteria that can cause death. Trump complains that
he was "viciously attacked" in Khizr Khan's Democratic convention
speech, says that he will not endorse House Speaker Paul Ryan for
reelection, and kicks a crying baby out of a rally in Virginia. As
Trump's poll numbers plunge, Republican candidates for the House
and Senate seek to distance themselves from the top of the ticket,
with one GOP congressman pledging in a commercial to "stand up
to Trump." "Do we run the risk of depressing our base by repudiating the guy, or do we run the risk of being tarred and feathered by
independents for not repudiating him?" wonders one Republican
pollster. The Clinton campaign sets up a special operation to moni-
tor news accounts that Republican leaders may be considering renouncing Trump, and one poll shows her leading in the reliably
Republican state of Georgia. The *Washington Post*'s Fact Checker
has awarded its worst ranking of Four Pinocchios to 16 percent of

Clinton's statements, compared to 64 percent of Trump's. "Essentially, Clinton is the norm for a typical politician," said the head of Fact Checker, and Thomas Wells, Trump's former lawyer, said, "The man lies all the time." On the first day of sailing competition in the Rio Olympics, sailors report the water is fine. A pediatric hospital in rebel-held northern Syria is destroyed in air strikes, killing thirteen. A suicide bomber in Pakistan kills a prominent attorney, then another suicide bomber attacks the hospital where dozens of other lawyers have gathered to mourn, killing at least seventy; a faction of the Pakistani Taliban claims credit for the attacks. Fifty senior Republican national security officials sign a letter declaring that Trump "lacks the character, values and experience" to be president, "would put at risk our country's national security and well-being," and "would be the most reckless president in history." Trump calls the officials, many of whom served in the George W. Bush administration, "failed Washington elite." Senator Marco Rubio opines that women infected with the Zika virus should not have the right to an abortion, and the number of "locally acquired" cases of Zika in Florida climbs to twenty-one. At a rally in Wilmington, North Carolina, Trump seems to endorse violence against Clinton by remarking, "If she gets to pick her judges, nothing you can do, folks. Although the Second Amendment people—maybe there is, I don't know." Democratic vice presidential nominee Kaine says that the ticket is "serious" about winning Texas, a state where no Democrat has won statewide office since 1994. A nineteen-year-old man from Virginia seeking an "audience" with Trump scales the glass facade of Trump Tower up to the twenty-first floor before police pull him inside, on a day when Trump is campaigning in Virginia. The Justice Department releases a scathing 163-page report on racial bias against African-Americans by the Baltimore Police Department, including such findings as 91 percent of those arrested for "discretionary offenses" such as failure to obey or trespassing were black; 82 percent of traffic stops involve black drivers; and of pedestrians stopped at least ten times in the past five years, 95 percent were black. Trump continues to repeat his allegation that President Obama founded ISIS, dismissing a conservative radio commentator's attempt to reframe the allegation as inferring that Obama's policies led to the creation of ISIS. "No," says Trump, "I meant he's the founder of ISIS. I do. He was the most valuable player." Ukraine puts its troops on combat alert along the de facto border of Russian-occupied Crimea, ISIS uses civilians as human shields as U.S.-backed forces close in on the ISIS-occupied city of Manbij, and a public health emergency is declared in Puerto Rico due to the Zika virus. In an early morning Twitter post, Trump says he was being sarcastic in alleging that President Obama founded ISIS, then later says, "But not that sarcastic." The mayor of Cannes, France, bans full-body "burkini" swimsuits, citing security concerns. A hacker calling itself Guccifer 2.0 posts online a trove of personal and official information related to hundreds of Democratic operatives; House minority leader Nancy Pelosi receives a deluge of obscene voicemails and text messages after her cell phone numbers are posted, and investigators blame Russia for the leak. The imam of a New York City mosque and his assistant are shot in the back of the head and killed in broad daylight as they leave afternoon prayers, and the leader of another local mosque says, "Read my lips: This is a hate crime." Temperatures reach 129 degrees in Basra, Iraq, and parts of the United Arab Emirates and Iran reach a heat index of 140. Stepping outside is like "walking into a fire," commented a resident of Basra, and an Iraqi meteorologist reveals that the number of days with temperatures of 118 degrees or higher in Baghdad has more than doubled in recent years. The *New York Times* reports that Paul Manafort may have received $12.7 million in "undisclosed cash payments" from Ukraine's pro-Russia ruling party from 2007 to 2012. Trump calls for "extreme, extreme vetting" of potential Muslim immigrants and visitors, and for a Cold War–style mobilization against "radical Islamic terror," which would include increased cooperation with Russia. A

University of Texas political science professor notes that the presidential polling leader coming out of the conventions has won the last sixteen popular votes, while a hot dog vendor in Rio says "the city has never felt so safe," referencing the eighty-five thousand security personnel mustered by the Brazilian government for the Olympics. Fox's Sean Hannity devotes an entire week of his show to questioning Clinton's medical fitness to be president, citing examples such as Clinton slipping on a stair and laughing "inappropriately" during her eleven hours of testimony before Congress on Benghazi. Evan McMullin, a former CIA officer and congressional aide, launches an independent campaign to offer "Never Trump" Republicans an alternative to Trump, and recently deposed Fox chairman Roger Ailes is advising Trump in his preparations for the presidential debates. Rudy Giuliani, mayor of New York on 9/11, claims that there were no "successful radical Islamic terrorist attacks" inside the U.S. until Barack Obama became president. July's average global temperature was the hottest on record and the fifteenth consecutive monthly heat record. Emails obtained by the Associated Press show that Paul Manafort's firm ran a covert lobbying operation on behalf of Ukraine's former ruling party, and failed to disclose its work as a foreign agent as required by law. Amid plummeting poll numbers, Trump names Steve Bannon, executive chairman of Breitbart News and a former Goldman Sachs banker, as his campaign's new chief executive, and Kellyanne Conway, a senior adviser and pollster, as his new campaign manager, while Manafort retains the title of "campaign chairman." In an email to campaign staff, Manafort describes the shakeup as an "exciting day for Team Trump," while a top aide to a conservative House Republican comments, "Rearranging the deck chairs is not an effective strategy . . . Problem is not staff. The problem is with Trump." Spanish and Italian ships rescue 534 African migrants from the Mediterranean in a single day, while U.S. Olympic swimmer Ryan Lochte vandalizes a gas station restroom in Rio, then attempts to cover up the incident by claiming he and three teammates were robbed at gunpoint. Record-breaking floods strike Baton Rouge less than a month after Gavin Long shot six Baton Rouge police officers, killing three, and in Southern California, the so-called Blue Cut Fire forces the evacuation of eighty thousand residents. "In forty years of fighting fire, I've never seen fire behavior so extreme," says the incident commander on the fire. CNN's "battleground map" gives 273 electoral votes to Clinton and 191 to Trump, with 74 electoral votes up for grabs in Florida, Ohio, North Carolina, Iowa, and Nevada. The Trump campaign makes major ad buys in Florida, Ohio, North Carolina, Pennsylvania, and Virginia, and Trump solicits African-American voters by asking, "What do you have to lose by trying something new, like Trump? You're living in poverty. Your schools are no good. You have no jobs. Fifty-eight percent of your youth is unemployed. What the hell do you have to lose?" Manafort resigns from the Trump campaign, and Colombia issues a new fifty-thousand-peso note bearing the image of the late Nobel Prize–winning writer Gabriel García Márquez. The New York City Department of Parks and Recreation removes a rogue statue of a naked Trump from Union Square, and a Parks spokesperson comments: "NYC Parks stands firmly against any unpermitted erection, no matter how small." Hillary Clinton, who has not held a press conference since early December 2015, embarks on an eleven-day megadonor fundraising blitz that includes private events in the Hamptons, Laguna Beach, the San Francisco Bay Area, Martha's Vineyard, and Beverly Hills, netting as much as $2 million at a single cocktail party, and a *Washington Post*/ABC News poll finds that 60 percent of voters do not see her as honest. U.S.-backed forces take control of Jarabulus, Syria, from ISIS, and a judge orders the State Department to release the nearly fifteen thousand new emails that the FBI discovered in its investigation into Clinton's email server. Killings by police and vigilantes in President Rodrigo Duterte's "war on drugs" leave eighteen hundred dead in the Philippines over a span of seven weeks. The

FDA orders all U.S. blood banks to start screening for Zika, and in Texas, a new law goes into effect allowing concealed handguns on college campuses. Rob Morrow, coauthor with Trump adviser Roger Stone of the 2015 book *The Clintons' War on Women,* is ousted as chairman of the Travis County, Texas, Republican Party, but will continue his bid for the presidency, running on a platform to "promote boobyliciousness every day," to have "bikini contests on the South Lawn of the White House," and to have wet T-shirt contests on the Fourth of July. On MSNBC's *Morning Joe,* Hillary Clinton describes the presidential race as "not a normal choice between a Republican and a Democrat," and the *New York Times* reports that new Trump campaign chief executive Steve Bannon was charged with domestic violence, battery, and attempting to dissuade a victim from reporting a crime in 1996, but the charges were dropped when prosecutors were unable to locate Bannon's then-wife, who was the alleged victim and main witness. Trump says he is willing to consider a "softer" approach to immigration, and Trump spokeswoman Katrina Pierson states: "He hasn't changed his position on immigration. He's changed the words that he's saying." Martha Stewart and Snoop Dogg announce they will host a new cooking series on VH1 called *Martha and Snoop's Potluck Dinner Party.* Real Clear Politics' average of polls shows a gain by Trump of 2.3 points over the past several weeks, and in one poll he trails Clinton by only 3 points. "Dwyane Wade's cousin was just shot and killed walking her baby in Chicago," Trump tweets on August 27. "Just what I have been saying. African-Americans will VOTE TRUMP!" Congressional Democrats begin to target affluent suburbs in hopes of turning normally solid Republican districts Democratic, and researchers report that the mortality rate for pregnant women in Texas has doubled in recent years. Clinton aide Huma Abedin separates from her husband, former congressman Anthony Weiner, after it's revealed that he has again been exchanging lewd messages with a woman on social media. Hillary Clinton's campaign raises $143 million for the month of August, including $2.5 million from an event in Sagaponack, New York, in which ten people paid at least $250,000 each to meet her, a dinner in Beverly Hills that required the attendees to "write, not raise" a contribution of $100,000 each, and a $100,000-per-couple lamb dinner at a Martha's Vineyard mansion. During the last two weeks of August, Clinton raises roughly $50 million at twenty-two private events. "It's the old adage," a prominent New York Democrat observes, "you go to where the money is." Senate minority leader Harry Reid asks the FBI to investigate evidence that Russia is trying to manipulate election results in November, based on recent classified briefings from senior intelligence officials. Reid notes that he has more leeway to speak on the issue than President Obama. "This is one of the strengths of Barack Obama. He waits and waits and waits until all the evidence is in."

# HILLARY DOESN'T LIVE
# HERE ANYMORE

## 1.

Charlemagne, a.k.a. Charles the Great, king of the Franks, king of the Lombards, emperor of the Romans, father of Europe, and, as he preferred it, "Charles, most serene Augustus crowned by God, the great, peaceful emperor ruling the Roman Empire," imposed order and stability over his far-flung state by requiring the teaching of . . . rhetoric. Not fancy talk, not the lip-spritz of flounce and folderol, but speaking based on logic, grammar, reasoned argument. The stuff, in other words, of public discourse, the means of useful give-and-take whereby civilization gets on with its proper business of furnishing people a decent shot at living long and happy lives.

For their guide Charlemagne's cadres looked to Aristotle's *Rhetoric* and his "modes of persuasion furnished by the spoken word." Aristotle identifies three distinct modes. *Ethos* depends on the character of the speaker, whether he or she appears to be credible. *Pathos* concerns the emotions that the speaker elicits from the audience. *Logos* relates to content and argument, the effectiveness of the "proof," whether it appeals to logical reason. "Persuasion is achieved by the speaker's personal character when the speech is so spoken as to make us think him credible," said Aristotle, and the speeches at the Democratic National Convention in Philadelphia, four days' worth, ten hours or more a day of droning and soaring, might be viewed collectively as an argument for the premise of the entire electoral exercise as much as a case for the election of a particular candidate. There was the candidate herself, of course, the arguments for, the *ethos-pathos-logos* trifecta deployed for the politics of the moment, but it seemed necessary, in this strangest of election years when someone or something was driving the people of America crazy, to affirm the basic worth of liberal democracy, and, by extension— sometimes implicitly, sometimes overtly—the values and attributes that it requires of us. Tolerance. Reason. Memory. Mutual respect. The tools—both intellectual and emotional—to engage with com- plexity. An elastic concept of polity and the common good, a sense of community larger than immediate self-interest. "Those bonds of affection," Obama declared in his convention speech, "that common creed." "Bonds of trust and respect," said the nominee herself. "We are all neighbors," said Tim Kaine, "and we must love neighbors as ourselves." Michelle Obama: "The vision that our founders put forth all those years ago that we are all created equal, each a be- loved part of the great American story." Cory Booker: "In this city our founders put forth a Declaration of Independence, but let me tell you, they also made a historic declaration of interdependence. They knew that if this country was to survive and thrive, we had to make an unusual and extraordinary commitment to one another." Obama again: "We have to listen to each other, and see ourselves in each other," and "democracy doesn't work if we constantly demon- ize each other."

As events would show, a large chunk of the electorate was in no mood to be appealed to in these terms. Events would show that an even larger chunk of the electorate was in no mood to listen at all, and had in fact tuned out some time ago, having decided that politics as practiced in America these past several decades is so remote, so stubbornly indifferent to their concerns and struggles, that they should join what the political scientist Walter Dean Burnham once called the country's "largest political party," those citizens who see no point in voting. Not enough hope out there, apparently. Not enough of the right kind of change trickling down, and much too much of the other.[1] Neither the Republicans' "morning in America" nor the Democrats' "bridge to the twenty-first century" had worked out for these people; had in fact excluded great numbers of poor, working-class, and middle-class Americans from the political calculus. And so they, the members of the country's largest political party, would choose in November to vote with their feet, so to speak, and absent themselves from the process.

But after the Republicans' days of rage in Cleveland—imagine an apoplectic old man, driven mad by cockroaches, strapping on a flamethrower to rid his house of the infestation—the Democrats' Philadelphia convention could at least claim the high ground of functional competence. This was the convention that had the non-fritzing lights and unplagiarized speeches, the A-list stars, the smooth runnings that hit prime time's sweetest spots. And it had, as we were told over and over, History. This was one of those rare obvious points that actually bore repeating, not least because it had been such a long time coming. Does anyone remember Shirley Chisholm? *Unbought and Unbossed*. On Thursday night, dressed entirely in white—the color of the suffragettes—Hillary stood before

---

[1] In presidential election years, roughly four out of every ten adults don't vote, and for midterm elections that number climbs to roughly six out of ten. Turnout is lower in the U.S. than in Canada, Mexico, and most of Europe. In the 2014 midterms, the national turnout fell to 36.7 percent, and in some states sank to levels not seen since the 1820s when poll taxes were in force. See Alicia Parlapiano and Adam Pearce, "For Every 10 U.S. Adults, Six Vote and Four Don't. What Separates Them?," *New York Times*, September 14, 2016. See also the United States Elections Project, www.electproject.org, and Walter Dean Burnham and Thomas Ferguson, "Americans Are Sick to Death of Both Parties: Why Our Politics Is in Worse Shape Than We Thought," Alternet, December 18, 2014.

the convention and accepted her party's nomination for president. If her oratory failed to scale up to the magnitude of the occasion, she at least did a serviceable job of staking out her turf as the candidate of adult demeanor and impulse control. "Yes, it's true, I sweat the details," she told us by way of apologizing for her coolish, grind-it-out approach. There were stronger together, the woman card, and the proverbial presidential finger on the nuclear button, along with a big shout-out to Bernie. "You put economic and social justice issues front and center, right where they belong!" she cried in his direction, and the TV cameras cut to Bernie sitting stone-faced in the shadows, then managing, with what seemed grim effort of will, to squeeze out the tightest of smiles. And there was this:

> *Americans are willing to work, and work hard. But right now an awful lot of people feel there is less and less respect for the work they do. And less respect for them, period. Democrats, we are the party of working people, but we haven't done a good enough job showing we get what you're going through.*

It seemed as if the point—itself somewhat fuzzy amid the syntactical muddle of the "we" and the "you" she spoke of, and to what extent this "we" and "you" were supposed to include or overlap with the "Democrats" whom she seemed to address directly—was to "get" what "you" (we? Democrats?) are "going through."[2] As if the point was to "feel your pain," to borrow a famous phrase, and the Democrats' fault lay in their failure to feel it enough, or maybe they *did* feel it, but muffed the essential political theatrics of display. This nod toward collective mea culpa was a nice way for Hillary to slide past some highly problematic history: to avoid the suggestion, and with it any obligation to explain or acknowledge, that much of "what you're going through" could be traced on a straight causal

---

[2] Cast a tight grammatical net to catch a slippery politician.

line back to the politics and policies of the Democratic Party of the past thirty years, a party that's as much the creation of Bill and Hillary Clinton as of any other pair of individuals.

That Hillary had an *ethos* problem, a credibility problem, was no secret in 2016. Informed, thoughtful people of eminent goodwill might reasonably doubt her perfect trustworthiness, quite apart from the right wing's delirium tremens accusations of witchcraft, pedophilia, murder, and other assorted mayhem. But this year was different. This year was worse. The credibility of the Democratic Party itself was in the dock, its establishment accused—quite accurately, as it turned out—of rigging the primary process in Clinton's favor. The bias implicit in the debate schedule, patently arranged to minimize risk to the front-runner, was borne out in the hacked emails of, among others, DNC chairwoman Debbie Wasserman Schultz and Clinton campaign chairman John Podesta, proof so blatant that the party suffered the humiliation—"embarrassment" doesn't do this train wreck justice—of its chairwoman resigning on the eve of the convention. Having fallen so low, the ex-chair would be brought even lower by the jeers that greeted her Monday-morning address to the Florida delegation, a further injury that was soon mirrored by her party. In due course it would be discovered that her replacement, interim DNC chairwoman Donna Brazile—presumably chosen for her strength in precisely those areas where Wasserman Schultz was deficient—had, thanks to inside information available to her as a paid commentator for CNN during the primary season, leaked questions to the Clinton campaign in advance of several town halls.

One was tempted to wail to the heavens, *Where do they find these people?* But these people have been around for years, building their nests and busily prospering within the bosom of the Democratic Party. Long before the 2016 election cycle, "the party of the people" had been slanting the nomination process toward insiders, hedging against possible eruptions of the popular will. The party's "superdelegate" innovation is one such hedge, the seven-hundred-plus unpledged delegates who come to every convention free of any duty to heed the millions of primary votes cast by their fellow Democrats. "Super Tuesday" is another, the stacking of Southern primaries early in the cycle to thwart the emergence of more liberal candidates. Let it be said that both hedges played significant roles in Bernie Sanders's eventual defeat, but not until 2017 would the radical cynicism of the party's establishment fully come to light. One such revelation was a lawsuit by Sanders supporters accusing the Democratic National Committee of election fraud. In response, DNC attorney Bruce Spiva argued in open court that the party was under "no contractual obligation" to conduct a fair and open presidential nominating process, this in spite of the "Impartiality Clause" of the DNC Charter, article 5, section 4, which plainly states:

> *The Chairperson shall exercise impartiality and*
> *evenhandedness as between the Presidential candidates and*
> *campaigns. The Chairperson shall be responsible for ensuring*
> *that the national officers and staff of the Democratic National*
> *Committee maintain impartiality and evenhandedness during*
> *the Democratic Party Presidential nomination process.*

Which, according to DNC lawyer Spiva, was one of "these general rules of the road" that was actually nothing of the sort, general or otherwise. "[T]here is no right to—just by virtue of making a donation, to enforce the party's internal rules," a presumably straight-faced Spiva argued to the judge. "And there's no right to not have your candidate disadvantaged or have another candidate advantaged. There's no contractual obligation here."[3]

This is cynicism of several magnitudes of decadence: think Dom

---

[3] Sean Adl-Tabatabai, "Court Documents Reveal DNC Forced Bernie Out to Appease Hillary," YourNewsWire.com, April 30, 2017.

Perignon for breakfast, diamond-encrusted push-up bras, orgies in the staterooms of ocean-going yachts. It is dynamic, this cynicism. It works to the advantage of a certain class of people, the same people whose influence could have been expected to grow when in 2015 Wasserman Schultz quietly lifted the party's long-standing ban on donations from PACs and lobbyists. Wasserman Schultz had moved so quietly, in fact, that for months the only people who knew were "leading Washington lobbyists," as the *Washington Post* reported when the news finally broke.[4] Included in the *Post*'s story was a description of the joint fund-raising committee that the Clinton campaign had formed with the DNC, the "Hillary Victory Fund," though the true significance of this fund would not be revealed until November 2017, when Donna Brazile disclosed that the Clinton campaign had, in exchange for shoring up the national party's disastrous finances, secretly assumed control of the party in August 2015, just as the race for the party's nomination was heating up.[5] Thanks to the "Joint Fund-Raising Agreement" among the DNC, the Hillary Victory Fund, and Hillary's campaign, her campaign took over the party's finances, strategy, data, analytics, and communications, and had the final say on staffing decisions. Virtually all of the millions of dollars raised by her campaign for the ostensible purpose of funding state parties and down-ballot candidates were quietly routed straight into the Clinton campaign, as was money raised with the national party through the Hillary Victory Fund.[6]

---

[4] Tom Hamburger and Paul Kane, "DNC Rolls Back Obama Ban on Contributions from Federal Lobbyists," *Washington Post,* February 12, 2016. In February 2017, the DNC voted down a proposal to reinstate the ban. See Andrew Cockburn, "It's My Party: The Democrats Struggle to Rise from the Ashes," *Harper's,* July 2017.

[5] Donna Brazile, "Inside Hillary Clinton's Secret Takeover of the DNC," *Politico,* November 2, 2017.

[6] In the summer of 2015, Hillary vowed to rebuild "the party from the ground up . . . when our state parties are strong, we win. That's what will happen." That is not what happened. According to Brazile, of the $82 million that the Clinton campaign raised jointly with state parties, the states kept less than half of 1 percent. For how one state, Nebraska, fared under Hillary's version of "ground up," see Cockburn, "It's My Party."

*Your Vote Counts!* chirp those public service announcements that always air around election time, but long before Donna Brazile added this latest chapter to the saga of a grievously rigged system, vast numbers of Americans, our everyday seers and savants, had already discovered the hollowness of democracy happy-talk. "We cannot afford to be tired or frustrated or cynical," Michelle Obama urged her fellow Democrats in Philadelphia. Truly we can't, but damn if our leaders don't make the cynicism easy.

A few weeks before the presidential election, George Packer of the *New Yorker* sat down with Hillary and asked her to elaborate on the passage in her convention speech about "showing we get what you're going through." Packer recounts her answer:

> *"We have been fighting out our elections in general on a lot of noneconomic issues over the past thirty years," she said— social issues, welfare, crime, war. "Sometimes we win, and sometimes we lose, but we haven't had a coherent, compelling economic case that needs to be made in order to lay down a foundation on which to both conduct politics and do policy."*[7]

This was not an accurate statement. In fact the dominant wing of the Democratic Party has for three decades had a coherent economic case—a quite compelling and lucrative case, for some—on which it has conducted politics and done policy, but by the fall of 2016 that case was looking tired; maybe no longer a winner, not in the face of so much evidence, both of politics and policy, to the contrary. There was little advantage to be had in acknowledging, much less pressing, that case, but it was the case off which the Clintons and their Democratic Party had lived for the past thirty years.

---

[7] George Packer, "The Unconnected," *New Yorker,* October 31, 2016.

## 2.

"If we lead with class warfare, we lose." So said Governor Bill Clinton of Arkansas after the 1988 presidential election in which George H. W. Bush thrashed Michael Dukakis by tallies of 426 Electoral College votes to 111, 40 states to 10, and 53.37 percent of the popular vote to 45.65 percent. For Democrats, this was progress. The previous two elections had been bona fide Republican landslides— "obliterations" is probably a truer description—with Ronald Reagan cleanly deposing Jimmy Carter by almost 10 percentage points in 1980, and winning every state but one in 1984, the lone holdout being Minnesota, Walter Mondale's home state, which Mondale won by fewer than 4,000 votes.[8]

Democrats had lost five out of the last six presidential elections. Something clearly wasn't working, and the "New Democrats" who'd begun to gain prominence in the 1970s tacitly identified that something as the party's allegiance to certain elements in its traditional constituency. In the early seventies, the party had already begun to distance itself from one of those constituencies, organized labor, diminishing the influence of this key New Deal partner in favor of a new coalition of minorities, feminists, and younger, affluent, college-educated whites. The New Deal itself was increasingly seen as an anachronism; the issues that gave 1930s economic populism its reason for being—corporate monopoly power, unchecked Wall Street speculation, too much of the country's wealth commanded by a small elite—seemed to reside in the distant past, and many of the old New Dealers and union bosses, dinosaurs by now, had more recently supported the Vietnam War and rammed Hubert Humphrey's nomination down the party's throat. Inflation, mounting deficits, corporate sclerosis, plus the rise of OPEC and increasing

---

[8] When asked what he wanted for Christmas that year, Reagan cracked, "Well, Minnesota would have been nice."

foreign business competition, all demanded a fresh economic vision from Democrats. The version put forward by the New Democrats would borrow heavily from the libertarian ideas of Milton Friedman and Alan Greenspan, in which "the market," rather than representative government, is the rightful arbiter of social good. Liberal economic gurus such as Alfred Kahn and Lester Thurow repackaged libertarian ideas for the left, eventually leading to a new "neoliberal" ideology that favored fiscal restraint, small government, a reduced social safety net, and the dismantling of much of the New Deal framework regulating banks, financial markets, and corporate monopolies.[9]

The journalist Randall Rothenberg explored the new movement in an *Esquire* cover story, "The Neoliberal Club," which profiled the cohort of up-and-comers who would provide much of the Democratic Party's leadership in the coming decades.[10] On social issues, at least rhetorically, the New Democrats were well within the liberal spectrum, particularly on civil and human rights, environmental protection, and foreign policy. The thing that set them apart from the New Dealers—that made them *New* Democrats—was faith in society's collective wisdom as expressed by market forces. Corporate monopolies were virtuous as long as they delivered low prices to consumers. Banking and finance were naturally "self-regulating," in the words of Alan Greenspan, always subject to the "ultimate regulator of competition in a free economy, the capital market." If a company or economic sector became reckless or inefficient, capital would inevitably start moving to more promising competitors.

On the heels of the Mondale obliteration of 1984, the New Democrats joined with big donors in a concerted, top-down effort to move the Democratic Party beyond New Deal liberalism. Several

---

[9] Matt Stoller, "How Democrats Killed Their Populist Soul," *Atlantic,* November 4, 2016.

[10] *Esquire,* February 1982. Among those profiled were Gary Hart, Al Gore, Bill and Hillary Clinton, Michael Dukakis, Paul Tsongas, and Richard Gephardt, all of whom would eventually run for president.

weeks after the election, twenty top Democratic fund-raisers met in Washington to discuss "1988 and how they could have more policy influence in that campaign, how they might use their fundraising skills to move the party toward their business oriented, centrist viewpoints."[11] Two days later, a group calling itself the Coalition for a Democratic Majority held a public forum pushing similar themes, and the star speakers at that forum—Governors Bruce Babbitt of Arizona and Charles Robb of Virginia—would, along with many others from Rothenberg's "Neoliberal Club," play crucial roles in the most influential organization to emerge from the movement, the Democratic Leadership Council. Established in 1985 by Al From and Will Marshall, the DLC was, in From's words, "really about modernizing liberalism and defining a new progressive center for our party, not simply pushing it further to the right."[12] What From and his fellow New Democrats meant by "modernizing liberalism" would be revealed in the fullness of time, but clear from the start was a close relationship with big donors and big business. The DLC's "executive council"—which required an annual donation of at least $25,000—included corporate giants such as ARCO, Chevron, Merck, DuPont, Microsoft, Philip Morris, and Koch Industries. Membership on the DLC's board of trustees required donations significantly greater than $25,000. Trustees were largely drawn from the ranks of corporate senior executives and finance industry centi-millionaires, and would eventually include among their number one Richard Harold Fink, nicknamed "the Pirate," the longtime chief political operative for Charles and David Koch.[13]

---

[11] Thomas Ferguson and Joel Rogers, *Right Turn: The Decline of the Democrats and the Future of American Politics* (Macmillan, 1987), p. 3, as referenced in Paul Rosenberg, "Clintonism Screwed the Democrats: How Bill, Hillary, and the Democratic Leadership Council Gutted Progressivism," *Salon*, April 30, 2016.

[12] Al From, "Recruiting Bill Clinton," *Atlantic*, December 3, 2013.

[13] Sam Smith, "How the Koch Brothers Helped Dismantle the Democratic Party," SamSmithArchives.wordpress.com, April 14, 2015; Joe Sudbay, "Koch Industries Gave Funding to the DLC and Served on Its Executive Council," *American Blog*, August 25, 2010. For more on the activities of Richard H. Fink, see the utterly essential *Dark Money*:

There was virtually no grassroots presence in the DLC; or you could call it a grassroots, rank-and-file, bottom-up organization for the private-jet crowd. It was big on deregulation, globalization, and "personal responsibility," particularly in the specific contexts of, as cofounder From put it, "the basic bargain of opportunity and responsibility," and "welfare reform and personal responsibility measures, including requiring kids to stay in school to get a driver's license and fining parents who missed their kids' parent-teacher conferences."[14] In 1990, Bill Clinton accepted From's offer to become chairman of the DLC, and at the organization's annual meeting the following year Clinton presided over the rollout of "the New Orleans Declaration." The declaration was essentially a manifesto for the kind of politics that Clinton and the DLC had begun calling "the third way," a centrist, business-friendly alternative to both New Deal liberalism and hard-core laissez-faire conservatism. "We believe *The New Orleans Declaration* represents a turning point for Democrats," stated the introduction, and under the heading "WHERE WE STAND" one finds such assertions as:

> *We don't need polls to tell us who we are . . .*
> *We believe the promise of America is equal opportunity, not equal outcomes.*
> *We believe the Democratic Party's fundamental mission is to expand opportunity, not government.*
> *We believe the right way to rebuild America's economic security is . . . to expand free trade, not restrict it.*
> *We believe that all claims on government are not equal. Our leaders must reject demands that are less worthy, and hold to clear governing priorities.*[15]

---

*The Hidden History of the Billionaires Behind the Rise of the Radical Right* by Jane Mayer (Doubleday, 2016).

[14] From, "Recruiting Bill Clinton."

[15] One wonders about the beef that went into this hunk of declamatory sausage.

*We believe in preventing crime and punishing criminals,
not explaining away their behavior.*

*We believe the purpose of social welfare is to bring the poor
into the nation's economic mainstream, not maintain them in
dependence.*[16]

The language here is too general to permit anything like policy analysis, but one detects a harrumphing sort of belligerence in the litany of *We believes*, something of the passive-aggressive, of resentments being aired at a rarefied pitch. This same prickliness could be detected in Al From's answer to a reporter at that same DLC conference in New Orleans—"We trust that a few people in the press have a brain in their heads"—when asked about the Reverend Jesse Jackson's assertion that he and the DLC "stand on common ground on many of these issues."[17]

Perhaps From was still smarting from Jackson's mocking name for the DLC, "Democrats for the Leisure Class." "[W]e don't think the Democratic Party should lead with class warfare," Bill Clinton again opined in New Orleans, yet his soon-to-be-launched presidential campaign would put the middle class at the rhetorical center of its goals and concerns, as if "middle class" was neutral ground, the Switzerland of the class wars. "The very burdened middle class," candidate Clinton would call it, "the forgotten middle class," "the people who pay the taxes, raise the kids, and play by the rules," or, taking a somewhat different tack, "the people who used to vote for us." But closer inspection of the candidate's views revealed a great deal less emphasis on the economic interests and anxieties of this besieged middle class than on its all-important "character" and "values." For Clinton, "middle class" meant "values that nearly every American holds dear—support for family, reward for work,

---

[16] Al From, "Waking the Democrats," *RealClearPolitics*, February 27, 2006.
[17] Robin Toner, "Eyes to Left, Democrats Edge Toward the Center," *New York Times*, March 25, 1990.

the willingness to change what isn't working," an echo of the New Orleans Declaration's trumpeting of "the moral and cultural values most Americans share." Cheek by jowl with planks advocating the New Democrats' "third way" and the "new social contract,"[18] the party's official 1992 platform would emphasize "work, family and individual responsibility," and endowing our children with "values, motivation and discipline." Social ills that had traditionally been viewed as the responsibility of government—"the old notion that there's a program for every problem"—might be more efficiently addressed by the private sector, such as the religious institutions and civic and charitable organizations where "the values and character of our citizens are formed."

Class, as the New Democrats chose to present it, was a battle of culture rather than economics; of "mainstream values" versus those other, presumably less virtuous values not held by "most Americans" or "nearly every American." The sharp class antagonisms that had galvanized New Deal liberalism—class as defined by economics: the material interests of the working and middle classes inevitably clashing with the interests of big business and big money—were smoothed over and rounded off, deftly reshaped to accommodate a more benign view of industrial capitalism. As for the contours of the new battleground, and the source of the threats to those cherished "middle class" values, the Clinton campaign furnished many helpful markers along the way. There was much talk of "entitlement reform," and "ending welfare as we know it." There were "deadbeat dads" to slam, and a Sister Souljah to call out, and planks in the party platform that included the inarguable, seemingly gratuitous propositions that "children should not have children" and "people who bring children into this world have a responsibility to care for them." To bolster Clinton's tough-on-crime stance—which included

---

[18] "We reject both the do-nothing government of the past 12 years as well as the big government theory that says we can hamstring business and tax and spend our way to prosperity."

his vow to put one hundred thousand more cops on the streets—
there was his determination, in the midst of his Gennifer Flowers
emergency, to return to Little Rock to preside over the execution of
convicted double-murderer Ricky Ray Rector, a black man rendered
so simple by a self-inflicted gunshot wound to the head that he put
aside the pecan pie dessert from his last meal, telling a guard that
he was "saving it for later." "I can be nicked a lot, but no one can
say I'm soft on crime," Clinton remarked after the execution. Then
there was his photo op at Stone Mountain Correctional Institute in
Georgia, just before the Georgia primary and a week before Super
Tuesday. In a campaign full of racist dog whistles, Stone Mountain
stands out for sheer dog-whistle gall; the episode's shamelessness and
cynicism are every bit the equal of Ronald Reagan's 1980 campaign
speech in Philadelphia, Mississippi.[19] Long ago Stone Mountain perfected its status as America's white-supremacist mecca: site of the Ku
Klux Klan's rebirth in 1915; of an enormous bas relief sculpture—
the largest in the world—depicting the Confederacy's holy trinity of
Stonewall Jackson, Jefferson Davis, and Robert E. Lee, known as the
"Confederate Rushmore"; and of the Klan's annual Labor Day cross
burning, as well as an annual "antebellum jubilee" celebrating the
pre–Civil War South. "Let freedom ring from Stone Mountain of
Georgia," Martin Luther King Jr. cried out in his "I Have a Dream"
speech, with the implication that if freedom could ring from that
bastion of white supremacy, it could ring anywhere in America.

But mere days before seven Southern states would hold their
primaries, Bill Clinton didn't go to Stone Mountain to talk about
freedom, civil rights, or the toxic legacy of slavery. He went there in
the company of three white male politicians[20] to talk about the need

---

[19] See "American Crossroads: Reagan, Trump, and the Devil Down South," *supra*.

[20] Georgia senator Sam Nunn, Georgia governor Zell Miller, and Georgia representative Ben
Jones, who played "Cooter" on the seventies TV show *The Dukes of Hazzard*. Jones was an
outspoken advocate for the display of the Confederate battle flag, claiming that it stood
for "courage and family and good times." See Nathan J. Robinson, "Bill Clinton's Stone
Mountain Moment," *Jacobin*, September 16, 2016.

for a law-and-order crackdown, and did so against a background of dozens of uniformed inmates standing in formation, the vast majority of them black. Of the photo that ran in the next day's newspapers, California governor Jerry Brown said that Clinton and his colleagues looked "like colonial masters" signaling "Don't worry, we'll keep them in their place." "Two [sic] white men and forty black prisoners, what's he saying? He's saying we've got 'em under control, folks." Clinton in turn accused Brown of playing "racial politics," just as he would later accuse Brown of letting "New York be split apart by race" when Brown announced prior to the New York primary that Jesse Jackson would be his first choice for vice presidential running mate.

"Clinton mastered the art of sending mixed cultural messages," Michelle Alexander would later write of the 1992 campaign.[21] He could dog-whistle to angry whites from Stone Mountain one day, and the next walk into a black church and belt out "Lift Every Voice and Sing" by heart, or slide on some Wayfarers and play the saxophone on *The Arsenio Hall Show*. "It seems silly in retrospect," Alexander wrote, "but many of us fell for that."

Clinton was, by any measure, an abnormally gifted politician. "Where I come from we know about race-baiting," he said when formally announcing his candidacy in Little Rock. "They've used it to divide us for years. I know this tactic well and I'm not going to let them get away with it." That Clinton's own race-baiting was part of a considered, precisely calibrated strategy was demonstrated by Joan Didion in her election reportage for the *New York Review of Books,* a strategy calculated, in the words of one Democratic operative, to signal to Reagan Democrats "that it is safe to come home to their party because poor, black, Hispanic, urban, homeless, hungry, and other people and problems out of favor in Middle America will no lon-

---

[21] Michelle Alexander, "Black Lives Shattered," *Nation,* February 29, 2016, posted online as "Why Hillary Clinton Doesn't Deserve the Black Vote" (https://thenation.com/article/hillary-clinton-does-not-deserve-blackpeoples-votes/).

Bill Clinton at Stone Mountain, Georgia, March 1992. Courtesy of the Associated Press

ger get the favored treatment they got from mushy 1960s and 1970s Democratic liberals."[22] Didion showed just how closely Clinton's pitch followed the lead of millions of dollars' worth of research into the white working- and middle-class voters, the "traditional Democrats," who had voted for Reagan. Focus groups, polling ("We don't need polls to tell us who we are"), and exhaustive data analysis mapped the psyche of a demographic that was fed up with welfare "freebies" and "rip-offs," with minorities getting "a free lunch" and "something for nothing." The "middle-class white guy" getting a "raw deal" was how Democratic pollster Stanley Greenberg summed up his findings from a famous 1985 study of Reagan Democrats in Macomb County, Michigan.[23] Didion quotes at length from one account of Greenberg's field research, an episode in which three dozen Reagan Democrats assembled for a focus group at a motel in Sterling Heights, Michigan.

---

[22] Joan Didion, "Eyes on the Prize," *New York Review of Books,* September 24, 1992, reprinted in Didion's *Political Fictions* (Knopf, 2001). The quote can be found on p. 145.

[23] Stanley Greenberg, "From Crisis to Working Majority," *American Prospect,* Fall 1991.

*The voters were broken into four groups. Each participant was paid $35 for two hours and fed cold cuts. The tone was set when Greenberg read a quote from Robert Kennedy, a man held in reverence by these heavily Roman Catholic voters. The quote was RFK's eloquent call for Americans to honor their special obligation to black citizens whose forefathers had lived through the slave experience and who themselves were the victims of racial discrimination . . .*

*"That's bullshit," shouted one participant.*

*"No wonder they killed him," said another.*

*"I'm fed up with it," chimed a third.*

*The resulting report sent a shudder through state and national Democrats. It was the first of a continuing series of research projects during the latter half of the decade that explained the problem, quite literally, in black and white.*

*The votes for Reagan among these traditional Democrats, Greenberg reported, stemmed from . . . a sense that "the Democratic Party no longer responded with genuine feeling to the vulnerabilities and burdens of the average middle-class person. Instead the party and government were preoccupied with the needs of minorities . . . They advanced spending programs that offered no appreciable or visible benefit" for middle-class people.*[24]

But there was more to the story than this particular subset of "traditional Democrats," as Greenberg himself would explain in 1991. In an article for the *American Prospect*, he elaborated on "the other side of the equation," namely, the extensive polling that showed "middle-class America's deep frustration with the ascendancy of the wealthy and the corporations." The Republican coalition that

---

[24] Didion, *Political Fictions*, pp. 159–60, quoting from *Minority Party: Why Democrats Face Defeat in 1992 and Beyond*, Peter Brown (Gateway Books, 1991).

had won five out of the last six presidential elections was "inherently unstable," depending as it did on an alliance of higher-income groups—whose priorities were smaller government, laissez-faire economics, and lower taxes—and middle-to-lower-income groups that might have shared the Republican establishment's cultural conservatism, but whose economic interests were fundamentally at odds with those of the wealthy. This mismatch created an opening for Democrats to exploit with a forthright appeal to, in Greenberg's borrowed phrase, the "majoritarian economic interests" shared by the working and middle classes across racial and cultural lines.[25]

This was a politics that spoke directly to economic class: more specifically, to class conflict, class struggle, class antagonism, class warfare, or whatever you want to call this abiding fact of the capitalist economy, the mention of which certain people, usually those with lots of money, seem to find unpatriotic. It was precisely this politics that Robert F. Kennedy ran on in 1968, the "black and blue" coalition—African-Americans and white blue-collar workers, along with students, Catholics, farmers, Hispanics, and college-educated whites—that was winning, and probably would have won, the Democratic nomination for Kennedy, bringing to life Richard Nixon's worst nightmare of a general-election matchup. As divided and tribalized as America was in the early nineties (or even in 2016), surely the fractures were no worse than in 1968, when the country was burning—the cities, literally—over Vietnam, the counterculture, civil rights, and racist backlash. At a time when so much of the rest of America was coming apart, Kennedy formed a mass movement based on common economic interests. No doubt his charisma had much to do with it, and the personal anguish that underlay his credibility—his *ethos*—but his unabashed liberal politics,

---

[25] Greenberg, "From Crisis to Working Majority." Greenberg is quoting from Thomas and Mary Edsall's book *Chain Reaction* with the phrase "majoritarian economic interests." Likewise, he quotes from E. J. Dionne's *Why Americans Hate Politics* in describing the "inherently unstable" Republican coalition.

firmly grounded in the New Deal, was essential to the glue that held his coalition together.[26]

By 1991, nearly twenty-five years after Kennedy's assassination, the notion of a similar black and blue coalition might well have seemed the stuff of nostalgic hippie dreams. *No wonder they killed him.* But Greenberg made a compelling empirical case that such a coalition could be built, citing polls, his own and others', showing voters believed (63 percent to 8 percent) that Republicans favor the rich over the middle class; that Democrats, more than Republicans, resist big special interests (48 percent to 21 percent); that Democrats do a better job of helping the middle class (by margins of two or three to one, depending on the poll); that the rich fail to carry "their fair share of the burden" (specific percentages not given); that just 18 percent of voters wanted a government that did "as little as possible"; that, "astonishingly" (Greenberg's word), 44 percent wanted a government that guarantees "a decent standard of living for everyone, including job creation and basic housing"; and that voters trusted Democrats over Republicans on health care (52 percent to 21 percent).

"It should be clear by now," Greenberg wrote in his 1991 assessment, "that the key to Democratic success is becoming a middle-class centered, bottom-up coalition—a mass party, encompassing the needs of the have-nots and working Americans, that centers on the values and interests of the middle class."

---

[26] "There is something going on here that has to do with real class politics," the sociologist Robert Coles told Kennedy during the campaign. See Richard Kahlenberg, "Harvard's Class Gap," *Harvard Magazine,* May/June 2017, for a useful discussion of the intersection of class and race in American politics. Kahlenberg sees in RFK's black and blue coalition the manifestation of Martin Luther King Jr.'s vision of economic and racial justice, as found in King's writings. "It is a simple matter of justice," King wrote, "that America, in dealing creatively with the task of raising the Negro from backwardness, should also be rescuing a large stratum of the forgotten white poor." And: "It is my opinion that many white workers whose economic condition is not too far removed from the economic condition of his black brother, will find it difficult to accept a 'Negro Bill of Rights,' which seeks to give special consideration to the Negro in the context of unemployment, joblessness, etc. and does not take into sufficient account their plight (that of the white worker)."

Thus the Democratic Party had a coherent, compelling economic case to make in 1992. Twelve consecutive years of Republican administration had resulted in one of the biggest redistributions of wealth in history, upward. Released from antitrust restrictions, corporate America had embarked on a mergers boom that undermined competition and led to massive concentrations of wealth and power in the private sector. Senior executives, big business, and Wall Street financiers had prospered mightily, while the bottom three-fifths of Americans saw their incomes stagnate or fall. Trickle-down economics hardly delivered even the promised, pathetic trickle, and the supply-side theory that prophesied magically balanced budgets from tax cuts had instead quadrupled the federal debt. Americans' economic dissatisfaction was amply reflected in Greenberg's polling, but the Democratic Party opted for a message that emphasized "culture" over class, and a shamefully low species of culture at that, one that aimed at the specific racist component within the larger complex of white resentment and grievance.

The afflictions of the working and middle classes—both white and black, it should be noted—owed a great deal less to welfare cheats and babies having babies than to the workings of a laissez-faire economics that channeled ever-greater wealth into fewer and fewer hands.[27] But making that case would have required Democrats to claim, forcefully and without apology, the New Deal and Great Society legacies that had dramatically transformed American life for the better.[28] Social Security, Medicare and Medicaid, unemployment insurance, the Centers for Disease Control, the National Institutes of Health, the National Science Foundation, these are all "welfare," parts of a social framework meant to provide for the basic well-being and economic security of everyone. Those much-reviled

---

[27] "The issue is not quotas. It is not reverse discrimination. It is not welfare queens. It is the need for a new American agenda to restore the country's economic base." Jesse Jackson, speaking in 1991, as quoted in Greenberg, "From Crisis to Working Majority."

[28] See "The Long Good Deal," *infra.*

food stamps—a program originated and administered by the Department of Agriculture—were part of the broader system of agricultural price supports designed to stabilize the incomes of Middle America's farmers. The New Deal's matrix of banking and securities regulation ushered in fifty years of stability and growth in finance, and the first major recision of that matrix—the deregulation of the savings and loan industry in the early 1980s—promptly resulted in the wholesale collapse of the industry, leaving taxpayers on the hook for $160 billion. The strong antitrust policy of the New Deal protected small and midsized companies—and the local communities they helped to sustain—from being overwhelmed by corporate giants. The framework of labor laws installed by the New Deal had delivered a living wage and upward mobility to three generations of American workers.

But Democrats had stopped making the case for government, and allowed the broad benefits made possible by the right kind of government to fade into the background of public consciousness. Instead, as Greenberg put it, "[f]or the public, the welfare state is welfare—AFDC [Aid to Families with Dependent Children] and food stamps . . . 'welfare queens' and the 'welfare mess.'" For the better part of two decades, Republicans had jammed up Democrats by shunting class into the highly flammable realm of morals, character, and "values," with racist dog whistles always piping in the background. "The last thing the Democratic Party has wanted to do is declare that there is a possibility for class struggle," Walter Dean Burnham observed in a 1988 interview. "The Republicans, however, are perfectly happy to declare class struggle all the time. They are always waging a one-sided class war against the constituency the Democrats nominally represent. In this sense, the Republicans are the only real political party in the United States."[29]

But it sounded good, all the Clinton campaign patter about

---

[29] Published in *New Perspectives Quarterly*, and quoted in Didion, *Political Fictions*, pp. 157–58.

opportunity and empowerment and putting people first, the hard sell on "mainstream values," those vaunted "middle-class values." Good enough for him to beat George H. W. Bush and Ross Perot that fall, taking 43 percent of the popular vote in an election in which approximately 60 percent of the voting-age population actually voted, which, to those of a perverse or skeptical frame of mind, meant that America's largest political party—the party of the people who don't vote—had won again.

As for "a coherent, compelling economic case," it was manifest in Bill Clinton's 1992 campaign in spite of how Hillary would, in 2016, characterize the last thirty years of Democratic politics. You could find it in the absence of an antimonopoly plank in the Democratic platform for the first time in over a hundred years, and in the plank admonishing workers to "be prepared to join in cooperative efforts to increase productivity, flexibility and quality,"[30] and in the fact that the sole reference to the minimum wage—whose real value (as measured in 2015 dollars) had fallen from $8.89 in 1980 to $7.16 by 1992[31]—was in support of an "indexed minimum wage." It was likewise to be found in Clinton's proud trumpeting of his associations with the militantly low-wage, antiunion Tyson Foods and Walmart, which made sense in light of Hillary's five years of service on the Walmart board of directors,[32] and also in light of the extensive antiunion record that Bill compiled as governor

---

[30] "Flexibility" is a loaded word in the context of labor-management relations. "[T]he term is generally understood to be a signifier of insecurity and impermanence of work within modern leftism. French sociologist Pierre Bourdieu referred to workplace flexibility as flexploitation, or in a less pithy manner, as 'a *mode of domination* . . . based on the creation of a generalized and permanent state of insecurity aimed at forcing workers into submission.'" From Isaac Effner, "The Limits of Cooperation: Social Conflict and the Collapse of the Democratic Party–Organized Labor Alliance," Undergraduate Honors Thesis, University of Colorado, Boulder, http://scholar.colorado.edu/honr_theses/1331, quoting "Job Insecurity Is Everywhere Now," in Pierre Bourdieu, *Acts of Resistance: Against the Tyranny of the Market,* trans. Richard Nice (The New Press, 1998).

[31] Annalyn Kurtz and Tal Yellin, "Minimum Wage Since 1938," Money.CNN.com, updated November 3, 2015.

[32] For which she received $100,000 worth of stock options, not unusual for serving on the board of a major company.

of Arkansas.[33] It could be found as well in the roster of big donors, both human and corporate, who made this "the best financed
Democratic presidential campaign ever," as Senator John D. Rockefeller IV (D-WV), the DNC's finance chairman, proclaimed from
the podium of the Democratic National Convention, a campaign
flush with the kind of cash that would buy "focus groups, polling, research, whatever it takes to get the message out."[34] That "the
message" itself was a con job—that the determined insistence on
bedrock American "values" regarding fairness, responsibility, and
hard work had a good deal less to do with the material needs of the
Democrats' traditional constituency than with selling that constituency a bill of goods—would be borne out in the years to come. The
holders of what might be called "minoritarian" economic interests
would grow stupendously rich. Surely for them the New Democrats' "third way" was both coherent and compelling. A swing back
toward genuine New Deal populism—to "majoritarian economic
interests"—would have served this new Democratic constituency
about as well as a pitchfork to the head.

## 3.

No one, least of all Hillary Clinton herself, would say she has been
a passive partner in her husband's career. They cultivated the same

---

[33] Bill Clinton played a leading role in destroying the long and extremely successful biracial
working-class coalition in Arkansas. Over a twenty-year period (1948–68), this coalition
increased voter turnout in presidential elections by 251 percent (despite the fact that the
state's population remained virtually the same), resulting in Arkansas's being one of only two
Southern states that were exempted from the preclearance provision of the Voting Rights Act
of 1965. This same progressive, biracial, labor-based coalition led to Arkansas's 1970s "liberal
heyday" that nurtured Clinton's early career. See Michael Pierce, "How Bill Clinton Remade
the Democratic Party by Abandoning Unions: An Arkansas Story," *Labor and Working-Class
History Association*, November 23, 2016, www.lawcha.org.

[34] As quoted in Didion, *Political Fictions*, p. 122.

donors, hammered the same talking points, and pushed the same agendas from Arkansas all the way to the White House, where Hillary dug the work of policy and politics with every bit as much gusto as Bill. Two of the signal progressive achievements of his presidency, the Family and Medical Leave Act and the State Children's Health Insurance Program, bear her stamp. There was, of course, her leadership of the spectacularly failed effort to reform health care, but she took the hit and continued the work: Medicare coverage for mammograms for breast cancer screening, more funds for research on prostate cancer and childhood asthma, a serious inquiry into Gulf War syndrome. She was a prime mover in the creation of the Justice Department's Office on Violence Against Women, and in Beijing to address the Fourth World Conference on Women, she resisted pressure from the Chinese as well as from the West Wing of the White House (one would like to know the man–woman ratio in *that* room) to state to representatives from 180 countries: "If there is one message that echoes forth from this conference, let it be that human rights are women's rights and women's rights are human rights, once and for all."[35] People cheered, pounded the tables; she was a hero for what she said that day.

More good works were to follow in foster care, adoption, children's health, and education. In the final years of Bill's presidency she became the administration's unofficial ambassador for the New Democrats' "Third Way," now capitalized, which was declared by buzzword ace Al From to be "the worldwide brand name for progressive politics for the Information Age."[36] In November 1997 Hillary led a nine-member delegation that included From and future Treasury secretary Larry Summers to Great Britain, where they were

---

[35] Patrick E. Tyler, "Hillary Clinton, in China, Details Abuse of Women," *New York Times,* September 6, 1995. For the positive long-term effect of the stand Clinton took that day, see Gayle Tzemach Lemmon, "The Hillary Doctrine," *Newsweek,* March 6, 2011.

[36] Curtis Atkins, "The Third Way International," *Jacobin,* February 11, 2016.

guests of Tony Blair at Chequers, the prime minister's country house retreat. There the New Democrats strategized with Blair and his "New Labour" coalition on how to build the "new progressivism" into an international movement for winning "the battle of ideas" as well as elections. In 1998 Hillary hosted a White House meeting of Democrats from across the spectrum in hopes of winning opponents over to Third Way ideology, and that fall she and From again traveled to Chequers for more meetings with Blair and New Labour. Higher-profile events were to follow: a Third Way forum in conjunction with the opening of that year's UN General Assembly, a DLC-sponsored conference in Washington attended by the leaders of virtually all the Western European democracies,[37] and a triumphant international conference held in Florence, Italy, in November 1999, at which the Third Way was declared to have superseded the "old left" of European social democracy.

"The most elite club in the world is becoming extremely fashionable," commented the *Guardian* after the Washington conference, and in fact the Third Way experiment in the U.S. looked like a glorious success. In February 2000, in his final State of the Union address, Bill Clinton assessed the country in near-utopian terms:

> *We are fortunate to be alive at this moment in history. Never before has our nation enjoyed, at once, so much prosperity and social progress with so little internal crisis and so few external threats . . .*

There was much for him to crow about. GDP growth averaged a robust 4 percent from 1993 to 2001, up from 2.8 percent under Reagan and Bush. The chronic deficits of the past thirty years had yielded to three straight years of budget surpluses, and the stock

---

[37] France was the major holdout. "The French left, like France, imitates no one," said Prime Minister Lionel Jospin. *L'esprit français vit.*

market, thanks to surging corporate profits and the dot-com boom, was hitting record highs. Twenty-two million new jobs had been created, inflation and interest rates were low, and unemployment hit a thirty-one-year low of 4 percent. Goldman Sachs called it the "best economy ever," and for those at the top it surely was. But a clue to the state of things for everyone else could be found in the strange confluence of low inflation and historically low unemployment. Workers' bargaining power normally rises as unemployment falls, leading to higher wages, then higher prices as businesses try to cover their increased labor costs, all of which create rising inflation. But the Clinton boom was different. The future Federal Reserve chair Janet Yellen, at the time a member of the Fed's Board of Governors, explained the anomaly: "While the labor market is tight, job insecurity also seems alive and well. Real wage aspirations appear modest, and the bargaining power of workers is surprisingly low."[38]

Federal Reserve chair Alan Greenspan put it more bluntly. Workers, he said, were "traumatized" by the twin pressures of globalization and technological advance, which together drove labor into a singularly weak bargaining position. This was due in no small part to NAFTA, the North American trade initiative carried over from the Reagan and Bush administrations that Clinton pushed through Congress despite the nearly unanimous opposition of labor. Corporate shareholders[39] and executives enjoyed the lion's share of NAFTA's benefits, while the average real wage for workers during Clinton's presidency, at $13.60 an hour (in 2001 dollars), was 2 percent lower than under Reagan and Bush, and nearly 10 percent lower than under Carter.[40] Likewise, the minimum wage—Clinton had engineered a two-step boost in 1996–97, from $4.25 to $5.15—

---

[38] Robert Pollin, "Note to Hillary: Clintonomics Was a Disaster for Most Americans," *Nation*, January 26, 2016.

[39] The wealthiest 10 percent of Americans own over 80 percent of stocks and mutual funds. See Paul Krugman, "A $700 Billion Trump Gift to Rich Foreigners," *New York Times*, October 27, 2017.

[40] Pollin, "Note to Hillary."

represented more backward movement for workers. The $5.15 wage in force when he left office in 2001 was 35 percent lower in real terms than in 1968.

In this brave new Third Way economy of mobile capital, free trade, and fast-evolving technology, the job you had this morning could be offshored or outsourced by afternoon. Income inequality was greater than at any time since 1929, and what *BusinessWeek* celebrated as the booming "New Age economy"[41] was pretty much the same old economy at the bottom, where the average poverty rate under Clinton, at 13.2 percent of the population, was only marginally better than the 14 percent rate under Reagan and Bush.[42] The record-low unemployment rate for African-Americans that Clinton loved to tout owed a great deal to the record-high incarceration rate for African-Americans: government statistics on unemployment and poverty exclude the incarcerated population, which had exploded after the passage of Clinton's 1994 crime bill, with African-Americans being pipelined into prisons in grossly disproportionate numbers.[43] Welfare "reform"—one of the DLC's most insistent themes, and a reliable talking point throughout Clinton's 1992 campaign—came to pass in August 1996, during the thick of his reelection effort. "[A] decent welfare bill wrapped in a sack of shit," as Clinton was said to have described the bill, which would ultimately decrease welfare rolls by 75 percent over the next two decades, though the poverty rate would remain virtually the same, and extreme poverty—defined as household income of less than $2 per person per day—would end

---

[41] As quoted in Stoller, "How Democrats Killed Their Populist Soul."

[42] Pollin, "Note to Hillary."

[43] The Violent Crime Control and Law Enforcement Act, which, among other provisions, allocated $10 billion for constructing new prisons, increased death-penalty-eligible crimes from two to fifty-eight, installed a hundred-to-one sentencing disparity between crack and powder cocaine, allowed for the execution of mentally incapacitated defendants, required mandatory life sentences for third offenses, severely restricted the use of parole, and eliminated Pell grants for inmates pursuing their college degree. By the time Clinton left office in 2001, the U.S. had the highest rate of incarceration in the world. See Alexander, "Black Lives Shattered," and Robinson, "Bill Clinton's Stone Mountain Moment."

up doubling.[44] The so-called Freedom to Farm Act of 1996 imposed the same laissez-faire economics on agriculture that had nearly destroyed American farmers in the early twentieth century, with the same results this time around: overproduction, plummeting crop prices, and disaster for independent farmers, though for the agribusiness giants like Cargill and ADM that buy their raw materials from farmers, it made for a great business model.[45] With antitrust policy largely moribund, wholesale consolidation took place across a range of industries that shape and control much of the daily lives of Americans, including media, energy, food production, telecommunications, technology, and retail. As competition from small and midsized companies was choked off, big business enjoyed ever-greater concentrations of wealth and monopoly power. And out there in the boonies, in Appalachia and the rural South and Midwest, the white working class started dying younger, of what we now call the "diseases of despair"—suicide, alcoholism, drug addiction—though it would be years before this unprecedented rise in American mortality would ping the national radar.[46]

---

[44] The Personal Responsibility and Work Opportunity Reconciliation Act of 1996. Bill Clinton, reportedly at Hillary's urging, had already vetoed two highly punitive Republican "reform" bills, and a third veto would have furnished Bob Dole a handy stick with which to beat Clinton all the way to Election Day. The new legislation replaced AFDC with Temporary Assistance to Needy Families (TANF), which channeled federal safety-net money to states in the form of block grants, in effect creating what two commentators have described as a "slush fund for states." The more people a state is able to move off its welfare rolls, the more TANF dollars that state can use to fund other programs or plug budget holes. In Texas, where the TANF-to-poverty ratio is 5 percent—that is, only 5 percent of poor families actually receive TANF help— the state uses much of its block grant to fund its child-welfare system, an expense that the state would otherwise have to bear on its own. Nationwide, three out of every four TANF dollars are spent on something other than assistance for needy families. See Kathryn Edin and H. Luke Shaefer, "20 Years Since Welfare 'Reform,'" *Atlantic*, August 22, 2016; Edin and Shaefer, *$2 a Day* (Houghton Mifflin Harcourt, 2015); Lily Rothman, "Why Bill Clinton Signed the Welfare Reform Bill, as Explained in 1996," *Time*, August 19, 2016; Max Ehrenfreund, "Bernie Sanders Is Right: Bill Clinton's Welfare Law Doubled Extreme Poverty," *Washington Post*, February 22, 2016. Clinton's expansion of the Earned Income Tax Credit mitigated some of the effects of welfare reform for the working poor, but for Americans who can't work, or can't find work, the 1996 bill has been catastrophic.

[45] Thomas Frank, *What's the Matter with Kansas?* (Picador, 2005), pp. 64–65.

[46] Anne Case and Angus Deaton, "Rising Morbidity and Mortality in Midlife Among White

For the Democratic Party's traditional constituency of the working class, the middle class, minorities, the poor, and immigrants—all those who throughout most of the twentieth century relied on the party's economic populism to give them a reasonably fair shot at achieving the American Dream—eight years of Bill Clinton's Third Way served them about as well as the second coming of Herbert Hoover. And just as Bill left office in January 2001, Hillary arrived in the Senate to continue the work. One would detect no appreciable softening in her ideology even as the New Economy boom of the 1990s quickly began its great unraveling. The stock market bubble burst in March 2001, marking the end of the long Clintonomics expansion, which, as it turned out, had been stoked by a massive run-up in household and business debt. Wages fell, unemployment rose, and major corporate scandals began to break, particularly in the recently deregulated telecom and energy sectors. Enron, World-Com, AOL Time Warner, Tyco, Reliant Energy, and Halliburton were among the companies whose rigged balance sheets suggested that the New Economy boom was less robust than advertised. Even bigger chickens would soon be coming home to roost, but for the One Percent, things were great—better than ever, in fact, as corporate consolidation and an explosion of exotic new securities on Wall Street channeled more and more wealth upward.

Hillary, meanwhile, stayed the course. She'd joined the Senate's New Democrat Caucus on taking office, instantly becoming its most prominent member, and continued to be a star speaker at DLC events. Free trade and free markets were her default positions, and during her first six years in office she introduced no bills aimed at regulating or otherwise overseeing Wall Street, which was literally on her senatorial turf. In 2005 she was tapped by the DLC to lead its "American Dream Initiative," a task force that would formulate a centrist platform for Democrats in the upcoming 2006 and 2008 elections. The result, widely viewed as a preview of Hillary's anticipated 2008 presidential run, was billed as—go crazy, DLC fans!—a "middle-class values agenda." It called for a strict pay-as-you-go budget process in Washington, along with incremental measures for making college and health care more affordable. Its most daring break with DLC orthodoxy was support for an increase in the minimum wage, although the document's basic conservatism could be easily identified in its omissions. There was no mention of the Iraq or Afghan wars, both of which the DLC fervently supported. It said nothing about remedying labor's anemic bargaining power, reversing the Bush administration's top-end tax cuts, bolstering antitrust policy, reining in Wall Street, or eliminating the carried-interest loophole that gave generous tax treatment to the billions in compensation that private equity executives and hedge fund managers were regularly taking home. The only concession to the reality of a clearly unbalanced financial system was a vague reference to holding CEOs accountable for the continuing skyward trend in executive pay.

This would still be Hillary's economic case when she ran for president in 2008, the year the biggest chickens of all returned to the roost. To get the proper measure of the New Democrats' role in creating the economic meltdown of 2008, it's useful to return to the early days of Bill's first presidential run, specifically to a dinner he had "with high-powered New York businesspeople" in the fall of 1991. The dinner was organized by Ken Brody, a Goldman Sachs banker,[47] and included Goldman Sachs's cochairman Robert Rubin, a man, as Clinton would later write, "whose tightly reasoned arguments for a new economic policy made a lasting impression on me."[48] A key economic adviser to Clinton during the campaign, Rubin would go on to serve Clinton for virtually the entire eight

---

[47] He would serve in the Clinton administration as president of the Export-Import Bank.
[48] Bill Clinton, *My Life* (Vintage Books, 2005), p. 497.

years of his presidency, first as chairman of the National Economic Council, then as secretary of the Treasury. This consummate Wall Street operator would be the administration's driving force for the systematic deregulation of banking and finance throughout the 1990s. In particular, Rubin sought to eliminate Glass-Steagall, the 1933 New Deal legislation that separated banks' traditional commercial activities—taking deposits and making loans—from riskier investment-banking operations, such as issuing and trading securities. Rubin's years-long effort ultimately succeeded with the passage of the Financial Services Modernization Act of 1999, a.k.a. the Gramm-Leach-Bliley Act, legislation that was greeted with great joy on Wall Street. John Reed and Sandy Weill, co-CEOs of bank giant Citigroup, released a statement lauding Washington for "liberating our financial companies from an antiquated regulatory structure," and predicted "this legislation will unleash the creativity of our industry and ensure our global competitiveness."[49]

If nothing else, the crash of 2008 demonstrated the preferability of boring bankers over the creative kind. But that would come later. In the "now" of 1999, Wall Street saw blue skies and big bucks ahead. Naturally it would, given that Wall Street had written the new rules. "Bob" Rubin left Treasury to join his friends John and Sandy at Citigroup, where he served as chairman of the executive committee for a cool $40 million a year. Hillary Clinton won a Senate seat from New York with the steadfast backing of Citigroup, her top contributor from the highly supportive financial sector. Bill Clinton would earn $104.9 million in speaking fees over the next twelve years, with the financial industry accounting for the largest share, $19.6 million.[50] And on Wall Street, the newly unleashed cre-

---

[49] Nomi Prins, "The Clintons and Their Banker Friends," TomDispatch.com, May 7, 2015, www.tomdispatch.com/blog/175993/. The Commodity Futures Modernization Act of 2000 would unleash further "creativity" in over-the-counter derivatives, including the credit default swaps that helped bring about the 2008 bust.

[50] Philip Rucker, Tom Hamburger, and Alexander Becker, "How the Clintons Went from 'Dead Broke' to Rich," *Washington Post*, June 26, 2014.

ativity was spinning out derivatives, collateralized debt obligations, securitized subprime mortgages, and other "products" that brought extraordinary wealth to the originators and handlers of these instruments. Much of it was junk, junk leveraged into more junk, and the goods got passed around in a daisy chain of banks, "Edge" affiliates (off-book bank subsidiaries), investment houses, and secondary markets, with insurance giants like AIG selling hedges against default. The market worked gloriously for them, until it didn't, and then they turned, all those scared-shitless brokers, bankers, hedge fund managers, auto-industry execs, insurance company CEOs, and the pols in Washington who'd sanctioned the whole sorry racket, to the rest of us to bail them out.

4.

It won't be the Communists who finally bring down capitalism. Nor will it be the socialists, the anarchists, the environmental movement, indigenous-rights advocates, labor unions, minorities, immigrants, hippies, heavy metal, or welfare cheats. The capitalists themselves will do it, by going too far. They nearly did it in 1929. Closer to our own time, the savings and loan bust of the 1980s could be viewed as a test run, and there was a brief, breathless dance along the abyss in 1998 when Long-Term Capital Management failed, a scare that was quickly and conveniently forgotten. Then 2008 happened, and for a while it looked as if this might be the real thing. The situation was dire enough that Bush's secretary of the Treasury, Henry Paulson, a veritable master of the universe if there ever was one,[51] got down on his knees to beg House Speaker Nancy Pelosi to support the $700 billion bank bailout bill.

Speaking on the floor of the Senate during debate on that same

---

[51] A former chairman of Goldman Sachs. Yes, them. Again.

bill, Senator Hillary Clinton of New York, by now in her second term, would see fit to lambast the "culture of recklessness in our financial markets, endorsed by an ideology of indifference in Washington." She would nevertheless vote in favor of the bill, putting taxpayers on the hook for Wall Street's very expensive spree. As for the constituency being served by the bill, she elaborated the next day to a New York City radio host: "I think that the banks of New York and our other financial institutions are probably the biggest winners in all this, which is one of the reasons why, at the end, despite my serious reservations about it, I supported it."[52]

It's worth remembering that as 2008 gave way to 2009, a new Democratic president, along with a Democratic Senate and a Democratic House of Representatives, would continue to cater first and foremost to those same banks and financial institutions that created the crisis. In short order, Wall Street was making big money again.[53] But for the many millions of "folks," as President Obama was fond of calling them, those same people who might be called the Democratic Party's "traditional" or by now "nominal" constituency, the people who "pay the taxes, raise the kids, and play by the rules," those avatars of "middle-class values" who lost their homes (as many as ten million), jobs (an estimated nine million), and household wealth (an estimated $16 trillion),[54] there was no comparable funding—not even close—for mortgage relief, economic stimulus, or housing assistance, the kinds of programs that would have put the rest of America on a similarly fast track to recovery.

[52] Jeff Gerth, "Hillary Clinton Told Wall Street to 'Cut It Out'—Not So Much, the Record Shows," *Politico*, November 15, 2015.

[53] See Ron Suskind, *Confidence Men: Wall Street, Washington, and the Education of a President* (Harper, 2011); Paul Street, "Barack Obama's Neoliberal Legacy: Rightward Drift and Donald Trump," *Truthdig*, January 3, 2017.

[54] See "The 2008 Housing Crisis Displaced More Americans Than the 1930s Dust Bowl," National Center for Policy Analysis, May 11, 2015; "Employment Loss and the 2007–09 Recession: An Overview," *Monthly Labor Review*, Bureau of Labor Statistics, April 2011; Lam Vo, "All the Wealth We Lost and Regained Since the Recession Started," Planet Money/National Public Radio, May 31, 2013.

"A blunt lesson about power," William Greider of the *Washington Post* called it, "who has it and who doesn't."[55] This disparity in treatment would be borne out by the numbers: 95 percent of the income gains during Obama's first term went to the One Percent.[56] Not a single high-ranking executive at a major bank or financial firm went to jail. A few were fired, but even these individuals could consider themselves lucky in light of the fact that more than eight hundred bankers went to jail for the savings and loan crisis of the 1980s.[57] No big banks were broken up. There would be no twenty-first-century version of Glass-Steagall. The "Big Six"[58] banks did end up paying over $150 *billion* in fines and settlements for their conduct leading to the 2008 crisis, but such is their profitability that these hits were absorbed with hardly a hitch in their balance sheets.[59] And as of 2013, Hillary would be back among these same bankers, mingling, giving speeches, raking in the big bucks with no apparent qualms about pocketing what was, in a very real sense, stolen money.[60]

"I run, I run to the whistle of money," a poet—American, of course—once wrote. Between 2013 and 2015 Hillary gave twelve speeches to Wall Street banks and investment firms, for which she was paid a total of $2,935,000.[61] When the speeches became an issue during the Democratic primaries, she pointed to her Senate record as evidence that she could be "tough" on Wall Street, though

[55] William Greider, "Obama Told Us to Speak Out, but Is He Listening?," *Washington Post*, March 22, 2009, referenced in Street, "Barack Obama's Neoliberal Legacy."

[56] Hibah Yousuf, "Obama Admits 95% of Income Gains Gone to Top 1%," Money.CNN.com, September 15, 2013, referenced in Street, "Barack Obama's Neoliberal Legacy."

[57] Gretchen Morgenson, "The Impunity That Main St. Didn't Forget," *New York Times*, November 13, 2016.

[58] JPMorgan Chase, Citigroup, Bank of America, Wells Fargo, Goldman Sachs, and Morgan Stanley.

[59] Nomi Prins, "Waking Up in Hillary Clinton's America," TomDispatch.com, October 27, 2016, www.tomdispatch.com/blog/176203/.

[60] See Amy Chozick, Nicholas Confessore, and Michael Barbaro, "Leaked Speech Excerpts Show a Hillary Clinton at Ease with Wall Street," *New York Times*, October 7, 2016; Ben White, "What Clinton Said in Her Paid Speeches," *Politico*, February 9, 2016; Prins, "Waking Up in Hillary Clinton's America."

[61] Prins, "Waking Up in Hillary Clinton's America."

the record is notably bare for her first six years in office. During 2007–2008, as the seriousness of the subprime crisis was becoming apparent—she also happened to be running for president at the time—she introduced five bills related to housing finance or foreclosure, all of which died in committee without discussion. In 2007 she cosponsored a bill to curtail executive compensation, which also quietly died in committee. While publicly calling for an end to the carried-interest loophole, she did not sign on to a 2007 bill that would have done exactly that. And when pressed by Bernie Sanders on her Wall Street ties during one of their debates, she recalled a meeting at the offices of the NASDAQ stock exchange in December 2007, where, by her account, she told a group of finance executives, "Cut it out! Quit foreclosing on homes! Quit engaging in these kinds of speculative behaviors!"[62]

Video of the meeting shows that she did call on the banks to voluntarily suspend foreclosures and freeze interest rates on adjustable subprime mortgages. She also acknowledged her "wonderful donors" in the audience, and praised Wall Street for its crucial role in building America's wealth. She assured the bankers that the brewing crisis wasn't mainly their fault, "not by a long shot," but Wall Street "certainly had a hand in making it worse" and "needs to help us solve it."[63] She would strike a similarly conciliatory tone in an October 2013 speech to Goldman Sachs employees, in which she said it was "oversimplification" to pin the 2008 bust on the banks. Blaming the banks "was conventional wisdom," she told her banker audience. "And I think that there's a lot that could have been avoided in terms of both misunderstanding and really politicizing what happened."[64]

That her nearly three million dollars' worth of Wall Street speeches would themselves be "politicized" in 2016 seemed to surprise her. She could, during that same 2013 Goldman Sachs speech,

---

[62] *Ibid.* See also Prins, "The Clintons and Their Banker Friends."

[63] Gerth, "Hillary Clinton Told Wall Street to 'Cut It Out.'"

[64] Chozick et al., "Leaked Speech Excerpts Show a Hillary Clinton at Ease with Wall Street."

describe her budding awareness of the "anxiety and even anger in the country over the feeling that the game is rigged" with no apparent appreciation that her presence among these bankers, for which she was paid $225,000, might itself be evidence, or at least contribute to the "feeling," that the game is rigged. Later, in *What Happened*, she would write of these lavishly compensated speeches, "I didn't think many Americans would believe that I'd sell a lifetime of principle and advocacy for any price."[65] But she gives herself too much credit with that statement. Many Americans viewed those speeches not as Hillary "selling out" but as Hillary doing business as usual, making her consummate striver's way in a morally bankrupt system that she'd played a large and active role in creating. This was the world she lived in, this system; to the extent that she was capable of seeing herself as a creature of the system, we can assume that she viewed it as benign rather than bankrupt, a force for the general good. We might also assume this benignity extended to her long-time friends in the system, the Lloyd Blankfeins and Bob Rubins and Sandy Weills who channeled tens of millions of dollars to the Clintons and their foundation over the years.

That it seems to have taken her until 2013 to appreciate the "anxiety and even anger in the country over the feeling that the game is rigged" is, on one hand, quite remarkable. But on the other, not so much: Hillary couldn't see the forest for the trees due to the elemental fact that she was one of the trees. Thus she could view her Wall Street buck-raking as entirely normal, and be surprised that it was even an issue. "That's what they offered!" she blurted when Anderson Cooper asked why she had accepted $225,000 for a single speech to Goldman Sachs, and her physical recoil in that moment—the wide eyes, the quick step backward, the flailing hands—suggests nearly as much as her words the depth of her cluelessness. Over time, as the issue persisted, her responses would show somewhat more

---

[65] Hillary Clinton, *What Happened* (Simon & Schuster, 2017), p. 45.

preparation, which had the effect of throwing their silliness into high relief. "Let everybody who's ever given a speech to any private group under any circumstances release them. We'll all release them at the same time." "Senator Sanders took about $200,000 from Wall Street firms. Not directly, but through the Democratic Senatorial Campaign Committee."[66] Or, more vaguely, she would "look into" releasing the transcripts of the speeches. Her campaign was just as feckless. "'Anybody who takes money from Goldman Sachs can't possibly be president.' You heard that, sort of, in the last debate," Bill Clinton said of Sanders's attacks on Hillary's Wall Street speeches. "Pure trolling," spokesman Brian Fallon said of the issue. "I don't think voters are interested in the transcripts of her speeches," offered Clinton pollster Joel Benenson.[67] And from DLC cofounder Will Marshall: "The idea that you have to excommunicate anybody who ever worked in the financial sector is ridiculous."[68]

No, not *excommunicate*. And it wasn't *pure trolling*, and it wasn't just *anybody*. And while these various propositions, as stated, were in fact ridiculous, that Clinton and her campaign refused to address the issue in a genuine way was surely taken by many Americans as yet more evidence that the game is rigged. All that blatant shiftiness, in plain sight. Such diving and dodging, with so little available pretense that it was anything but. The political calculation in all this must have been excruciating for her, weighing the cost-benefit

---

[66] In 2006, the year of Sanders's first Senate campaign, the DSCC raised approximately $121,376,000 from scores of different donors. The Sanders campaign received $37,300 directly from the DSCC; the national Democratic Party spent $60,000 on ads supporting Sanders, and gave $100,000 to the Vermont Democratic Party. Sanders appears to have received no money from the DSCC for his 2012 reelection campaign. Center for Responsive Politics data on the DSCC, opensecrets.org.

[67] A June 2016 Bloomberg Politics poll showed that half of all registered voters were bothered "a lot" by Hillary's paid speeches. Chozick et al., "Leaked Speech Excerpts Show a Hillary Clinton at Ease with Wall Street."

[68] See White, "What Clinton Said in Her Paid Speeches," and Nick Timiraos, "Parties' Divide on the Economy Widens," *Wall Street Journal*, November 15, 2015, both referenced in Michael Corcoran, "Hillary Clinton's Ghosts: A Legacy of Pushing the Democratic Party to the Right," *Truthout*, December 2, 2015.

ratio of muddling through against that of releasing the transcripts and speaking directly to the conflict they represented. Facing up to the conflict: on some level the idea must have terrified her. The contradictions were too great to reconcile short of a frank admission that the contradictions existed, and to admit this would have forced her to confront the possibility that her "lifetime of principle and advocacy," for all the good it had wrought, had been chiefly in the service of a system that benefited the rich and powerful at the expense of everyone else. But say she'd dared to open up this way: imagining this requires us to enlarge our notion of what politics could be, its potential for authenticity. To witness a candidate questioning herself, embarking on a genuine soul-search in the midst of running for the highest office in the land—what an extraordinary moment in America that could be. What a gamble! Hillary putting it all on the table, heart and soul, hopes, history, ambition, staking everything on the chance of a better politics. With all her armor and careerist caution, all the layers of personae built up over a lifetime of trench-warfare politics, Hillary Clinton might be the last politician we could expect this from, and yet, and yet . . . As things stood, her *ethos,* her credibility, wasn't worth spit in the eyes of the majority of Americans. Simply as a matter of practical politics, maybe nothing short of a gamble on this scale could have given her the credibility to smash Trump in the way he deserved.

The Wall Street speeches were "bad 'optics,'" she goes so far as to admit in *What Happened.*[69] The optics were bad indeed, and we're talking about more than mere spin or window-dressing here. "Optics" in a democracy go to the guts of the thing. For people to buy into the premise of democracy—for them to care enough to participate in an informed, thoughtful way—they need some basic level of confidence that their government is truly representative, and as such works in the genuine public interest. Hillary hanging out with the

---

[69] Page 46.

bankers, hoovering up their cash—this same crowd who caused the crash and walked away clean—the optics do damage not just to her but to the entire *ethos* of democracy. Same for the sprawling enterprise of the Clinton Foundation, the chronic overlap of its global-elite donor base with the elite's business before Hillary Clinton's Department of State. Human rights certifications, approvals for arms deals and oil pipelines, interventions on behalf of foreign banks: under Hillary's leadership the State Department showed an uncanny knack for coming through for friends of the Clinton Foundation.[70] Maybe there was influence, maybe not. It's hard to tell when the parties possess a certain degree of sophistication, but it *looks* bad, and that alone does damage. Inflict enough of this kind of damage, and people lose faith. They might opt out and join America's largest political party, or maybe they find themselves drawn to a thug candidate who states plainly that the system is rigged rotten and he alone can fix it. Maybe he's not perfect—maybe he's a perfect horror show, actually—but there's that one big truth he's got on his side, and anyway nihilism's a blast for people who've been lied to all their lives.

Hillary's career is emblematic of the past thirty-five years of New Democrat politics, a period when the party became not so much the champion of the working and middle classes as the party that made things worse a little more slowly than Republicans did. By now it's clear who neoliberalism's big winners are. The One Percent's income has skyrocketed since the late 1980s, and their power and influence have grown accordingly. Neoliberalism's losers—the poor, and the working and middle classes that were once the Demo-

---

[70] See, for instance, Simon Head, "The Clinton System," *New York Review of Books,* January 30, 2016, www.nybooks.com/daily/2016/01/30/clinton-system-donor-machine-2016-election/; Nathan J. Robinson, "The Clinton Foundation's Problems Are Deeper Than You Think," *Current Affairs,* August 31, 2016; "Weapons, Pipelines & Wall St.: Did Clinton Foundation Donations Impact Clinton State Dept. Decisions?," *Democracy Now!,* August 25, 2016 (transcript of radio interview among Amy Goodman, David Sirota, and Paul Glastris). For a more sanguine view of the Clinton Foundation, see, for example, Paul Krugman, "Clinton Gets Gored," *New York Times,* September 5, 2016.

cratic Party's natural, now nominal, constituency—have seen their incomes barely budge in real terms during that time.[71] Even with their modest income gains of the last two years, life is precarious. The Federal Reserve reports that 22 percent of American workers are holding down two or more jobs, and almost half say they lack the ready cash to meet a hypothetical emergency expense of $400.[72] Four hundred bucks. That's a fairly routine car repair, or a plumbing trauma, or maybe your out-of-pocket expense for a trip to the emergency room to get your kid's broken arm fixed, and that's if—*if, if, if*—you're lucky enough to have decent insurance. And it's not recent, this state of affairs. This is how it's been for a generation and more, with no relief in sight. Politics is broken, work is tenuous, education equals debt, and the very rich—how do they do it?—just keep getting richer and richer. The institutions that are supposed to work for everyday people, to speak for them, to provide orderly channels for change and redress, they have become indifferent and distant, if not actively hostile.

"For most Americans," Matt Stoller wrote in the *Atlantic* two weeks before the election,

> *the institutions that touch their lives are unreachable. Americans get broadband through Comcast, their internet through Google, their seeds and chemicals through Monsanto. They sell their grain through Cargill and buy everything from books to lawnmowers through Amazon. Open markets are gone, replaced by a handful of corporate giants. Political groups associated with Koch Industries have a larger budget than either political party, and there is no faith in what was once the most democratically responsive part of government: Congress. Steeped in centralized power and mistrust . . .*

---

[71] Branko Milanovic, *Global Inequality: A New Approach for the Age of Globalization* (Belknap Press, 2016), referenced in Packer, "The Unconnected."
[72] Morgenson, "The Impunity That Main St. Didn't Forget."

*Americans feel a lack of control: They are at the mercy of*
*distant forces, their livelihoods dependent on the arbitrary*
*whims of power.*[73]

In Trump, some forty-six million Americans saw their chance to throw a wrench into the workings of the power machine, and they took it. Many more than that, what we might call the coalition of the alienated, the detached, the disgusted, the know-betters, and the just-don't-give-a-damns who comprise America's largest political party, once again they sent their own form of fuck-you to the machine. They stayed home.

## 5.

*The house seemed as lifeless and undisturbed as some Etruscan*
*tomb, silent with the gods. Jay stood for a moment in the*
*dining room, remembering his first visit here in the early*
*weeks of the Governor's campaign. They had been served an*
*incredible meal, and Arthur Fenstemaker sat in the big chair,*
*stretching and talking: "This is what you have to watch out*
*for, Jay. Remember it. You sit here in these carpets up to your*
*ankles with a fire crackling in a corner and these black men*
*serve you red wine and rare roast beef—and there's crepes*
*suzettes comin' later—and tell me, now. Can you get all*
*wrought up about the poor folks?"*

BILLY LEE BRAMMER, *THE GAY PLACE*

In his convention speech in Philadelphia, Bill Clinton described at length the young Hillary's good works on behalf of poor people. She worked in the legal services project at Yale Law School. She

---

[73] Stoller, "How Democrats Killed Their Populist Soul."

spent a summer interviewing farm workers in migrant camps for a Senate subcommittee. She helped develop procedures for handling suspected child-abuse cases for the Yale New Haven Hospital, and spent an extra year of law school at the Yale Child Study Center writing about the legal rights of children. In the summer of 1972 she smoked out the bogus tax-exempt status of an all-white academy in Alabama, then went door to door in South Texas registering Hispanics to vote.[74] The next year she was in South Carolina investigating the jailing of black juveniles with adults, and in 1974 she was in Massachusetts, trying to track down kids who'd shown up in the census but weren't registered for school. She went knocking on doors again, which was how she found one such child, wheelchair-bound, sitting alone on her porch.

"[M]aking change from the bottom up," was how Bill described the work. God knows there's no glory in it, and no money, and anybody who's gone door to door knows how brutal the work can be. It's foot-blisters-and-sweat, doors slamming-in-your-face, mean-dogs running-you-out-of-the-yard kind of work, not for fakers or the faint of heart. The work has to be a powerful thing in you, a *burning* thing, and so at some point during the 2016 campaign it might have crossed our mind that Bernie Sanders would be the liberation of Hillary. Maybe that populist wave he was riding, that groundswell of youth from the left, would return her to her true self, that young Christian soldier slogging door to door. The wave would give her cover to break free of all the corporate assholes and bankers she'd served all these years, having believed, perhaps correctly, that serving them and their money had to be done in order to get where she and Bill were meant to be.

As the campaign unfolded, a certain amount of repositioning was on display. "People rightly believe that corporations and the powerful have stacked the deck in their favor and against everybody

---

[74] With her Bible in her hand, George Packer tells us in "The Unconnected."

else," Hillary said at a November 2015 debate.[75] By then, with Sanders breathing down her neck, she'd already stated her opposition to the Trans-Pacific Partnership. At various points she endorsed tuition-free public universities, criminal justice reform, universal health care, bringing "accountability" to Wall Street, and, ultimately, after much pushing and prodding, she would agree to a plank in the party's platform calling for "an updated and modernized version" of Glass-Steagall.

While many in the Sanders-Warren wing of the party doubted her complete sincerity, the New Democrats themselves didn't seem terribly worried. "Everyone knew *where she was on that and where she will be,*" said Representative Ron Kind, chairman of the New Democrat Coalition in Congress, speaking of her opposition to the Trans-Pacific Partnership. "But given the necessities of the moment and a tough Democratic primary, she felt she needed to go there *initially.*"[76] In a similar vein, Hillary's old friend Al From assured a reporter from the *Guardian,* "Hillary will bend a little bit but not so much that she can't get herself back on course in the general [election] and when she is governing."[77]

From and his peers apparently think this sort of tacking and trimming, long a feature of U.S. politics—Mitt Romney vividly described it with his Etch A Sketch riff in 2012—happens in a vacuum, sealed off from the eyes and ears of a magically tranced electorate; as if this normalized "pivoting" from the primaries to the general election might not itself be part of a larger "trustworthiness" problem, if not a source of outright public disgust and alienation. The professional Democratic class, all those consultants and "donor advisors," the think tankers and data whizzes, perhaps they live on

[75] Dan Roberts, "'New Democrats' Sound Alarm over Sanders and Clinton's Leftward March," *Guardian,* November 8, 2015.

[76] *Ibid.* (emphasis added), referenced in Corcoran, "Hillary Clinton's Ghosts."

[77] Roberts, "'New Democrats' Sound Alarm." See also Jim Tankersley, "There's Actually a Big Economic Fight Happening in the Democratic Party," *Washington Post,* October 29, 2015.

distant planets. These same political pros who didn't see Trump coming also seemed not to notice their role in creating the anger and frustration that a demagogue like Trump could exploit. For thirty years they'd made it their business to shrink politics down to one or two particular subsets of "swing" voters who, it was agreed, could be swayed by just the right alchemy of codes, messages, signals. Great numbers of Americans were left out of the political calculation, or— most often in the case of minorities—taken for granted. Call it the political equivalent of "small ball," the Democrats' strategy in presidential elections of cobbling together just enough states to squeeze out a win in the Electoral College while conceding vast swaths of the country to Republicans.[78]

"A two-party system in which both parties are committed to calibrating the precise level of tinkering required to get elected is not likely to be a meaningful system," Joan Didion observed in 1992.[79] Equipped with their reams of voter-data analysis and microtargeting models, the tiny minds of the Democratic establishment lacked space for the larger thought that meaningful success in politics might depend on such things as education, consciousness-raising, and movement-building. Thus an establishment player like David Brock and his American Bridge organizations get $75 million from the party in 2016 to carry out negative attacks on Trump, while the entire state of Nebraska limps along with an unpaid director and a "staff" of two:

> *These days Kleeb operates on a "shoestring budget," with $7,500 a month from party headquarters in Washington making up the bulk of the funding—just enough to pay two staffers, hold town halls, and train candidates. "We don't have a ton of money for all the things we should be doing . . . like*

---

[78] The fifty-state strategy pushed by Howard Dean during his time as DNC chairman was an exception.

[79] Didion, *Political Fictions*, p. 153.

> *really intensive voter-registration programs." She especially*
> *regrets not being able to hire a Spanish-speaking staffer, since*
> *some Nebraska towns are now 50 percent Latino.*[80]

*Really intensive voter-registration programs* would seem like a good place to start, given that over half of nonvoters, 52 percent, either identify as Democrats or lean Democratic.[81] But for the New Democrats, bringing nonvoters into the process has always been a touchy proposition; nonvoters, when they do vote, tend to show an alarming independence from New Democrat orthodoxy. Jesse Jackson's surprising strength in the 1984 and 1988 primaries owed much to the new voters he inspired to register. Jerry Brown's campaign for the nomination in 1992 was likewise keyed to bringing new voters into the process, both by making it easier to vote and by giving people a reason to vote, e.g., restoring their faith in electoral politics in part by kicking big money out of elections. It was a stance he insisted on even in defeat. At the convention, he pledged to endorse the Clinton-Gore ticket so long as the party platform was revised to include "a $100 ceiling on all political contributions, a ban on political action committees (PACs), universal [voter] registration undertaken by the government itself (together with same-day registration), and finally election day as a holiday."[82]

The votes are out there. By not trying for them—by deliberately narrowing the scope of its politics over the past several decades—the Democratic Party seems to have made matters needlessly difficult for itself. Then again, the small-ball strategy has had the advantage

---

[80] Cockburn, "It's My Party."
[81] Compared to 27 percent of nonvoters who identify as Republican or lean Republican. Pew Research Center, "Nonvoters: Who They Are, What They Think," November 1, 2012.
[82] The party platform was not revised. Didion, *Political Fictions*, pp. 128–29, 147–48. In 2017 Bernie Sanders was still pounding the theme. "The party's main thrust must be to make politics relevant to those who have given up on democracy and bring millions of new voters into the political process." Bernie Sanders, "How Democrats Can Stop Losing," *New York Times*, June 14, 2017.

for Democratic elites of limiting their obligations. If you can win without the help of a particular demographic or interest group, then you won't be beholden to them once you're in power. In this sense the "pragmatists" of the establishment are true to the name, but over the long haul they're peddling a dud proposition. For twenty years Democrats have been losing even when they were winning; the party's 2016 debacle was merely the bang at the end of the long, steady slide of the New Democrat era. In 1994, two years after Bill Clinton was elected president with 43 percent of the vote in an election in which 40 percent of eligible voters stayed home, Democrats lost their majority in the House, a body they'd controlled for all but four of the past sixty years. They wouldn't regain the House until 2006, then promptly lost it again in 2010 in what Obama, two years into his first term, famously called a "shellacking." The Senate would likewise slip in and out of Democratic control, mostly out, thanks largely to Republican primacy in those Southern and Midwestern states that the Democratic establishment had long ago ceded to the Republican Party. State legislatures, historically dominated by Democrats, began to shift in the early 1990s to the GOP. Democrats lost over a thousand legislative seats during Obama's eight years as president, and after the 2014 midterms Republicans controlled state legislatures to an extent not seen since Reconstruction. After 2016, the GOP held thirty-four governorships, thirty-two state legislatures (including seventeen with veto-proof majorities), and the governorship and both chambers of the legislature in twenty-six states.[83] In twenty-four states, the Democratic Party has practically no influence to speak of, and its "thin bench," the paucity of new talent

---

[83] See Nick Hillman, "Party Control in Congress and State Legislatures," blog post, https://web.education.wisc.edu/nwhillman/index.php/2017/02/01/party-control-in-congress-and-state-legislatures/ (Dr. Hillman is associate professor of educational leadership and policy analysis at the University of Wisconsin–Madison), and K. K. Rebecca Lai, Jasmine C. Lee, and Karl Russell, "In a Further Blow to Democrats, Republicans Increase Their Hold on State Governments," *New York Times,* November 11, 2016.

at the national level, is one consequence of its long local decline. What Stanley Greenberg could describe in 1991 as "the Democrats' continuing hold on politics below the presidential level" had, even before 2016, been reduced to fond memories and wishful thinking.

That Al From would publish a book in 2015 celebrating the movement he helped found, and title it *The New Democrats and the Return to Power,* might seem like a particularly unlucky bit of timing in light of 2016, but the record shows that From and his New Democrat–dominated Democratic Party have been losing power for decades. It hasn't been for lack of money.[84] The Democratic establishment has for years been awash in oceans of money, another reason for regular Americans to distrust, if not flatly despise, that establishment. There's been plenty of money to "get the message out," as Senator Rockefeller told his fellow Democrats way back in 1992, and that message, disastrous as it's been, was still very much in play in 2016. The DLC closed up shop in 2011,[85] but the Third Way, its self-appointed successor organization, has carried on not only the DLC's agenda but its organizational skew toward big money.[86] In late October 2015, the Third Way published a thick policy paper titled "Ready for the New Economy"—even the verbiage gets recycled—making yet again the old New Democrat case for "centrist" politics. "[T]he narrative of fairness and inequality has, to put it mildly, failed to excite voters," the paper asserted, which "should compel the party to rigorously question the electoral value of today's populist agenda."

Throughout the summer and fall of 2015 there was—to put it

---

[84] The party, Hillary's campaign, their joint fund-raising committees, and Super PACs raised $1.4 billion for her campaign, compared to the Republicans' $957.6 million for Trump. Anu Narayansamy, Darla Cameron, and Matea Gold, "Election 2016: Money Raised as of December 31," *Washington Post,* February 1, 2017.

[85] Its archive went to the Clinton Foundation, "an appropriate and fitting repository" in the opinion of Al From. See Corcoran, "Hillary Clinton's Ghosts."

[86] See Corcoran, "Hillary Clinton's Ghosts," and Lee Fang, "Third Way: 'Majority of Our Financial Support' from Wall Street, Business Executives," *Nation,* December 11, 2013.

mildly!—a *great deal* of excitement, red-*hot* excitement, football-rivalry, stomp-their-heads-and-smash-'em-flat *excitement* for the "narrative of fairness and inequality" put forward at Trump's rallies, and the same could be said for Bernie Sanders as well. The air must be thin out there, on whatever planet the Third Way has set up shop. Meanwhile, here on planet Earth, great numbers of poor, working-class, and middle-class Americans who were once the Democratic Party's traditional and natural, now nominal, constituency, turned Republican, stopped voting, or became casual Democrats, voting occasionally in presidential election years and rarely, if ever, in the midterms. The coalitions that put Clinton and Obama in the White House failed to cohere even long enough to give them Congress beyond their first two years in office, much less grow into lasting movements. Now Democrats look to the country's changing demographics to sweep them into power, as if the coming "minority-majority" were a force of nature, sufficient in itself to flip the country. But people need a reason to vote. African-Americans, Hispanics, immigrants, there's no law requiring them to choose between the two major parties. They can do exactly as millions have been doing for years, opt out on Election Day. And for those who do want to vote, it's getting harder, thanks to your local GOP. Stringent ID laws, shorter periods for early voting, fewer polling places, and onerous registration procedures all mean we're going to need more motivation than ever to get out and vote.

Remaking the Democratic Party into a vital popular force would take time. Movements always do. Women's suffrage and civil rights were many decades in the making. The New Deal's farm policies grew out of the Farmers' Alliance and the People's Party of the late nineteenth century. The American labor movement reaches back to the very beginnings of the Industrial Revolution in England. Movements happen through education, organizing, recruiting: grassroots work, the kind of work young Hillary did, back in the day. Historical awareness is essential, as an antidote for lies and fantasies. And rhetoric, of course, is equally essential, the classic *ethos, pathos,* and *logos* that we see working in the best of the plain-speaking American style. In the very fine essay that Matt Stoller published in the *Atlantic* shortly before the election, we learn of an old flyer in the archives of Wright Patman, a populist Texas congressman of the New Deal era. Stoller writes of the flyer:

> *"Here Is What Our Democratic Party Has Given Us" was the title. There were no fancy slogans or focus-grouped logos. Each item listed is a solid thing that was relevant to the lives of conservative white Southern voters in rural Texas: Electricity. Telephone. Roads. Social Security. Soil conservation. Price supports. Foreclosure prevention . . . Packaged together, these measures epitomized the idea that citizens must be able to govern themselves through their own community structures, or as Walt Whitman put it: "train communities through all their grades, beginning with individuals and ending there again, to rule themselves." Patman's ideals represented a deep understanding that sovereign citizens governing sovereign communities were the only protection against demagoguery.*[87]

What Stoller describes—*sovereign citizens governing sovereign communities*—is the exact inverse of neoliberalism, whose most striking feature may be citizens and communities with no practical sovereignty, subject to the mercy of distant powers and interests. Now a demagogue lives in the White House. The Democratic Party helped put him there. If the party can't transform itself into an instrument of genuine resistance and renewal, then let it die and make way for the necessary new thing.

---

[87] Stoller, "How Democrats Killed Their Populist Soul."

# BOOK OF DAYS

SEPTEMBER

After saying within a span of two days that his stance on immigration was "softening" and then "hardening," Trump travels to Mexico City to meet with Mexican president Enrique Peña Nieto, who previously compared Trump to Mussolini and Hitler. Afterward, Trump says the two leaders did not discuss the wall, while President Peña Nieto tweets, "I made it clear that Mexico will not pay for the wall." Two Indian climbers were found to have faked photographs showing they reached the summit of Mount Everest, ISIS's senior propagandist and strategist is killed by a U.S. drone strike, and the North Korean deputy premier for education is executed for showing "disrespectful posture" during a meeting led by North Korean leader Kim Jong Un. Regularly scheduled passenger flights between Cuba and the U.S. resume after more than fifty years. *Foreign Affairs* magazine publishes an analysis that concludes Trump is the "preferred candidate" of ISIS, stating, "[J]ihadists are rooting for a Trump presidency because they believe that he will lead the United States on a path to self-destruction." After making sweeping generalizations about drug use and ethnicity, and then wishing "it were 1825" so he could duel a lawmaker who criticized the remarks and "point" his gun "right between his eyes," Maine governor and Tea Party favorite Paul LePage refuses to resign, declaring, "I'm not an alcoholic, and I'm not a drug addict, and I don't have mental issues." LePage also says that he is seeking "spiritual guidance," and that he "will no longer speak to the press ever again after today." Brazilian president Dilma Rousseff is impeached and removed from office for allegedly manipulating the federal budget to conceal the country's economic problems. After four travel-related cases of Zika are reported in the area, Dorchester County, South Carolina, authorizes aerial spraying of an insecticide intended to kill mosquitoes, which results in the deaths of millions of honeybees. Ninety homicides occur in Chicago in the month of August, the highest monthly total in twenty years. Speaking in Phoenix, Trump sets forth a hard-line ten-point plan on immigration that includes "ideological certification" of immigrants seeking citizenship. Conservative commentator Ann Coulter praises the speech as "the most magnificent" ever given, and David Duke, a former grand dragon of the Ku Klux Klan, calls it "excellent." "We don't need to convince Muslims in the Middle East that the West is against them. They already know," a former ISIS fighter tells *Foreign Affairs* magazine. Fred Hellerman, the last surviving member of the Weavers, dies at age eighty-nine. Protestors banging on pots and pans and yelling that they are hungry chase Venezuelan president Nicolás Maduro during an event celebrating the opening of new public housing units on Margarita Island. Palo Alto, California, mayor Patrick Burt seeks to enforce an obscure zoning regulation that bans companies whose primary business is research and development, including software coding, from the town's center. A 5.6-magnitude earthquake in Oklahoma ties a record for the strongest in state history, and studies show a sharp increase in "sunny day" flooding in coastal communities on the Atlantic and Gulf coasts. Two weeks after San Francisco 49ers reserve quarterback Colin Kaepernick begins refusing to stand for the pre-game national anthem, his jersey is the fifth-best seller at the NFL's online merchandise store. Kaepernick previously stated that he would not "stand up to show pride in a flag for a country that oppresses black people and people of color." Two bombings near the Afghan Defense Ministry kill at least forty in Kabul, including two generals, several colonels, and numerous other soldiers and police officers, and ISIS bombings targeting Syrian government and Kurdish troops kill at least forty-eight. Phyllis Schlafly dies at age ninety-two, and North Korea fires three ballistic missiles over the Sea of Japan. Fox News agrees to pay $20 million to settle the sexual harassment lawsuit brought by Gretchen Carlson that forced the ouster of Fox chairman Roger Ailes. Trump calls for ninety thousand additional soldiers for the army and seventy-five new ships for the navy, which would require up to an additional $90 billion a year, and vows to order "my generals" to devise a new plan to defeat ISIS "immediately upon taking office." The same evening, at an NBC "Commander in Chief Forum," Trump praises Vladimir Putin and says there is no evidence that Russia played a role in hacking the Democratic National Committee. "If he says great things about me," Trump remarks, "I'm going to say great things about him." A suspected chlorine gas attack in Aleppo's rebel-held areas kills at least two and sickens more than 120. Recent polls show Clinton with modest leads in Wisconsin and Michigan, down from her double-digit leads a month ago. President Obama calls the trends in climate change "terrifying," and Wells Fargo is fined $185 million for creating bank and credit card accounts for its customers without their knowledge. A car full of gas cylinders and jerry cans of diesel fuel is found abandoned near Notre Dame Cathedral, and French police subsequently arrest three women, ages nineteen, twenty-three, and thirty-nine, in connection with a suspected terror plot involving the car. Gary Johnson, the Libertarian Party's presidential nominee, asks, "What is Aleppo?" in response to a question about how he would address the refugee crisis in the embattled Syrian city. Two North Carolina men associated with the hacking group "Crackas with Attitude" are arrested in connection with the hack of the personal email account of John Brennan, the current director of the CIA. The federal government temporarily halts construction on the Dakota Access Pipeline in response to protests by members of 280 Native American tribes. At a $1,200-minimum-a-plate fund-raiser at Cipriani in Manhattan, Hillary Clinton remarks, "You could put half of Trump's supporters into what I call the basket of deplorables, right? The racist, sexist, homophobic, xenophobic, Islamophobic—you name it." The Trump campaign demands an apology, while a Clinton campaign talking-points memo advises campaign aides to emphasize that Clinton intended to say "some" rather than "half." As a nationwide cease-fire brokered by the U.S. and Russia is set to begin in Syria, Russian and Syrian government air strikes kill at least ninety-one, many of them civilians, in rebel-held areas around the country. "When we hear there is a cease-fire, we say, 'God help us,'" remarks an aid worker in Aleppo. In Manhattan, Clinton abruptly leaves a ceremony marking the fifteenth anniversary of the 9/11 attacks, and video shows her legs buckling as she is helped into a van by Secret Service agents; later that day her doctor reports that she became "overheated and dehydrated" at the 9/11 event, and is being treated for pneumonia, an explanation dismissed by various Clinton critics who have claimed in recent months that she has Parkinson's disease, epilepsy, and/or advancing dementia, that the head of her Secret Service detail is actually her hypnotist as well as a medical doctor, and that she has a body double. The Census Bureau reports that median household income in 2015 was $56,500, up 5.2 percent from 2014, and the largest single-year increase since record-keeping began in 1967. Poverty fell, health insurance coverage continued to increase, and incomes rose most sharply for the poor and middle class. In response to North Carolina's "bathroom law," the NCAA decides to move elsewhere the seven championship events the state was scheduled to host this academic year. Speaking in support of Clinton, President Obama says of the election, "We cannot afford, suddenly, to treat this like a reality show." Carla D. Hayden, formerly the chief librarian of Baltimore, becomes the first woman and first African-American to lead the Library of Congress. The email account of retired four-star general and former secretary of state Colin Powell is hacked, bringing to light emails in which he calls Donald Trump "a national disgrace and an international pariah," calls Donald Rumsfeld an "idiot," calls Dick Cheney and his daughter Liz "idiots," and attributes to Hillary Clinton "a long track record, unbridled ambition, greedy, not transformative." "I will speak out when I feel it appropriate and not after every idiot thing he says," Powell wrote of Trump, and "everything H.R.C. touches she kind of screws up with hubris," he wrote of Clinton, then complained about "the gig I lost at a university" because the college could not afford his speaking fee after paying Clinton for her appearance. A CNN/ORC poll finds that by a margin of fifteen percentage points, voters consider Trump "more honest and trustworthy" than Clinton, and other polls show the race tightening. "Hillary Clinton's lead in the polls has been declining for several weeks," Nate Silver writes, "and now we're at the point where it's not much of a lead at all." Dr. Harold Bornstein, the gastroenterologist who last December provided a brief, glowing letter on Trump's health that gave no specifics, authors a new, two-page letter asserting that Trump is in "excellent physical health," and Trump discloses the letter on an episode of *The Dr. Oz Show*. Trump appears on *The Tonight Show* and allows host Jimmy Fallon to muss his hair. After promising a major disclosure about President Obama's birthplace, Trump gets nearly an hour of uninterrupted coverage on cable news networks to promote the new Trump International Hotel in downtown Washington, then announces, "President Barack Obama was born in the United States, period," and adds: "Hillary Clinton and her campaign of 2008 started the birther controversy. I finished it." "We got played," CNN's John King says, and Representative James Clyburn of South Carolina, a member of the Congressional Black Caucus, says of Trump's birther statements, "One of the things that we are all used to in this business is dog whistles. But the thing that we are not used to, and I'm finding it very difficult to get used to, are the howls of wolves. These are howls. These are not dog whistles." Reading from a teleprompter, Trump claims that Clinton wants to "abolish the borders around the country" and "give lifetime welfare and entitlements to illegal immigrants." A two-mile underground beer pipeline opens in Bruges, Belgium, and Swiss researchers report that drinking a glass of beer enhances empathy. The U.S. apologizes to the Syrian government for killing sixty-two government soldiers in an air strike that was intended to support Syrian rebels fighting ISIS, six days after the negotiation of a cease-fire. A pipe bomb explodes in a garbage can near the start of a charity 5K race in Seaside Park, New Jersey; eleven hours later a homemade bomb explodes under a Dumpster in Manhattan's Chelsea neighborhood, injuring twenty-nine, and a second bomb four streets away fails to explode; five more bombs are found the next evening near an Elizabeth, New Jersey, train station, and the following morning a suspect, Ahmad Khan Rahami, a U.S. citizen who was born in Afghanistan, is arrested after exchanging gunfire with police. An ISIS "soldier" disguised as a security guard stabs and wounds nine people in a Minnesota shopping mall before being shot and killed by an off-duty police officer. The Syrian government declares the seven-day partial cease-fire over, and immediately bombs a thirty-one-truck humanitarian convoy delivering medicine and supplies to Aleppo. Tyre King, thirteen years old, black, is shot and killed in Columbus, Ohio, by police when he displays a BB gun designed to look nearly identical to a Smith & Wesson military and police semiautomatic pistol. Putin's United Russia party gains an absolute majority in Parliament, and German chancellor Angela Merkel's Christian Democratic Union suffers its second defeat in regional elections in a span of two weeks, in votes largely seen as a backlash against her decision to welcome refugees from Syria and other war-torn countries. In less than three months, the Trump campaign surpasses $100 million in donations from "small" donors—those who give $200 or less—far more than previous GOP nominees Romney and McCain raised from small donors during their entire campaigns. Terence Crutcher, an unarmed black man, is shot and killed by police officers in Tulsa, Oklahoma, after his SUV stalls out; police video shows Crutcher walking away from officers with his hands up, then dropping to the ground after being shocked with a stun gun, then being shot. Federal authorities in Mexico discover a van outfitted with a bazooka, apparently used to launch packages over the border to the U.S. Donald Trump Jr. posts on Twitter an image of a bowl full of multicolored Skittles, with the comment: "If I had a bowl of skittles and I told you just three would kill you. Would you take a handful? That's our Syrian refugee problem." Researchers from Harvard and Columbia estimate that over one hundred thousand people died last year in Southeast Asia from a "haze disaster" brought on by fires set to clear land for agriculture, and the National Oceanic and Atmospheric Administration reports that August 2016 was the hottest August on record, and also extended the streak of consecutive record-warm months to sixteen. Keith Scott, a black man, is shot and killed in an apartment complex parking lot by police in Charlotte, North Carolina; protests erupt amid conflicting accounts of whether Scott did or did not have a firearm. On the same day that Scott is killed, Trump calls for use of stop-and-frisk tactics across the country. In findings published in *Nature,* three separate teams of geneticists conclude that all non-Africans are descended from a single population of early humans who migrated out of Africa between fifty thousand and eighty thousand years ago. The Institute for Health Metrics and Evaluation reports that the rate of maternal mortality in the U.S. has risen by more than half since 1990. "The first time I saw our results for the United States, I thought there must be some error," commented the head of the institute's maternal and child health research. Yahoo announces that in 2014 a "state-sponsored actor" hacked into the company's computer network and stole the account information of at least five hundred million customers. An analysis carried out by the RAND Corporation and the Commonwealth Fund finds that Clinton's health care proposal would provide coverage for an additional nine million people, while Trump's proposal would cause about twenty million people to lose coverage. Ted Cruz, who once called Trump "a sniveling coward," and who dismissed previous speculation about whether he would endorse Trump by saying he is not "a servile puppy dog" and "I don't make a habit of supporting people who attack my wife and my family," endorses Trump. "After many months of careful consideration, of prayer and searching my own conscience, I have decided that on Election Day I will vote for the Republican nominee," explains Cruz, who began renting his donor email list to the Trump campaign in June. In a speech dedicating the new National Museum of African American History and Culture, President Obama says, "Hopefully, this museum can help us talk to each other." Syrian and Russian forces relentlessly bomb rebel-held eastern Aleppo for the fourth straight day in what residents and aid workers describe as the worst bombardment of the five-year war. After fifty-two years of civil war, the government of Colombia and the rebel group FARC sign a peace agreement. The first Clinton-Trump debate draws a record audience of eighty-four million viewers who witness Trump citing his temperament as his "strongest asset." The day after, Trump claims that his microphone malfunctioned, that moderator Lester Holt asked him "unfair questions," and that he was justified in denigrating a former Miss Universe because "she gained a massive amount of weight and it was a real problem." Former New York mayor and presidential candidate Rudolph Giuliani, who informed his second wife that he was separating from her via a news conference, and whose own presidential campaign in 2008 ended in January of that year, says Hillary Clinton is "too stupid to be president." Dutch investigators conclude that the missile used to shoot down a Malaysia Airlines plane over Ukraine two years ago, killing all 298 aboard, was deployed by Russia at the request of Russian-backed separatists. Congress passes a ten-week spending bill, narrowly averting a government shutdown; the bill includes funds to combat the Zika virus seven months after President Obama's request, and the promise of money to fix Flint's water systems sometime in the future. Speaking in Novi, Michigan, Trump says "the wealthy donor, the large corporations and the media executives [are] all part of the same corrupt political establishment. And they nod along when Hillary Clinton slanders you as 'deplorable' and 'irredeemable.'" Afterward, one attendee, sixty-seven-year-old Rebecca Nickel of Fenton, Michigan, says of the political and corporate establishment: "Honey, they built an ark. They didn't make any room for us, though."

# TWO AMERICAN DREAMS

For one summer in the early 1980s, I was a New Yorker. I lived with two law school classmates in a brownstone on Barrow Street In Greenwich Village, and worked in the downtown office of Sullivan & Cromwell, one of the "silk stocking" Wall Street firms that sits at the center of American commerce. I was that rarefied legal commodity known as the summer associate, overpaid and indulged, courted as sweetly as any debutante ever was for her production potential, though in my case it wasn't babies but billable hours. Two summers before I'd been making $2.30 an hour as a fry cook in Raleigh, and now it was $900 a week, free lunch every day, plus dinner and a cab ride home if I worked past eight. I bought two suits, four shirts, and four ties at J. Press, drank black-and-tans at Chumley's, and read the *Village Voice*, which was sounding the alarm that summer over the mysterious "gay cancer" that was ravaging the community, soon to be known as AIDS. New York's seemingly hopeless death spiral of the 1970s had been checked, but it was still a rough place. It wasn't unusual to see homeless people lying on the sidewalk who looked dead. Muggings were common. The Lower East Side and parts of the Village were no-go zones, and the subway was hot, dirty, always breaking down. If you had to be somewhere at a certain time, safer to take a cab.

I was a Southerner in the North. I arrived at seven thirty A.M. for my first day of work and cooled my heels in the lobby for thirty minutes, waiting for someone to come along and unlock the doors. First lesson: farmer's hours don't cut it in New York. Sullivan & Cromwell was supposed to be the ultimate establishment firm in the city—therefore the country?—and that's why I was there, I wanted to see this ultimate world for myself. I was a tourist, just passing through for the summer, but there was always the chance that I'd like it, that I'd want to stay and have a certain kind of life, a New York corporate lawyer's life of making money. It turned out to be a formal, fairly paranoid place, a thicket of unspoken bicultural codes that served as the keys to genuine entry. A kind of funeral-home hush presided over the halls, which were hung with the firm's collection of original Currier & Ives prints, said to be worth several million dollars. The first woman partner in the firm's history was named that summer. I don't recall a single person of color among the lawyers. Archival photos and a framed handwritten note from Theodore Roosevelt commemorated William Nelson Cromwell's pivotal role in the transnational intrigues that produced the Panama Canal, and incidentally (thanks to a marine expeditionary force), the new country of Panama.[1] The Dulles brothers, John and Allen, were lionized alumni of the firm. John had presided over Cold War policy as Eisenhower's secretary of state;[2] Allen did policy's bidding as longtime director of the CIA, his tenure marked by agency-sponsored coups d'état, interventions, black operations, and "wet"

---

[1] According to the firm's centennial history, *Sullivan & Cromwell 1879–1979: A Century at Law* (1979, privately printed), William Cromwell was described by a congressman "as the most dangerous man the country had produced since the days of Aaron Burr, and it is likely that Cromwell took it as a compliment."

[2] John Foster Dulles: "Do nothing to offend the dictators; they are the only people we can count on." Alex von Tunzelmann, *Red Heat: Conspiracy, Murder, and the Cold War in the Caribbean* (Henry Holt, 2011), p. 61.

jobs across the globe. Later I would encounter the brothers, and Sullivan & Cromwell itself—"the Dulles family lawfirm"—in the poems of Allen Ginsberg:

> The Ghost of John F. Dulles hangs
> over America like dirty linen
> draped over the wintry red sunset,
> Fumes of Unconscious Gas
> emanate from his corpse
> & hypnotize the Egyptian intellectuals—
> He grinds his teeth in horror & crosses his
> thigh bones over his skull
> Dust flows out of his asshole
> his hands are full of bacteria
> The worm is at his eye—
> He's declaring counterrevolutions in the Worm-world,
> my cat threw him up last
> Thursday.[3]

These were serious people. By the end of the summer I was just beginning to realize how deeply serious they were, and the nature of the stakes in the work they were about. This was finance on the scale of ocean currents and tectonic plates, the nearly irresistible force that comes of vast amounts of money applied with purpose. Capital requires structure—government, laws, banks, markets—and the lawyers at Sullivan & Cromwell were part of the elite professional class that would overhaul these structures beginning in the late 1970s. Private equity, leveraged buyouts, takeovers, all facilitated by exotic new securities and government deregulation, these transformed the American economy in the space of a generation. The business of

---

[3] "Who Will Take Over the Universe?," *Collected Poems, 1947–1980*, p. 265. See also "Wichita Vortex Sutra" and "Elegy Che Guevara," among other poems.

America became less about the production and exchange of goods and much more about finance, finance as an end in itself as opposed to a tool for creating and building companies.[4]

I was clueless about the history happening around me, but naturally I would be with my clerk's-eye view of things, moiling away in the lower reaches of the machinery. Investment banks—Goldman Sachs was one of the firm's blue-chip clients—were on the cusp of a monumental feed that continues to this day, an era where big leverage and quick cash-out produce mind-boggling profits for the people who own the deals. A friend of mine from that Sullivan & Cromwell summer, a fellow summer associate, went on to get his MBA and a job at Goldman Sachs. He must have seen something I didn't. We lost touch around the time he made partner, but I'm guessing he's a very rich man by now.

**THAT WAS THE SUMMER DONALD TRUMP FIRST ENTERED MY** mind. His mark was everywhere, the TRUMP logo on his buildings, the signage urging us to "Enter the World of Trump" with his head blown up to billboard proportions, the image as fixed as an icon of the Eastern Orthodox Church: tawny spun-sugar hair, pouty lips, the command-mode scowl with the faintest glint of fun in the eyes, a clue—though we could never be sure—that he was better than his shtick, like he knew only mopes would fall for his low-rent line of upscale puff. Which raised the question, did people buy the condos because of Trump or in spite of him? I was sufficiently Southern and small-town to consider this kind of thing to be in bad taste, blasting your name everywhere, proclaiming your greatness. The feeling I got from his ads can be summed up as: whenever I saw one of his ads, I wished I hadn't seen it. They weren't neutral. They produced a brief but distinctly unhappy effect. With each exposure

---

[4] See the very fine and essential *American Amnesia: How the War on Government Led Us to Forget What Made America Prosper* by Jacob Hacker and Paul Pierson (Simon & Schuster, 2016), pp. 174–88.

an ounce or two of psychical drag was added to your day. He was an annoyance, a blowhard, a bore; certainly New Yorkers didn't seem to take him seriously. Whenever his name came up in the lawyers' lunchroom, people would shrug and smirk, default to irony. Trump was a joke, a rich, successful joke to be sure, but that was part of the joke, how easy it was to get rich if you were shameless enough.

A celebrity is a creature that inhabits our mind. It doesn't much matter if the creature is welcome or not, or good or bad, or loved or loathed, or even whether it has a flesh-and-blood analogue walking around on earth. It's simply part of the modern condition, this celebrity village we all carry around in our heads, and surely the goal of every resident of this village is to occupy as much space in the village as possible. That's where the money is, the glory, the fans, "the fan base," and sometime during the eighties or nineties a technical term was coined for this process of mental occupation, "branding." Every year we have more and better systems for delivering brands, systems now considered essential to daily life, some that fit in the palm of our hand. We never have to be without these systems. Another way of saying this is that we can't get away from them, short of renouncing most of the mass technology of the past twenty years.

At some point during my New York summer, I began reading *The Ambassadors* on the subway to and from work.[5] I suppose I was showing off, trying to make some sort of futile nerd-punk statement: I was the pin-striped dude on the subway reading Henry James. Near the end of the book, simultaneous with Chad Newsome revealing himself to be a heartless spineless bastard and a cad and a jerk, he and Lambert Strether have this conversation on a Paris street about the new "science" of advertising:

> *He [Chad] appeared at all events to have been looking into*
> *the question and had encountered a revelation. Advertising*

---

[5] Signet Classic paperback, $2.50. I still have it.

*scientifically worked presented itself thus as the great new force.*
*"It really does the thing, you know."*

*They were face to face under the street-lamp as they had*
*been the first night, and Strether, no doubt, looked blank.*
*"Affects, you mean the sale of the object advertised?"*

*"Yes—but affects it extraordinarily; really beyond what*
*one had supposed. I mean of course when it's done as one*
*makes out that, in our roaring age, it* can *be done. I've been*
*finding out a little. It's an art like another, and infinite like*
*all the arts." He went on as if for the joke of it—almost as*
*if his friend's face amused him. "In the hands, naturally, of*
*a master. The right man must take hold. With* him *to work*
*it*—c'est un monde!"

Given the kind of man Chad shows himself to be in this scene,
it's clear that James, writing in the earliest years of the twentieth
century, meant to portray advertising as a degrading, maybe even
insidious, force. Poor old Henry James, I thought on reading those
pages in 1982, trying to imagine what he'd make of the world now
that advertising was the basic landscape of life. Would he break
down weeping? Throw up? Both at once? I suspect Trump was on
my mind at that particular subway moment of reading and thinking. On some level, surely; after a couple of months of living in
TRUMP Manhattan, I don't see how he couldn't have been. But
rereading that scene all these years later, it strikes me that James
was onto something more than the cheapening effects of advertising, or that it worked, that it was "the great new force." The scene
continues:

*Strether had watched [Chad] quite as if, there on the*
*pavement, without a pretext, he had begun to dance a fancy*
*step. "Is what you're thinking of that you yourself, in the case*
*you have in mind, would be the right man?"*

> *Chad had thrown back his light coat and thrust each of*
> *his thumbs in to an armhole of his waistcoat; in which position*
> *his fingers played up and down. "Isn't he what you yourself*
> *took me for when you first came out?"*
>   *Strether felt a little faint, but he coerced his attention.*
> *"Oh yes, and there's no doubt that, with your natural parts,*
> *you'd have much in common with him. Advertising is clearly,*
> *at this time of day, the secret of trade. It's quite possible it*
> *would be open to you—giving the whole of your mind to*
> *it—to make the whole place hum with you . . ."*

Henry James, that tireless student of the modern psyche, shows Chad transforming right before Strether's eyes, becoming a new man, "the right man" for our "roaring age." Chad is jilting—quite casually, even cheerfully—an extraordinary woman in order to return to America, to the family business, to his rich mother's money. To advertising, which seems to excite him very much. James drives home the psychology of the moment with the use of the third person. "'Isn't *he* what you yourself took me for . . .'" "'Oh yes . . . you'd have much in common with *him*.'" It's not that Chad is failing to be true to himself; rather, he's assuming—deliberately, expediently, effortlessly—a new and different self, this aspiring master of advertising. Where his heart and soul should be there's only ego, and the blithe, careless cruelty of the narcissist.

Writing this in 2017, I confess that 1982 seems as quaint to me now as 1900 seemed in the summer of 1982. The roaring age has blasted along for thirty-five more years at exponentially faster speeds, and the new science that so captivated young Chad, it's long since overwhelmed the neat conceptual boundary contained in the term *advertising*. Now it's everything, a sprawling industrial complex that saturates life, the hardware of it embedded in our public and private spaces, its omnipresence usurping personality's rightful domain. Our poor human psyche, built for walking and single-tasking on the African savannah, hardly stands a chance. We're too susceptible to sparkly things, to bright colors, beautiful faces, to sex and simple stories. To fantasy. The human talent for distraction has always been with us, but the Fantasy Industrial Complex, the "FIC," to put a name to it, challenges our grasp of reality as nothing ever has. All these screens everywhere going 24/7 with movies, TV, internet, email, texts, tweets, news saturation, ad saturation, sports and celebrity saturation, social media, Amazonian sewers of sex and political porn, the entire onslaught of media and messaging that numbs us out and dumbs us down—that dims our capacity for understanding the world as it actually is. The FIC is relentless, infinite, *an art like any other*. The old distinctions start to break down, the boundary between reality and fantasy. It becomes increasingly difficult to know what's real anymore, especially *there,* inside those screens where so much of our daily existence takes place.

Cary Grant, *né* Archibald Leach, famously said: "Everyone wants to be Cary Grant. Even I want to be Cary Grant." For Archie Leach the fantasy stopped at the edge of the movie screen, but Donald J. Trump, born Donald J. Trump, solved that problem by constructing a real-life fantasy with himself in the lead role. His entire career has played out on stage sets with top-of-the-line props: the Versailles-style triplex on Fifth Avenue, the country club honky paradise of Mar-a-Lago, the bombshell wives, the planes, the beauty pageants, all the gold-gilt, Mafia-don-meets-Liberace glitz. *Make the whole place hum with you.* He was selling the fantasy by living it, his entire being devoted not so much to the art of the deal as to the art of branding, the cutting-edge science of the FIC. And for a price, we, too, could have a piece of the fantasy, could "enter the world of Trump," as the advertisements had it.

You can be sure someone is a definite, no-doubt, top-shelf celebrity when you can't get them out of your life, short of hunkering down in a convent or Himalayan cave. The FIC transcends time and space, and Trump has worked that free-floating realm as hard as any human who ever lived, to the point that his celebrity, the name, the brand, became the engine of his wealth, more than the steel and glass buildings he actually held title to. The man is clearly brilliant at something, though whether that was ever the real estate *business* is an open question—there are all those bankruptcies and bailouts, and the nearly billion-dollar loss he claimed on his tax return in 1995.[6] But at understanding and manipulating the FIC he may be the best alive, and his starter career in real estate provided excellent training. Success at the high end of real estate is much less a function of intrinsic or "use" value than it is of socially constructed value, the perception of value. A savvy upmarket developer like Trump boosts the price of a project with various signifiers of style and taste: a star architect, "prestige" design references, ornamental doodads, high-gloss advertising. This is the kind of value that exists in the mind; it's real as long as people agree that it's real.[7] Trump was so good at this racket that merely his name came to signify value, hence the global phenomenon of developers paying big money to put TRUMP on their creations, projects that Trump himself had little or no active role in.

With the debut of *The Apprentice* in January 2004, Trump could plow the sweetest of all the FIC's fertile spots, that soft, pliable region in the American mind where the most calculated artifice goes by the name of "reality." For fourteen seasons he honed the message and management of his brand on TV sets in millions of homes, eventually doubling down on the whole self-contradicting concept of "reality TV" with *Celebrity Apprentice*. Think about it: "reality" TV, starring . . . celebrities. As if! And it was genius.

The surest sign that he would run for president was his decision

---

[6] See, for instance, Adam Davidson, "Donald Trump Promises to Bring Business Acumen to Washington," *New York Times Magazine,* June 12, 2016.

[7] Here I am shamelessly and gratefully pillaging *The See-Through Years: Creation and Destruction in Texas Architecture and Real Estate, 1981–1991* by Joel W. Barna (Rice University Press, 1992). Chapter 1, "J. R. McConnell Died for Our Sins," is especially revelatory.

in February 2015 not to commit to another season of the show. He'd flirted with presidential runs many times,[8] a near-perennial teaser candidate, in it for the foreplay and ego boost, not to mention the power surge to the brand. Totally natural, this notion of a billionaire with zero government experience running for high office. By the eighties, America had rebounded from its failed romance with the counterculture and fallen in love with capitalist heroes. They solved problems. They cut through bullshit. What better proof of executive excellence than a huge pile of dough? Ross Perot won 19,740,000 votes when he ran for president in 1992, and he merely made computer systems. By comparison, the first episode of *The Apprentice* drew 20.7 million viewers—yes, I'm comparing vote totals to Nielsen ratings, such is the reach of the FIC in our national life—but Trump kept drawing that robust twenty million week after week. The season finale clocked 28 million viewers, and over the next decade, for thirteen more seasons, this was how America came to know him, as the glowering, blustering, swaggering boardroom action figure who would draw 24 million viewers—a record, of course—for the first Republican debate of the 2016 election season.

Trump's earlier presidential runs were all about ego flexing and bigging up the brand, and there's evidence that his 2016 run began with the same limited goals. In "An Open Letter to Trump Voters from His Top Strategist-Turned-Defector" (*xoJane*, March 28,

---

[8] Beginning in 1987 with the publication of *The Art of the Deal*, which he promoted by floating his name as a possible candidate, and going to New Hampshire to make speeches denouncing the Reagan administration's failures. As Trump biographer Michael D'Antonio noted on *PBS NewsHour*, July 20, 2016: "He was one of the first people actually to use running for president as a business tactic." In 2000 he was briefly a candidate for the Reform Party's nomination, receiving over fifteen thousand votes in the party's California primary. He hinted again at runs in 2004 and 2008. A *Wall Street Journal*/NBC News poll released in March 2011 showed Trump leading all potential Republican contenders, a development that coincided with his flurry of public statements giving credence to the birther movement. After several months of dalliance, he announced that he would not be a candidate in 2012. See Cooper Allen, "Donald Trump and White House Bids: A Long History of Not Running," *USA Today*, June 15, 2015.

2016), Stephanie Cegielski, the former communications chief of Trump's Super PAC, wrote:

> *I sat in Trump Tower being told that the goal was to get The Donald to poll in double digits and come in second in the delegate count. That was it. The Trump camp would have been satisfied to see him polling at 12 percent and taking second place to a candidate who might hold 50 percent. His candidacy was a protest candidacy.*

Protest? Branding seems closer to the mark, but let's take Ms. Cegielski at her word. There was plenty to protest in 2015–16, just as there was in the cycles of 1988, 2000, 2004, 2008, and 2012, just as there was always a brand to burnish and promote. But ripeness is all. Something had turned in America by 2015. Thirty-five years of stagnant wages for the working and middle classes, then the economic carnage of 2008 from which the elite had escaped miraculously unscathed, sparked off a populist outcry such as hadn't been seen in this country since the 1930s. Rage, disgust, a vast sense of betrayal fueled the Tea Party and the Occupy movements, to name just two of the more hot-blooded reactions. Trump spoke to the outrage. Bernie too, but Trump had a career's worth of high-wattage celebrity going for him, capped by twelve years as a reality TV star, mojo that no professional politician could touch. And if, over the long course of the campaign, Trump's regard for the truth proved even more erratic than that of the professional pols, we should have expected no less. In the realm of the FIC, reality happens on a sliding scale. The truth is just another possibility.

**THERE'S FANTASY, AND THEN THERE'S THE HOMEGROWN PHE-**nomenon known as the American Dream, which is real, and one of the greatest inventions of all time. After millennia of pharaohs, kings, queens, sultans, caesars, and czars, with all their attendant aristocracies and buttoned-up social structures, a country was founded where birth and lineage didn't matter so much; where by application of your talents, energy, labor, and willingness to play by the rules, you could improve your material lot and achieve a measure of autonomy for yourself and your family. Just like it says on the dollar bill—*Novus ordo seclorum*—this was an entirely new order in human affairs. Peasants and proles could aspire to more than mere survival. Radical!

The now-obscure historian James Truslow Adams coined the term in his book *The Epic of America,* defining "the American dream" as

> *a dream of a social order in which each man and each woman*
> *shall be able to attain to the fullest stature of which they are*
> *innately capable, and be recognized by others for what they are,*
> *regardless of the fortuitous circumstances of birth or position.*

Adams was writing in 1931, but the dream was there from the start, in Jefferson's "pursuit of happiness" formulation in the Declaration of Independence, "happiness" residing in its eighteenth-century sense of prosperity, thriving, well-being. Nobody ever came to America with a starry-eyed dream of working for starvation wages. Plenty of that available in the old country, where the system in whatever its local form—feudalism, serfdom, enclosure, indenture, outright slavery—bondage by whatever name—limited freedom for the many while granting vast license and prerogative to a few. The practical result, always, was a nautonomic order[9] that channeled the profits of our labor upstream to the Man, the freedom-profits-plunder equation doing its grinding work: profit proportionate to freedom, plunder correlative to subjugation. We came to America to do better, and for millions—mostly for white males at first, and then slowly, sputteringly, still insufficiently, for women and people of color—that's

---

[9] On nautonomy, see "Iowa 2016: Riding the Roadkill Express," pp. 90-92, *supra.*

the way it worked out, nothing less than a revolution in the human condition.

The notion of upward mobility has always been central to the American Dream, the possibility of rising from working to middle class and middle to upper on the model of a (fictional) Horatio Alger or an (actual) Andrew Carnegie. This kind of social movement—what sociologists call "relative mobility"—happens, but much less frequently than the Horatio Alger myth would have us believe. Relative mobility peaked in the U.S. in the late nineteenth century. "Structural mobility" has played a far greater role in American life, people's fortunes moving up or down en masse due to major economic and social changes. Most of the upward mobility in America during the twentieth century was structural: it was less a phenomenon of great numbers of people rising from one class to the next than it was standards of living rising sharply for all classes.[10] You didn't have to be exceptional to rise. Hard work and steadiness would do, along with tacit buy-in to the social contract, buy-in proceeding on the assumption that the system was basically fair. The biggest gains occurred in the post–World War II era of the GI Bill, affordable higher education, strong labor unions, and a progressive tax code. From 1950 through 1980, the average income of the bottom 90 percent of Americans increased by 75 percent. Income grew faster at the bottom and middle than the top, and income inequality hit historic lows. The average CEO salary was approximately 30 times that of the lowest-paid employee, compared to today's gold-plated multiple of 370. The top tax bracket ranged in the neighborhood of 70 to 90 percent. Granted, we had fewer millionaires in those days, and hardly any billionaires, but somehow the nation survived.[11]

---

[10] James Surowiecki, "The Mobility Myth," *New Yorker,* March 3, 2014.

[11] See Bill Moyers, "We, the Plutocrats vs. We, the People," TomDispatch.com, September 11, 2016, http://www.tomdispatch.com/blog/176184/; Nicholas Lemann, "Unhappy Days for America," *New York Review of Books,* May 21, 2015 (review of *Our Kids: The American Dream in Crisis* by Robert D. Putnam); and Harold Meyerson, "When Tea Party Wants to Go Back, Where Is It To?," *Washington Post,* October 27, 2010.

"America is a dream of greater justice and opportunity for the average man and, if we can not obtain it, all our other achievements amount to nothing." So wrote Eleanor Roosevelt in her syndicated column of January 6, 1941, an apt lead-in for the State of the Union address that her husband would deliver later that day. This was the famous speech in which Franklin Roosevelt enumerated the four freedoms essential to American democracy, among them "freedom from want." In his State of the Union address three years later, Roosevelt expanded on this essential "freedom from want" with his proposal for a "Second Bill of Rights," an "economic" bill of rights to counteract the potential for tyranny in the modern economic order:

> *This Republic had at its beginning, and grew to its present*
> *strength, under the protection of certain inalienable political*
> *rights—among them the right of free speech, free press, free*
> *worship . . . As our nation has grown in size and stature,*
> *however—as our industrial economy has expanded—these*
> *political rights have proved inadequate to assure us equality.*
> *We have come to a clear realization of the fact that* true
> individual freedom cannot exist without economic security
> and independence.[12]

Political rights notwithstanding, "freedom" rings awfully hollow when you're getting nickel-and-dimed to death in your everyday life. The Roosevelts recognized that wage peonage, or any system that inclines its people toward subsistence level, is simply incompatible with self-determination. Subsistence is, by definition, a constrained, desperate state; one's horizon is necessarily limited to the present day, to getting enough of what the body needs to make it to the next. In 2016, a minimum-wage worker in New York City

---

[12] Emphasis added. See John Nichols, "Seventy Years On, Let Us Renew FDR's Struggle for an Economic Bill of Rights," *Nation*, April 14, 2015.

clocking forty hours a week (at $9 per) earned $18,720 a year, well under the Federal Poverty Level of $20,160 for a family of three. That's a scrambling, anxious existence, narrowly bounded. Close to impossible to decently feed, clothe, and shelter yourself on a wage like that, much less a family; much less buy health insurance, or save for your kids' college, or participate in any of those other good American things like dignity and hope and self-determination. Workplace goods that were common a generation ago have all but vanished for unskilled and blue-collar workers. Paid vacation? Forget it. Sick days? Suck it up. Pension? Benefits? Overtime? Ha ha ha. Down at peon level, the pursuit of happiness comes across as a bad joke. "It's called the American dream," George Carlin once cracked, "because you have to be asleep to believe it."[13]

We have, many of us, returned to the land of nautonomy, the peonage imposed by a social order in which tremendous wealth and power reside at the top, and the little people scrounge for crumbs. Had they known this is what it would come to, maybe our ancestors would have saved themselves the trouble and stayed in the old country. We do enjoy political rights that were unknown to many of them—free speech, freedom of worship, the right to vote, and so on—but a certain kind of lapdog democracy sits quite comfortably in the gut of a nautonomic order. Elections are held, votes cast and counted, leaders are chosen, but the fundamental order—the values in the freedom-profits-plunder equation—is not disturbed. In this kind of "minimalist" democracy, the ability of a people to determine the direction of their government is severely curtailed by "private actors who are not subject to democratic control and accountability,"

---

[13] See Peter Van Buren, "Nickel and Dimed in 2016," TomDispatch.com, February 16, 2016, http://www.tomdispatch.com/blog/176104/. Van Buren, who lived it, found himself literally nickel-and-dimed by a nasty phenomenon known as "time theft." See also Scott Burns, "Most of Us Are Sliding Downhill," *Dallas Morning News,* May 22, 2016. Citing data from the Federal Reserve Bank of St. Louis, Burns notes that labor's share of business-sector wealth peaked in 1960, and began a steep decline in 2000 even as executive salaries and corporate profits have soared.

as one astute scholar put it.[14] In such a system, these powerful private actors have essentially captured the democratic process. Change might happen here and there around the edges, but the distribution of power remains the same, and the freedom-profits-plunder equation keeps channeling wealth and power up to the top.

If we went looking for these private actors in the U.S., we would find them among the banks and investment firms that paid $2.9 million in speaking fees to Hillary Clinton in 2013–2015, and the Koch brothers' billionaire donor network that aimed to spend almost $1 billion on the 2016 elections, and all the other human and corporate actors funding the PACs and Super PACs that have overrun American politics in the few short years since *Citizens United*. We would also find them gathered wherever laws are made, whether in Washington, DC, or in the fifty state capitols; private actors don't take a break between elections. Between 1998, when lobbying disclosure requirements took effect, and 2014, the health care industry reported spending more than $6 billion on lobbying the federal government and lawmakers. In the same period, the FIRE industries (finance, insurance, and real estate) also spent more than $6 billion on lobbying. In 2009 alone, oil and gas interests spent $175 million on lobbying, and the U.S. Chamber of Commerce spent over $300 million in 2009–2010.[15] Unsurprising (but still depressing) to learn that this kind of big-bucks lobbying works, as shown by a comprehensive study published in 2014 of 1,800 different policy

---

[14] Alex Dupuy, *The Prophet and Power* (Rowan & Littlefield, 2007), p. 14. For an instructive discussion of minimalist vs. maximalist democracy and the role of economic power, see chapter 1, "Globalization, the 'New World Order Imperialism,' and Haiti," especially pp. 13–20. Dupuy writes of post-Duvalier Haiti: "The proponents of [maximalist] democracy understood that without securing economic or redistributive rights, the exercise of all other rights would be limited for most citizens because the profound inequities in wealth, income, and resources . . . would maintain them in conditions of nautonomy." Martin Luther King Jr. was making the same case when he began emphasizing economic issues near the end of his life. "Now our struggle is for genuine equality, which means economic equality." See Eugene Robinson, "MLK's Prophetic Call for Economic Justice," *Washington Post,* January 15, 2015.

[15] Hacker and Pierson, *American Amnesia,* pp. 278, 283, 290, and 296.

initiatives proposed between 1981 and 2002. The study's authors concluded: "economic elites and organized groups representing business interests have substantial independent impacts on U.S. government policy while mass-based interest groups and average citizens have little or no independent influence."[16]

If the U.S. hasn't yet achieved lapdog-democracy status, it's gone a far way there. In April 2009, even as the wreckage of the 2008 crash was still settling, Senator Dick Durbin, Democrat of Illinois and the number two man in the Senate, said during a radio interview: "And the banks—hard to believe in a time when we're facing a banking crisis that many of the banks created—are still the most powerful lobby on Capitol Hill. And they frankly own the place."[17]

One of the New Deal's main thrusts—and very arguably, its overriding purpose—was combating the "private actors" of the day, who with their great concentrations of power and wealth were threatening to emasculate American democracy. When proposing a tough new antimonopoly law to Congress in 1938, Roosevelt declared: "The liberty of a democracy is not safe if the people tolerate the growth of private power to a point where it becomes stronger than their democratic state itself. That, in its essence, is fascism."[18] Roosevelt and his fellow New Dealers understood that wealth concentration served both to disempower and to impoverish the average citizen. Big money can buy the kinds of elections and laws, not to mention lawmakers, that will privilege its wealth, and, correspondingly, its power. And in a laissez-faire system, big money can use unchecked monopoly power to steamroll small and midsized competitors, leaving local communities dependent on—in effect, at the mercy of—distant masters.

[16] Martin Gilens and Benjamin I. Page, "Testing Theories of American Politics: Elites, Interest Groups, and Average Citizens," *Perspectives on Politics* 12, no. 3 (September 2014), pp. 564–81. Bill Moyers's "We, the Plutocrats vs. We, the People" led me to this study.

[17] Hacker and Pierson, *American Amnesia*, p. 299.

[18] Matt Stoller, "How Democrats Killed Their Populist Soul," *Atlantic*, October 24, 2016.

"We must make our choice," wrote Supreme Court justice Louis Brandeis. "We may have democracy, or we may have wealth concentrated in the hands of a few, but we can't have both."[19] Brandeis spent his entire career, first as a private lawyer, then as a jurist, articulating a legal philosophy that would safeguard democracy against the tremendous wealth created by industrial capitalism. Brandeis's friend and ally in Congress, Wright Patman, worked to put that philosophy into law. Among other legislation, he sponsored the Robinson-Patman Act of 1936, an antimonopoly measure that cracked down on the price discrimination and manipulation that the A&P retail chain—"the Walmart of its day"—was using to drive local retailers out of business.[20] Breaking up monopolies, regulating banks and utility companies, enacting laws that gave labor a fighting chance at the bargaining table, these were the means by which the New Deal gave working people a way out of modern peonage. A chance, in other words, at the pursuit of happiness, as opposed to the Old World's perpetual treadmill of subsistence.

"Necessitous men are not free men," Franklin Roosevelt said in that 1944 State of the Union speech. "People who are hungry and out of a job are the stuff of which dictatorships are made." A dire statement, demonstrably true, and especially unsettling now, a point in time when the American Dream seems more viable as nostalgia—make America great again!—than as present reality. Income inequality, wealth distribution, mortality rates: by every measure, the "average man" that Eleanor Roosevelt celebrated is sinking. A recent study by the Pew Research Center shows that the middle class has shrunk to the point where it may no longer be the economic majority in the U.S.[21] And with widespread decline in economic prospects comes disillusionment: A recent poll shows nearly three-quarters of

---

[19] Raymond Lonergan, ed., *Mr. Justice Brandeis, Great American* (The Modern View Press, 1941), p. 42.

[20] Stoller, "How Democrats Killed Their Populist Soul."

[21] "The American Middle Class Is Losing Ground," Pew Research Center, December 9, 2015.

Americans across the economic and political spectrum believe that the U.S. economy is rigged. A quarter of these same respondents hadn't had a vacation in at least five years. Over half worried about missing their mortgage payment, and 60 percent of the renters expressed concern about making the monthly rent.[22] Exceptional individuals continue to rise, but overall mobility is stagnant at best. More and more it comes down to the birth lottery. If you're born poor in Flint or Appalachia, chances are you're going to stay that way. And if your early memories are of July Fourth fireworks at the Nantucket Yacht Club and ski lessons at Deer Valley, you're likely going to keep your perch at the top of the heap.[23]

Income inequality, impoverishment, gross disparities in outcomes for the "winners" and "losers": we're told daily, incessantly, that these are the natural and necessary consequences of the free market, as if the market were a force of nature like weather or ocean tides, and not the entirely man-made construct that it is. But let's assume for the moment that the market, like the weather, must "be borne with resignation,"[24] and ignore, also for the moment, that blind acceptance of this laissez-faire economics would, in light of the crash of 2008, seem to require a firm commitment to stupidity: so let us agree, all of us, for the moment, that the free market exists as a universe unto itself, as immutable in its workings as the laws of physics. Does that universe include some ironclad law that requires inequality of opportunity? That consigns babies, children, adolescents in all their potential and innocence to wasted lives? I've

[22] Andrea Seabrook, "Americans' Anxiety Around the Economy Grows," Marketplace.org, June 27, 2016, citing Marketplace-Edison Research poll.

[23] Jeff Madrick, "Goodbye, Horatio Alger," *Nation,* January 21, 2007; "Ever Higher Society, Ever Harder to Ascend," *Economist,* December 29, 2004. Thanks to Bill Moyers for pointing me in the direction of these two articles.

[24] "The prevalence of the corporation in America has led men of this generation to act, at times, as if the privilege of doing business in corporate form were inherent in the citizen; and has led them to accept the evils attendant upon the free and unrestricted use of the corporate mechanism as if these evils were the inescapable price of civilized life, and, hence, to be borne with resignation." Justice Brandeis, dissenting, *Liggett Co. v. Lee,* 288 U.S. 517 (1933).

yet to hear the case for that, though doubtless some enterprising think tanker could manufacture one out of this same laissez-faire economics. We'd get an earful about incentivizing job creators, the efficient movement of capital, disparities in labor markets, and so on, perhaps with hints of genetic determinism as it relates to intelligence and qualities of discipline and character. And it would be bogus, that case. And against the American grain. And more than that, immoral. That we should allow for wildly divergent opportunities due to accidents of birth ought to strike us as a crime equal to child abuse.

Franklin Roosevelt: "[F]reedom is no half-and-half affair. If the average citizen is guaranteed equal opportunity in the polling place, he must have equal opportunity in the market place." The proposition goes deeper than sentiment, deeper than policy, deeper even than faithfulness to the principles of equality and "the pursuit of happiness" as set forth in the Declaration. It cuts all the way to the nature of democracy, and to the prospects for its continued existence in America. All packaging and cheap mythology aside, the American Dream is central to the democratic project, "the American Dream" as it embodies the idea of autonomy, of liberation from peonage: as the expression of a standard of living above subsistence, and with it the margin of freedom that allows for the development of gifts, talents, mind, soul. In this sense the American Dream is democracy's best guarantee. Justice Brandeis, of course, knew it:

> *Those who won our independence believed that the final end of the state was to make men free to develop their faculties, and that in its government the deliberative forces should prevail over the arbitrary.* They valued liberty both as an end and as a means.[25]

---

[25] Concurring, *Whitney v. California*, 274 U.S. 357 (1927) (emphasis added).

This, then, is democracy's premise, which dares us with its fundamentally optimistic view of human nature: its faith in the notion that, over the long term, the collective wisdom of the majority will prove right more often than wrong. That given sufficient opportunity in the pursuit of happiness, your population will develop its talents, its intellect, its better judgment; that over time its capacity for discernment and self-correction will be enlarged. Life is improved, liberty strengthened, and life is improved again. *Liberty both as an end and as a means.* The form of your union will be more perfect, to borrow a phrase. But if a critical mass of your population is kept in peonage? All its vitality spent in the ditch of day-to-day survival, with scant opportunity to develop the full range of its faculties? Then how much poorer the prospects for your democracy will be.

Economic rights can no more be divorced from the functioning of democracy than the ballot. Jefferson, Brandeis, the Roosevelts all recognized this home truth. For the country to survive and thrive, the American Dream has to be the lived reality of the people, not just a pretty story we tell ourselves.

**THE VAST MAJORITY OF AMERICANS HAVE DONE THEIR PART. WE** went to school, worked, paid taxes, obeyed the laws, raised our kids the best we could and tried to educate them in a manner that befits themselves and society. We lived up to our side of the social contract in the not-outlandish expectation of participating in the American Dream, but nobody told us the contract's broken. We had to figure that out for ourselves. It took a while, the better part of four decades. The crash of 2008 was one of the more bracing clues.

Actually, there were a few people who did sound the alarm about that broken contract. The late Richard Rorty, professor of philosophy at Harvard, was one, and his warning has proved so apt and prophetic that he had something of a comeback in 2016, nine years after his death. One passage in particular from his 1998 book *Achieving Our Country* shows especially spooky prescience. Mark

Danner quoted it at length in one of his election reports, and there was social media buzz, and after Trump's election the book was in such high demand that Harvard Press reprinted it for the first time since 2010.[26] The passage that Danner quoted is worth repeating in full here. Rorty envisions a near future in which "the old industrialized democracies . . . [are] heading into a Weimar-like period":

> [M]embers of labor unions, and unorganized unskilled workers, will sooner or later realize that their government is not even trying to prevent wages from sinking or to prevent jobs from being exported. Around the same time, they will realize that suburban white-collar workers—themselves desperately afraid of being downsized—are not going to let themselves be taxed to provide social benefits for anyone else.
>
> At that point, something will crack. The nonsuburban electorate will decide that the system has failed and start looking around for a strongman to vote for—someone willing to assure them that, once he is elected, the smug bureaucrats, tricky lawyers, overpaid bond salesmen, and postmodernist professors will no longer be calling the shots . . .
>
> One thing that is very likely to happen is that the gains made in the past forty years by black and brown Americans, and by homosexuals, will be wiped out. Jocular contempt for women will come back into fashion. . . . All the resentment which badly educated Americans feel about having their manners dictated to them by college graduates will find an outlet.[27]

Many millions of Americans feel betrayed. Contemporary accounts of our life and times describe disillusionment on a vast scale,

---

[26] Mark Danner, "The Magic of Donald Trump," *New York Review of Books*, May 26, 2016. See also Jennifer Senior, "A Book From 1998 Envisioned 2016 Election," *New York Times*, November 21, 2016.
[27] *Achieving Our Country: Leftist Thought in Twentieth-Century America*, pp. 89–90.

not to mention anger, fear, hostility, and confusion, along with widespread, destabilizing anxiety. *Necessitous men . . . the stuff of which dictatorships are made.* Roosevelt wasn't indulging in rhetorical flourish when he spoke those words. At the time the country was fighting a global war that had its roots in the desperation of necessitous men, fueled by a keen sense of betrayal that one of history's most notorious dictators had masterfully exploited to gain power. The careers of Roosevelt and that dictator ran in striking parallel starting in 1933, when Hitler became chancellor of Germany in January, and Roosevelt was sworn in as president five weeks later. Both leaders pledged to lead their respective countries out of misery. One succeeded, and the other failed spectacularly.

Trump, too, promises to lead us out of "the carnage" and make America great again. He aims his pitch particularly at the shafted, pissed-off working class, but his professed devotion to working people stumbles over the simplest proofs. On whether to raise the federal minimum wage of $7.25 an hour, Trump's moral compass has spun from an implied no (wages are already "too high"), to an implied yes (wages are "too low"), to weasel words (leave it up to the states), to yes and no in the same breath ("I would leave it and raise it somewhat"), and, finally, when pressed in an interview with Bill O'Reilly in July 2016, to yes-but (raise it to $10, but it's still best left to the states).[28] All this from a candidate, now president, firmly in favor of abolishing the estate tax, to the great benefit of heirs of multimillionaires and none at all to the vast majority of us.

But facts, lies, contradictions, it's all the same to the maestro of America's mighty FIC. Trump is peddling a certain kind of American "dream" whose trail was blazed by sellers of Florida swampland, Hollywood studio executives, and alleged scholars of so-called race science. Meanwhile, it bears noting that the 2016 election season

---

[28] Dave Jamieson, "Donald Trump's Stance on the Minimum Wage Is Indecipherable," *Huffington Post*, July 27, 2016.

was very, very good for the FIC's bottom line. Hundreds of millions of dollars' worth of TV and radio ads were sold. Twitter, Facebook, YouTube, and their social media peers made money hand over fist while platforming the most insane sorts of conspiracist fantasies.[29] In the midst of all this came a report that the number of full-time daily journalists had, as of 2015, dropped by almost half since 2000,[30] but journalism, in the strict, old-fashioned sense of gathering facts and accurately reporting them, has never been part of the FIC. Whether journalism will survive in the U.S. as a viable endeavor is an open question. The FIC, however, is clearly a growth industry. Speaking at a Morgan Stanley investors' conference in March 2016, one of the FIC's commanders, Leslie Moonves, the chief executive of CBS whose 2015 compensation totaled $56.8 million, said of the Trump campaign: "It may not be good for America, but it's damn good for CBS. The money's rolling in and this is fun . . . this [is] going to be a very good year for us. Sorry. It's a terrible thing to say. But bring it on, Donald. Keep going."[31]

---

[29] "POPE FRANCIS SHOCKS THE WORLD, ENDORSES DONALD TRUMP FOR PRESIDENT'" was one of the less lurid fakes. Among many others, there was the Clinton campaign's plan for a radiological attack that would halt voting (and save Hillary from defeat), the child-sex ring masterminded by Clinton's campaign chairman located in the basement of a Washington, DC, pizza parlor, and Clinton paying pollsters to skew their results in her favor. All of the foregoing were shared on Twitter by people close to the Trump campaign, and in some instances by people named Trump. See Amanda Robb, "Anatomy of a Fake News Scandal," *Rolling Stone,* November 16, 2017; Marc Fisher, John Woodrow Cox, and Peter Hermann, "Pizzagate: From Rumor, to Hashtag, to Gunfire in D.C.," *Washington Post,* December 6, 2016; and Jim Rutenberg, "Media's Next Challenge: Overcoming the Threat of Fake News," *New York Times,* November 6, 2016.

[30] Rutenberg, "Media's Next Challenge: Overcoming the Threat of Fake News."

[31] Eliza Collins, "Les Moonves: Trump's Run Is 'Damn Good for CBS,'" *Politico,* February 29, 2016.

# BOOK OF DAYS
## OCTOBER

The World Health Organization reports that Russian and Syrian government bombardments of Aleppo killed 338 people in the past week, including more than 100 children, and that many of the more than 800 wounded are expected to die due to lack of medical care. Alabama Supreme Court chief justice Roy S. Moore is suspended for the remainder of his term for instructing the state's probate judges to refuse to issue marriage licenses to same-sex couples. "She's nasty, but I can be nastier than she ever can be," Trump says of Hillary Clinton after she defends former Miss Universe Alicia Machado, whom Trump has called "Miss Piggy," "Miss Housekeeping," and "disgusting." "Hillary Clinton was married to the single greatest abuser of women in the history of politics . . . and it's something that I'm considering talking about more in the near future," says Trump, who also asserts that infidelity was "never a problem" in his three marriages. The *Arizona Republic* endorses Clinton for president, its first endorsement of a Democratic nominee since its founding in 1890. The *New York Times* reports that Trump claimed a loss of $916 million on his tax returns in 1995 due to mismanagement of his three Atlantic City casinos, his failed Trump airline, and losses associated with his purchase of the Plaza Hotel in Manhattan. In a nationwide referendum, Colombian voters reject the peace deal recently negotiated by the government and FARC to end a five-decade-long war in which 220,000 people were killed and 6 million were displaced. FiveThirtyEight's polls-only model puts Clinton's chances of winning the election at 75 percent, her best position since late August, and other polls show Trump trailing badly in Pennsylvania and by smaller margins in Florida and North Carolina. In Paris, Kim Kardashian is tied up, gagged, and robbed of jewelry worth nearly $9 million. The Taliban overruns central neighborhoods in the provincial capital of Kunduz, taunting American and Afghan government forces on social media. "What is point of backing a regime holed up in Kabul, riven with old rivalries & useless as a turd," reads one Twitter post. The attorney general of New York issues a "notice of violation" to Trump's foundation and orders it to stop soliciting charitable donations. Julian Assange announces that Wikileaks will release "significant material" in the next ten weeks, and promises that all U.S.-election-related documents will appear before November 8. Hurricane Matthew wreaks havoc on southern Haiti, the president of the Philippines says that President Obama "can go to hell," and bacterial diseases and skin rashes are on the rise in Flint as residents are reluctant to use tap water for washing hands and bathing. The Pew Research Center reports that nearly seven in ten Democrats believe climate change is mainly the result of human activity, while fewer than 25 percent of Republicans believe so. News media report the FBI's arrest of Harold T. Martin of Glen Burnie, Maryland, for allegedly stealing highly classified computer codes developed by the National Security Agency for hacking into the networks of foreign governments. Israel approves plans for a new settlement on the West Bank three weeks after signing a lucrative military aid package with the U.S., and the European Union announces that it will send tens of thousands of Afghan refugees back to Afghanistan, in apparent violation of international conventions on refugees. Indian police shut down a call center outside Mumbai where callers posing as IRS agents have been collecting as much as $150,000 a day from U.S. citizens. In the vice presidential debate, Kaine and Pence clash over which presidential candidate has the most "insult-driven campaign," and Republicans privately express hopes for a "lose-close" result in the presidential race that will prevent a Democratic landslide in down-ticket races. "Two weeks ago I would have said Republicans would hold control of the Senate," says one Republican pollster, "but there's just so many seats up and nobody is getting separation." The Department of Homeland Security and the Office of the Director of National Intelligence release an unprecedented joint statement announcing that "the U.S. Intelligence Community (USIC) is confident that the Russian Government directed the recent compromises of e-mails from US persons and institutions, including from US political organizations." The statement says that releases of hacked emails on DCLeaks.com and Wikileaks, and by Guccifer 2.0, are "consistent with the methods and motivations of Russian-directed efforts." The statement continues:

> *These thefts and disclosures are intended to interfere with the US election process. Such activity is not new to Moscow — the Russians have used similar tactics and techniques across Europe and Eurasia, for example, to influence public opinion there. We believe, based on the scope and sensitivity of these efforts, that only Russia's senior-most officials could have authorized these activities.*

On this same day, also a day on which Trump asserts, without evidence, that the Obama administration is allowing illegal immigrants into the U.S. in order to vote in November, and also tells CNN that he believes the exonerated African-American men known as "the Central Park Five" are guilty of a 1989 rape of a female jogger despite DNA evidence proving otherwise, the *Washington Post* releases an *Access Hollywood* tape from 2005 in which Trump, who had recently married for the third time, can be heard telling host Billy Bush of an unidentified woman:

> *I moved on her, actually . . . I moved on her, and I failed. I'll admit it. I did try and fuck her. She was married . . . I moved on her like a bitch. But I couldn't get there. And she was married. Then all of a sudden I see her, she's now got the big phony tits and everything . . .*

And:

> *You know, I'm automatically attracted to beautiful—I just start kissing them. It's like a magnet. Just kiss. I don't even wait. And when you're a star, they let you do it. You can do anything . . . Grab 'em by the pussy. You can do anything.*

Trump responds to the tape's release with a statement declaring, "This was locker room banter, a private conversation that took place many years ago. Bill Clinton has said far worse to me on the golf course—not even close. I apologize if anyone was offended." On the evening of this same day, excerpts of speeches that Hillary Clinton delivered to Wall Street executives are uploaded to Wikileaks, including a Clinton comment about the necessity for politicians to have "both a public and a private position." Responding to the *Access Hollywood* tape, at least thirty-five Republican governors and members of Congress withdraw their support for Trump, including Senators John Thune, John McCain, Susan Collins, and Kelly Ayotte. House Speaker Paul Ryan says he is "sickened" by the *Access Hollywood* tape but will continue to support Trump. "Oh yeah we can win—we will win," Trump says in a telephone interview. "We have tremendous support. I think a lot of people underestimate how loyal my supporters are." "The Republican Party is caught in a theatre fire," says one longtime GOP operative, "people are just running to different exits as fast as they can," and senior Democratic officials urge Clinton to target traditionally Republican states. Trump lambasts defecting Republican lawmakers as "self-righteous hypocrites," and holds a surprise news conference featuring three women who have previously accused Bill Clinton of either sexual assault or sexual harassment. Secretary of State John Kerry calls for a war crimes investigation into the recent bombing campaign in Syria by Russian and Syrian government forces that repeatedly targeted hospitals and other medical facilities. After killing more than a thousand people in Haiti, Hurricane Matthew kills twenty-two in the U.S. and leaves 1.2 million people without power. Oklahoma governor Mary Fallin amends an executive proclamation to invite people of all faiths, not just Christians, to pray for the oil and gas industry on Oilfield Prayer Day. Shortly after Trump's *Access Hollywood* tape is released, author Kelly Oxford tells women, "[T]weet me your first assaults," and continues: "I'll go first: Old man on city bus grabs my 'pussy' and smiles at me, I'm 12." Within three days more than twenty-seven million people have responded or visited Oxford's Twitter page, with as many as fifty "first assault" responses coming in per minute. Wikileaks releases thousands of emails from the Clinton campaign and Democratic operatives, House Speaker Paul Ryan says he will no longer campaign alongside Trump, and German police arrest a Syrian refugee suspected of plotting a bomb attack. During the second presidential debate, Trump points at Clinton and declares that she "has tremendous hate in her heart," and he vows to prosecute and jail her if he is elected president. Also during the debate, Trump asserts that his remarks in the *Access Hollywood* tape were only "locker room talk," and that he has never engaged in behavior that could be construed as sexual assault. The following day he calls Clinton "the devil" and says that her election would lead to "the destruction of our country." GOP vice presidential nominee Mike Pence squelches speculation that he might withdraw from the race by proclaiming he is "proud to stand with Donald Trump." Texas congressman Blake Farenthold, a Trump supporter, is asked on MSNBC whether he would withdraw his support if Trump were heard on tape saying, "I really like to rape women." "That would be bad and I would have to consider it," the congressman responds. British police increase anti-clown patrols after dozens of incidents in which people dressed as clowns, sometimes carrying axes or chain saws, acted aggressively or menacingly; in response to the clown scare in Britain and the U.S., McDonald's announces it will stop displaying its Ronald McDonald character in public. The World Health Organization urges countries to tax sugary drinks to fight the growing worldwide obesity epidemic. An NBC/*Wall Street Journal* poll shows Trump trailing Clinton by nine percentage points, and drawing just 37 percent of the popular vote. "We have to make sure that this election is not stolen from us," Trump urges the crowd at a campaign rally, and he claims that polls showing him down by double digits are "rigged." Responding to fierce backlash from Trump supporters, four Republican members of Congress, including Senator John Thune, reverse their recent decision to withdraw their support from Trump. More than one hundred Afghan police officers and soldiers are massacred by the Taliban after negotiating safe passage in Helmand Province. A study by Human Rights Watch and the ACLU shows that arrests in the U.S. for possessing small amounts of marijuana exceeded those for all violent crimes in 2015, and that African-Americans are far more likely to be arrested and prosecuted than whites, even though whites smoke marijuana at rates similar to African-Americans. Nine women come forward to publicly accuse Trump of groping and forcibly kissing them in past years, allegations that Trump asserts are part of a conspiracy by "the establishment and their media neighbors" against him. "Anyone who challenges their control is deemed a sexist, a racist, a xenophobe and morally deformed," Trump says. Bob Dylan is awarded the Nobel Prize in Literature, and President Obama lifts the $100 limit on Cuban rum and cigars that can be brought into the U.S. Trump, who called his then-twenty-three-year-old daughter Ivanka "a piece of ass" in an on-air interview with radio host Howard Stern, told a group of fourteen-year-old girls that he would be dating them in "a couple of years," and walked unannounced into a room where Miss Teen USA beauty pageant contestants—some as young as fifteen—were changing clothes, characterizes the growing number of sexual harassment and assault claims against him as "lies, lies, lies," and dismisses two of the claimants as not being attractive enough to have interested him. "Check out her Facebook page, you'll understand," he says of one, and "Believe me, she would not be my first choice," he says of the other, and of Clinton passing in front of him at their most recent debate, he says: "I'm standing at my podium and she walks in front of me, right. She walks in front of me, and when she walked in front of me, believe me, I wasn't impressed." ISIS-linked attacks kill dozens in Iraq, and Saudi Arabia admits that one of its jets mistakenly bombed a funeral procession in Sana, Yemen, killing more than one hundred people. Trump accuses Clinton of being on drugs during their second debate, and calls for both Clinton and himself to be drug-tested before their next debate. An Associated Press poll finds that only one-third of Republicans have a great deal of confidence that their votes will be counted fairly. "The election is absolutely being rigged by the dishonest and distorted media pushing Crooked Hillary—but also at many polling places—SAD," Trump writes on Twitter. Trump surrogates Newt Gingrich and Rudy Giuliani suggest that Democrats plan to cheat in the presidential election, Senator Jeff Sessions warns that Democrats "are attempting to rig this election," and Trump supporter David Clarke Jr., sheriff of Milwaukee County, posts on Twitter that it's "Pitchforks and torches time," along with a photo of an angry mob brandishing weapons. The American Psychological Association reports that 52 percent of adult Americans are suffering high levels of stress because of the presidential election. Iraqi government forces, supported by U.S. troops and air power, begin the battle to retake Mosul, Iraq's second-largest city, from ISIS. In an attempt to push Clinton's growing advantage in the polls and bolster down-ballot candidates, the Clinton campaign announces that it is "dramatically expanding" its efforts in traditionally right-leaning states such as Arizona, Indiana, Missouri, and Nebraska, and is making forays into long-shot states such as Texas and Utah. Sheriff Joe Arpaio of Maricopa County, Arizona, is charged with criminal contempt of court for willfully defying a judge's orders to stop targeting Latinos in traffic stops and other law enforcement actions. Ecuador shuts down Julian Assange's access to the internet at its London embassy, where he sought asylum in 2012 and has lived ever since, and Austria seizes the house where Adolf Hitler was born, with plans to raze it now that it has become a pilgrimage site for neo-Nazis. President Obama advises Trump to "stop whining and go make [your] case" to win votes. "If you start whining before the game's even over," Obama added, "if whenever things are going badly for you and you lose, you start blaming somebody else, then you don't have what it takes to be in this job." Phil Chess, cofounder of Chess Records, dies at age ninety-five. Kellyanne Conway, Trump's campaign manager, criticizes Clinton for not being farther ahead in the polls, and Trump pledges, "I will totally accept the results of this great and historic presidential election—if I win." In their third debate, Trump interjects, "What a nasty woman," as Clinton discusses his avoidance of taxes, triggering an eruption of pro-Clinton "Nasty Woman" T-shirts, bumper stickers, and campaign buttons, and a resurgence of Janet Jackson's song "Nasty" from 1986. "That was the greatest Republican debate performance since Abraham Lincoln!" claims a Trump campaign operative on Trump's Facebook Live show, a broadcast that the *New York Times* describes as "like state television produced by QVC." "We can't just beat this guy," a Clinton spokeswoman writes to potential donors, "we've got to beat him so definitively that Hillary's victory is undeniable." A U.S. soldier is killed on the third day of the Iraqi offensive to retake

Mosul. A tenth woman comes forward to accuse Trump of groping her, and emails released by Wikileaks show that Donna Brazile, the current interim Democratic Party chairwoman and former paid CNN commentator, tipped off the Clinton campaign about questions Clinton would face during a primary town hall, and again at a primary debate with Bernie Sanders. Private security researchers at Dell SecureWorks conclude that the email account of Clinton campaign chairman John Podesta was hacked by the GRU, Russia's foreign intelligence service. Dyn, a company that manages crucial parts of the internet's infrastructure, suffers a denial-of-service attack that disrupts accessibility to Amazon, Netflix, and a number of other major websites, and the attack appears to have relied on infections of hundreds of thousands of internet-connected devices such as baby monitors, cameras, and home routers. AT&T offers to buy Time Warner for $85 billion, and the bid is unanimously approved by the boards of both companies. Polls show that Missouri secretary of state Jason Kander, the state's Democratic U.S. Senate nominee and a former military intelligence officer, has pulled within a few percentage points of his opponent, incumbent senator Roy Blunt, thanks in part to a commercial in which a blindfolded Kander assembles an AR-15 assault rifle while critiquing Blunt's hardline position against gun control. An eleventh woman—an adult film actress—comes forward to claim that Trump hugged and kissed her without permission at a charity golf event in Lake Tahoe, Nevada, then offered her $10,000 to join him in his hotel room. Trump vows to sue every woman accusing him of sexual assault. The *New York Times*'s "Upshot" model gives Trump a 7 percent chance of winning the election, FiveThirtyEight puts Trump's chances at 16 percent, or about the same as the chance of losing at Russian roulette, and RealClearPolitics shifts Texas from solid Trump to "tossup." "Just in case you haven't heard," Trump said at a campaign rally in St. Augustine, Florida, "we're winning not only in Florida, but we're winning everywhere." In Amherst, Wisconsin, a woman is charged with disorderly conduct after smearing peanut butter on thirty vehicles parked out-side a gathering she mistook for a Trump rally. The American Bar Association refuses to publish a report characterizing Trump as a "libel bully" who has filed numerous meritless suits to punish and silence his critics, citing "the risk of the A.B.A. being sued by Mr. Trump." A study published in the journal *Nature Neuroscience* finds that people who tell small lies are likely to progress to bigger lies as the brain becomes desensitized to dishonesty over time. ISIS moves hundreds of civilians from surrounding villages into Mosul to use as human shields, sixty people are killed in an attack on a police academy in Quetta, Pakistan, and a Russian missile company rolls out the RS-28, a one-hundred-ton ballistic rocket with a nearly seven-thousand-mile range nicknamed "Satan 2," which the com-pany claims can "wipe out parts of the earth the size of Texas or France." In a live interview with Trump supporter and former House Speaker Newt Gingrich, Fox News anchor Megyn Kelly says sexual assault allegations against Trump raise the issue of whether Trump is "a sexual predator," and Gingrich accuses her of "being fascinated with sex, and you don't care about public policy." Kelly responds that she is "fascinated by the protection of women," then suggests that Gingrich "take your anger issues and spend some time working on them." Ammon Bundy and six other defendants are acquitted of charges of conspiracy to impede federal employees and weapons violations in connection with their six-week occupation of the Mal-heur National Wildlife Refuge headquarters in Oregon. Authorities arrest more than 140 Native Americans and other protestors near the Standing Rock Sioux reservation in North Dakota, the latest clash in the ongoing protests against the proposed Dakota Access Pipeline. In a letter sent to members of Congress eleven days before the presidential election, FBI director James Comey discloses that the agency is revisiting its dormant investigation of Clinton's use of a private email server after possibly relevant emails are found on devices owned by ex-congressman Anthony Weiner, the estranged

husband of top Clinton aide Huma Abedin, in the course of the
Bureau's investigation into Weiner for allegedly sending lewd text
messages to a fifteen-year-old girl in North Carolina. The FBI
"cannot yet assess whether or not this material may be significant,"
Comey's letter states, after saying that the emails "appear to be perti-
nent" even though the Bureau has yet to review them. "I think it's
the biggest story since Watergate," Trump says of the news. "I think
this changes everything." "We are calling the FBI to release all the
information that it has," Clinton says in an evening news conference. "The FBI has a history of extreme caution near Election Day
so as not to influence the results," Senator Dianne Feinstein, Democrat of California, says in a statement. "Today's break from that
tradition is appalling." Senate minority leader Harry Reid accuses
Comey of breaking the law by making the announcement this close
to the election, and George J. Terwilliger III, deputy attorney general under President George W. Bush, comments: "There's a long-
standing policy of not doing anything that could influence an
election. Those guidelines exist for a reason." Richard W. Painter,
chief White House ethics lawyer under President Bush from 2005
to 2007, files a complaint with the Office of Government Ethics and
the Office of Special Counsel against the FBI for violations of the
Hatch Act, which bars the use of an official position to influence an
election. Speaking at a rally in Golden, Colorado, Trump accuses
Clinton of "criminal action" that was "willful, deliberate, inten-
tional, and purposeful," then he refers to a comment from one of
Clinton campaign director John Podesta's thousands of hacked
emails. "As Podesta said, she's got bad instincts. Well, she's got bad
instincts when her emails are on Anthony Weiner's wherever."

# THE LONG GOOD DEAL

America's collective memory is short. During the 2010 midterms, it seemed like every other house in my North Dallas neighborhood sported a "Had Enough? Vote Republican!" sign in the yard. As if it had been two hundred years, instead of two, since the U.S. economy was on the brink of collapse, with panicked credit markets, big banks and insurance companies about to topple into the void, a flatlining auto industry, the Dow Jones plunging toward 6,500, job losses topping 700,000 a month, and two wars that had turned the budget surpluses of the late Clinton years into massive deficits, all courtesy of a two-term Republican president whose party had controlled Congress for six of his eight years in office. Yes, please! Vote Republican! Take us back to the good old days of 2008!

Two years. The perpetual fog of American forgetting-gas had done its work. If two years are all it took to erase the memory of the worst economic meltdown since the Great Depression, then we shouldn't hope for much awareness of that earlier crisis some eighty years ago, though there are still a few old heads around who lived it, and the experience of those times can be found readily enough in the archives and histories of the era. The country, to put it mildly, was different back then. Life was harder, and in places like the Texas hinterland—which today forms the big beating heart of the state's Republican base—it was a close approximation of fourteenth-century peasant hell. The vast majority of rural Texans lived without electric power, which meant no refrigeration, no water pumps, no indoor plumbing, no furnaces, no electric stoves, no incandescent lights, no motors to power machines for milking or shearing. Even for those of us only a generation or two removed from the farm, it's almost impossible to conceive just how different life was, although the phrase "nasty, brutish, and short" comes to mind. Among the best guides to that time is the "Sad Irons" chapter of *The Path to Power,* the first volume of Robert Caro's biography of Lyndon Johnson, which delivers a harrowing portrait of life as a medieval slog plunked down in the middle of twentieth-century America.[1] To take just one aspect of the slog: water. "Packing water" to the house from the source—a stream or a well—was a daily beatdown that often fell to the farmwife. As Caro writes:

> *A federal study of nearly half a million farm families . . . would show that, on the average, a person living on a farm used 40 gallons of water every day. Since the average farm family was five persons, the family used 200 gallons, or four-fifths of a ton, of water each day—73,000 gallons, or almost 300 tons, in a year. The study showed that, on the average, the well was located 253 feet from the house—and that to pump by hand and carry to the house 73,000 gallons of water a year would require someone to put in during that year 63 eight-hour days, and walk 1,750 miles.[2]*

Laundry was done outside, in a vat of boiling water suspended over a roaring fire—imagine *that* on a July day in Texas—next to

---

[1] Robert A. Caro, *The Path to Power* (Knopf, 1990), pp. 502–15.
[2] *Ibid.*, p. 504.

which the farmwife would stand "punching" the clothes with a paddle or broomstick, the human equivalent of an automatic washing machine.[3] Cooking was done with woodstoves, which were kept burning most of the day—summer and winter—and required constant tending: firewood in, ashes out. Because of the lack of refrigeration, most meals had to be prepared from scratch. In order not to starve in winter, a family had to can fruit and vegetables as they ripened in summer, a hellish process that went on for days at a time, indoors, during the hottest weeks of the year, and required the utmost precision in timing and technique.[4] The woodstoves were also used to heat irons for pressing clothes, six- or seven-pound slabs of actual iron that had to be scrubbed, sanded, and scraped every few minutes to remove the soot, and inevitably left the ironer's hands blistered and burned. Farmwives dreaded ironing day; hence, "the sad irons."[5] Caro goes on:

> *A Hill Country farm wife had to do her chores even if she was ill—no matter how ill. Because Hill Country women were too poor to afford proper medical care they often suffered perineal tears in childbirth. During the 1930s, the federal government sent physicians to examine a sampling of Hill Country women. The doctors found that, out of 275 women, 158 had perineal tears. Many of them, the team of gynecologists reported, were third-degree tears, "tears so bad that it is difficult to see how they stand on their feet." But they were standing on their feet, and doing all the chores that Hill Country wives had*

---

[3] Then the clothes went into the "rinse" tub for more punching, then to a third tub for "bluing," then each item would be hand-wrung and hung out to dry. "'By the time you got done washing, your back was broke.'" *Ibid.*, p. 509.

[4] "'You got so hot that you couldn't stay in the house. You ran out and sat under the trees. I couldn't stand it to stay in the house. Terrible. Really terrible. But you couldn't stay out of the house long. You had to stir. You had to watch the fire. So you had to go back into the house.'" *Ibid.*, p. 508.

[5] "'Washing was hard work, but ironing was the worst. Nothing could ever be as hard as ironing.'" *Ibid.*, p. 510.

*always done—hauling the water, hauling the wood, canning, washing, ironing, helping with the shearing, the plowing and the picking.*

*Because there was no electricity.*[6]

This state of affairs wasn't limited to Texas. In the early 1930s, more than 6 million of America's 6.8 million farms were without electricity.[7] From sundown to sunup these farmers and their families lived virtually in the dark. Most kerosene lamps provided twenty-five watts of light at best, barely sufficient for reading, and they were dirty, difficult to use, and dangerous. Many farmers did their pre-dawn chores in the dark rather than risk having a kerosene lamp in the barn with all that hay, all those animals with their restless feet. Radio, of course, was out of the question. The news and entertainment available to urban America were as effectively blacked out in most rural areas as if they were truly still stuck in the Dark Ages.

The Great Depression transformed what was an extremely hard life into an impossible one. With prices for crops, in real terms, falling below what they'd been in Colonial times, financial disaster began to overwhelm rural America. By the end of 1931, twenty thousand farms a month were being foreclosed on. A quarter of Mississippi had already been auctioned off, and a third of Iowa, with even greater numbers of foreclosures on the horizon.[8] Farmers' pleas for relief—among them, a moratorium on foreclosures—were rejected by President Hoover, who in effect told America to quit whining and go chew on its moral fiber. The president himself and Mrs. Hoover continued their ritual of dressing formally for dinner every night and consuming seven full courses, reasoning that any downscaling of the White House lifestyle would hurt the

---

[6] *Ibid.*, p. 511.
[7] *Ibid.*, p. 516.
[8] *Ibid.*, pp. 241–42.

country's morale.[9] But Hoover seemed oblivious to a basic fact of human nature: people tend not to be models of obedience when they're starving to death, and by the winter of 1931–32, starvation was what millions of Hoover's constituents were facing. "They had put their faith in government," as one contemporary reporter said of the farmers, "and government had failed . . . they reached a point where they could stand the strain no longer and moved toward open rebellion."[10]

You're not likely to find this episode of American history in the schoolbooks. It's too raw to fit the standard uplift narrative, and it might give the kids ideas, this story of patient, hardworking farmers driven to direct action. In Iowa, the Farmers' Holiday Association organized a boycott in which farmers refused to bring food to market for thirty days, but the "holiday" quickly morphed into a full-fledged strike. Roads were picketed, and when that didn't work, barricaded with spiked telegraph poles and logs. Bootleg milk was taken off trucks and poured into ditches, and more than once farmers turned back convoys of trucks escorted by armed lawmen. Telephone operators coordinated with striking farmers to warn them when soldiers or police were headed their way. Within weeks the strike spread to the Dakotas, Kansas, Minnesota, Missouri, Nebraska, and beyond. When sixty strikers were arrested in Council Bluffs, Iowa, a thousand farmers marched on the jail and forced their release. Four thousand men occupied the Lincoln, Nebraska, statehouse, and another seven thousand marched on the statehouse in Columbus, Ohio, with the intention of establishing a "workers' and farmers' republic." Across the Midwest, farmers banded together in armed groups to stop foreclosures. Lawyers and judges were stripped and beaten, threatened with hanging, and in at least one case, murdered.[11]

---

[9] *Ibid.*, p. 247.

[10] Mary Heaton Vorse, "Rebellion in the Cornbelt," *Harper's*, December 1932. See also Caro, *The Path to Power*, pp. 241–48, and Ira Katznelson, *Fear Itself: The New Deal and the Origins of Our Time* (Liveright Publishing, 2013), pp. 37–40.

[11] See Vorse, "Rebellion in the Cornbelt," and Caro, *The Path to Power*, pp. 248–52.

The cities were no calmer. Unemployment had leaped from 3 percent of the workforce in October 1929 to 24 percent in 1932, with as many as seventeen million men out of work in the cities.[12] In Seattle, five thousand protestors occupied the municipal building. Thousands of unpaid teachers in Chicago mobbed the city's banks, and a Communist Party rally in New York's Union Square drew thirty-five thousand.[13] In Washington, twenty-five thousand destitute World War I veterans—the "Bonus Marchers"—marched up Pennsylvania Avenue, then occupied the National Mall with their families, camping out for the next three months until Hoover had them routed out by U.S. soldiers using tear gas and fixed bayonets.[14] Campaigning for reelection that fall, the president was greeted by crowds chanting, "Hang Hoover!" A gridlocked Congress dithered and bickered, inspiring one columnist to call it "the Monkey House," and Americans questioned whether their government had the structural and practical abilities to address the crisis. There was growing speculation that perhaps liberal democracy was obsolete, a historical phase whose time had passed. Italian Fascism, Japanese militarism, the Bolshevik Communism of the USSR, and, soon, the rise of Nazi Germany all seemed to present fresh alternatives for dealing with modern problems. Mussolini himself predicted that "the liberal state is destined to perish." Constitutional democracies were "worn out," he declared, being "deserted by the peoples who feel [they will] lead to ruin." "[A]ll the political experiments of our day are antiliberal."[15]

By early 1933, *Barron's*, the financial establishment's weekly bible, was calling for "a mild species of dictatorship [that] will help us over the roughest spots in the road ahead." The American Legion claimed that the crisis could not be "promptly and efficiently met by exist-

[12] Katznelson, *Fear Itself*, p. 37; Caro, *The Path to Power*, p. 245.

[13] Caro, *The Path to Power*, p. 248.

[14] *Ibid.*, pp. 245–46.

[15] Katznelson, *Fear Itself*, p. 5. See also pp. 98–127.

ing political methods," and U.S. senator David Reed, Republican of Pennsylvania, stated: "If this country ever needed a Mussolini, it needs one now . . . The country wants stern action, and action taken quickly." The prominent American theologian Reinhold Niebuhr asserted that "our western society is obviously in the process of disintegration." "A dying capitalism," he wrote, "is under the necessity of abolishing or circumscribing democracy not only to rob its foes of a weapon, but to save itself from its own anarchy."[16]

SPECIALISTS KNOW IT AS "THE MIXED ECONOMY," THE COMBI-nation of free markets, effective government, and organized labor that characterizes the world's most prosperous nations. Laissez-faire capitalism created extraordinary wealth in late-nineteenth- and early-twentieth-century America. It also created extraordinary concentrations of power that threatened to undermine democracy, along with such virulent side effects as frequent bank panics, wild vacillations of boom and bust, extreme social and income inequality, and monopoly control of major industries. The Gilded Age robber barons—the Goulds, the Vanderbilts, the Morgans and Rockefellers—did quite well under laissez-faire. And as Jacob Hacker and Paul Pierson show in their indispensable *American Amnesia,* most of the rest of Americans were still stuck in the ditch, with little or no economic security and a life expectancy of roughly forty-five years, only marginally better than that of our ancestors in the Neolithic era.[17]

By the turn of the century, recognition was growing that concentrations of power in the hands of a few were fundamentally at odds with the country's foundational idea of equality. Without question,

---

[16] All four quotes are lifted from Katznelson, *Fear Itself,* pp. 12, 32, 114–15. See also pp. 30–40, 43–57, and 98–127 for a sobering description of the challenges to its legitimacy that American liberal democracy faced throughout the 1930s.

[17] Jacob S. Hacker and Paul Pierson, *American Amnesia: How the War on Government Led Us to Forget What Made America Prosper* (Simon & Schuster, 2016). On the "public-private arrangements" characteristic of mixed economies, see pp. 3–7. On life expectancy, see r 7–9, 45–47.

laissez-faire industrial capitalism was producing remarkable wealth. It was also driving American farmers and workers into exactly the kind of Old World peonage that generations of immigrants had come here to escape. Laissez-faire—literally, "to let you do"—gave the wealthiest members of society tremendous freedom to act as they wished with everyone else, and, as always throughout history, this broad freedom for the few led to plunder of the many. If America was to stay true to its aspiration of equality, the social contract had to be updated to account for the new and extraordinary pressures of industrial capitalism. Theodore Roosevelt acknowledged as much when he said in 1910, "The citizens of the United States must effectively control the mighty commercial forces which they have called into being."[18] But it took another Roosevelt, Franklin, along with the existential crisis of the Great Depression, to galvanize the political will that brought about this transition from laissez-faire capitalism to the mixed economy.

Roosevelt gave it a name, the New Deal, and its remaking of the social contract transformed American life so thoroughly that it's become invisible to us, as taken for granted as the air we breathe or the ground beneath our feet. Or as, for instance: electricity. As Caro shows in *The Path to Power,* thirty million farmers and their families lived in the preindustrial dark not because of technological obstacles (many lived within sight of power lines) or prohibitive cost to the utility company (plenty of farmers offered to pay the expense of running a line out to their homes) or because utility companies couldn't make a profit on rural lines (studies in Minnesota and Alabama showed that rural lines were profitable) but because rural electric service wouldn't be *as* profitable for utility companies urban market. The companies based their decision, as compa-, on capital risk and rate of return. Considerations of fairness, fellow feeling, or the greater social good simply didn't factor into the corporate calculus.[19]

This is known among economists as "market failure." Sam Rayburn, the Texas congressman who led the legislative fight to bring electricity to rural America, stated it plainly during debate on the House floor: "When free enterprise had the opportunity to electrify farm homes—after fifty years, they had electrified three percent."[20] The Public Utility Holding Company Act of 1935 and the Rural Electrification Act of 1936—crucial New Deal legislation— "brought the lights" to rural America over the strenuous opposition of the utility lobby, which put out fake "spontaneous" mass mailings to members of Congress (one of the first instances of Astroturfing in American politics) and pushed a whisper campaign alleging that President Roosevelt was insane. John Carpenter, president of Texas Power & Light—there's a freeway named after him in Dallas—so loathed Sam Rayburn that he offered to spend any amount of money to defeat him in the next election. Rayburn won. The lights went on.[21]

The air we breathe. The ground beneath our feet. Along with: banks, and more broadly, the entire system of banking and finance on which market capitalism depends for its lifeblood. With scant regulation, no deposit insurance, and no national bank, America's laissez-faire financial system endured no fewer than six major bank panics between 1873 and 1907, and the overall economy endured seven major depressions or recessions during the same period. Boom-and-bust was the norm continuing into the twentieth century, culminating in the stock market crash of 1929, marking the start of the mother of all depressions. By January 1933, some 5,500 banks had gone bust, and most of the remaining 13,000 were teetering on

---

[19] Caro, *The Path to Power,* pp. 517–19.

[20] *Ibid.,* pp. 520–21.

[21] *Ibid.,* pp. 326–27.

the brink, collectively holding $6 billion in cash against $41 billion in deposit obligations. That February, the dreaded panic began in Michigan when the governor, hoping to save the shaky Union Guardian Trust Company, declared a banking moratorium and closed all of the state's 550 banks. As the news spread, people across the country rushed their own banks to withdraw their money, starting runs in Baltimore, then Indianapolis and Akron, and then in the country's two major financial cities, New York and Chicago. Banks began locking their doors to stave off collapse, and by March 1, governors in seventeen states had declared statewide bank "holidays" in hopes that a cooling-off period would prevent wholesale disaster.[22]

Roosevelt took office on March 4. The first bill of his administration enabled banks to reopen under Treasury Department licenses that guaranteed their soundness, effectively putting the federal government's warranty on all deposits. When banks began reopening on March 13, there were no runs, and within days people were making deposits again. Over the next several years Roosevelt and Congress would create a comprehensive regulatory system for banking—deposit insurance, capital requirements, the Glass-Steagall Act (separating commercial and investment banks)—and for the financial industry in general, such as the Securities Act of 1933, also known as the "Truth in Securities Act," and the Securities Exchange Act of 1934 (if you think Wall Street is a rigged game these days, it's a seminary compared to the fraud-fest of the Roaring Twenties), that would make bank panics and market crashes a thing of the past. From the mid-1930s into the early 1980s, U.S. banking and finance enjoyed remarkable stability. Bank failures were rare, isolated events. The bipolar booms and busts of laissez-faire capitalism became the much more manageable phenomenon of the business cycle. This began to change with deregulation, starting with the bipartisan overhaul of the savings and loan industry in the early

---

[22] Caro, *The Path to Power*, pp. 250–52.

1980s. "All in all, I think we hit the jackpot," said a beaming President Reagan in 1982 as he signed the Garn–St. Germain Act into law.[23] Not quite. By the end of the decade there would be *no* savings and loan industry, thanks to the frenzy of speculation and self-dealing that followed passage of Garn–St. Germain. The industry boomed, busted, and disappeared, all within the span of eight years. The biggest bank crisis since the Great Depression had erased an entire sector of American finance, leaving taxpayers on the hook for $160 billion; this seemed like a huge amount of money at the time, but it was just chump change compared to what was coming. The New Deal framework continued to be dismantled throughout the 1990s—Glass-Steagall bit the dust in 1999—and, just as importantly, regulation was never extended to new markets in financial exotica like credit default swaps and derivatives.[24] Banking and finance grew increasingly volatile, culminating (so far?) in the Great Recession of 2008, when only massive government intervention saved the economy.[25]

The air we breathe. The ground beneath our feet. New Deal initiatives produced much of the infrastructure that we rely on to this day, the roads, waterways, bridges, sewers and water mains, courthouses, libraries, and power grids. The omnibus Farm Relief Act of 1933 saved and stabilized American agriculture, and began establishing the institutions that would make farming an economically feasible way of life for future generations. The national framework of social insurance—Social Security, unemployment and disability benefits, work programs and workers' compensation—not only protected citizens from risks that private markets couldn't or wouldn't insure, but also tempered downturns in the business cycle, as well

---

[23] See Paul Krugman, "Reagan Did It," *New York Times,* May 31, 2009.
[24] Warren Buffet famously warned that derivatives were "weapons of mass financial destruction." Hacker and Pierson, *American Amnesia,* p. 284.
[25] For more on the deregulation of banking and finance, and the 2008 crash, see "Hillary Doesn't Live Here Anymore," *supra.*

as preventing the kind of mass destitution that threatened the country's stability in the early 1930s. The final piece of the mixed economy got its due with the Wagner Act (1935), which established the rights of workers to unionize and bargain collectively with employers, enabling labor to get its fair share of the benefits of rising productivity.[26]

The New Deal saved capitalism—saved it from the big-time capitalists who by 1932 had nearly run it into the ground, though many of the big-timers didn't see it that way. Fred Koch, the multimillionaire father of the future multibillionaire brothers Charles and David, opined in 1938 that "the only sound countries in the world are Germany, Italy, and Japan." He found Germany to be a heartening counterexample to Roosevelt's New Deal: "When you contrast the state of mind of Germany today [1938] with what it was in 1925, you begin to think that perhaps this course of idleness, feeding at the public trough, dependence on government, etc., with which we are afflicted is not permanent and can be overcome."[27]

The comparison is instructive. Adolf Hitler became chancellor of Germany in January 1933, and had gained dictatorial powers by late March of that year. In the meantime, Franklin Roosevelt was sworn in as U.S. president. Two leaders, both taking office at the same time, both faced with the economic and social chaos of the Great Depression. To say that they took vastly different approaches, with correspondingly divergent outcomes, would be an understatement on the order of a piano falling on your head. History shows that Fred Koch was about as wrong as a human being can be, and Nazi Germany is only the half of it. Roosevelt reinvented the American social contract, and he did it by working within the bounds of a constitutional democracy that was already some 140 years old when

---

[26] See Caro, *The Path to Power,* pp. 321–26, 252–60, 416–17, 497–501; Hacker and Pierson, *American Amnesia,* pp. 115–19, 136; Thomas Frank, *What's the Matter With Kansas?* (Picador, 2004), pp. 62–66, 76, 78–80.

[27] Hacker and Pierson, *American Amnesia,* p. 230.

he took office.[28] By every measure—life expectancy, infant mortality, income, education, productivity, scientific and technological innovation—the mixed economy ushered in by the New Deal was a huge success. Corporate America thrived, notwithstanding conservative alarm over "creeping socialism," or the slippery slope thereto, that greeted virtually every New Deal initiative.[29] Within a generation, the United States was enjoying the fastest sustained growth of any society in recorded history, and the prosperity was shared broadly, with income rising faster at the bottom and middle of society than at the top.[30] Even so, gross racial and gender disparities in income remained. No doubt this failing was the New Deal's silver lining for many of its conservative opponents.[31]

By the 1950s, there was broad bipartisan consensus that the mixed economy was "an established and useful reality," to borrow a phrase from a Roosevelt-era president of the Chamber of Commerce (he was referring to collective bargaining). President Dwight Eisenhower, Republican, five-star army general, and no flaming liberal, much less a Communist (though he was accused of being one by the John Birch Society, which counted Fred Koch—he seems to

----

[28] John Gunther called it "one of the few gradualist revolutions in history." Isaiah Berlin reflected in 1955 that "Mr. Roosevelt's example strengthened democracy everywhere—that is to say, the view that promotion of social justice and individual liberty does not necessarily mean the end of all efficient government." Both quotes are gratefully lifted from Katznelson, *Fear Itself*, p. 6. Ira Katznelson himself credits the New Deal with "an import almost on par with that of the French Revolution. It becomes . . . not merely an important event in the history of the United States, but the most important twentieth-century testing ground for representative democracy in an age of mass politics." *Ibid.*, p. 9.

[29] The National Association of Manufacturers warned that Social Security would lead to "ultimate socialistic control of life and liberty," and the U.S. Chamber of Commerce launched an inquiry "to determine whether such legislation may be demonstrated as leading definitely to the complete socialization of the United States." The Liberty League, the voice of America's conservative industrial elite, issued pamphlets attacking the New Deal as fascist, socialist, and un-American, and compared Roosevelt to Hitler, Mussolini, and Stalin. Hacker and Pierson, *American Amnesia*, pp. 132, 136–37.

[30] Bill Moyers, "We, the Plutocrats vs. We, the People," TomDispatch.com, September 11, 2016, http://www.tomdispatch.com/blog/176184/.

[31] One would like to know the extent to which midcentury American prosperity was built on the back of such disparities.

have had a special gift for shedding darkness onto light—among its founders), expanded Social Security, increased federal support for science and technology, and pushed for major infrastructure programs.[32] Such was the political consensus of the day that his legislation initiating the interstate highway system passed Congress with one dissenting vote in the Senate, and by voice vote in the House. In private, he mocked the archconservatives who dreamed of dismantling the New Deal. "There is a tiny splinter group . . . that believes you can do such things," he wrote. "Among them are H. L. Hunt . . . a few other Texas oil millionaires, and an occasional politician or business man from other areas. Their number is negligible and they are stupid."[33]

**"YOU DON'T MISS YOUR WATER TILL YOUR WELL RUNS DRY,"** THE late, great Otis Redding sang in one of his heartbreak songs. Around 2009, 2010, around the time we were crawling out from under the wreckage of 2008 and saw that the One Percent had come through just fine, thank you, that seems to be when a critical mass of America began to realize that we were missing something; that maybe our well was running dry. People were angry. They had good reason to be. They saw great prosperity at the top, scant trickle-down toward the bottom, and impunity—not to mention bigger incomes—for the very same Wall Street crowd who'd nearly wrecked the world economy. In Texas, and especially in rural Texas—where, by the way, electric appliances, electric lights, radio, television, and more recently, the internet have been settled facts of life for years—the Tea Party rose with a mighty roar to rage against liberals, the federal government, and a newly elected Democratic president.

---

[32] As for the "useful reality" of collective bargaining, Eisenhower stated: "[U]nions have a secure place in our industrial life. Only a handful of unreconstructed reactionaries harbor the ugly thought of breaking unions. Only a fool would try to deprive working men and women of the right to join the union of their choice." Hacker and Pierson, *American Amnesia,* p. 150.
[33] *Ibid.*, pp. 149–51.

If that rage seems somewhat misdirected, there's a reason: forty years of well-funded, expertly guided government-bashing have done a number on the American mind. The story of this bashing, of its funding and organizing and the people behind it, offers a *Game of Thrones* sort of scale and intricacy, with scores of characters, intrigues, and fiefdoms sprawled across a vast expanse. The telling, like *Game of Thrones,* requires multiple volumes. There is, for instance, Jane Mayer's *Dark Money,*[34] an exhaustively researched and sourced exploration into the rich people's movement that founded and funded the think tanks, institutes,[35] conferences, and media outlets that worked to replace the broad postwar consensus on the mixed economy with "free-market absolutism."[36] There is *Democracy in Chains,* Nancy MacLean's deep dive into the story of libertarian economist James Buchanan, whose "public-choice theory," with its premise of public servants and elected officials as self-aggrandizing actors less concerned with the common good than with their own interests, was taken on and advanced by the movement, and particularly by Charles Koch, who, among other acts of patronage, donated $10 million to support the Center for Study of Public Choice

---

[34] *Dark Money: The Hidden History of the Billionaires Behind the Rise of the Radical Right* (Doubleday, 2016).

[35] The Orwellian names are a kick. There is, for instance, the "Center to Protect Patients' Rights," which existed as a PO box in the Boulder Hills post office in Phoenix, Arizona, and through which some $62 million in Koch-network donations flowed in 2010, mostly to fund Astroturf attacks on Obamacare. Then there is the "Institute for Humane Studies," whose founder, F. A. "Baldy" Harper, was a free-market fundamentalist who called taxes "theft," welfare "immoral," and labor unions "slavery," and fought court orders to enforce integration. Charles Koch, the chairman and a major funder of IHS, eulogized Harper thus: "Of all the teachers of liberty, none was as well-beloved as Baldy, for it was he who taught the teachers and, in teaching, taught them humility and gentleness." Among those affiliated with the IHS was the libertarian historian Leonard Liggio, who presented a paper at a Koch-sponsored conference calling for a libertarian youth movement based on the Nazi model. "National Socialist Political Strategy: Social Change in a Modern Industrial Society with an Authoritarian Tradition" was the title of his paper, which portrayed the Nazis' youth movement as crucial to their creation of a group identity and eventual capture of the state. Charles Koch's own contribution to the conference was a paper analyzing the strengths and weaknesses of the John Birch Society. *Ibid.,* pp. 54–56, 150, 188–91.

[36] *Ibid.*, p. 156.

at George Mason University.[37] There is *American Amnesia*'s narrative of corporate America's repudiation of the mixed economy, and the bipartisan political consensus that underlay it, in favor of an increasingly aggressive partisan role in politics and government.[38] And there are the one-off profiles of the key players bankrolling the whole thing, the Art Popes, the Kochs, the Robert and Rebekah Mercers, the planets and moons of this sprawling billionaire movement.[39]

Certain threads bind all these stories into one: abiding hostility to labor unions, antitrust laws, environmental and financial regulation, the minimum wage. Special loathing is reserved for taxes; it seems the richer you are, the more personal it gets. Action in the public interest is regarded as naive and pointless at best, more often actively malign. The free market is revered as the ultimate arbiter of wisdom and worth, as well as inherently "self-regulating," in the famous phrase of former Fed chairman Alan Greenspan.[40] Ayn

[37] *Democracy in Chains: The Deep History of the Radical Right's Stealth Plan for America* (Viking, 2017). MacLean focuses especially on Buchanan's application of public-choice theory to support the resistance to integration in Virginia, such as his plan for tax-funded vouchers for private schools that would have enabled the state to avoid complying with *Brown v. Board of Education;* to support the privatization of virtually all government functions and programs, including schools, Social Security, and Medicare; and to provide the intellectual basis for challenging the principle of majority rule.

[38] Chapters 7, 8, and 9, "We're Not in Camelot Anymore," "This Is Not Your Father's Party," and "The Modern Robber Barons," respectively.

[39] See, for instance, Jane Mayer, "Trump's Money Man," *New Yorker,* March 27, 2017; Jane Mayer, "New Koch," *New Yorker,* January 25, 2016; Jane Mayer, "State for Sale," *New Yorker,* October 10, 2011; and Jane Mayer, "Covert Operations," *New Yorker,* August 30, 2010. Ms. Mayer's exposés of the billionaire's movement have, predictably, drawn the ire of her subjects. See Jim Dwyer, "What Happened to Jane Mayer When She Wrote About the Koch Brothers," *New York Times,* January 26, 2016, and "Koch Propaganda Machine Tries Unsuccessfully to Discredit Jane Mayer (Again!)," Daily Kos, January 13, 2016.

[40] Greenspan, who has described himself as a "lifelong libertarian Republican," was chairman of the Federal Reserve Board from 1987 to 2006, where his devotion to laissez-faire principles was demonstrated by his steadfast opposition to financial regulation. Testifying on the subprime crisis before a congressional committee in October 2008, he acknowledged that events had revealed a "flaw" in his ideology. "Those of us who have looked to the self-interest of lending institutions to protect shareholder's equity—myself included—are in a state of shocked disbelief." Ayn Rand was a formative influence on Greenspan, and is standing at his side in a 1974 photograph taken with President Gerald Ford in the Oval Office on the

Rand, author of romance novels for business moguls, is venerated for her depictions of rugged capitalist heroes taking on wimpy liberals and obstructionist bureaucrats. Rand's philosophy of "ethical egoism," which holds that the morally correct action in any situation is the one that advances your self-interest, fits nicely with the social Darwinism of the free-market absolutists, a worldview in which laissez-faire capitalism is nothing less than part of the natural order. Inequality, gross disparities of wealth and power, these are not only inevitable but good: they are the mechanism by which natural selection culls the weak from the strong, the takers from the makers. As hedge fund billionaire Ray Dalio explained in his *Principles*:

> . . . *when a pack of hyenas takes down a young wildebeest, is this good or bad? At face value, this seems terrible; the poor wildebeest suffers and dies. Some people might even say that the hyenas are evil. Yet this type of apparently evil behavior exists throughout nature through all species . . . like death itself, this behavior is integral to the enormously complex and efficient system that has worked for as long as there has been life . . . [It] is good for both the hyenas, who are operating in their self-interest, and the interests of the greater system, which includes the wildebeest, because killing and eating the wildebeest fosters evolution, i.e., the natural process of improvement. Like the hyenas attacking the wildebeest, successful people might not even know if or how their pursuit of self-interest helps evolution, but it typically does.*[41]

*Evolution, i.e., the natural process of improvement.* Extreme success proves your extreme superiority in the natural order; or perhaps

---

occasion of the appointment of Greenspan as chairman of Ford's Council of Economic Advisors.

[41] *Principles: Life and Work* (Simon & Schuster, 2017), as quoted in Moyers, "We, the Plutocrats vs. We, the People."

for those of a religious cast of mind, God's blessing. How this Darwinist worldview plays out in the context of American democracy leads to some problematic results. Billionaire investor Tom Perkins has bluntly suggested a system of voting weighted by wealth: "You don't get to vote unless you pay a dollar of taxes . . . If you pay a million in taxes, you should get a million votes."[42] The billionaire movement's efforts to limit access to the polls could be viewed as a slightly different application of the same logic.[43] Voter suppression is hardball politics, nothing new about that; and what's hardball politics if not the pursuit of raw self-interest? How much more soothing to the conscience, then, to believe that your self-interest serves the interests of that larger *natural process of improvement*.[44]

In an interview published in *Slate*, Nancy MacLean, author of *Democracy in Chains*, had this to say about the billionaire movement's voter suppression efforts:

> *[It's] not just money. I think it's also much more about this psychology of threatened domination. People who believe it will harm their liberty for other people to have full citizenship and be able to work together to govern society. And that somehow goes much deeper than money to me. It's hard to find the right words for it, but it's a whole way of being in the world and seeing others. Assuming one's right to dominate . . . this is a messianic cause, with a vision of the good society and*

---

[42] As quoted in Hacker and Pierson, *American Amnesia*, p. 188.

[43] In addition to *Dark Money* and *Democracy in Chains*, see, for example, Ari Berman, "Why the Koch Brothers and ALEC Don't Want You to Vote," *Nation*, November 11, 2011; Lauren Harmon and Sarah Baron, "The Academy Awards of Voter Suppression," Center for American Progress Action Fund, February 20, 2015; and Robert Greenwald, "Exposing the Koch Brothers and the Price We All Pay," *Huffington Post*, May 20, 2014.

[44] Ray Dalio: "Self-interest and society's interests are generally symbiotic. Society rewards those who give it what it wants. That is why how much money people have earned is a rough measure of how much they gave society what it wanted." Dalio, *Principles: Life and Work*, as quoted in Hacker and Pierson, *American Amnesia*, p. 186.

*government that I think most of us would find terrifying, for the practical implications and impact that it will have on our lives.*[45]

Whether or not one buys the hyena theory of capitalism, its assumptions cannot be reconciled with the founding principles of American democracy. We the People. All men created equal. Right to life, liberty, and the pursuit of happiness. These are the principles of full citizenship, the foundational guarantee against subjugation, peonage, plunder—against nautonomy.[46] The New Deal was a deliberate, systematic effort to adapt that foundational guarantee to the new reality of industrial capitalism. Whatever the motives of the free-market absolutists—rank money grubbing, or sincere belief in the righteousness of their vision; good luck figuring out the difference!—their dismantling of the New Deal and the mixed economy inevitably ushers in a new Gilded Age, a society in which tremendous power for a few results, as it always has, in plunder of the many.

Right now the absolutists are winning. When *Forbes* magazine published its first list of the 400 wealthiest Americans in 1982, there were two billionaires on the roster, and the entire 400 had a combined net worth of $225 billion in today's dollars. By 2014, 113 billionaires were *left off* the list because they didn't make the cut ($1.55 billion), and the combined net worth of the 400 was $2.3 trillion. Meanwhile, earnings for working- and middle-class Americans stagnated even as we worked longer hours, took fewer vacations, and kept increasing our productivity. Paying for college is more of a challenge than ever. Retirement security is a receding mirage. More of us have

---

[45] Rebecca Onion, "What Is the Far Right's Endgame? A Society That Suppresses the Majority," *Slate*, June 22, 2017 (transcript of interview with Nancy MacLean).

[46] Abraham Lincoln: "As I would not be a slave, so I would not be a master. This expresses my idea of democracy. Whatever differs from this, to the extent of the difference, is no democracy." As quoted in Ronald C. White, "Notes to Self: Lincoln's Private Thoughts on Fate, Failure, Slavery, and Belief," *Harper's*, February 2018.

health insurance thanks to Obamacare, but the political climate and perpetually rising medical costs put the long-term viability of that lifeline in doubt. Where I live in Texas, median income doesn't get you into the middle class, which means two-thirds of my fellow North Texans lack the basic security—psychological and material—that *middle-class* denotes.[47] The two things that working Americans can look to as hedges against a destitute old age are Social Security and Medicare, both of which we pay for all our lives through payroll taxes, both abhorred as "entitlements" by free-market absolutists.

A "milk cow with 310 million tits!" was how one former chief of staff to Bill Clinton has described Social Security. "America's life-style expectations are far too high and need to be adjusted so we have less things and a smaller, better existence," we were recently advised by Jeff Greene, American billionaire; he made his pile going short on subprime mortgages. We've been getting this line for quite some time now, since at least as long ago as 1982, when then-millionaire, soon-to-be-billionaire Pete Peterson published an article in the *New York Times Magazine* titled "No More Free Lunch for the Middle Class."[48] Cut Social Security and Medicare, Peterson argued; it was time for the government to stop "subsidizing" the middle class. He's been saying the same thing ever since, even as the middle class disappears around us like the deck of a slowly sinking ship.

**IT'S EASY TO IMAGINE HOW SEEING YOURSELF AS THE LOVE** child of Ayn Rand and natural selection might encourage a certain

---

[47] See Lisa M. Virgoe, "Is American Dream Still Affordable?," *Dallas Morning News,* January 20, 2016. The excellent Ms. Virgoe walks us through a step-by-step analysis of the costs of a middle-class lifestyle in the Dallas area, which she defines as "decent housing in a reasonably safe neighborhood, decent school system, reliable transportation, an annual family vacation (whether a long weekend camping or a trip to the beach) and some cash left to save for retirement and kids' college." Even using the higher U.S. median income of $54,000 at the time (the Dallas median was about $48,000), Virgoe showed that a thrifty North Texas family of four came up about $30,000 short of the income needed for a middle-class life.

[48] The milk-cow, Greene, and Peterson references are all shamelessly and gratefully pillaged from Hacker and Pierson, *American Amnesia,* pp. 190–93.

inflation of self-regard, along with a corresponding enlargement of prerogative. "Competition . . . is the law of nature," declared William Graham Sumner, professor of political economy at Yale during the Gilded Age. Nature "grants her rewards to the fittest, therefore, without regard to other considerations of any kind."[49] Finding yourself at the top of the capitalist hyena heap, showered with nature's rewards, it's understandable that a sense of privilege might come with the view. Or perhaps not so much privilege as obligation, the mandates of ethical egoism. A responsibility to extend your will, your self-interest, even your DNA, as far as they will go. Evolution, "i.e., the natural process of improvement," might well demand it, in "the interests of the greater system."

Maybe this was what Nancy MacLean was getting at when she spoke of that "whole way of being in the world and seeing others. Assuming one's right to dominate." And how much easier to justify domination when those to be subjugated are moochers, takers, losers, the free-lunch crowd, the 47 percent for whom Mitt Romney expressed his contempt in 2012. So much more logical and even ethical, in evolutionary terms, to exclude them from "full citizenship," a status properly reserved for the rugged individualists of the producer and maker class. Except they aren't as rugged and independent as they think; they need the rest of us more than they seem to know. Riding high on the finance boom of the early 2000s, Citigroup CEO and chairman Sanford Weill, who sacked $785 million during those heady years, declared, "We didn't rely on somebody else to build what we built." In fact it was the collective (proper Randians break out in hives at the word) enterprise of the mixed economy that built the world where Weill's success was possible. Government oversight and regulation were part of it, starting seventy years ago with the New Deal. And within a few years of the Clinton-era deregulation of the banking industry, including the

---

[49] As quoted in Moyers, "We, the Plutocrats vs. We, the People."

repeal of Glass-Steagall in 1999, a bankrupt Citigroup would be rescued by the taxpayers to the tune of $476 billion in cash and guarantees.[50]

In 2012, President Obama famously overstated the case when he said, "If you've got a business—you didn't build that." Margaret Thatcher, Great Britain's ideological twin to Ronald Reagan, overstated the opposite case with her famous pronouncement, "There is no such thing as society," in effect reducing human endeavor to a bundle of "markets." The truth is we need it all, markets, government, collective effort, and there's no readier example of this than the cell phone most of us are never without. In *American Amnesia* we find the story of Dr. Vannevar Bush, Roosevelt's science czar during World War II, and how Bush, at Roosevelt's urging and with strong bipartisan support from Congress, set the path for America's huge postwar government spending on research and development in science, technology, and medicine. As Hacker and Pierson write:

> *The fruits of these investments ranged from radar and GPS, to advanced medical technology, to robotics and the computing systems that figure in nearly every modern technology. Far from crowding out private R&D, moreover, these public investments spurred additional private innovation. The computer pioneers who developed better and smaller systems not only relied on publicly fostered breakthroughs in technology; they also would have found little market for their most profitable products if not for the internet, GPS, and other government-sponsored platforms for the digital revolution.*[51]

[50] See Hacker and Pierson, *American Amnesia*, pp. 186–87, and Barry Eichengreen, *Hall of Mirrors: The Great Depression, the Great Recession, and the Uses—and Misuses—of History* (Oxford University Press, 2014), pp. 69–70. In his office, Weill displayed a four-foot-wide piece of wood featuring his portrait and the sobriquet "The Shatterer of Glass-Steagall."

[51] Hacker and Pierson, *American Amnesia*, p. 39. For more on Vannevar Bush and the government's role in tech development, see also pp. 65–67, 98–102, 119–20, 128–30.

If, as the authors of *American Amnesia* point out, you crack open that smartphone, you'll find that every component is the product of research that the U.S. government either funded or carried out directly: lithium-ion batteries, GPS, cellular technology, touch-screens and LCDs, internet connectivity, algorithmic applications. The internet itself is a government creation; the Department of Defense developed its precursor, the ARPANET, in order to connect with computing centers at major universities.[52] So we can only be amazed at the Olympian chutzpah of Silicon Valley billionaires who dream of libertarian utopias that would be free of government. Venture capitalist Tim Draper has proposed making Silicon Valley its own semiautonomous state. Google's Larry Page wants to construct a "Google Island," where tech research can proceed without government meddling. PayPal's Peter Thiel, whose fortune was built not just on the internet but through helpful government regulation (such as the Securities Exchange Commission's rule limiting losses on identity theft; how many of us would put our credit card information on the internet at the risk of losing everything we own?), is a prime mover of the Seasteading Institute, dedicated to the creation of man-made island nations beyond the reach of government.[53]

When faced with this sort of nonsense, one thinks of little boys who declare independence from their families, then run away as far as the tree house in the backyard. Their worldview is about as juvenile as that, a kind of nerdy romanticism that recalls the capitalist fantasies of Ayn Rand. "If companies shut down, the stock market would collapse," tech venture capitalist Chamath Palihapitiya asserted in 2013 when the debt-limit impasse between Obama and Congress closed down the federal government. "If the government shuts down, nothing happens, and we all move on, because it just doesn't matter."[54]

---

[52] *Ibid.*, p. 66.
[53] *Ibid.*, pp. 188–89.
[54] *Ibid.*, p. 189.

For centi-millionaires like Palihapitiya, it probably doesn't matter much, at least for the short term. But the industry in which he so fabulously prospered wouldn't function for long—wouldn't exist in the first place—without the institutions and social structures that only well-functioning governance can provide, such as: Laws, both civil and criminal. Courts and police to enforce those laws. Private property rights. Secure and enforceable contracts, copyrights, and patents. A stable system of banking and finance. Orderly international commerce, governed by treaties, trade agreements, secure borders, and customs controls. Orderly movement of people among countries. "I can guarantee that if you don't have a legal structure you will not have innovation," said Jim Dempsey, executive director of the Berkeley Center for Law and Technology, in a 2015 article in *Wired*. "Instead you will have chaos . . . every innovator survives on the oxygen of multiple regulatory systems."[55]

But it's even more basic than that, as basic, for most of us, as family history, the deflection point where some form of social good—cheap college tuition, union membership, the GI Bill, a WPA job—boosted a generation out of subsistence level. We of the current generation might bask in our achievements and claim to be self-made men and women, but it couldn't have happened without that boost two or three or four generations ago that got our grandparents out of the tar-paper shack, off the used-up farm. And what's just as basic as that deflection point: health. The development and widespread availability of vaccines and antibiotics are due in large part to initiatives begun and in many instances carried out by the National Institutes of Health, the National Science Foundation, the Department of Agriculture, and the Centers for Disease Control and Prevention, among other government agencies. We don't even think about horrors like tuberculosis or polio anymore, and the in-

[55] Kyle Denuccio, "Silicon Valley Is Letting Go of Its Techie Island Fantasies," *Wired*, May 16, 2015.

fections that used to put us in mortal danger. Now we pop some antibiotics and go on about our day.[56]

Longevity, quality of life: like wealth creation, these are social constructs as much as they are the products of private initiative. But it's even more basic than modern medicine, and reaches back before the New Deal, to some of the very first initiatives of progressive government. The sharp drop in mortality that began in the early years of the twentieth century was largely the result of many more children surviving into adulthood. The reason is simple, though it took huge investments by government to make happen: cities began to clean up their water supplies.[57] Filtration. Chlorination. Sewers. Basic stuff we take for granted every time we turn on the faucet, every time we flush the toilet. That we're alive and well today, walking and talking and in some cases making a career out of bashing the government, it's because Great-Grandpa didn't die from cholera or typhoid back in the day.

The air we breathe. The ground beneath our feet.

THE NEW DEAL GOAL OF BROADLY SHARED PROSPERITY HAS taken a beating the past forty years, and the damage shows. By virtually every measure relative to other rich nations, the U.S. has lost ground since the 1970s. We're shorter (height is a prime indicator of social conditions), we don't live as long, more of our babies die before their first birthdays, wages and educational achievement have stagnated, and inequalities of wealth and opportunity are higher than at any time since the late nineteenth century. Mortality rates for middle-aged white Americans have actually risen the past fifteen years, especially for non-college-educated whites. Maternal

[56] See Hacker and Pierson, *American Amnesia*, pp. 39, 51–56, 116, 126–28.
[57] *Ibid.*, pp. 49–51. See also Anya Groner, "The Politics of Drinking Water," *Atlantic*, December 30, 2014, and "A Century of U.S. Water Chlorination and Treatment: One of the Ten Greatest Public Health Achievements of the 20th Century," Centers for Disease Control and Prevention, https://www.cdc.gov/healthywater/drinking/history.html.

mortality rose 27 percent nationwide between 2000 and 2014. In Texas, the maternal mortality rate doubled between 2010 and 2014.

The very rich, of course, can buy what they need—health care, clean water, political clout. Now they're building luxury survival bunkers, where they can retreat when the societal apocalypse comes.[58] As for the rest of us—for instance, all the good citizens out there in rural Texas, Tea Party Texas, the hard country that was transformed by the New Deal—one tries to imagine how it might look in seventy or eighty years if current trends continue. Crumbling roads, jerry-rigged bridges, worn-out farms. A grudging, "market-based" energy grid. Clean water a rarity, and health care that's hit and miss. Perineal tears, perhaps, are once again commonplace. A far-fetched scenario, surely, but no harder to imagine in 2016 than the lived reality of rural Texas eighty years ago.

---

[58] Evan Osnos, "Survival of the Richest," *New Yorker*, January 30, 2017. "I think people who are particularly attuned to the levers by which society actually works understand that we are skating on really thin cultural ice right now." "I keep a helicopter gassed up all the time, and I have an underground bunker with an air-filtration system." "I will probably be in charge, or at least not a slave, when push comes to shove." "Saying you're 'buying a house in New Zealand' is kind of a wink, wink, say no more." "I would guess fifty-plus percent" of Silicon Valley billionaires have some form of "apocalypse insurance," said the cofounder and CEO of Reddit. And this from an East Coast venture capitalist: "Anyone who's in this community knows people who are worried that America is heading toward something like the Russian Revolution."

# BOOK OF DAYS
## NOVEMBER

In response to a petition by his surviving ninety-five-year-old half
sister, the Swedish government declares Raoul Wallenberg, the
Swedish diplomat who saved thousands of Hungarian Jews during
World War II, dead some seventy-one years after his disappearance
during the closing days of the war. Dutch far-right politician Geert
Wilders refuses to attend his own trial on charges of hate speech, and
instead issues a series of posts on Twitter that includes the assertion
that the Netherlands has a "huge problem with Moroccans." Gunther Oettinger, Germany's representative on the European Commission, the executive arm of the European Union, refers to Chinese
people as "slit-eyes" and "sly dogs" in a speech to Hamburg business
leaders, and makes disparaging remarks about homosexuals as well.
An explosion on the Colonial gas pipeline in Alabama injures at
least seven workers, not far from the site of another blast in September. Early vote totals in several states, including North Carolina,
appear to favor Clinton, and private polls show Clinton still leading
in North Carolina despite the FBI's renewed investigation into her
use of a private email server. Speaking in Michigan, a state no Republican presidential candidate has won since 1988, Trump tells

voters, "When you look around your state and you see the rusted-out factories, the empty buildings and the long unemployment lines, remember Hillary Clinton did much of this to you." CNN accepts the resignation of interim Democratic National Committee chairwoman Donna Brazile for divulging questions for CNN-sponsored candidate events to the Clinton campaign. "I didn't want to put CNN in the middle of what has been a real invasive cyberintrusion," Brazile explained, referring to emails between herself and the campaign released by Wikileaks. As polls show the race tightening, President Obama criticizes FBI director James Comey for disclosing the renewed investigation into Clinton's private email server, and in the same speech urges North Carolina college students to vote because "the fate of the world is teetering." Two police officers in Urbandale, Iowa, are ambushed and killed by a man who several weeks before was escorted out of a high school football game for waving a Confederate flag in front of black students. Trump, who avoided the draft during Vietnam, has bragged that he learns foreign policy from TV shows, and once said that sleeping around during his bachelor days and risking venereal disease was "my own Vietnam," leads Clinton by nineteen percentage points among military veterans registered to vote, according to a Fox News poll. "The Iraq War was a disaster," said one veteran, explaining his support for Trump. "He at least is not trying to tiptoe around it." The Chicago Cubs win the World Series for the first time since 1908. In Iran, a former high-ranking official is sentenced to 135 lashes for misappropriation of public funds. A 110-year-old predominantly African-American church in Greenville, Mississippi, is burned, and "Vote Trump" is spray-painted on the side of the church sanctuary. The Centers for Disease Control and Prevention report that the suicide rate for children ages ten to fourteen now surpasses their death rate from traffic accidents, with the suicide rate nearly doubling since 1999. Two American soldiers and thirty Afghans are killed in fighting near Kunduz, Afghanistan, and migrants evicted from the "Jungle" migrant camp near Calais, France, are moving to Paris at an estimated rate of one hundred per day. Less than a week before the election, a *New York Times*/CBS News poll shows that among likely voters, Clinton leads Trump 45 percent to 42 percent, with Gary Johnson polling 5 percent and Jill Stein 4 percent. Eighty-two percent of likely voters said the campaign left them feeling "more disgusted," 13 percent said the campaign made them feel "more excited," and 3 percent reported "neither." A number of Republican senators, including John McCain, Ted Cruz, and Richard Burr, say they will fight any Supreme Court nominee put forward by Hillary Clinton if she is elected president, and Melania Trump, in a rare solo campaign appearance, calls for more civility in public discourse. Two former allies of New Jersey governor Chris Christie are convicted of all charges of conspiracy and wire fraud in connection with the 2013 lane closing on the George Washington Bridge. The Labor Department reports that unemployment fell to 4.9 percent in October, the lowest level since February of 2008, and that hourly wages rose 2.8 percent compared to a year ago, the best year-to-year gain in more than seven years. At a campaign rally in New Hampshire, Trump calls the jobs report "an absolute disaster" and says "nobody believes the numbers anyway." An Ontario court places the Trump International Hotel and Tower—a project that Trump did not develop and has never owned—into receivership after its owners default on debt payments. Iraqi government troops push into eastern Mosul in the face of heavy opposition from ISIS, and three American military trainers are shot dead at a Jordanian air force base. In a development widely seen as favorable to Clinton, Hispanics surge to the polls in the final days of early voting, while Democrats' hopes of retaking the Senate fade as races tighten in New Hampshire, North Carolina, and elsewhere. "Trump deserves the award for Hispanic turnout," says Senator Lindsey Graham, Republican of South Carolina. "He did more to get them out than any Democrat has ever done." Nikolai Tolstoy, chancellor of the International Monarchist

League, urges Americans to consider installing a monarch as head of the U.S. government. Two days before the election, FBI director Comey clears Clinton regarding the latest batch of emails, saying they don't warrant any change to his earlier conclusion that she should face no charges over her handling of classified information. The Ku Klux Klan's official newspaper endorses Trump, Iranian state television broadcasts U.S. presidential debates as anti-American propaganda, and Trump's aides take away his Twitter access. A recovering heroin addict in Buffalo sues to stop the presidential election, and FiveThirtyEight characterizes Clinton as "the probable but far-from-certain winner." Leonard Cohen dies at age eighty-two. In New Delhi, eighteen hundred primary schools close due to heavy air pollution, exposure to which is said to be the equivalent of smoking forty cigarettes a day. As Election Day arrives, slightly more than half of Americans have an unfavorable view of Clinton, while six in ten have an unfavorable view of Trump. Polls show extremely tight races in battleground states such as Florida, New Hampshire, Nevada, and North Carolina. Trump is jeered and booed as he arrives at his midtown Manhattan precinct to vote; inside, where a group of topless women protestors appeared earlier, voters waiting in line openly laugh at him; one man shouts, "You're gonna lose!"; and cameras capture Trump sneaking a look at Melania's ballot as she votes. Clinton is cheered as she arrives at her Chappaqua, New York, precinct; among the crowd is Coline Jenkins, the great-great-granddaughter of suffragette leader Elizabeth Cady Stanton. Prince Harry of Great Britain, fifth in line to the throne, attacks the "racial undertones" of news coverage and social media commentary on his girlfriend Meghan Markle, whose mother is black and father is white, and the federal judge presiding over the murder trial of avowed white supremacist Dylann Roof orders Roof to undergo a competency evaluation. In Haiti, a large-scale vaccination program to battle cholera begins in the midst of new outbreaks following Hurricane Matthew. Late on Tuesday night, November 8, the website of Canada's immigration department crashes due to "a significant increase in the volume of traffic," and at 2:40 A.M. on November 9 news media begin reporting that Clinton has called Trump to concede the election. At 3:00 A.M., flanked by his family and close advisers, Trump delivers a victory speech at the Hilton hotel in midtown Manhattan in which he says Americans owe Clinton "a major debt of gratitude for her service to our country," that "now is the time for America to bind the wounds of division," and that he "will be president for all Americans." Russia's Duma, or parliament, bursts into applause at the news of Trump's election. "We are all now rooting for his success," Obama says of Trump, and Clinton tells her supporters that Americans owe Trump "an open mind and a chance to lead." Anti-Trump rallies erupt in a number of cities, and on Fox News former New York City mayor Rudy Giuliani says of the protestors, "The reality is they're a bunch of spoiled crybabies." Final results show that Trump won Pennsylvania, Ohio, Wisconsin, Iowa, and Michigan, all states carried by Obama in 2008 and 2012, and the Republican Party retains control of both houses of Congress, wins control of more state legislatures than at any time in history, and wins more governor's offices than in a century, while in Maricopa County, Arizona, Sheriff Joe Arpaio loses his bid for a seventh term. Mason Williams, professor of history at Albright College, writes: "Trump exploited the moral and psychic anxieties stemming from very real working-class precarity by mobilizing a white-nationalist identity politics. The political agency of the white working class was not channeled into a project of moderate national reform, even to the degree it had been during the Obama years. Instead, it issued forth as a primal scream of despair and rage that will reverberate around the world and down through history." As vote totals come in, Hillary Clinton is on track to win the popular vote by more than two million votes, while New York City mayor Bill de Blasio, speaking of new security measures being put in place around Trump Tower, says, "Yeah, there will be some disruption, but look on the bright side—the holidays are coming anyway, and Midtown is going to be all messed up anyway." San Antonio Spurs coach Gregg Popovich calls Trump's victory "disgusting." The UN warns that 250,000 residents in rebel-held eastern Aleppo are in danger of starvation, and implores all sides in the conflict to allow food deliveries to the area. Russia's deputy foreign minister tells the Interfax news agency that the Russian government maintained contacts with members of Trump's "immediate entourage" during the campaign, adding, "We continue to do this and have been doing this work during the election campaign." A Trump spokeswoman responds, "We are not aware of any campaign representatives that were in touch with any foreign entities before yesterday, when Mr. Trump spoke with many world leaders." Vice President–Elect Pence takes over as head of Trump's transition team, replacing Chris Christie, who as U.S. attorney prosecuted and jailed real estate developer Charles Kushner, whose son Jared Kushner is now married to Ivanka Trump. In a thirty-minute conference call with donors, Hillary Clinton blames her loss on FBI director James Comey's announcement eleven days before the election that he was reviving the inquiry into her use of a private email server. ISIS claims credit for a suicide-bomb attack that kills at least fifty-two people and wounds at least one hundred more at a Sufi shrine in southwestern Pakistan, and a suicide bomber kills two American soldiers and two American contractors at Bagram air force base in Afghanistan. Appearing on prime-time TV for the first time since his election victory, Trump repeats his promise on *60 Minutes* to appoint a Supreme Court justice who will help overturn *Roe v. Wade*. When asked about the consequences for women seeking abortions, Trump answers, "Well, they'll perhaps have to go—they'll have to go to another state." The FBI reports that attacks against Muslim Americans rose 67 percent from 2014 to 2015, driving an overall increase in hate crimes against all groups. Trump appoints as chief White House strategist his campaign director Steve Bannon, who in a radio interview in 2011 praised Ann Coulter and Sarah Palin by saying they were not "a bunch of dykes that came from the Seven Sisters schools up in New England." A bald eagle flies into a sewer in Orlando and dies. Howard Schultz, CEO of Starbucks and a prominent Clinton supporter, reports that he received a picture of a swastika on social media two days after the election, and more than 4.3 million Americans sign a petition asking state electors to pick Hillary Clinton over Trump for president. As Trump's transition team experiences delays, infighting, and firings, foreign leaders resort to blindly calling Trump Tower in their attempts to speak with him. The Labatt brewery announces an end to its long-standing policy of offering free beer for life to its retired employees. The first "supermoon" in seventy years occurs as the moon reaches perigee during full waxing, and House Speaker Paul Ryan tells reporters, "Welcome to the dawn of a new unified Republican government," after he is renominated for another term as Speaker. Workers at Walmart stores in China organize strikes and boycotts against the company to protest low wages and a new scheduling system that they say leaves them poorer and exhausted, and the International Energy Agency warns that the Paris climate accord targets are too weak to keep global temperatures from rising more than two degrees Celsius above preindustrial levels. Congressional Democrats say they will release a number of populist economic and ethics initiatives in the coming weeks, such as more spending on infrastructure, punishing American companies that move jobs overseas, and ending the carried-interest loophole for hedge fund and private equity managers. "This is an acknowledgment that it is very shortsighted to blame this loss on a letter from the FBI, or what states Hillary went to," says Senator Amy Klobuchar (D-MN). "We need to do a better job of having a bold sharp focus on the economy." The *Washington Post* reports that eight days before the election, the White House used the nuclear "hotline" to warn Russia against trying to hack into U.S. polling or registration systems, or otherwise trying to affect the outcome of the election. Trump names as his national security advisor retired lieutenant general Michael Flynn, who has characterized the Islamic faith as being no more than a "political ideology," posted a video on his Twitter account that includes the statement "Fear of Muslims is rational," and claimed that sharia law is spreading in the U.S. Speaking by phone with British prime minister Theresa May, Trump tells her, "If you travel to the U.S., you should let me know." In an interview with the *Hollywood Reporter,* Steve Bannon describes the incoming administration's plans for a huge infrastructure spending package and says that "the conservatives are going to go crazy . . . With negative interest rates throughout the world, it's the greatest opportunity to rebuild everything—shipyards, ironworks, get them all jacked up. It will be as exciting as the 1930s, greater than the Reagan revolution." Trump agrees to pay $21 million to settle two Californian class-action suits and $4 million to the New York attorney general to settle fraud claims against his now-defunct Trump University. Following a performance of *Hamilton,* the entire cast appears onstage to appeal to Vice President–Elect Pence, who is in the audience, to "uphold our American values" and "work on behalf of all of us." The 2012 GOP presidential nominee, Mitt Romney, who has described Trump as "a phony" and "a fraud," disparaged Trump's "bullying, the greed, the showing off, the misogyny, the absurd third-grade theatrics," and said when Trump won the GOP nomination that "the prospects for a safe and prosperous future are greatly diminished," meets with Trump amid speculation that Romney may be offered the post of secretary of state. At a federal building named for Ronald Reagan a few blocks from the White House, white supremacists hold a one-day conference at which one speaker describes white people as "children of the sun" who must "conquer or die," and America as a country that "was, until this last generation, a white country designed for ourselves and our posterity. It is our creation, it is our inheritance and it belongs to us." An analysis finds that propaganda, or "fake news," websites generate more traffic on Facebook than major news outlets, and the *New York Times* runs a story on censorship software being developed by Facebook intended to help the company enter the Chinese market. Trump drops his pledge to prosecute Hillary Clinton. The Turkish government, which has closed down 129 media outlets and jailed thousands of political opponents since the attempted July coup, fires an additional 15,000 civil servants and soldiers, and proposes to issue an amnesty to as many as 4,000 men convicted of child abuse and rape, provided that they have married their victims. With Clinton's lead in the popular vote continuing to grow, supporters urge her to seek recounts in Michigan, Pennsylvania, and Wisconsin. In Texas, a federal judge blocks a new Labor Department rule that would have enabled as many as 4.2 million workers to start earning time and a half for overtime. Fidel Castro dies of natural causes at age 90, after having survived no fewer than 634 assassination attempts, and three days later the first regularly scheduled flight in 50 years from the U.S. lands in Havana. On Twitter, Trump claims that Clinton won the popular vote only because "millions of people" voted illegally, and the Clinton campaign says it will participate in a recount effort in Wisconsin, and possibly similar efforts in Michigan and Pennsylvania, being undertaken by Green Party candidate Jill Stein. Trump, who explored business possibilities in Cuba during the 1990s arguably in violation of the trade embargo, threatens on Twitter to "terminate deal" with Cuba. A student at Ohio State, Abdul Razak Ali Artan, a Somali refugee, intentionally rams his car into pedestrians and then slashes at passersby with a butcher knife, injuring eleven, before being shot and killed by a university police officer; in a manifesto posted on Facebook earlier that day, Artan wrote that he was "sick and tired of seeing my fellow Muslim brothers and sisters being killed and tortured EVERYWHERE." Dylann Roof is granted permission to represent himself at his trial on charges of killing nine African-American parishioners in Charleston, South Carolina, last year. In an interview with editors of the *New York Times,* Trump indicates he is rethinking his support for revising the law to make it easier to sue for libel. "Somebody said to me on that, they said, 'You know, it's a great idea, softening up those laws, but you may get sued a lot more.' I said, 'You know, you're right, I never thought about that.'" Oxford Dictionaries announces that the word of the year for 2016 is "post-truth."

# TRUMP RISING

## KING DONALD SADDLES UP WITH THE WRECKING CREW

And so we voted, some of us, and the votes got counted, and the morning after, *on this grimmest of mornings* a friend wrote, we rose to ponder this strange new thing we'd wrought, *this bloodbath of an election.* Email was at it early. *Like watching someone get murdered. Like nine-eleven got voted in.* And this, from a Vietnam vet:

> *The third Vietnam Draft Dodger is now commander in chief.*

Welcome to the full flowering of the Era of Trump, which began with that now-mythic glide down the escalator at Trump Tower, where our president-elect commenced his candidacy with the historic words:

> *When Mexico sends its people, they're not sending their best . . . They're sending people that have lots of problems, and they're bringing those problems with us [sic]. They're bringing*

*drugs. They're bringing crime. They're rapists. And some, I
assume, are good people.*

If ever a monument is erected to the Trump presidency, then
surely these words—shades of Gettysburg!—will be carved in marble,
along with "blood coming out of her wherever," "nasty woman," and
"I would bring back a hell of a lot worse than waterboarding."
Like a true demagogue, Trump bypassed the head and spoke directly to the gut, to the biles and bubbling acids of emotion. He
said things that many civil, temperate Americans would never say,
would hardly admit (at least to pollsters) we carried in ourselves—
perhaps we hadn't even known just how deeply we resented our
own niceness, how angry our interior lives had become with all this
stuff bottled up, years and years of internalized microaggression
from a culture that kept insisting on diversity, inclusiveness, tolerance. Many discovered over the course of the campaign just what
a drag political correctness had been all these years, and to be free
of it, freed from this code that was jamming us up? That was relief
akin to a lung-cleansing primal scream. From the start Trump's rallies had the air of the tent revival, that same holy heat of exorcism
and ecstasy.

*Let's not fool ourselves,* another friend wrote—

*I can't stand anything but cold honesty right now. This is not a
Repub winning the election, which would be bad enough. This
is white supremacy winning.*

And on the phone, women sobbing. Trying to talk, failing, sobbing. It's okay, we wanted to say. Maybe it's not that bad. Stances are
taken, things get said in the heat of a campaign, and we could take
heart in the newly gracious, conciliatory Trump on display for several days after the election. Then came the news that Steve Bannon,
erstwhile chairman of the Trump campaign who bears a striking

resemblance to Otis, the town drunk on the old *Andy Griffith Show*,[1] was named "senior counselor and chief strategist" for the incoming Trump administration. The mainstream press still feels compelled to explain what *alt-right* means, but we *know* already, *we know **we know WE KNOW:*** white "nationalism," a.k.a. honky "purity" (don't dig too deep into the family DNA!), along with generous lardings of apocalyptic racism, and a style sense that falls somewhere between "Springtime for Hitler" and *Queer Eye for the Straight Guy*.[2] Prior to joining the Trump campaign, Bannon was chairman of Breitbart News, which he proudly declared to be "the platform for the alt-right." There he presided over such charming headlines as "Gabby Giffords: The Gun Control Movement's Human Shield," "Birth Control Makes Women Unattractive and Crazy," and, two weeks after a white nationalist murdered nine members of a Bible study group at a black church in Charleston, South Carolina, "Hoist It High and Proud: The Confederate Flag Proclaims a Glorious Heritage."[3]

*The faces on the subway today, I will never forget. And, the world as we knew it just died. And, the first president endorsed by the Ku*

[2] Just so we're clear, two thoughtful commentators have described the alt-right as "an amalgam of conspiracy theorists, techno-libertarians, white nationalists, Men's Rights advocates, trolls, anti-feminists, anti-immigration activists, and bored young people" who adhere to "a self-referential culture in which anti-Semitism, occult ties, and Nazi imagery can be explained either as entirely sincere or completely tongue-in-cheek." Alice Marwick and Rebecca Lewis, *Media Manipulation and Disinformation Online* (Data & Society Research Institute, 2017).

[3] See Dana Milbank, "Donald Trump's New Loose Cannon," *Washington Post*, August 24, 2016; Jill Disis, "Ten of Breitbart's Most Incendiary Headlines," Money.CNN.com, November 15, 2016; Daniel Victor and Liam Stack, "Stephen Bannon and Breitbart News, in Their Words," *New York Times*, November 14, 2016; Editorial Board, "Steve 'Turn On the Hate' Bannon, in the White House," *New York Times*, November 15, 2016.

*Klux Klan.* Then there was Obama being Obama the day after the election: "We have to remember that we're actually all on one team." A man's character is his fate, as Heraclitus said, and what a sick, twisted fate indeed that Barack Obama—cerebral, disciplined, cool, ever seeking to reconcile and accommodate (as an African-American pastor in Charleston drily commented, once his presidency is over, Obama will no longer have "to be the least threatening black man in America"[4])—has had to contend these past eight years with a political opposition that regards him as very much *not on the team.* Not even American: "His grandmother in Kenya said, 'Oh, no, he was born in Kenya and I was there and I witnessed the birth.' She's on tape. I think that tape's going to be produced fairly soon."[5] Or not a "real" American, but a "man who is a closet secular-type Muslim, but he's still a Muslim. He's no Christian. We're seeing a man who's a Socialist Communist in the White House, pretending to be an American."[6] That terrorist fist-bump, remember? Oh, and he was the founder of ISIS, an aspiring tyrant aiming for a Nazi- or Soviet-style dictatorship, and looks like a skinny ghetto crackhead.[7] "All this damage he's done to America is deliberate," said Marco Rubio during a Republican debate,[8] which had to be one of the dumbest things anyone said during the whole campaign. If Obama wanted to destroy the U.S., all he needed to do was sit on his hands in 2009 and let the hot mess of the Bush economy melt the country down to slag.

But the issue is bigger than any particular president. After his "all on one team" remark, Obama continued:

---

[4] David Remnick, "After Charleston," *New Yorker,* September 28, 2015.

[5] Donald Trump, April 7, 2011, on MSNBC's *Morning Joe.*

[6] Christopher S. Parker and Matt A. Barreto, *Change They Can't Believe In: The Tea Party and Reactionary Politics in America* (Princeton University Press, 2013), p. 2, quoting Tea Party activist and radio host Laurie Roth.

[7] ISIS comment by Donald Trump, August 9, 2016; dictator comment by Representative Paul Broun, Republican of Georgia, November 11, 2008; crackhead comment by Brent Bozell, Fox News guest, December 22, 2011.

[8] February 6, 2016.

*The point, though, is that we all go forward with a presumption of good faith in our fellow citizens, because that presumption of good faith is essential to a vibrant and functioning democracy.*

This goes to the heart of the matter. The American system of constitutional government is based on deliberate fragmentation of power, the "separation of powers" and "checks and balances" that we learned about in high school civics. For government to be effective—for government to meet the needs of the people—the U.S. constitutional order requires a healthy measure of good-faith cooperation among the players. Throughout the big middle of the twentieth century that's how it worked, and then good faith began to fray in the early 1990s. GOP leaders, Newt Gingrich and Tom DeLay chief among them, set out to win control of Congress by any means necessary, trashing traditions and protocols that for generations had enabled the House and Senate to function in spite of the natural frictions of party politics. One Republican congressman called the new tactics "kind of scary stuff," citing Gingrich's "belief that to ultimately succeed you almost had to destroy the system so that you could rebuild it."[9]

Democrats, in Gingrich's world of moral absolutes, were "the enemy of normal Americans." He and his allies were fighting no less than a "civil war" with liberals, and as he declared in a speech to the Heritage Foundation, "this war has to be fought with a scale and a duration and a savagery that is only true of civil wars."[10] And so began the constitutional hardball and scorched-earth tactics that have characterized the past quarter-century of American politics.

---

[9] Jacob S. Hacker and Paul Pierson, *American Amnesia: How the War on Government Led Us to Forget What Made America Prosper* (Simon & Schuster, 2016), p. 261. For more on this institutional shift, see the very fine *It's Even Worse Than It Was* by Thomas E. Mann and Norman J. Ornstein (Basic Books, expanded edition 2016), especially pp. 31–80, 170–91, and, by the same authors, *The Broken Branch* (Oxford University Press, 2006), especially pp. 64–140.

[10] Hacker and Pierson, *American Amnesia,* p. 260.

You may recall the Gingrich-orchestrated government shutdowns of 1995 (November, five days) and 1995–96 (December and January, three weeks) over budget disputes, and the party-line impeachment of Bill Clinton in 1998.[11] In more recent times, there was the famous dinner at a Washington fine-dining steakhouse on the evening of January 20, 2009—the day of Obama's inauguration—at which a group of leading GOP congressmen (along with Gingrich, by then a highly paid K Street lobbyist) vowed to sabotage Obama's presidency by opposing every, single, item, on the new president's agenda— this at a time when seven hundred thousand Americans were losing their jobs every month—including items previously supported or even proposed by the GOP.[12] ("We're all rooting for him," Obama said of Trump at their postelection meeting in the Oval Office. "Because if he succeeds, America succeeds.") In separate meetings, Senate Republican leader Mitch McConnell demanded total opposition to Obama, as later confirmed by three former GOP senators. "If he [Obama] was for it, we had to be against it," said former senator George Voinovich. "[McConnell] wanted everyone to hold the fort. All he cared about was making sure Obama could never have a clean victory."[13] McConnell himself would later admit to the strategy when he stated publicly, "The single most important thing we want to achieve is for President Obama to be a one-term president."[14]

*The single most important thing.* Burying Obama was the goal, and if bringing him down meant shredding the constitutional or-

---

[11] See Mann and Ornstein, *The Broken Branch*, pp. 116–20, for a description of the painstakingly crafted bipartisan support for Richard Nixon's impeachment in 1974, in contrast to the stark partisanship of the Clinton impeachment.

[12] See Robert Draper, *Do Not Ask What Good We Do: Inside the House of Representatives* (Free Press, 2012), pp. xv–xxii ("Prologue: Evening, January 20, 2009"). See also Azmat Khan, "Frank Luntz: How '21st-Century Republicans' Changed Washington," Frontline, February 12, 2013 (interview with Republican strategist Frank Luntz).

[13] Michael Grunwald, *The New New Deal* (Simon & Schuster, 2012), pp. 148–49.

[14] Andy Barr, "The GOP's No-Compromise Pledge," *Politico*, October 28, 2010. For a nuanced parsing of McConnell's remarks, see Glenn Kessler, "When Did Mitch McConnell Say He Wanted to Make Obama a One-Term President?," *Washington Post*, January 11, 2017.

der, then to hell with 220 years of constitutional order. The filibuster, once reserved for only the most major policy disputes, became McConnell's go-to weapon, routinely deployed even for small-bore matters. By withholding funding or refusing to consider appointments to government posts, the Senate effectively nullified laws that had been duly enacted in accordance with the Constitution. At a time when the federal courts had record numbers of vacancies, scores of judicial seats went unfilled; Republicans' refusal even to consider Obama's nominee to fill the late Justice Scalia's Supreme Court seat would be merely the most high-profile example of intransigence.[15] Government shutdowns and debt-ceiling crises—once unthinkable—became so endemic that for the first time in its more than 150-year history, Standard & Poor's downgraded the credit rating of the U.S., citing the "recent" phenomenon of "political brinkmanship." Even then, GOP lawmakers matter-of-factly continued to use the threat of government default as a bargaining chip, a nuclear option that, if carried out, would have had catastrophic effects on the world economy.[16]

Had the Founding Fathers wanted gridlock, they wouldn't have replaced the Articles of Confederation with the Constitution. But gridlock's been great for the Republican Party, which has mastered a crude but so-far-effective trick: campaign on a platform decrying government as dysfunctional and ineffective, and once you're in power do everything you can to make government dysfunctional and ineffective. Maybe this is why Congress has lower approval ratings than cockroaches, head lice, and zombies, and why Mitch McConnell has the perpetually serene look of a man who sleeps well at night. Those low approval ratings mean his side is winning. That all this has happened at the expense of the constitutional order, and of the spirit

---

[15] See Mann and Ornstein, *It's Even Worse Than It Looks,* pp. 81–103.

[16] For the United States to default on its debts would result only in a "short-term market correction," opined Senator Tom Cotton, Republican of Arkansas. Hacker and Pierson, *American Amnesia,* p. 267.

of comity and good faith so necessary for the functioning of that order, seems not to trouble McConnell or his colleagues in the least.

To call these people "conservative" is a joke. They seek to conserve precious little. Much more accurate to call them the wrecking crew.

I SAT AS FAR AWAY FROM THE TV AS I COULD. AND, I HAVE NEVER *been laid so low by a political event.* And as for the man soon to be our president, he is *about as ignorant as a turnip.*

I called Mom, eighty-seven years old, born under the sign of Hoover, three months before the Great Crash of 1929. How are you feeling about all this? I asked.

There was a pause. *Philosophical.*

Maybe he'll be better than we think, I offered.

*Nah. He showed us who he is. He's not changing.*

The people want change. Can you blame us? We've been sucking wind for thirty-five years while the One Percent rides higher and higher, a trend that began with the "Reagan Revolution," a sea change in American politics that the Democratic establishment accepted all too readily. *It is the poorest people in the world who will pay for this, over and over.* Trickle-down economics, free trade, government-is-the-problem, kick labor and the social safety net to the curb: the whole supply-side package became the default center of American politics, and the increasingly corporate Dems offered less and less to regular people as the years went by. *Our generation missed this. Woke up at 3 A.M. thinking, I've failed my kids.* That the Clinton campaign wrote off the working class was not only a political failure but a moral failure as well, and emblematic of the past several decades of Democratic leadership.[17] *Tell her to go hang out with George W. Bush in hubris hell.* Trump's campaign spoke to our economic fear and anger with a rawness that Clinton's didn't even try to match. In hindsight, it's no surprise that she lost the Wisconsin and Michigan

---

[17] See "Hillary Doesn't Live Here Anymore," *supra.*

primaries to Bernie Sanders, an independent who tapped into the same populist angst that would deliver 306 Electoral College votes to Trump. Though one wonders whether all those working folks who voted for Trump realized they were endorsing a huge tax cut for the One Percent, and a man whose election has made K Street as giddy as a girl asked to the prom by the handsomest boy in school.

*I wish I thought things would seem even slightly less terrifying in a day or month.*

*Limit your news intake for a while. It will only make you feel worse.*

*Try some escapist literature. I find detailed accounts of World War I and disastrous Arctic expeditions very readable at times like this.*

This system we have, this "free market" system that grinds huge numbers of people to bits, it seems so vast and monolithic, a planetary machine steered by distant, mysterious forces. Trump seemed to offer a rare chance to throw a wrench into the works, and many took it. That there's an even bleaker side to his victory—racist, misogynist, xenophobic—owes much to a complex of feelings and impulses that have been central to American life from the very beginning. Those feelings and impulses, so carefully nurtured by the Republican Party through the last fifty years of social change,[18] they were Trump's fuel, the combustible stuff of the fire this time. Old demons we hoped we'd pushed to the fringe, it turns out they've been right here with us all along, biding, waiting for their hour to come around again. That's the heartache. And for many of us, more than heartache: it's a clear and present danger.

*For a minute, tribal identity looked not to be everything. Fond little daydream—nothing optimistic comes to mind, stunned beloveds.*

**EGO WILL BE THE GUIDING PRINCIPLE OF THE TRUMP PRESI-**dency. In this respect he's much more like a monarch than the duly

---

[18] See "American Crossroads: Reagan, Trump, and the Devil Down South," *supra,* and "A Familiar Spirit," *infra.*

elected servant of a representative democracy, and, as monarchs do, he will keep his heirs close to the center of power: Ivanka, Don Jr., Eric, and that budding Cardinal Richelieu of a son-in-law, Jared Kushner. Top security clearances and advisory roles are contemplated for the kids, who at the same time will be running the for-profit entities of the sprawling Trump Organization. It's hard to imagine a more ethically fraught, legally explosive situation for the children, managing a vast consortium of transnational businesses while being privy to the country's most sensitive secrets, along with easy access to the most powerful man in the world. How will it all play out? Badly. Look to Shakespeare for a taste of the awful potential here, to the tragedies and history plays, those coils of ego and empire and wealth (and sex and sex and sex!) that end with bodies lying all over the stage. The best thing Trump could do for his children would be to put his assets in a blind trust and send the kids away—far, far away from Washington—to do their own thing. Limit visits to holidays and weekends, bounce the grandkids on his knee, breathe not a word about business or affairs of state.

But that's not how monarchies roll. That Trump would put his children in such a legally tenuous position gives us a clear idea—as if we needed it from a man who used to rely on the bottom-feeder Roy Cohn for legal counsel—of his appreciation for the rule of law. Here again we can expect the monarchical model. *L'état, c'est moi.* People rarely grow in humility once they reach the White House. To the extent that Trump attempts to game, spin, and mutilate the rule of law, his most immediate potential check will be a Congress that's firmly in Republican hands, led by the same wrecking crew that's already shown such faint regard for the constitutional order, with a fire-breathing rank-and-file—think "Freedom Caucus"—egging them on to new lows.

The institutions, structures, and traditions of American governance are about to be tested as they haven't been in generations. You say you want change? Here it comes. Brace for impact.

# BOOK OF DAYS
## DECEMBER

Jim Delligatti, inventor of the Big Mac, dies at age ninety-eight, and McDonald's says it will move its tax base to Britain from Luxembourg in response to a European Union inquiry into the food chain's tax arrangements. Scientists report that the Great Barrier Reef has suffered the most significant coral bleaching ever recorded, with large swaths of the reef's northern reaches dead after a season's worth of warm summer waters. The first German-language edition of *Charlie Hebdo* goes on sale, with a cover depicting a fatigued-looking Chancellor Angela Merkel lying on a hydraulic lift, with a caption saying Volkswagen "stands behind Merkel," and that "with a new exhaust pipe, she'll be good to go for another four years." The UN issues an apology for its role in the 2010 cholera outbreak in Haiti that has so far killed more than ten thousand people. A recount of presidential ballots begins in Wisconsin, where Trump beat Clinton by 22,177 votes, and Texas imposes regulations requiring abortion facilities to pay for the cremation or burial of fetal remains. Jeffrey Zucker, president of CNN, which is on track to make $1 billion in profits this year, is heckled by reporters as well as by aides to Marco Rubio, Ted Cruz, and Jeb Bush at a postelection conference at Harvard, while Trump begins a two-week "thank you" tour with a campaign-style rally in Cincinnati. After a series of Taliban offensives, the chief of U.S. Central Command says the Afghan government controls only about 60 percent of the country. Stolen in 2014, the wrought-iron gate from the Dachau concentration camp bearing the infamous phrase "*Arbeit Macht Frei*," or "Work Sets You Free," is located in a suburb of Bergen, Norway, after an anonymous tip alerts Norwegian police. Trump's official council of business advisers, called the "President's Strategic and Policy Forum," will include the current or former CEOs of Walmart, JPMorgan Chase, Boeing, General Electric, and General Motors, and will be chaired by private equity multibillionaire Stephen Schwarzman, who once compared President Obama's tax policy to the German invasion of Poland. No representatives of labor or consumers are named to the council. Trump accepts a call from Taiwanese president Tsai Ing-wen, becoming the first U.S. president or president-elect since 1979 to do so; news of the call, which breaks with nearly four decades of U.S. diplomatic convention that regards Taiwan and China as a single nation, is reacted to with "surprise, verging on disbelief," in Beijing, while Taiwanese media report that the Trump Organization is exploring the possibility of building a luxury hotel in Taiwan. In a conversation with Philippine president Rodrigo Duterte, who once called President Obama a "son of a whore," Trump praises Duterte's "war on drugs," in which more than two thousand Filipinos have been killed by police since June. Far-right Austrian presidential candidate Norbert Hofer loses by 6.6 percentage points to Green Party candidate Alexander Van der Bellen in an election widely viewed as a measure of the "Trump effect" in Europe. Trump, whose campaign aired a commercial portraying Goldman Sachs chairman Lloyd Blankfein as the embodiment of the global elite that "robbed our working class, stripped our country of its wealth and put that money into the pockets of a handful of large corporations and political entities," chooses as his secretary of the treasury Steve Mnuchin, the son of a former Goldman Sachs banker who is himself a former Goldman Sachs banker, and whose film financing company, Dune Capital Management, is named after the beach dunes near his mansion in the Hamptons. "THE UNITED STATES IS OPEN FOR BUSINESS," Trump tweets. The Presidential Inaugural Committee offers two tickets to an "intimate policy discussion" with cabinet members for between $100,000 and $249,000, and eight tickets for $1 million to a "candlelight" dinner with an appearance by Trump. North Carolina governor Pat McCrory blames his ten-thousand-vote loss on "massive voter fraud" and challenges the eligibility of forty-three voters, alleging that they are felons; Democracy North Carolina, a voting rights group, establishes that nearly half of those voters are, in fact, eligible. Kanye West visits Trump at Trump Tower. "We've been friends for a long time," Trump tells reporters after the meeting, and adds, "We discussed life." John Glenn, who flew 149 combat missions in World War II and Korea, was the first American to orbit Earth, and served four terms in the U.S. Senate, dies at age ninety-five. Trump mocks American intelligence assessments that Russia interfered in the election on his behalf, and his transition office releases a statement saying "these are the same people that said Saddam Hussein had weapons of mass destruction." ExxonMobil chairman Rex Tillerson, who received Russia's "Order of Friendship" from Vladimir Putin in 2013, is chosen by Trump to be secretary of state. In an interview with *Time* magazine reporters, Trump says of the election-related hacks, "It could be Russia. And it could be China. And it could be some guy in his home in New Jersey." The United Nations Children's Fund reports that more than a half billion children, or roughly one in four, currently live in conflict or disaster zones. South Korea's parliament votes to impeach President Park Geun-hye because of an influence-peddling scandal, and in the Netherlands, Geert Wilders, the far-right leader viewed as a contender to be prime minister in next year's elections, is convicted of inciting discrimination. Trump names Gary D. Cohn, president of

Goldman Sachs, as his chief economic policy adviser. Former Texas governor Rick Perry, who once described Trump as "a barking carnival act" and "a cancer on conservatism," who called climate-change science a "contrived, phony mess" in a 2010 book, and whose 2012 presidential campaign was derailed when he could not remember that the third cabinet-level federal agency he wanted to abolish (along with Education and Commerce) was the Department of Energy, is named by Trump to be secretary of energy. Russia declares that the four-year battle for Aleppo is over after rebel forces agree to surrender their remaining territory; as Syrian government forces move in, there are multiple reports of atrocities and execution-style killings of rebels and civilians. The Trump transition team circulates a seventy-four-point questionnaire at the Department of Energy requesting the names of all employees and contractors who have attended climate-change policy conferences during the past five years, and Ivanka Trump and Jared Kushner will likely take on formal roles in the Trump administration. "The anti-nepotism law apparently has an exception if you want to work in the West Wing," Trump adviser Kellyanne Conway explains to reporters. When House minority leader Nancy Pelosi calls Trump to discuss issues relating to women and families, Trump reportedly hands the phone to Ivanka. Representative Peter King of New York meets with Trump at Trump Tower, and after the meeting proposes that the Trump administration implement a national counterterrorism strategy based on a discredited New York Police Department surveillance program that targeted Muslims. Democratic congressional candidates in Florida, Pennsylvania, North Carolina, New Hampshire, Ohio, Illinois, and New Mexico were targeted by a Russian influence operation in which hackers working under the Guccifer 2.0 name stole thousands of documents from the Democratic Congressional Campaign Committee, then used social media to invite individual reporters and bloggers to request specific caches of documents relating to the candidates, some of whom were running in the most competitive House races in the country. The *New York Times* reports that the Obama administration spent months deliberating whether to publicly blame Russia for cyberattacks on the Democratic National Committee and other organizations; the delay was partly due to President Obama's aversion to being seen as politicizing intelligence or otherwise interfering in the election on behalf of Hillary Clinton, and partly due to the bureaucratic process of getting confirmation from seventeen different government agencies that they had high confidence that Russia was in fact responsible. In response, Trump tweets, "If Russia, or some other entity was hacking, why did the White House wait so long to act? Why did they only complain after Hillary lost?," a statement that PolitiFact rates as "Pants on Fire!," pointing to the October 7 joint statement by the Department of Homeland Security and the Office of the Director of National Intelligence, as well as the third presidential debate exchange in which Clinton accused Trump of being Putin's "puppet." In an interview with NPR, Obama, who has five weeks left in his term, says the U.S. will retaliate for Russia's efforts to influence the election "at the time and place of our choosing." A hacking collective dispersed across Eastern Europe is selling on the Dark Web the records and personal information of more than one billion users of Yahoo's email system. Pope Francis compares spreading fake news to "the sickness of coprophilia," and a North Carolina man faces federal charges after firing an AR-15 assault rifle inside a Washington, DC, pizza restaurant while investigating an internet conspiracy theory linking Hillary Clinton to child trafficking. Michael G. Flynn, the son of retired lieutenant general Michael T. Flynn, Trump's proposed national security advisor, tweets, "Until #Pizzagate is proven false, it'll remain a story." A woman in Tampa, Florida, is charged with transmitting threats in interstate commerce after she sends messages such as "You gonna die" to the parent of one of the twenty children killed in the Sandy Hook school shooting, which she believes is a hoax promoted by the Obama administration to justify gun control. In Minneapolis, the Mall of America hires its first African-American Santa. Cuba offers to pay its $276 million debt to the Czech Republic in rum. Trump says he does not need daily intelligence briefings because he is "like, a smart person." The Electoral College elects Donald Trump president with 304 votes to 227 for Hillary Clinton; Bernie Sanders, Ron Paul, John Kasich, Colin Powell, and Faith Spotted Eagle also receive votes as seven presidential electors, the most ever, vote for someone other than their party's nominee. New Orleans settles Katrina-era police brutality lawsuits for $13.3 million. In Ankara, an off-duty Turkish police officer assassinates the Russian ambassador to Turkey at an art gallery; before he is killed by security forces, the gunman shouts, "God is great!" in Arabic, and "Don't forget Aleppo, don't forget Syria!" in Turkish. A stolen semitrailer truck slams into a crowded outdoor Christmas market in Berlin, killing twelve and injuring at least forty-eight, and ISIS claims that the driver, a Tunisian national, is "a soldier" acting on its behalf. In Zurich, a man enters a Muslim prayer center and opens fire, wounding at least three people; the gunman is a Swiss citizen of Ghanaian descent who is later found dead of an apparent suicide. ISIS claims credit for an attack in Karak, Jordan, that kills ten, including a Jordanian general who was head of the military's special forces. Carrie Fisher dies at age sixty. Trump inauguration planners prepare for a wave of protestors, and Carl Paladino, a Trump ally and former candidate for governor of New York, emails racist comments about the Obamas to a Buffalo, New York, weekly, *Artvoice,* that he intended to send only to friends; in the email, Paladino says he wants Barack Obama to die of mad cow disease, and would like for Michelle Obama to "return to being a male and let loose in the outback of Zimbabwe where she lives comfortably in a cave with Maxie, the gorilla." It is reported that the number of people giving guns for Christmas gifts is up compared to 2015, and one gun-shop owner comments: "It is a significant gift, to arm the ones that you love." Volunteers in Denver give away a thousand rolled joints to the homeless on Christmas Eve, New York City experiences the warmest Christmas Day on record, and Queen Elizabeth II misses Christmas Day church services for the first time in nearly thirty years because of a bad cold. After the UN Security Council votes to condemn Israeli settlements, Israel vows to move ahead with thousands of new homes in East Jerusalem. "Israel is a country with national pride," says Prime Minister Benjamin Netanyahu, "and we do not turn the other cheek." Debbie Reynolds, age eighty-four, dies one day after the death of her daughter, Carrie Fisher. Taking note of Trump's willingness to lash out at well-known brands such as Boeing, *Vanity Fair,* and Lockheed Martin, marketing executives have begun drafting contingency plans to deal with a possible Trump attack. In response to Russian efforts to influence the election, President Obama announces the ejection of thirty-five suspected Russian intelligence operatives from the U.S., and imposes sanctions on Russia's two leading intelligence agencies. The head of the foreign affairs committee of the upper house of Russia's parliament characterizes Obama's actions as "the agony not even of 'lame ducks' but of 'political corpses,'" and Trump responds to news of the sanctions by saying it is time to "move on." As the Year of the Rooster approaches in China, the northern Chinese city of Taiyuan installs a twenty-three-foot-tall statue of a rooster that bears a striking resemblance to Donald Trump.

# A FAMILIAR SPIRIT

They were called patrollers, or, variously, "paterollers," "paddyrollers," or "patterolls," and they were meant to be part of the solution to Colonial America's biggest problem, labor. Unlike Great Britain, which had a large, basically immobile peasant class that could be forced to work for subsistence wages, there weren't enough cheap bodies in America to do the grunt work. If you were a planter looking to make your fortune in rice or tobacco—the New World's cash crops—you had to size up to industrial scale, and for that you needed bodies, armies of bodies, a labor force that could be made to work for terms no less brutal than those inflicted on the miserables of Europe.

Native Americans weren't the solution, not after disease, war, and murderous forms of forced labor reduced their number by half. Indentured servants were imported, but in numbers too few to fill the void, and they had a habit of running off: the wide frontier beckoned, all that empty space for sass-mouths and malcontents to vanish into. So it became Africans. Jamestown received its first cargo of enslaved humans in 1619, a dozen years after the colony's founding: "20 and odd Negroes," according to records, the first installment on the estimated 455,000 who would eventually land in North America.[1] Control of this new labor force would be key, as shown by the free society that sprang up under the Virginia planters' noses within forty years of the arrival of those first Africans. South of the great plantations lay the Dismal Swamp, and beyond that the backwater regions of the Albemarle, which by the 1660s had become a haven for anyone seeking relief from the oppressions of Virginia. "[A] Rabble of the basest sort of People" was how one Virginia grandee characterized his troublesome neighbors to the south. "[I]dle debtors, theeves, Negroes, Indians and English servants," they tended to be "stubborne and disobedient to superiors," and, taken as a whole, "a very mutinous people."[2]

Mutiny was indeed the great fear; our American tradition of paranoia got off to an early start. The fear increasingly came to focus on the African labor force that the English colonists imported with such industry into their midst. The Albemarle outliers weren't even the most egregious incarnation of the fear. The people of Albemarle mainly wanted to be left alone; much more terrifying to Virginians was the prospect of slave revolt, not Africans running away but Africans rising up. For plantation society, enforcing the racial hierarchy was considered as much a matter of self-preservation as of economic

---

[1] According to the Trans-Atlantic Slave Trade Database (www.slavevoyages.org), an estimated total of 12.5 million Africans were put on ships destined for North America, the Caribbean, and South America between 1525 and 1866, of whom an estimated 10.7 million survived passage. Approximately 455,000 of these survivors disembarked in North America.

[2] A phrase Noeleen McIlvenna takes for the title of her fine and useful book *A Very Mutinous People: The Struggle for North Carolina, 1660–1713* (UNC Press, 2009). The "rabble," for its part, saw fit to declare, "Wee will have noe Lords noe Landgraves noe Cassiques we renounce them all." Informed by the egalitarian ideas of Oliver Cromwell's Interregnum, the "poor Virginia precinct" of Albemarle is striking as much for its racial equality as its economic and social leveling. Native Americans, blacks, and whites made common cause against attempts by the Virginia elite to assert control, and cross-racial solidarity was apparently such a problem that Virginia enacted a law prescribing especially onerous penalties for indentured servants who ran off "in company with any negroes." Albemarle's history, McIlvenna writes, should leave "us wondering why eighteenth-century planters get credit for developing philosophies of liberty. More than a century before wealthy Virginia slave owners debated the meaning of liberty, the Dismal Swamp country sheltered the most free society in the European purview." *A Very Mutinous People*, pp. 1–5, 20, 22–24, 41, 45, 69–70, 83. In the same vein, see McIlvenna's *The Short Life of Free Georgia: Class and Slavery in the Colonial South* (UNC Press, 2015).

advantage. By the time the Virginia governors brought Albemarle to heel in the early 1700s, a comprehensive system of racially directed law enforcement was well on its way to being fully developed.

This was, in fact, the first systematic form of policing in the land that would become the United States. The northeast colonies relied on the informal "night-watch" system of volunteer policing, and on private security to protect commercial property.[3] In the Southern colonies, policing's origins were rooted in the slave economy and the radically racialized social order that invented "whiteness" as the ultimate boundary. "White," no matter how poor or low, could not be held in slavery. "Black" could be enslaved by anyone—whites, free blacks, and people of mixed race. The distinction—and the economic order that created it—was maintained by a legally sanctioned system of surveillance, intimidation, and brute force whose purpose was the control of blacks. Slave patrols were the chief enforcers of this system, groups of armed, mounted whites who rode at night among the plantations and settlements of their assigned "beats"—the word originated with the patrols—seeking out runaway slaves, unsanctioned gatherings, weapons, contraband, and generally any sign of potential revolt.[4] They were the stuff of lore and songs.

> *Run Nigger run, Patty Roller will catch you,*
> *Run Nigger run*
> *I'll shoot you with my flintlock gun.*
> *Run nigger run, Patty Roller will catch you,*
> *Run, nigger run, you'd better get away.*[5]

---

[3] The first publicly funded, full-time police force wouldn't be organized until 1838, in Boston. See Olivia B. Waxman, "How the U.S. Got Its Police Force," *Time*, May 18, 2017. See also Gary Potter, "The History of Policing in the United States, Part 1," Eastern Kentucky University Police Studies, June 25, 2013.

[4] I am shamelessly and gratefully pillaging from the chilling, scholarly, and instructive *Slave Patrols: Law and Violence in Virginia and the Carolinas* by Sally E. Hadden (Harvard University Press, 2001).

[5] Lyrics from sheet music, c. 1867, quoted in Hadden, *Slave Patrols*, pp. 119–20. As Hadden

Slave patrols usually consisted of three to six white men on horseback equipped with guns, rope, and whips. "A mounted man presents an awesome figure, and the power and majesty of a group of men on horseback, at night, could terrify slaves into submission." Among other duties, paddyrollers enforced the pass system, which required all slaves absent from their master's property to have a pass, or "ticket," signed by the master indicating his permission for travel.[6] Any slave encountered without a pass was subject to detention and beating on the spot, although possession of a valid pass was by no means a guarantee against beating. Certain people, granted power, can be counted on to abuse those under their authority just because they can; one imagines moreover that gratuitous beatings relieved the tedium and fatigue of nightlong patrols, and served to reinforce the notion of who was boss. The paddyrollers' authority extended to patrolling plantation grounds and entering slave quarters, where the presence of books, writing paper, weapons, liquor, luxury items, or more than the usual store of provisions was cause for beating. "Gatherings"—weddings, funerals, church services—were grounds for beating. Mingling with whites, especially poor whites, or any "loose, disorderly or suspected person": beating. Back talk: beating. Dressing tidily: beating. Singing certain hymns: beating.[7] Even best behavior could earn you a lick: "Elige Davison, another former Virginia slave, remembered that as bondsmen lay asleep in their own quarters, patrollers would enter and lightly hit them with a whip to see if they were truly tired and asleep at the end of the work day."[8] For an enslaved woman, a beating might well be the least of her worries.

---

notes, there are a number of variations of this song. Among others, she references a 1920s recording by Gid Tanner and His Skillet Lickers (Rounder Records No. 1005).

[6] Hadden, *Slave Patrols*, pp. 110–14, 121, 123. In some Southern counties, all white men were required by law to check the pass of any black person they encountered on the road, day or night. See Christian Parenti, "Policing the Color Line," *Nation*, September 13, 2001.

[7] Hadden, *Slave Patrols*, pp. 107–24.

[8] *Ibid.*, p. 107.

The system continued largely intact after Emancipation and the defeat of the Confederacy. Legally sanctioned slave patrols were replaced by night-riding vigilantes like the Ku Klux Klan, whose white robes, flaming torches, and queer pseudo–ghost talk were intended for maximum terrorizing effect. Lynching and shooting took their place alongside the more traditional punishments of beating and whipping; blacks' economic value as slaves had evaporated, and with it the constraints on lethal force that had offered some measure of protection under the old system. White supremacy continued as the dominant order for the next hundred years, a social and psychological reality maintained by terror, surveillance, and the letter of the law. Its power was such that even the New Deal—the most profound reordering of American society since the Civil War—left white supremacy intact.[9] Twenty-six lynchings were recorded in Southern states in 1933. An antilynching bill was defeated in Congress in 1935. Southern blacks' awareness of antebellum history was acute, naturally enough given that they were living it. "Even seventy years after freedom came, one former bondsman declared he still had his badge and pass to show the patrol, so that no one could molest him."[10]

We don't have to know the particulars of history in order to live it in our bones. Perhaps history arrives as a sense of the uncanny, the peculiar weight of certain words and acts, a suffusion of dreadful power.[11] We might suppose the pass system is long gone, but there it is in stop-and-frisk, in racial profiling, in the reflexive fear and violence of our own time. Trayvon Martin, seventeen years old, walking down the street just minding his own, killed by a

---

[9] "The Roosevelt administration pursued a strategy of pragmatic forgetfulness with regard to racial matters as long as it could." Southern legislators generally supported New Deal legislation as long as the South's "racial arrangements" were not disturbed. Ira Katznelson, *Fear Itself: The New Deal and the Origins of Our Time* (Liveright Publishing, 2013), pp. 161–76.

[10] Hadden, *Slave Patrols*, p. 114.

[11] "In a study they did with mice, researchers concluded what we already knew: that trauma lives in our blood." Morgan Parker, "How to Stay Sane While Black," *New York Times*, November 19, 2016.

self-anointed, night-riding, so-called neighborhood watchman. Sandra Bland, dead in a Texas jail after being pulled over for failure to signal a lane change. Walter Scott, stopped by police in North Charleston for an allegedly broken taillight, shot to death with eight bullets in his back. Philando Castile, popular school cafeteria supervisor, shot dead in Falcon Heights, Minnesota, during a traffic stop for, allegedly, a broken taillight (accounts differ); records reveal that he'd been pulled over no fewer than *fifty-two* times by local police in the preceding fourteen years, and owed over $6,000 in outstanding fines.[12] That $6,000 in fines opens the window onto another ugly echo of times past, the use of law enforcement to extract profit from black and brown people. Michael Brown's death at the hands of Ferguson police led to the exposure of a municipal regime that deployed police less for the sake of public safety than as a means of plundering the African-American community. In 2010, Ferguson's finance director informed the police chief that "unless ticket writing ramps up significantly before the end of the year, it will be hard to significantly raise collections next year." A new "I-270 traffic enforcement initiative . . . to fill the revenue pipeline" is plainly documented, and by October 31, 2014, the municipal courts of Ferguson, a town of twenty-one thousand residents (two-thirds of whom are black), had handled no fewer than fifty-three thousand traffic cases that year. By 2015, more than one-fifth of the town's revenue would come from fines and fees. The community's frustration after years of harassment, abuse, and humiliation at the hands of the police would finally explode in the protests that followed Michael Brown's death.[13]

---

[12] Darryl Pinckney, "Black Lives and the Police," *New York Review of Books,* August 18, 2016; Kyle Potter, "Racial Profiling Suspected," *Dallas Morning News,* July 14, 2016.

[13] Chris Hayes, "Policing the Colony," *Nation,* April 17, 2017. See also Pinckney, "Black Lives and the Police" ("police forces and their relation to black people in general is a long tale about the enforcement of whiteness and blackness"); Jelani Cobb, "The Matter of Black Lives," *New Yorker,* March 14, 2016 ("Ferguson as a case study of structural racism in America"); and Elizabeth Hinton, "Equal Protection," *New York Times Book Review,* July 30, 2017 ("when

Some facts sit heavier in the gut than others. It may be that the American brain is wired for certain cues, or maybe it's just the nature of systems of control, systems that grant or withhold sanction to move about, to work, to vote, to be secure in your home and body; to be free of suspicion absent evidence to the contrary. Sanction, in other words, to exercise your full humanity. Slave patrols and passes, the Klan, Jim Crow, these are historical incarnations of a social order that held people of color to less-than status, the necessary corollary to white supremacy. One doubts that Donald Trump knew the first thing about the pass system and paddyrollers when he took up the birther movement in 2011,[14] employing lies and the cheapest sorts of innuendo to mainstream the allegation— the outright fantasy—that Barack Obama was not a genuine U.S. citizen. Trump, that master plumber of the American psyche, intuited the heat in the allegation, its potential for exciting the country's ingrained racism. You couldn't very well send night riders in full conehead regalia to burn a cross on the White House lawn in hopes of running the Obamas out of town, but you could harass and attack by other means, wage a twenty-first-century version of vigilante warfare on behalf of white supremacy.

And so it went: the black man didn't belong in the White House because he wasn't a real American. He was an interloper, a pretender. Less than American. Which of course has been exactly the issue for people of color in America for four hundred years, the issue brought into high relief—the schizophrenia inscribed by the country's own hand, in effect—by the fine ideals expressed in the founding documents. *All men created equal. Certain inalienable rights.* So who is a "man"? Who is to be counted among "we the people"? Who is

---

citizenship rights are extended to African-Americans, policy makers and officials at all levels of government historically used law and incarceration as proxy to exert social control in black communities").

[14] Until then, the chief promoter of so-called birtherism was a far-right commentator whose previous assertions included claims that soybeans cause homosexuality and that the attacks of 9/11 were a judgment from God.

entitled to full enjoyment of the God-given rights of life, liberty, and the pursuit of happiness, and the protection and exercise of those rights as provided by the laws of the country? Trayvon Martin clearly wasn't. Zimmerman walked, and it became necessary to say what in a just society would go without saying: *black lives matter.*[15]

The great divide in America has always been the color of skin, the presumptive and usually final criterion. Whiteness is law, legitimacy, citizenship; the benefit of the doubt. Not-white is doubt. Not-white has to *prove,* not just once but over and over. *Fifty-two* traffic stops. Can a white person even imagine? Fifty-two times Philando Castile had to stop and show his papers, keep his cool, say *yes sir, no sir.* Had to check the fury that surely rose in him with every stop, every new harassment and humiliation. This remarkable record of self-control should properly be called superhuman. A certain kind of gasbag politician loves to yatter at minorities for their alleged dearths of "personal responsibility," yet these pols remain blind to a form of strenuous *personal responsibility* that's enacted in some fashion several million times a day by people of color in America.

By attacking Obama's claim to citizenship—by insisting that he produce a particular piece of paper in form and substance satisfactory to the race police, in their sole discretion—Trump tapped into the core of the American anthropology, the peculiarly toxic confluence of racism and economics that's organized life in America from the very beginning. That the birther claim lacked even the slightest basis in fact was surely part of its power; that it existed so blatantly in the realm of racial animus. No night riders, no burning crosses, but there are other, marginally less florid means of making the point. Dog whistles and codes. Racism hiding in plain sight. Birtherism was a dog whistle blown through a megaphone, and

---

[15] "I continue to be surprised at how little Black lives matter," Alicia Garza posted on social media on the day of George Zimmerman's acquittal. Garza's friend Patrisse Khan-Cullors saw the post and was inspired to create the hashtag #BlackLivesMatter. Cobb, "The Matter of Black Lives."

Trump rode it to the top of the polls in 2011, only to decline going head-to-head with Obama when he had the chance. He was still riding the birther wave as 2016 approached,[16] but with the official launch of his candidacy in June 2015, Trump did something no mainstream candidate for president had done in a generation. He threw away the dog whistle.

*They're bringing drugs. They're bringing crime. They're rapists.*

An agenda he elaborated over the next eighteen months with the wall, the illegal-immigrant-atrocity stories, the proposal to ban all Muslim immigrants, his smirking approval when his supporters beat Black Lives Matter protestors, and the assertion that President Obama was "the founder" of ISIS, and, in the wake of the Orlando massacre, that Obama either "doesn't get it or he gets it better than anybody understands." For those of us of a certain age it was a time warp, a fever-dream blast from the past. Who would have thought that George Wallace would be reincarnated in American politics as a New York City real estate tycoon? Wallace, that Brylcreemed banty rooster of a man, fighting cock of the racist Southern walk, and four-term governor of Alabama who thundered in his first inaugural address, "Segregation now, segregation tomorrow, segregation forever!" He flamed across the national stage for twenty years, a dart-eyed, snarling prophet of the honky apocalypse, his plump lips a cracker version of Mick Jagger's. He had a flair for the grand gesture—shouting down hippies, taunting the feds, standing in

---

[16] In August 2013, when asked about his birther comments on ABC's *This Week:* "I think that resonated with a lot of people . . . Was there a birth certificate? You tell me . . . Nobody knows." His tweet of December 12, 2013: "How amazing, the State Health Director who verified copies of Obama's 'birth certificate' died in a plane crash today. All others lived." Speaking at the CPAC Conference in February 2015, he questioned the validity of Obama's long-form birth certificate posted on the White House website. In July 2015 on CNN, in response to Anderson Cooper's question as to whether he accepted that Obama was born in the U.S.: "I really don't know. I don't know why he wouldn't release his records . . ." See Alison Kite, "Five Years of Donald Trump's 'Birther' Statements," *Wall Street Journal,* July 16, 2016, and Gregory Krieg, "Fourteen of Trump's Most Outrageous 'Birther' Claims—Half from After 2011," CNN.com, September 16, 2016.

schoolhouse doors to keep children of color from entering—and a demagogue's strop of a tongue, a gift for lashing and teasing his crowds to the point of violence. "It was very scary. My father's rallies, they could be right rough," his daughter Peggy would have occasion to recall in 2016.[17]

He ran for president four times. As the American Independent Party's nominee in 1968, he won five Deep South states and forty-six Electoral College votes. That same year, Norman Mailer mused on the volcanic potential that Wallace touched but couldn't fully tap, the power immanent in white America's obsession with "the Negro problem" and its simmering, psychopathically suppressed guilt over the demonstrably valid claim that, as Mailer put it, "America's wealth, whiteness, and hygiene had been refined out of the most powerful molecules stolen from the sweat of the black man."

> . . . *political power of the most frightening sort was obviously waiting for the first demagogue who would smash the obsession and free the white man of his guilt. Torrents of energy would be loosed, yes, those same torrents which Hitler had freed in the Germans when he exploded their ten-year obsession with whether they had lost the war through betrayal or through material weakness. Through betrayal, Hitler had told them: Germans were actually strong and good. The consequences would never be counted.*
>
> *Now if suburban America was not waiting for Georgie Wallace, it might still be waiting for Super-Wallace.*[18]

Wallace ran too hot for the sixties and seventies. Times had changed, and the racial concerns of variously aggrieved, enraged,

[17] Margaret Newkirk, "Trump's Appeal to White Anger Echoes Campaigns of George Wallace," *Bloomberg Politics*, March 24, 2016.
[18] *Miami and the Siege of Chicago* (New York Review Books, 2008), pp. 51–52.

neurotic whites had to be addressed by cooler means.[19] But in 2016 Trump brought back the heat, and won, and so we're forced to consider the prospect that the time of the Super-Wallace has come around at last. It seems that history has led us in a circle back to Alabama days, a circle so wide, so encompassing of far horizons, that we hadn't known this journey that looked so much like progress was in fact a fantasy, a happy story we told ourselves along the way.

**"OUR COUNTRY HAS CHANGED," WROTE JOHN ROBERTS, CHIEF** justice of the United States Supreme Court, in 2013. The case was *Shelby County, Alabama v. Eric H. Holder, Jr., Attorney General,*[20] and the chief justice, author of the majority opinion, was insistent on this point. "'[T]hings have changed in the South.'" "[H]istory did not end in 1965." "Nearly 50 years later, things have changed dramatically." "[O]ur Nation has made great strides." At issue in *Shelby County* was the constitutionality of sections 4 and 5 of the Voting Rights Act of 1965 (as reauthorized by Congress for the fourth time in 2006), which required states and certain counties with histories of racial discrimination to obtain "preclearance" from the Department of Justice before implementing changes to their election laws. Preclearance had been crucial in curbing racial discrimination in voting, Roberts conceded, but the remedy was no longer relevant to current conditions. Congress had reauthorized the Voting Rights Act in 2006 based on facts "having no logical relation to the present day," wrote the chief justice. "'Blatantly discriminatory evasions of federal decrees are rare.'"

Smart white men acting stupid will be the death of America. John Glover Roberts Jr. is a white man, by all accounts a very smart one: *summa* from Harvard College, *magna* Harvard Law, Supreme

---

[19] For a discussion of those cooler means, see "American Crossroads: Reagan, Trump, and the Devil Down South," *supra.*

[20] 570 U.S. 2 (2013).

Court clerk, impressively useful to his bosses in the Reagan-era Department of Justice, highly successful in private practice. His demeanor, obliged by pleasant, wholesome features and untroubled blue eyes, projects warmth, decency, and thoughtfulness, traits amply confirmed by peers and subordinates alike. In order to rule as he did in *Shelby County*—that Congress acted irrationally in reauthorizing the Voting Rights Act, which renders the preclearance remedy unconstitutional—Chief Justice Roberts had to place his own judgment over that of Congress (where the vote was 390–33 in the House, and 98–0 in the Senate, for reauthorization), President George W. Bush (who signed the bill into law within a week of its passage), and a legislative record that exceeded fifteen thousand pages, a record packed with reports, case studies, and the sworn testimony of scores of witnesses in support of the bill. During debate preceding the 2006 House vote, Representative James Sensenbrenner, Republican of Wisconsin, chairman of the House Judiciary Committee, and nobody's idea of even a little bit liberal, piled the volumes of legislative material on the table before him, and as the piles became unsteady and began sliding to the floor, said that the record comprised

> one of the most extensive considerations of any piece of
> legislation that the United States Congress has dealt with in
> the $27^1/_2$ years that I have been honored to serve as a Member
> of this body. All of this is part of the record that . . . has [been]
> assembled to show the need for the reauthorization of the
> Voting Rights Act . . . In fact, the extensive record of continued
> abuse compiled by the committee over the last year, which I
> have put on the table here today, echoes that which preceded
> congressional reauthorization of the VRA in 1982.[21]

---

[21] 152 Congressional Record H5143 (2006). See also Kristen Clarke, "The Congressional Record Underlying the 2006 Voting Rights Act: How Much Discrimination Can the Constitution Tolerate?," *Harvard Civil Rights–Civil Liberties Law Review* 43 (2008), pp. 386–433.

Chief Justice Roberts disagreed, in effect preferencing his own version of reality for that portrayed in those fifteen thousand pages of testimony, as vetted and endorsed by both houses of Congress, and further endorsed by the president. The hubris of it takes your breath away. Here is a white man who has spent his youth and adult life in the highest reaches of the American establishment, a world where the security of one's body is rarely at issue, a world of offices, computers, climate control, of orderly meetings and civil discourse, starched shirts, polished shoes—"hygiene," to echo Norman Mailer—a world where people take their showers before work, not after. You don't go hungry in that world; you don't worry where your next meal is coming from, or the rent money, or whether you can go to the doctor when you're sick. You work hard, no question, and it's the best kind of work, interesting, stimulating, remunerative. It's an entirely reasonable life to lead, nothing mean or dishonorable about it, and yet in the final analysis it's a relatively narrow slice of experience. It can encourage a kind of innocence—*fantasy* might be the better word—about the fact of one's whiteness. Its neutrality. Its basic disinterest. What could be fairer, more equitable, more quintessentially American than color-blindness? A level playing field for all, no preferences or special treatment. Measures such as affirmative action and racial quotas—however necessary, and necessarily temporary, they may be—are viewed as aberrations, departures from the universal neutral of the good American norm, justified only by the most extraordinary circumstances.

But affirmative action and racial quotas have always been the American norm. To borrow a phrase from H. Rap Brown, racial preference is as American as cherry pie. For proof we have the long history of racial preference that for hundreds of years produced all-white juries, city councils, legislatures, police forces, electorates, student bodies, faculties, executive suites, and labor pools. The country has changed, Chief Justice Roberts insisted in *Shelby County*. "If Congress had started from scratch in 2006, it plainly could not have enacted the present coverage formula." As if the "scratch" that Congress would have started from in 2006 would not, in the absence of the Voting Rights Act, have looked a lot like the America of 1965.[22] But to a well-nourished, physically and financially secure white man comfortably settled in the lap of the establishment, it doubtless does look pretty good on the race-relations front. Though not perfect, no. "[V]oting discrimination still exists; no one doubts that." Still and all, how far we've come as a country, yes indeed. Somewhat. Sort of. Some of the time. The record before the court provided a vast and detailed chronicle of the extent to which the country hasn't changed, and the relentless pressure to undo the changes won. Yet in the chief justice's judgment—in his experience, for what is judgment but the sum of experience brought to bear in the moment—Congress had acted irrationally, those fifteen thousand pages of evidence aside, in reauthorizing preclearance.[23]

You could call this the "soft" psychology of white supremacy, as opposed to the more febrile mentality of neo-Nazis, Klanners, the alt-right crowd. White supremacy by default; a failure to see beyond whiteness as the presumptive norm, as the neutral and natural order of things. This is, ultimately, a failure of empathy, which is to say a failure of moral imagination, but Chief Justice Roberts didn't even have to exert so very much of his imagination to clue into the state of things. Evidence of racist revanchism was as close as his right elbow every time he gaveled the court into session, for there sat Antonin Scalia, who as the senior associate justice occupied the seat of honor at the chief's right. Amid his long career of professional skep-

---

22 "There are two neuroses that I consider particularly American: the habit of forgetting, and the inability to imagine what has not been." Parker, "How to Stay Sane While Black."

23 One wonders if actual evidence ever had the slightest chance of swaying Chief Justice Roberts. As long ago as 1981 he was working zealously in the Department of Justice to roll back the protections of the Voting Rights Act. See Ari Berman, "Inside John Roberts' Decades-Long Crusade Against the Voting Rights Act," *Politico*, August 10, 2015, adapted from his book *Give Us the Ballot: The Modern Struggle for Voting Rights in America* (Farrar, Straus and Giroux, 2015).

ticism toward civil rights and affirmative action, Scalia was capable of such openly racist screamers as this, offered during oral argument in an affirmative action case, when he said minority students would benefit by attending "a less advanced school, a slower-track school where they can do well."[24] And this, during oral argument for *Shelby County* itself, when Scalia observed of the 2006 reauthorization:

> *And this last enactment, not a single vote in the Senate against it. And the House is pretty much the same. Now, I don't think that's attributable to the fact that it is so much clearer now that we need this. I think it is attributable, very likely attributable, to a phenomenon that is called perpetuation of racial entitlement. It's been written about. Whenever a society adopts racial entitlements, it is very difficult to get out of them through normal political processes. I don't think there is anything to be gained by any senator to vote against continuation of this act. And I am fairly confident that it will be re-enacted in perpetuity unless—unless a court can say it does not comport with the Constitution.*[25]

*A phenomenon that is called perpetuation of racial entitlement.* And *it's been written about.* Justice Scalia spoke the truth, though not in the way he intended, which is to say he didn't know what he was talking about. There is in fact *a phenomenon of perpetuation of racial entitlement* in America, and *it's been written about,* by, among others, James Baldwin, Toni Morrison, Albert Murray, Frederick Douglass, Michelle Alexander, Zora Neale Hurston, Ta-Nehisi Coates, Mark Twain, Jean Toomer, Alice Walker, Claudia Rankine, Ralph Ellison,

---

[24] As well as taking up the argument "that most of the black scientists in this country don't come from schools like the University of Texas. They come from lesser schools where they do not feel they're being pushed ahead in classes that are too fast for them." *Fisher v. University of Texas at Austin,* 579 US __ (2016) (pp. 67–68, transcript of oral argument, available at www.supremecourt.gov).

[25] Page 47, transcript of oral argument in *Shelby County,* www.supremecourt.gov.

Tiphanie Yanique, August Wilson, Jesmyn Ward, Angela Flournoy, Tarell Alvin McCraney, Colson Whitehead, Morgan Parker, and many more. *Very difficult to get out of them through normal political processes.* Justice Scalia was channeling the wisdom of the ages that day. We are for a fact still mired in the *racial entitlements* that came in with that slave ship in 1619, a social order that has so far produced the deadliest war in America's history and many thousands of casualties before and after, the victims of conflicts that might be safely described as not *through normal political processes.*

Scalia and Roberts were adhering to a fantasy, a perfect inversion of the reality that those writers on the phenomenon of perpetuation of racial entitlement have always insisted on. The reality—the indisputable record, if you will—of black duress, black suffering, the theft of black labor, the fullness of black humanity, all the strands of the counternarrative to the heroic American fantasy that places whiteness in the starring roles; that makes whiteness the very definition of "American." Trump bulled his way to the presidency on the power of that fantasy, all of the potent, half-mad paranoias bound up in birtherism, the wall, the blaming and berating of Mexicans, Muslims, immigrants, Obama, Black Lives Matter, all the people and powers who'd supposedly betrayed the "real" America. The "real" America, white America, was strong and good and guiltless. "Real" America had nothing to apologize for. Trump's belligerence mocked the very idea, as did his gleeful willingness to trash every standard of common decency in sight. This was showmanship, a way to keep us tuned in—who would he insult next?—but more than that it served as proof of his authenticity, proof that he understood the confusions and grievances of white America and had the guts to speak them in the plainest language.

"The grand aim of the [Voting Rights] Act," Justice Ginsburg wrote in her *Shelby County* dissent, "is to secure to all in our polity equal citizenship stature." *Equal citizenship stature.* Not less-than; not contingent; not the old American anthropology of dehumanizing, of *decitizenizing*, people of color, but full recognition of one's humanity under the law, with equal right to life, liberty, and the pursuit of happiness. Black Lives Matter gets at the same point. When Trayvon Martin's killer walked, "black lives matter" located America's failure with surgical precision. There would be no recourse for this young man's unjustified death, no punishment, no assignment of guilt, no recognition by the system of this ultimate wrong. A starker demonstration of the less-than status of Trayvon Martin's right to life cannot be imagined.

Trump reserved his special contempt for "political correctness," which seemed to represent for him not just an agenda for supplanting the "real" America, but a very real and present threat to his ego. When it comes to the national psyche, Trump has great instincts—give him that. He was entirely right to identify political correctness as his enemy, insofar as it aspires—as it does—to a reinvention of American identity. And therein lies the revolution, "the deep and mighty transformation" that James Baldwin saw as America's only hope. "Political correctness" denotes far more than linguistic temporizing and hypersensitive undergrads, but if the term has lately been rendered too small to carry its genuine revolutionary weight, we could try for a substitute. "Historical correctness," say. Or "reality connect." "Eyes." "Knowledge." "Getting a fucking clue." Because at its heart, the phenomenon known as "political correctness" is the struggle to supplant the default American identity of mythic whiteness with a truer, more complex, more various identity, one that contains all of America's historical reality as it plays out in the life of the country with each new day.

MARY BOYKIN CHESNUT, BORN 1823, DAUGHTER OF A SOUTH Carolina planter and U.S. senator, and wife to another South Carolina planter and U.S. senator, wrote in her diary on March 18, 1861:

*I wonder if it be a sin to think slavery a curse to any land . . .*
*Like the patriarchs of old our men live all in one house with*
*their wives and their concubines, and the mulattoes one sees in*
*every family exactly resemble the white children—and every*
*lady tells you who is the father of all the mulatto children in*
*everybody's household, but those in her own she seems to think*
*drop from the clouds.*[26]

Mary Chesnut's fellow Southerner Edgar Allan Poe was onto it too, white people's talent for denying the reality happening right under our nose. At a time when various nitwits were celebrating the South as an idyll of courtly love and Arthurian chivalry, Poe was mining realer stuff. Dungeons, hauntings, torture, murder, people buried alive or sealed up in walls, these were his specialty. In Poe, disease and madness proceed from suppressed guilt; grand families and houses are cursed; dread atmospherics signal universal corruption and decay. His was the only lasting art to emerge from the antebellum South, and in the mid-twentieth century another Southerner, William Faulkner, would cast Poe's horrors in more literal form. In particular, his books contain much human information on that dropping-from-the-clouds business that Mary Chesnut alluded to. Faulkner explores sexual servitude through all its grades of duress and coercion, including the vilest forms of rape. It always turns out badly in Faulkner, the denial of crimes, connections, intimacies, and like a curse the consequences wreak havoc on successive generations.[27] But of course they would. "The past is never dead," Faulkner famously said. "It's not even past."[28]

---

[26] Mary Boykin Chesnut, *The Private Mary Chesnut: The Unpublished Civil War Diaries*, ed. Elisabeth Muhlenfeld and C. Vann Woodward (Oxford University Press, 1984), p. 42. Thomas Powers's perceptive "The Big Thing on His Mind," *New York Review of Books*, April 20, 2017, led me to this passage in Mary Chesnut's diaries.

[27] As deftly pointed out in Powers, "The Big Thing on His Mind."

[28] Jean Stein, "William Faulkner, the Art of Fiction No. 12," *Paris Review* 12 (Spring 1956) (interview with Faulkner).

James Baldwin was even more direct. "We *are* our history," he wrote of the American nation. "If we pretend otherwise, to put it very brutally, we literally are criminals."

> I attest to this:
> the world is not white;
> it never was white,
> cannot be white.
> White is a metaphor for power,
> and that is simply a way of describing
> Chase Manhattan Bank.[29]

Which is another way of describing our history: profit proportionate to freedom; plunder correlative to subjugation. *White is a metaphor for power, and that is simply a way of describing Chase Manhattan Bank.* James Baldwin is handing us a bomb with those words, all the truth of America compressed in that sentence like a teaspoonful of dead-star matter that weighs more than a thousand Earths. American society, the American anthropology, has from the start been organized on the invention of white supremacy. Allegiance to a certain kind of economics required it, and to ignore or deny the implications of these basic facts is to choose to live in a fantasy.[30] "Make America Great Again" was yet another stroke of Trump's salesman genius. "Great" for whom, exactly? "Again," with reference to which particular era? Trump gave us the answers plainly enough over the course of his campaign, he was no less clear in his agenda than a George Wallace or a David Duke, and his election

---

[29] James Baldwin, "Black English: A Dishonest Argument," text of a 1980 speech delivered at Wayne State University, as published in *The Cross of Redemption: Uncollected Writings*, ed. Randall Kenan (Vintage International, 2011), pp. 154, 158. These lines are rendered as verse, to powerful effect, in *I Am Not Your Negro*, ed. Raoul Peck (Vintage International, 2017), p. 107, and are so presented here. The financial giant formerly known as Chase Manhattan Bank now goes by the name JPMorgan Chase.

[30] Needless to say, but saying it anyway: those on the bottom don't get to choose.

should be viewed—must be viewed—as a triumph of that brutal anthropology.

Baldwin, again:

> *What white people have to do is try and find out in their own hearts why it was necessary to have a "nigger" in the first place, because I'm not a nigger, I'm a man. But if you think I'm a nigger, it means you need him. The question that you've got to ask yourself, the white population of this country has got to ask itself . . . If I'm not the nigger here and you invented him, you the white people invented him, then you've got to find out why. And the future of the country depends on that, whether or not it is able to ask that question.*[31]

Trump's election represents a great turning away from that question. Trump sold us, or a good many of us, on the fantasy, but for a consummate salesman such as he it wasn't all that hard a sell. Fantasy offers certainty, affirmation, instant gratification, a way to evade—for a while, at least—the reality right in front of our face. It's so much easier that way, but perhaps we're fast approaching the point where the fantasy can no longer be sustained. The evidence won't shut up; it insists and persists, and in this all those writers on the phenomenon of the perpetuation of racial entitlement, the James Baldwins and Toni Morrisons, have succeeded. And for the hard-core fantasists, we have video: the last moments of Walter Scott, Eric Garner, and Tamir Rice are now part of the record. Consciousness—historical consciousness, political consciousness—has been raised to critical mass, and to suppress it, to try to stuff it back in the box along with all its necessary disruptions and agitations, will destroy the best part of America. The promise of it, the ongoing project. The possibility.

---

[31] Transcription of Baldwin's comments from telecast of "The Negro and the American Promise," 1963, as published in *I Am Not Your Negro*, pp. 108–9.

# ACKNOWLEDGMENTS

In November 2015, David Taylor of the *Guardian* got in touch to ask if I'd be interested in writing a series of pieces in the coming year on the U.S. presidential election. I didn't have to think long; ever since Trump had emerged from the summer leading the Republican field, I'd felt that we were heading into strange political waters—uncharted, in some respects, though there was also the suspicion that Trump was the entirely logical result of certain long-standing forces in the life of the country. Throughout 2016, David proved to be unfailingly thoughtful, supportive, and wise, and it's due to his encouragement and guidance that this book exists. I offer my sincerest thanks to him, and to all of the fine editors and writers at the *Guardian* whom I encountered in the course of 2016. It was a privilege to work alongside these outstanding journalists.

Thanks are also owed and cheerfully offered to Dan Halpern and Megan Lynch of Ecco, who supported and guided this book from the start, and to my tireless agent, Heather Schroder, who provided her usual excellent counsel every step of the way. Sincere thanks as well to Nicole Dewey for all she's done to launch this book out into the world, and to Lee Boudreaux for that first break, and several more besides. I'm also tremendously grateful to the faculty and students in the writing program at Texas State University, and at the Michener Center for Writers at the University of Texas in Austin, with special thanks to Tom Grimes at Texas State and Jim Magnuson at the Michener Center for inviting me to teach at those fine institutions.

In my life I've been extremely lucky to have been close to a number of preternaturally gifted observers and practitioners of the political arts. Foremost among them have been my paternal grandparents, Ben Fountain Sr. and Emmie Green Fountain; my father, Dr. Ben Fountain Jr.; my great-uncle Ted Jack Green; and my good friend Dr. Frantz Large of Haiti. I owe them all a tremendous debt of gratitude. Chief among the writers whose work I turn to time and again when trying to make sense of American political life are James Baldwin, Joan Didion, Norman Mailer, and Garry Wills. If you're looking for answers, read their work. Then keep on reading; we never know enough.

Fiercest thanks of all go to Sharie, John, and Lee. I love you very much.

# CREDITS

The following essays were previously published in a different form in the *Guardian:*

"The Phony in American Politics" (February 13, 2016)

"American Crossroads: Reagan, Trump, and the Devil Down South" (March 5, 2016)

"American Exceptionalism and the Great Game: At Play in the Fields of the Lord" (April 9, 2016)

"Doing the Chickenhawk with Trump: Talking Fast and Loose in the Time of Endless War" (May 28, 2016)

"Cheerleaders of the Star-Spangled Apocalypse: Fear and Loathing with the NRA in Louisville, Kentucky" (June 25, 2016)

Portions of "Cleveland Fear Factory" appeared as "The Madman in His Castle" (July 23, 2016)

"Two American Dreams" (September 17, 2016)

"The Long Good Deal" (November 5, 2016)

"Trump Rising: King Donald Saddles Up with the Wrecking Crew" (November 22, 2016)

# INDEX